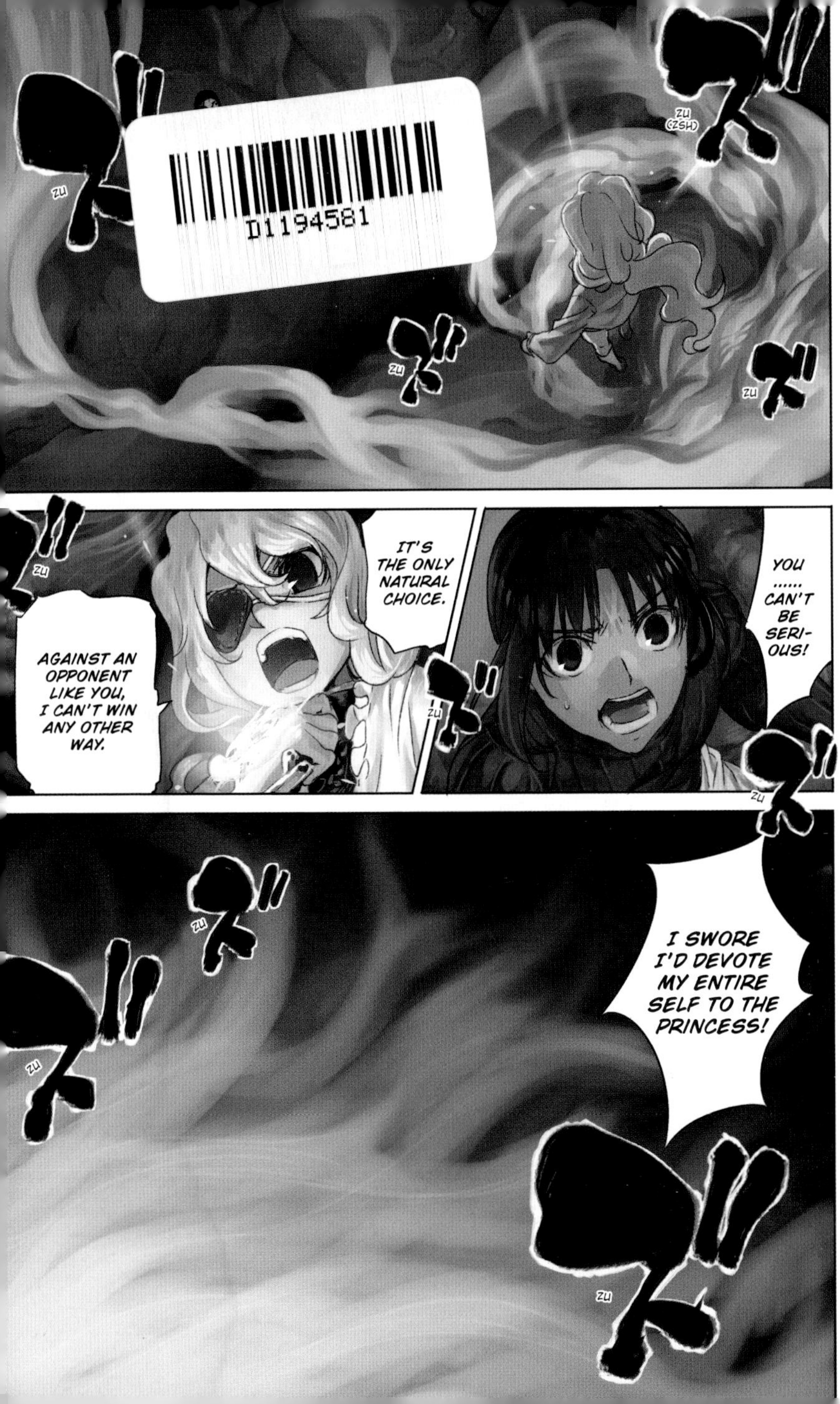
ZU
(ZSH)
ZU
ZU
ZU
ZU
YOU ...... CAN'T BE SERI- OUS!
ZU
IT'S THE ONLY NATURAL CHOICE.
AGAINST AN OPPONENT LIKE YOU, I CAN'T WIN ANY OTHER WAY.
ZU
ZU
I SWORE I'D DEVOTE MY ENTIRE SELF TO THE PRINCESS!
ZU
ZU
ZU

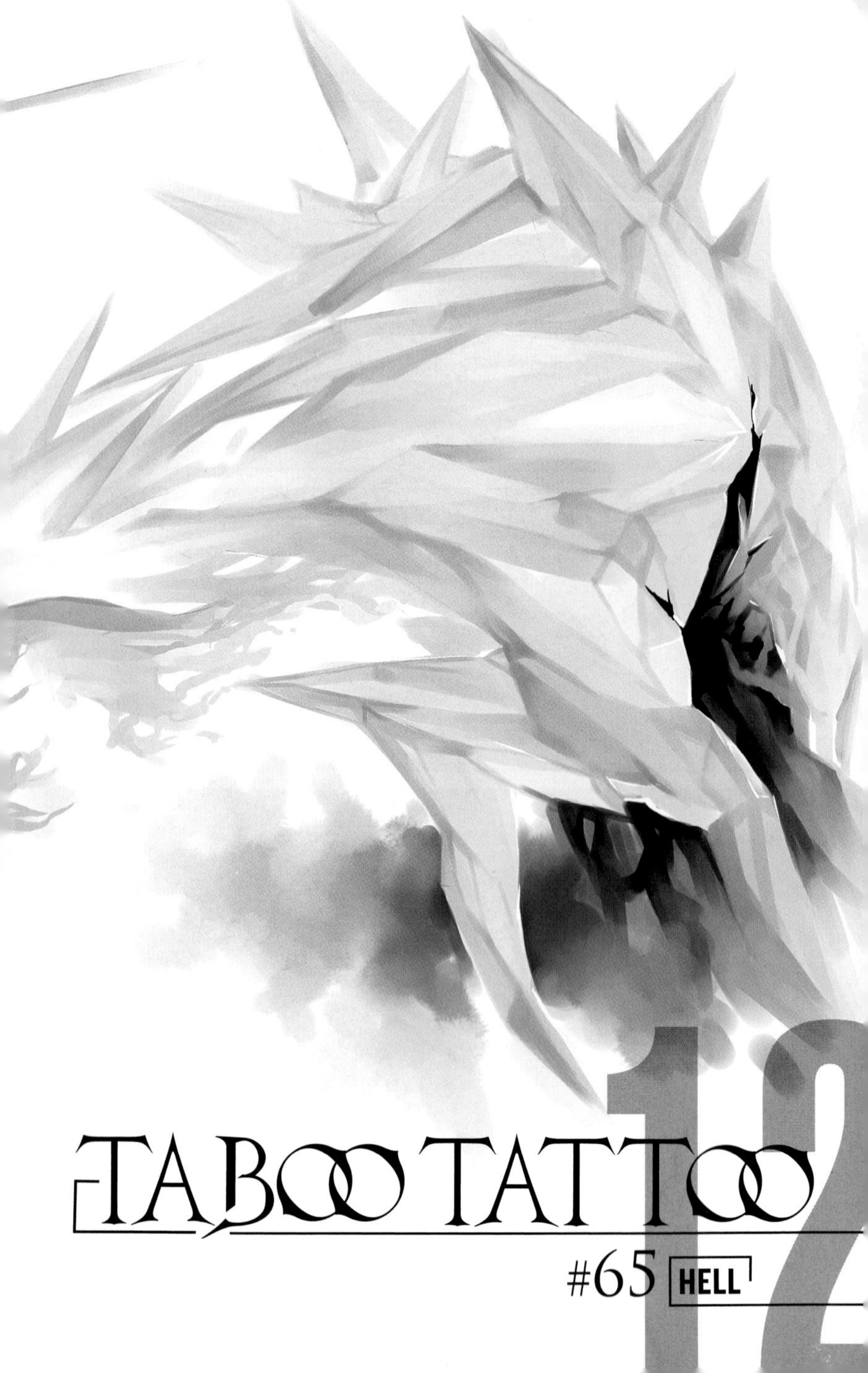

TABOO TATTOO 12

#65 HELL

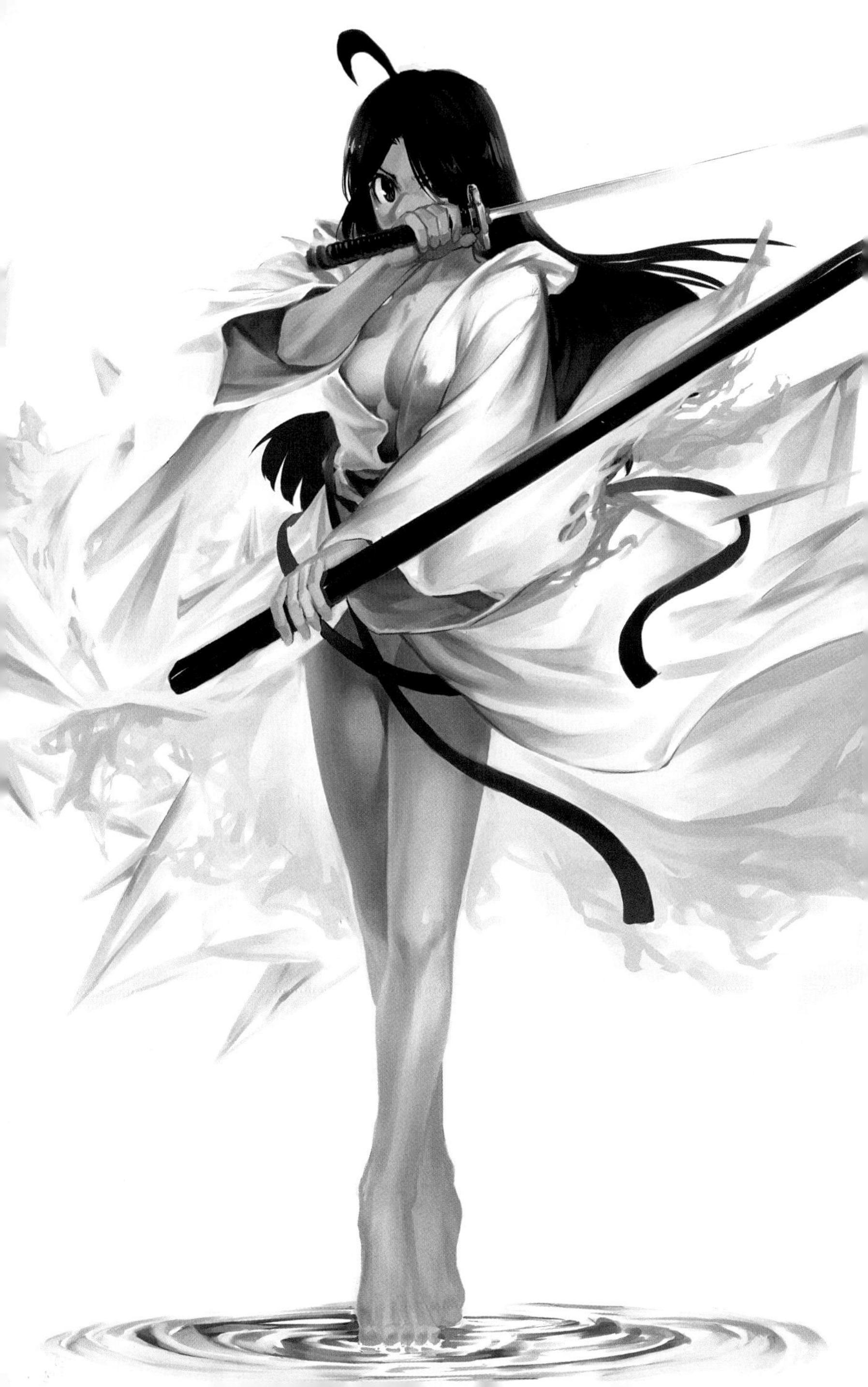

TABOO TATTOO

12

CONTENTS

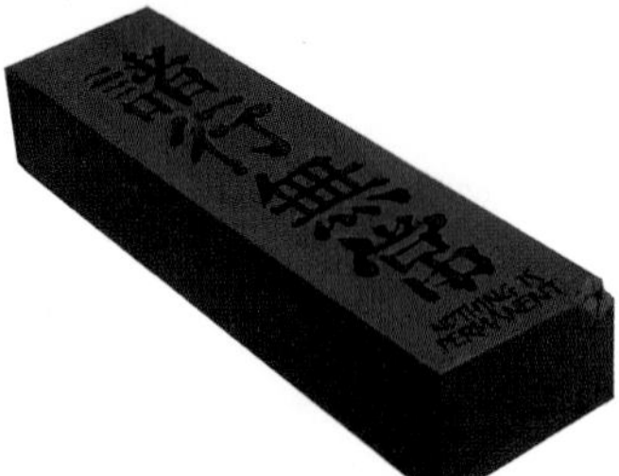

諸行無常
NOTHING IS PERMANENT

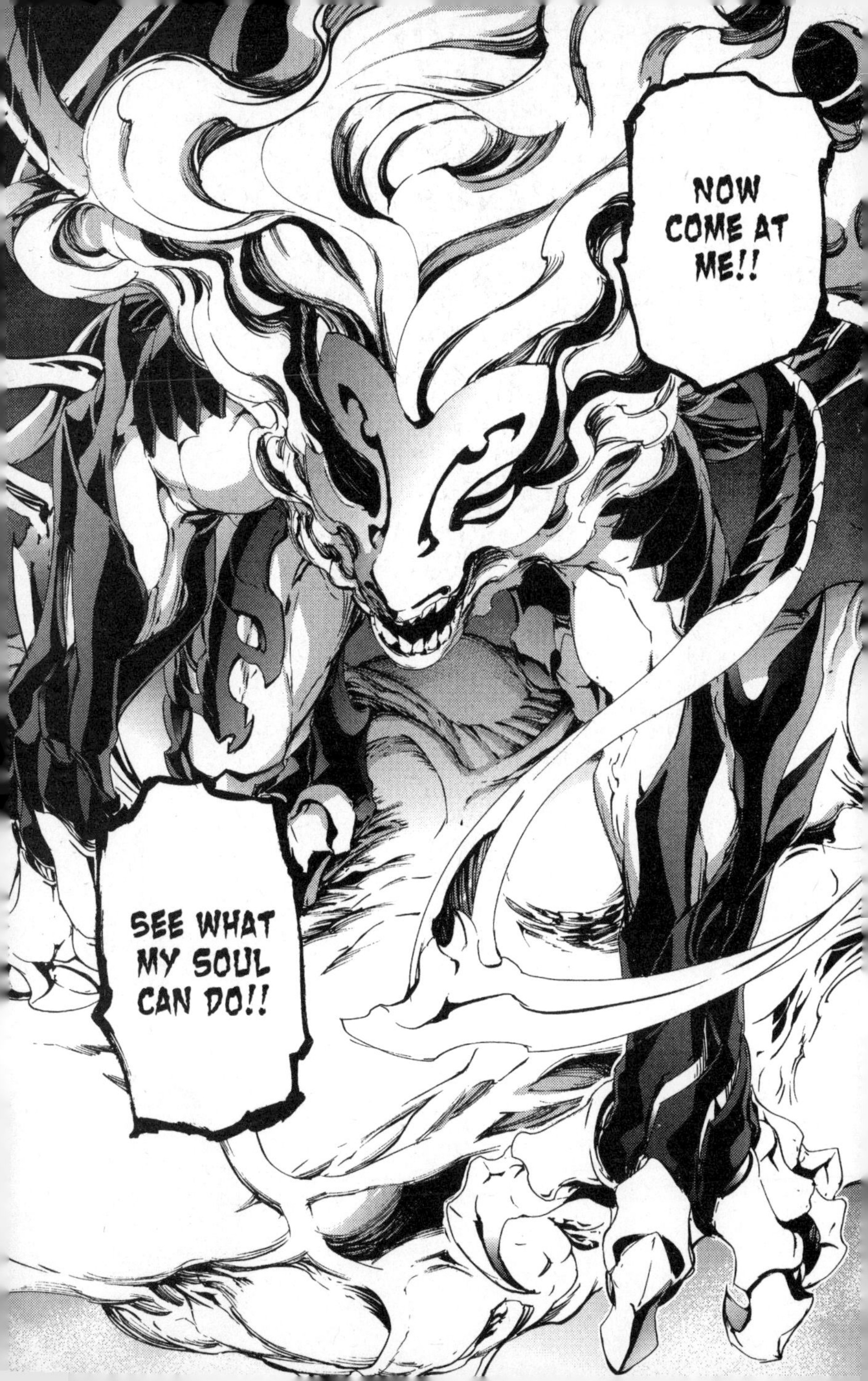
NOW COME AT ME!!
SEE WHAT MY SOUL CAN DO!!

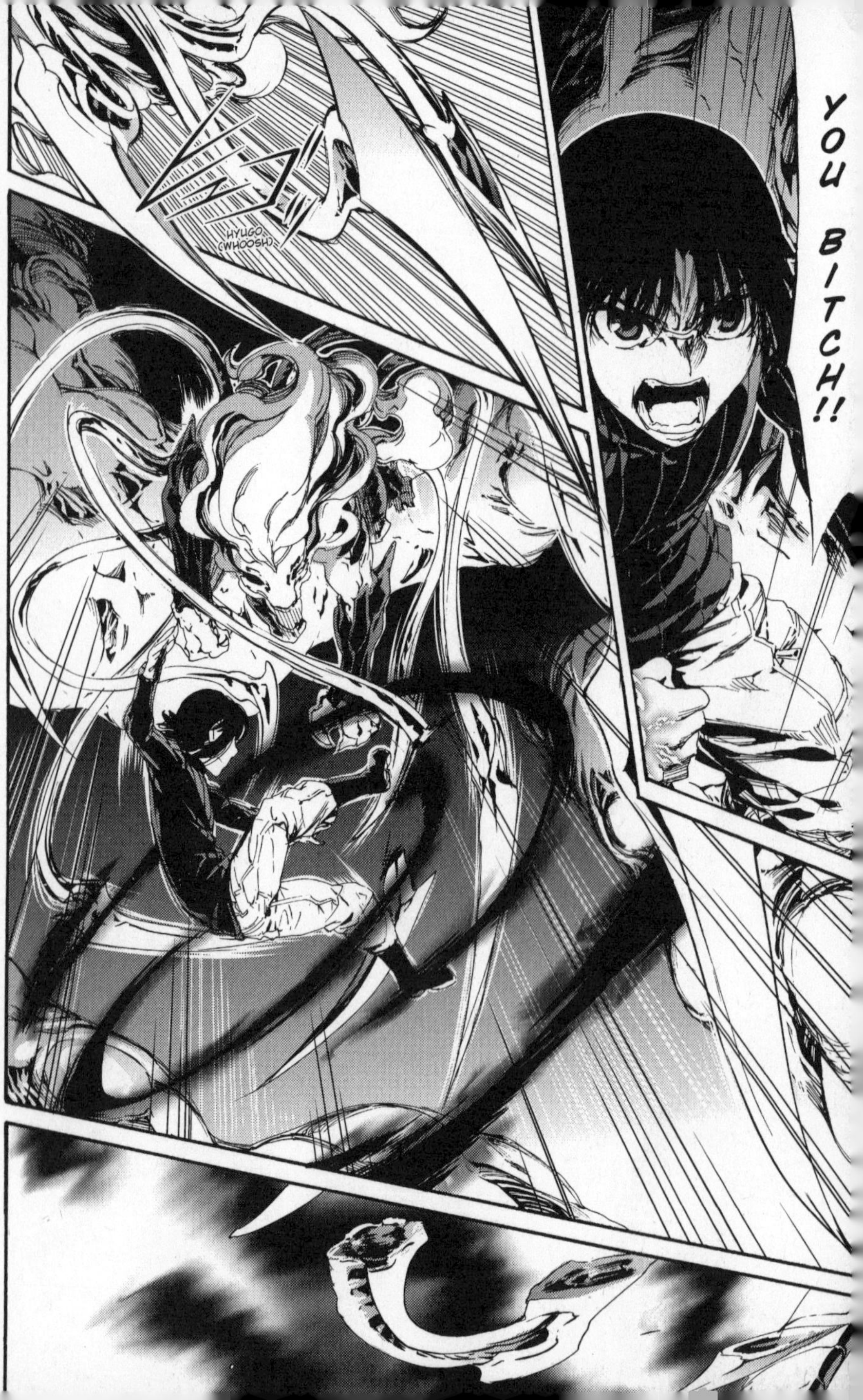
YOU BITCH!!
HYUGO (WHOOSH)

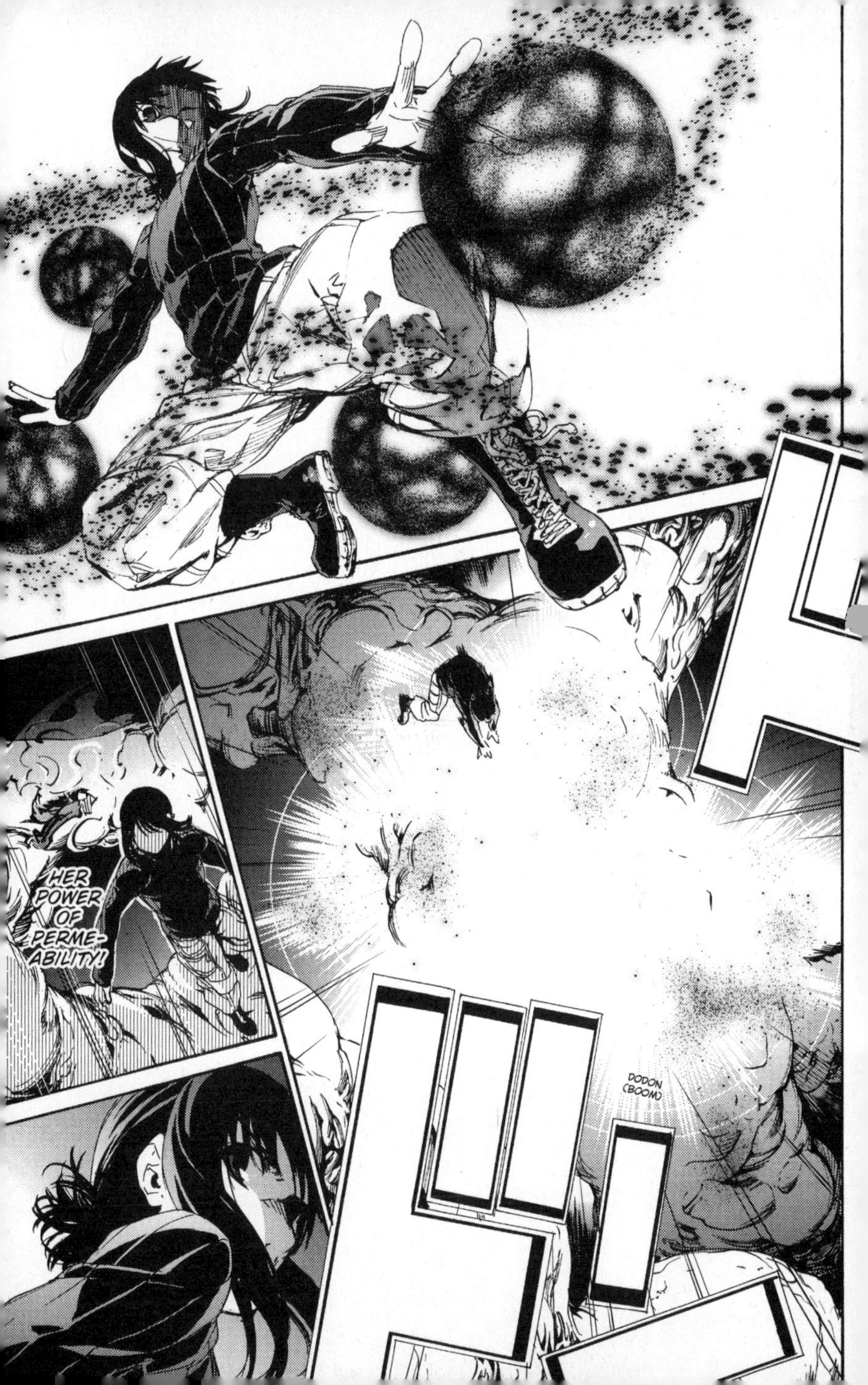
DODON (BOOM)
HER POWER OF PERME-ABILITY!

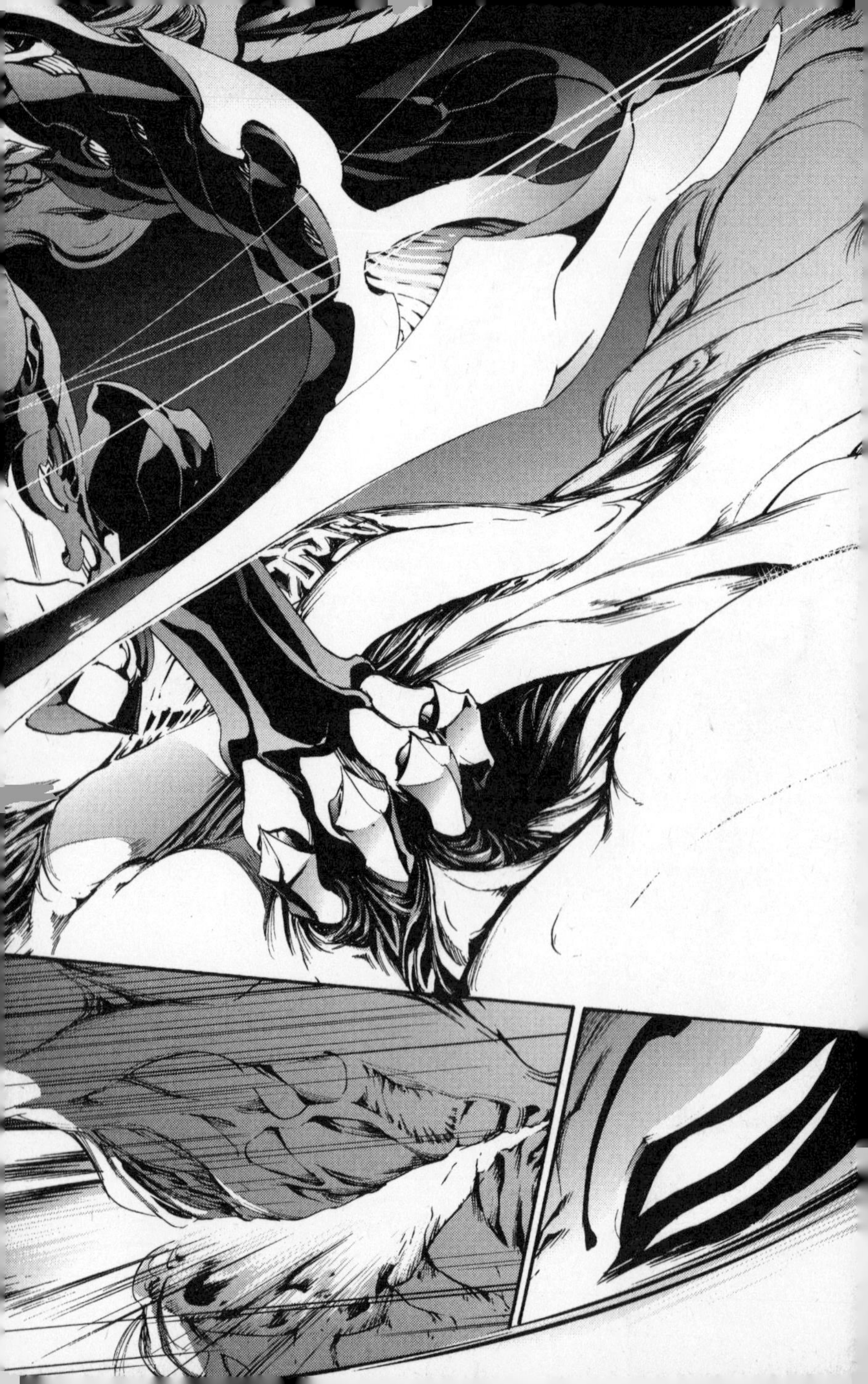

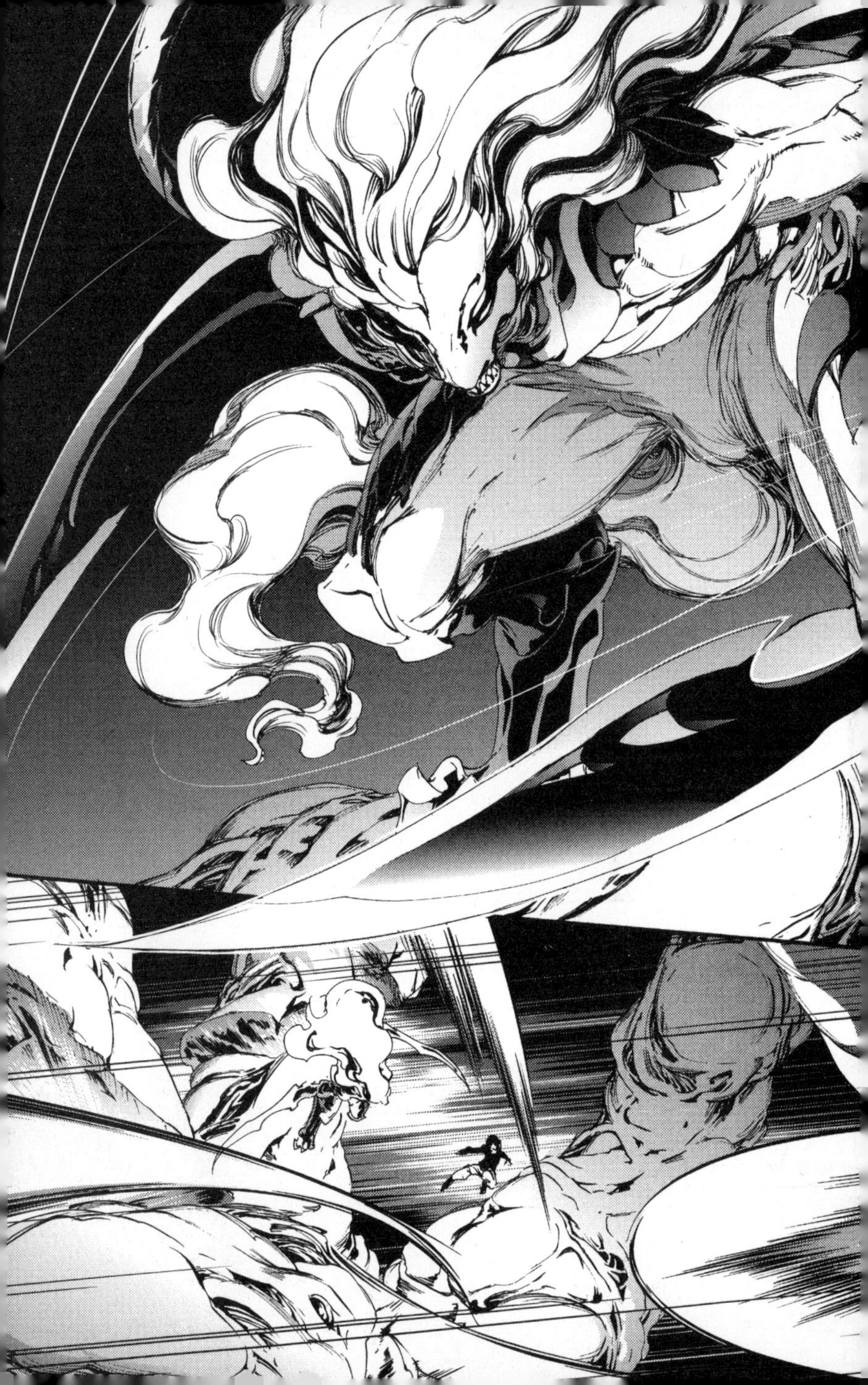

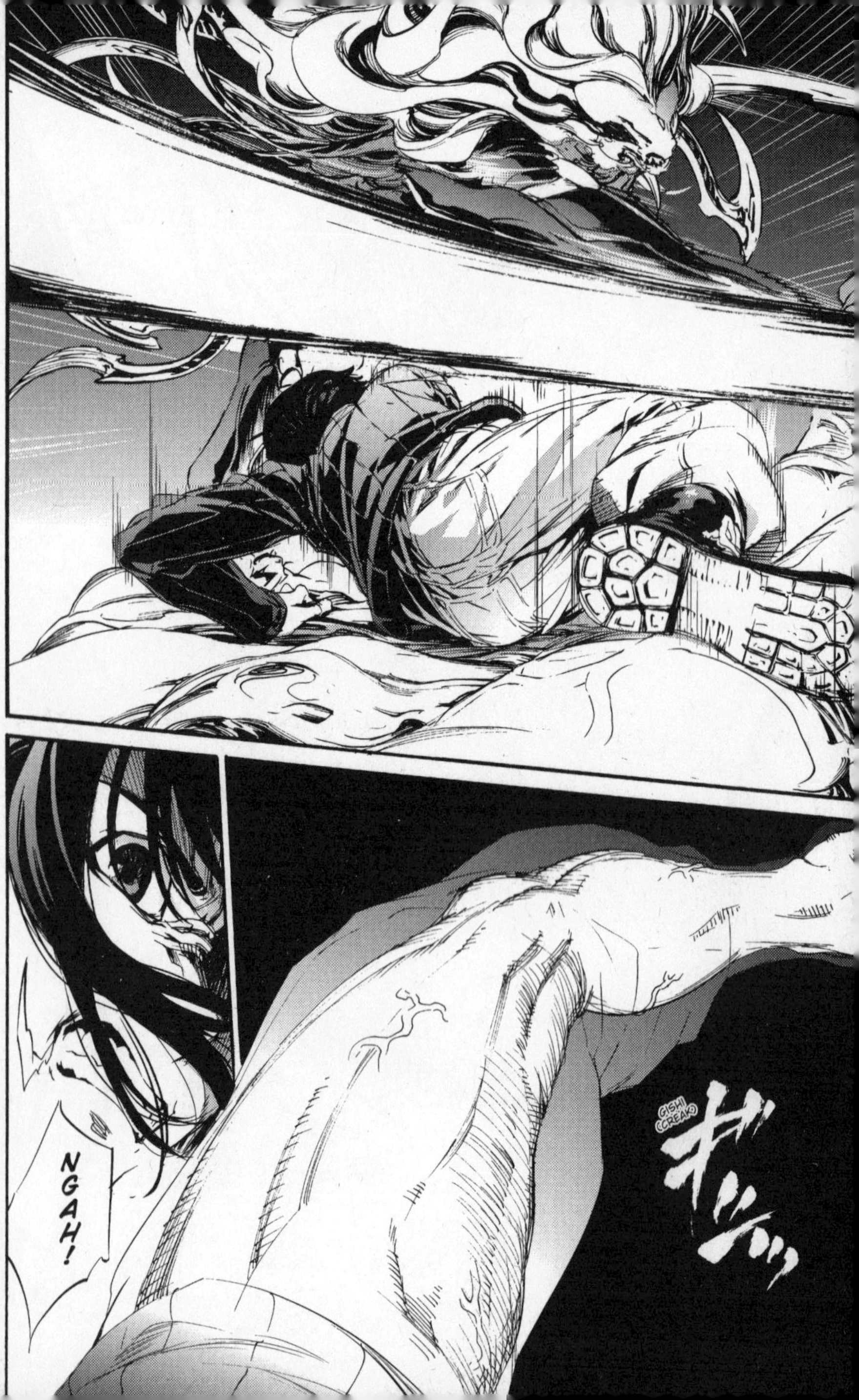
GISHI (CREAK)
NGAH!

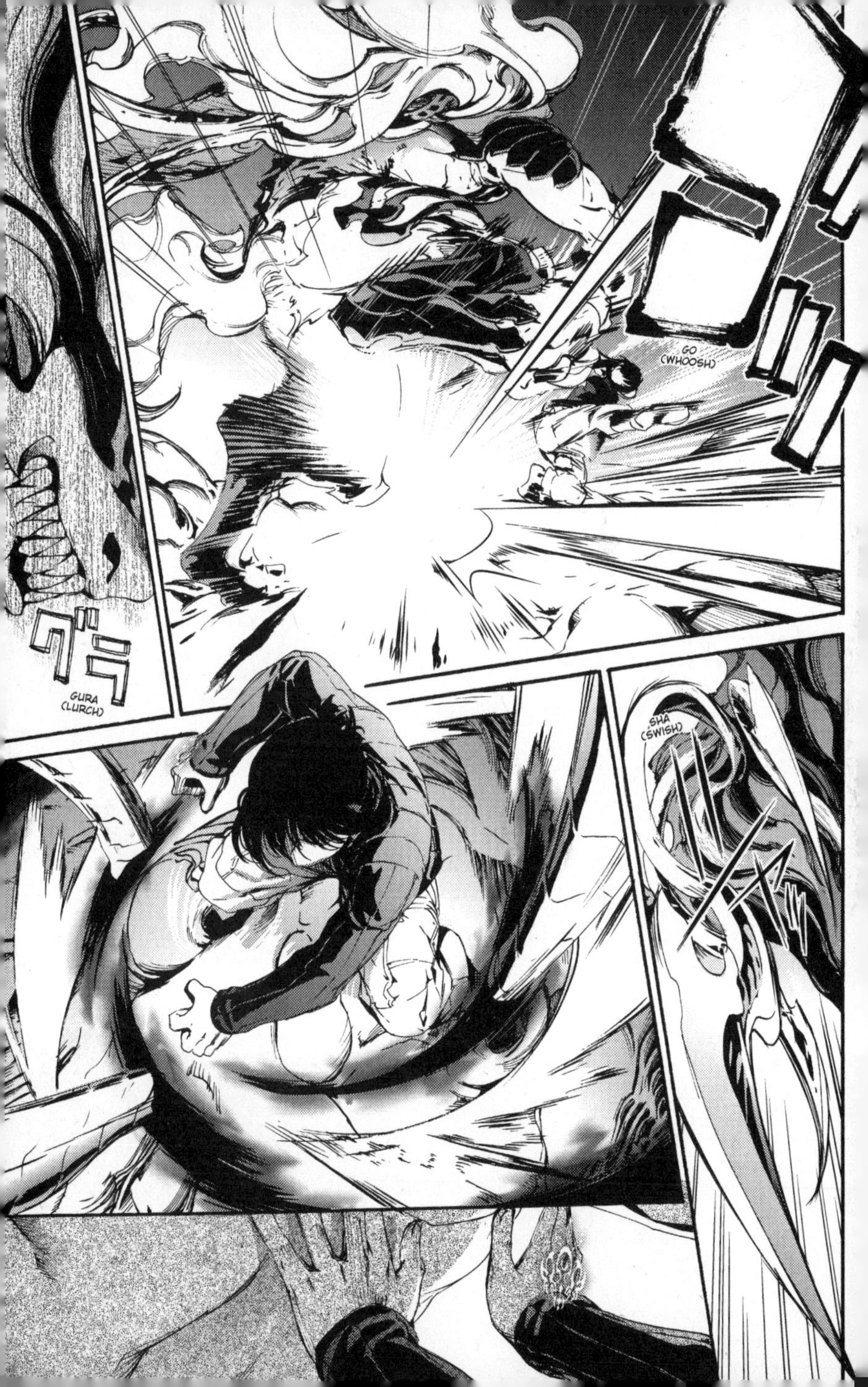
ゴ
GO
(WHOOSH)
グラ
GURA
(LURCH)
シャ
SHA
(SWISH)

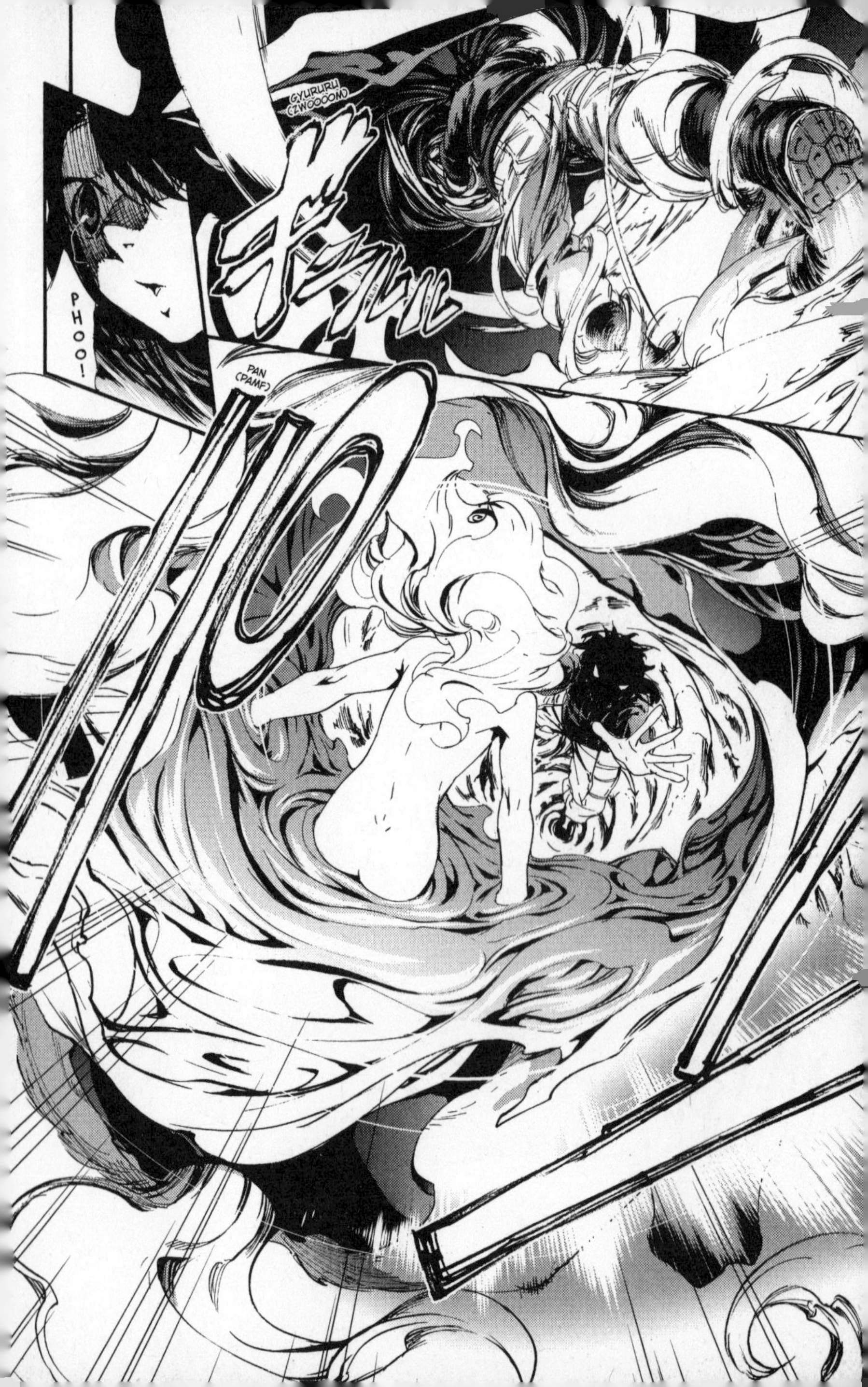
GYURURU (ZWOOOOM)
PHOO!
PAN (PAMF)

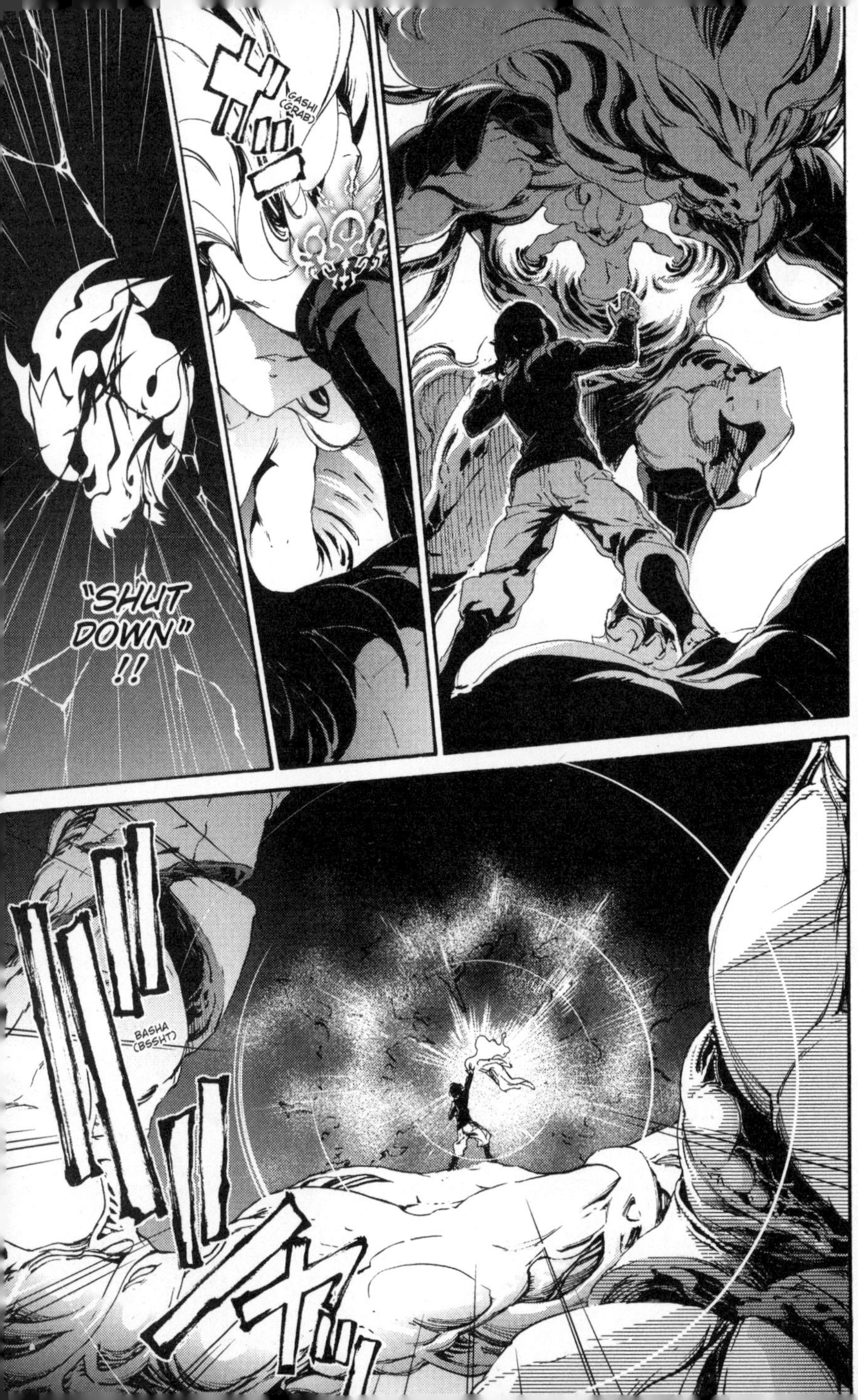
GASHI (GRAB)
"SHUT DOWN"!!
BASHA (BSSHT)

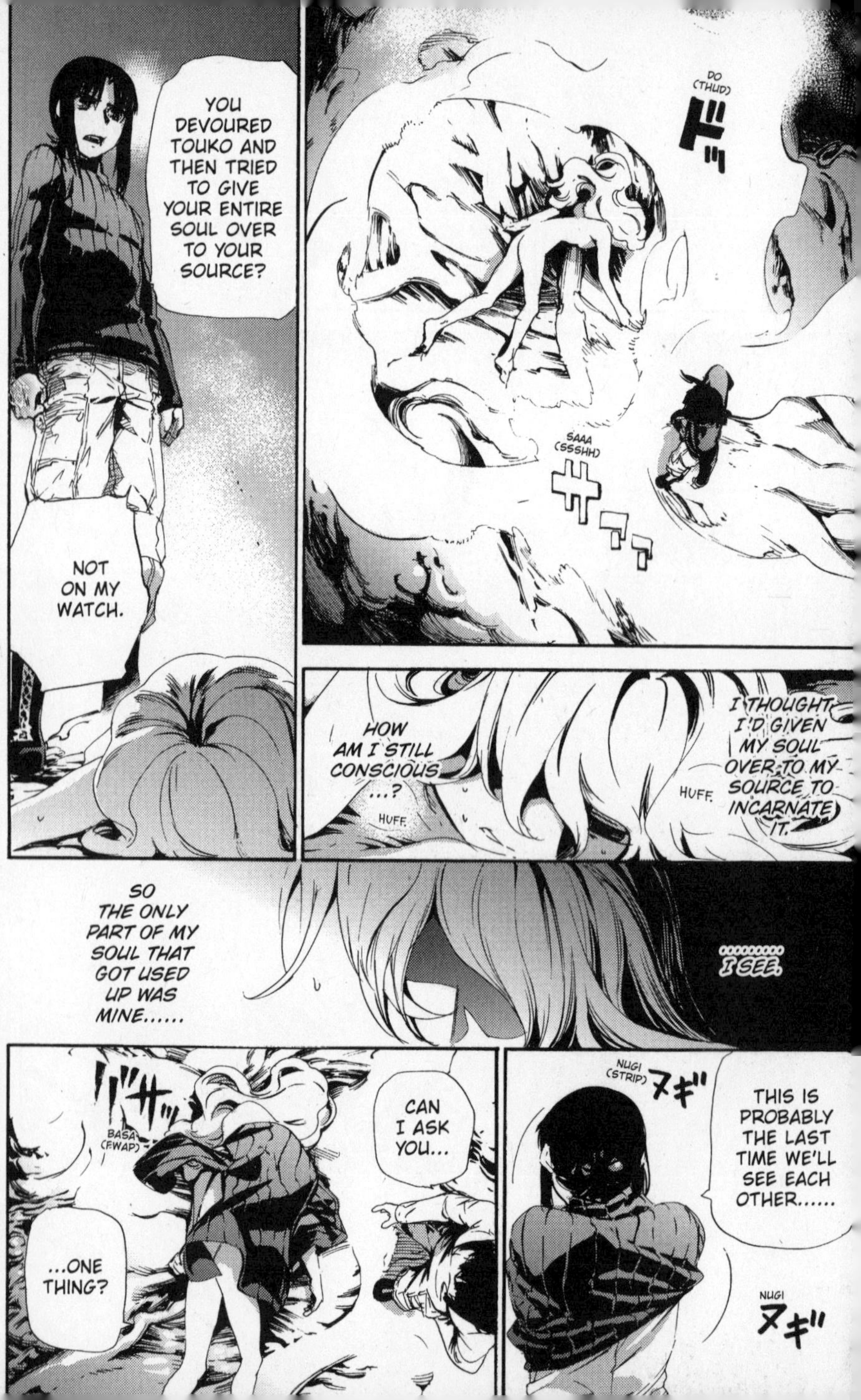
DO (THUD)
ドッ
SAAA (SSSHH)
サァァ
I THOUGHT I'D GIVEN MY SOUL OVER TO MY SOURCE TO INCARNATE IT.
HUFF.
HOW AM I STILL CONSCIOUS...?
HUFF.
YOU DEVOURED TOUKO AND THEN TRIED TO GIVE YOUR ENTIRE SOUL OVER TO YOUR SOURCE?
NOT ON MY WATCH.
..........I SEE.
SO THE ONLY PART OF MY SOUL THAT GOT USED UP WAS MINE......
NUGI (STRIP)
ヌギ
THIS IS PROBABLY THE LAST TIME WE'LL SEE EACH OTHER......
NUGI
ヌギ
CAN I ASK YOU...
バサッ
BASA (FWAP)
...ONE THING?

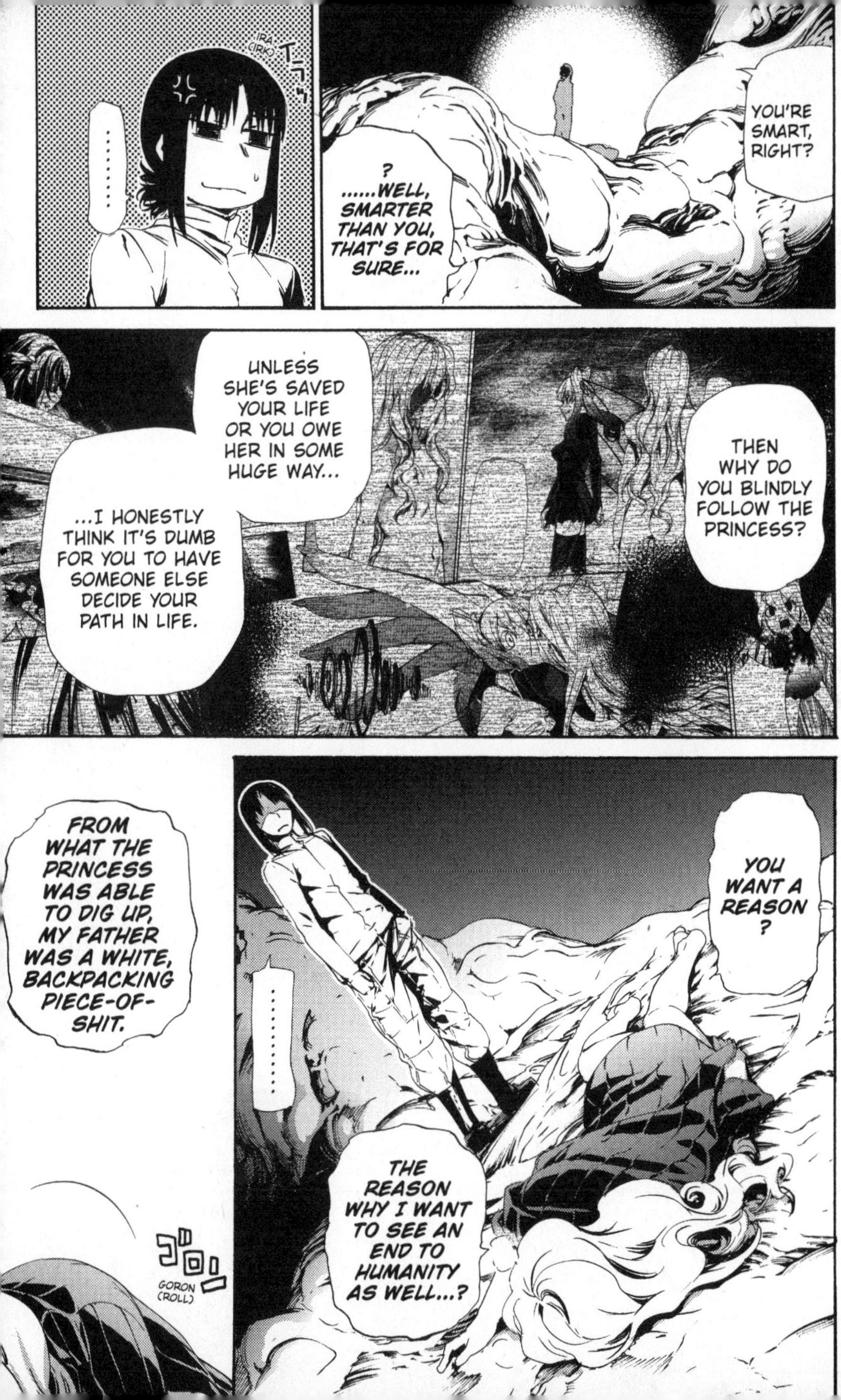
YOU'RE SMART, RIGHT?
? ......WELL, SMARTER THAN YOU, THAT'S FOR SURE...
IRA (IRK)
....
THEN WHY DO YOU BLINDLY FOLLOW THE PRINCESS?
UNLESS SHE'S SAVED YOUR LIFE OR YOU OWE HER IN SOME HUGE WAY...
...I HONESTLY THINK IT'S DUMB FOR YOU TO HAVE SOMEONE ELSE DECIDE YOUR PATH IN LIFE.
YOU WANT A REASON?
....
THE REASON WHY I WANT TO SEE AN END TO HUMANITY AS WELL...?
FROM WHAT THE PRINCESS WAS ABLE TO DIG UP, MY FATHER WAS A WHITE, BACKPACKING PIECE-OF-SHIT.
GORON (ROLL)

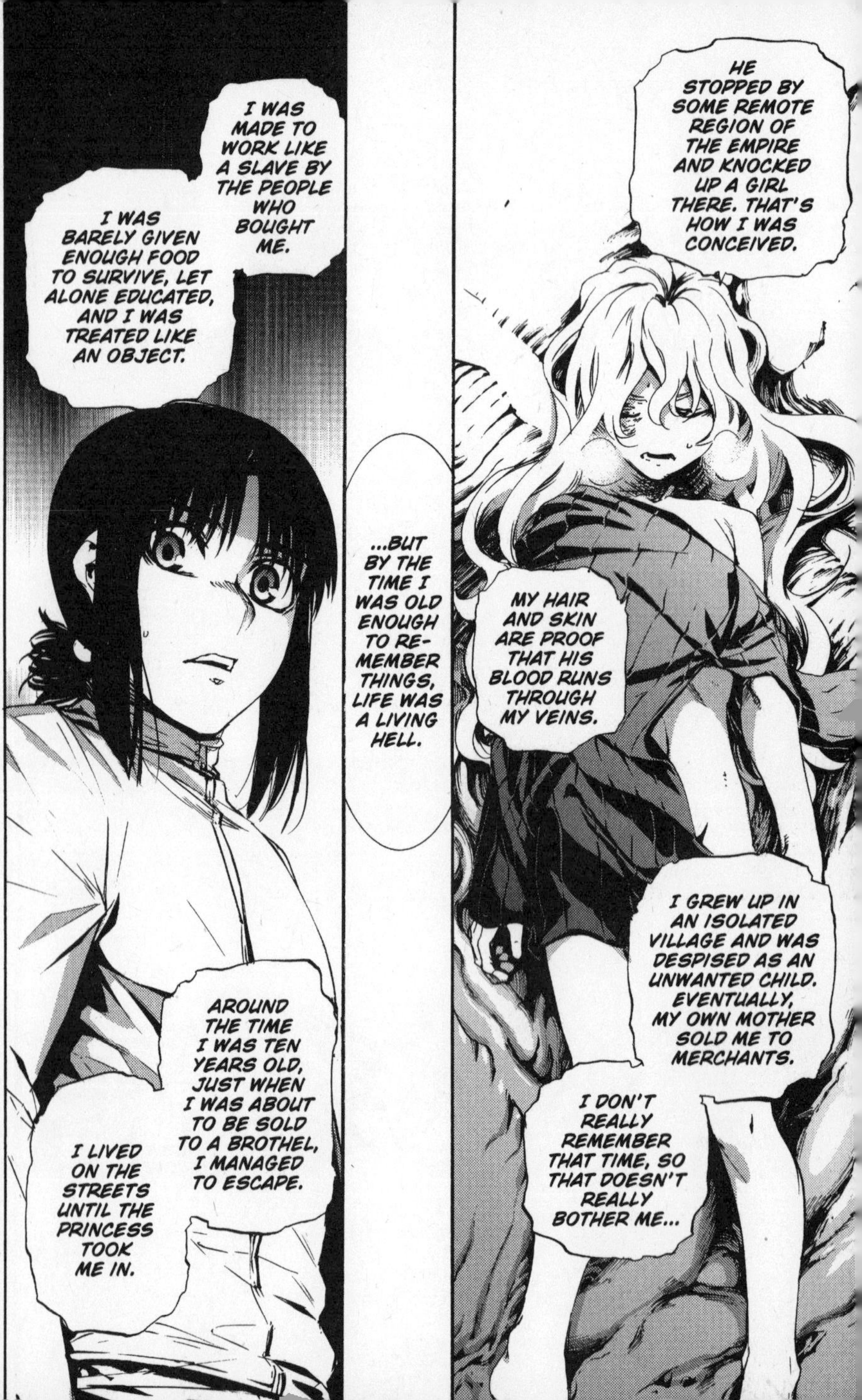
HE STOPPED BY SOME REMOTE REGION OF THE EMPIRE AND KNOCKED UP A GIRL THERE. THAT'S HOW I WAS CONCEIVED.
MY HAIR AND SKIN ARE PROOF THAT HIS BLOOD RUNS THROUGH MY VEINS.
I GREW UP IN AN ISOLATED VILLAGE AND WAS DESPISED AS AN UNWANTED CHILD. EVENTUALLY, MY OWN MOTHER SOLD ME TO MERCHANTS.
I DON'T REALLY REMEMBER THAT TIME, SO THAT DOESN'T REALLY BOTHER ME...
...BUT BY THE TIME I WAS OLD ENOUGH TO RE-MEMBER THINGS, LIFE WAS A LIVING HELL.
I WAS MADE TO WORK LIKE A SLAVE BY THE PEOPLE WHO BOUGHT ME.
I WAS BARELY GIVEN ENOUGH FOOD TO SURVIVE, LET ALONE EDUCATED, AND I WAS TREATED LIKE AN OBJECT.
AROUND THE TIME I WAS TEN YEARS OLD, JUST WHEN I WAS ABOUT TO BE SOLD TO A BROTHEL, I MANAGED TO ESCAPE.
I LIVED ON THE STREETS UNTIL THE PRINCESS TOOK ME IN.

FOR PEOPLE LIKE ME, UNTIL SOMEBODY OFFERS A SAVING HAND, THE WORLD IS LIKE HELL ITSELF.

EVEN IF 99.9% OF PEOPLE LIVE A PEACEFUL AND SAFE LIFE...

...FOR THE .1% LIVING IN HELL, IT'S HARD TO BELIEVE ANYTHING LIKE THAT COULD EXIST.

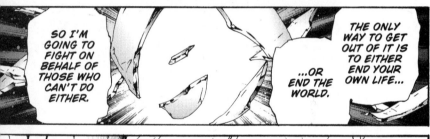

THE ONLY WAY TO GET OUT OF IT IS TO EITHER END YOUR OWN LIFE...

...OR END THE WORLD.

SO I'M GOING TO FIGHT ON BEHALF OF THOSE WHO CAN'T DO EITHER.

TO CARRY THE LOGIC TO THE EXTREME... FOR THE INDIVIDUAL, DEATH IS THE SAME AS THE END OF THE WORLD.

WHEN IT COMES TO LIFE, THE WORLD IS ONLY EITHER A ONE OR A ZERO.

DON'T YOU THINK THAT'S MORE THAN ENOUGH REASON?

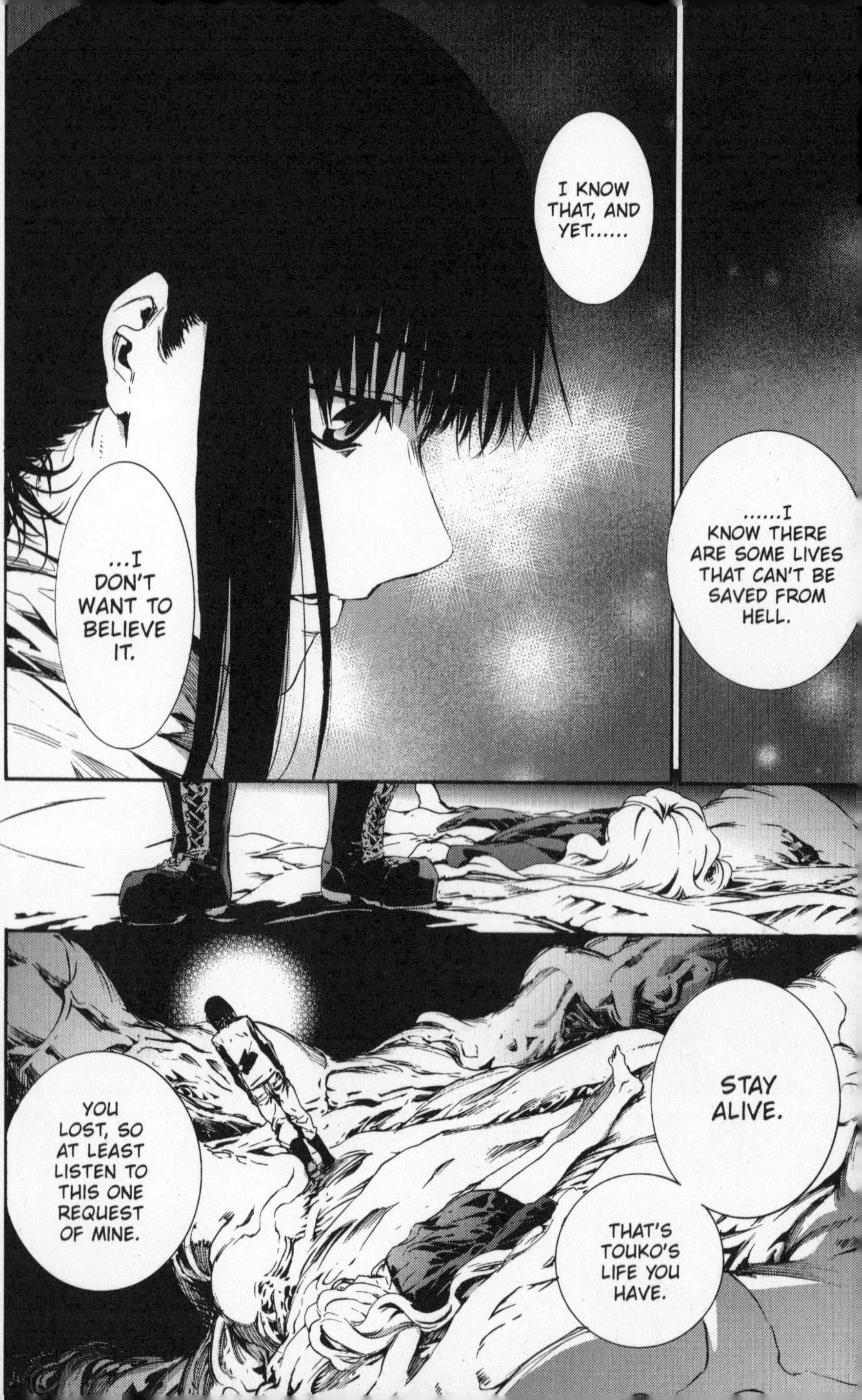
......I KNOW THERE ARE SOME LIVES THAT CAN'T BE SAVED FROM HELL.
I KNOW THAT, AND YET......
...I DON'T WANT TO BELIEVE IT.
STAY ALIVE.
THAT'S TOUKO'S LIFE YOU HAVE.
YOU LOST, SO AT LEAST LISTEN TO THIS ONE REQUEST OF MINE.

MEOW.

SQUEAK.
SNUFFLE.

PURRRRR.

……HMPH.

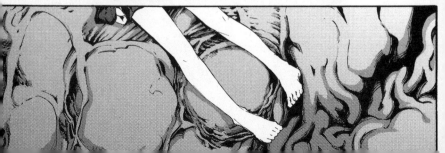

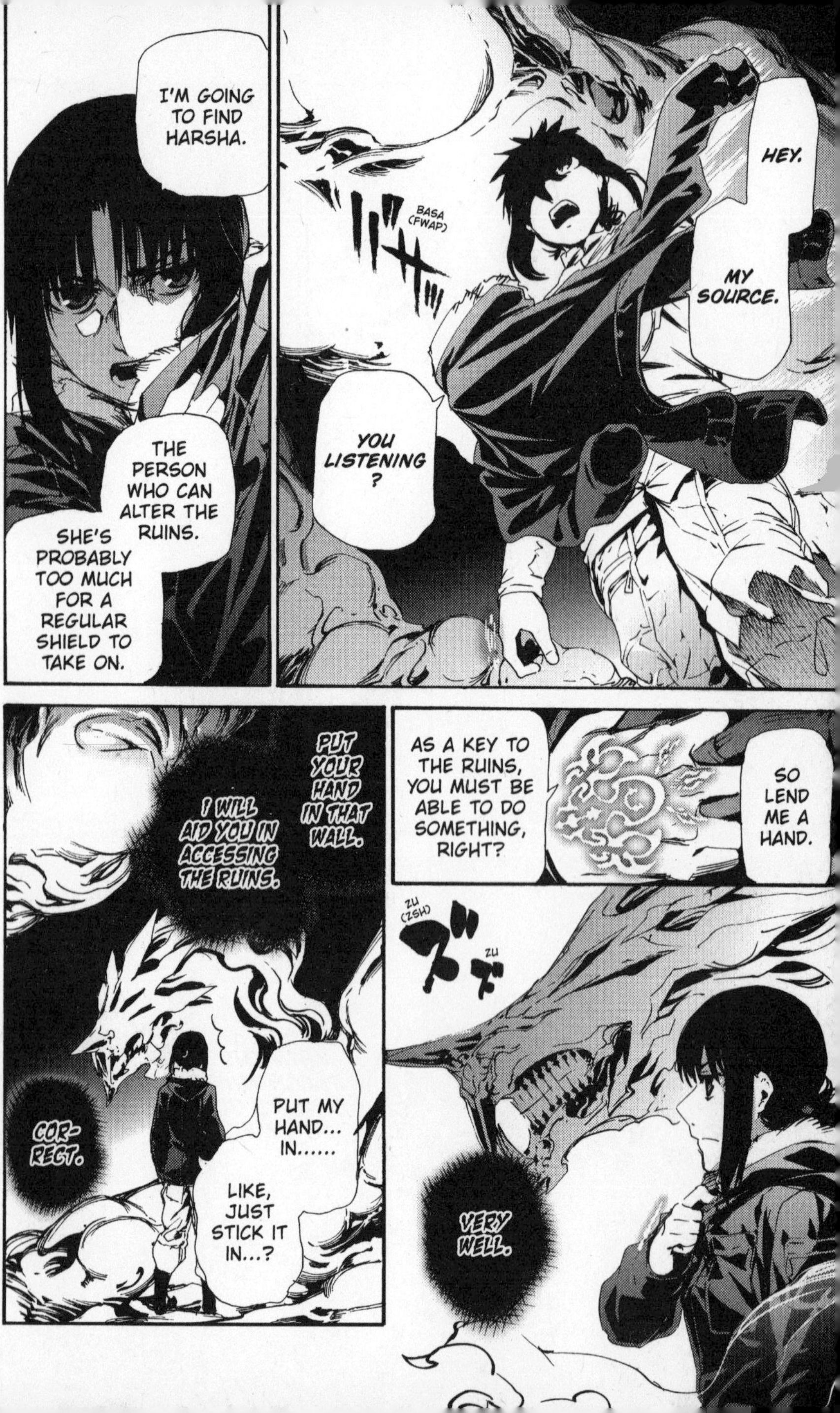
HEY.
MY SOURCE.
BASA (FWAP)
YOU LISTENING?
I'M GOING TO FIND HARSHA.
THE PERSON WHO CAN ALTER THE RUINS.
SHE'S PROBABLY TOO MUCH FOR A REGULAR SHIELD TO TAKE ON.
SO LEND ME A HAND.
AS A KEY TO THE RUINS, YOU MUST BE ABLE TO DO SOMETHING, RIGHT?
ZU (ZSH)
ZU
VERY WELL.
PUT YOUR HAND IN THAT WALL.
I WILL AID YOU IN ACCESSING THE RUINS.
PUT MY HAND... IN......
LIKE, JUST STICK IT IN...?
COR-RECT.

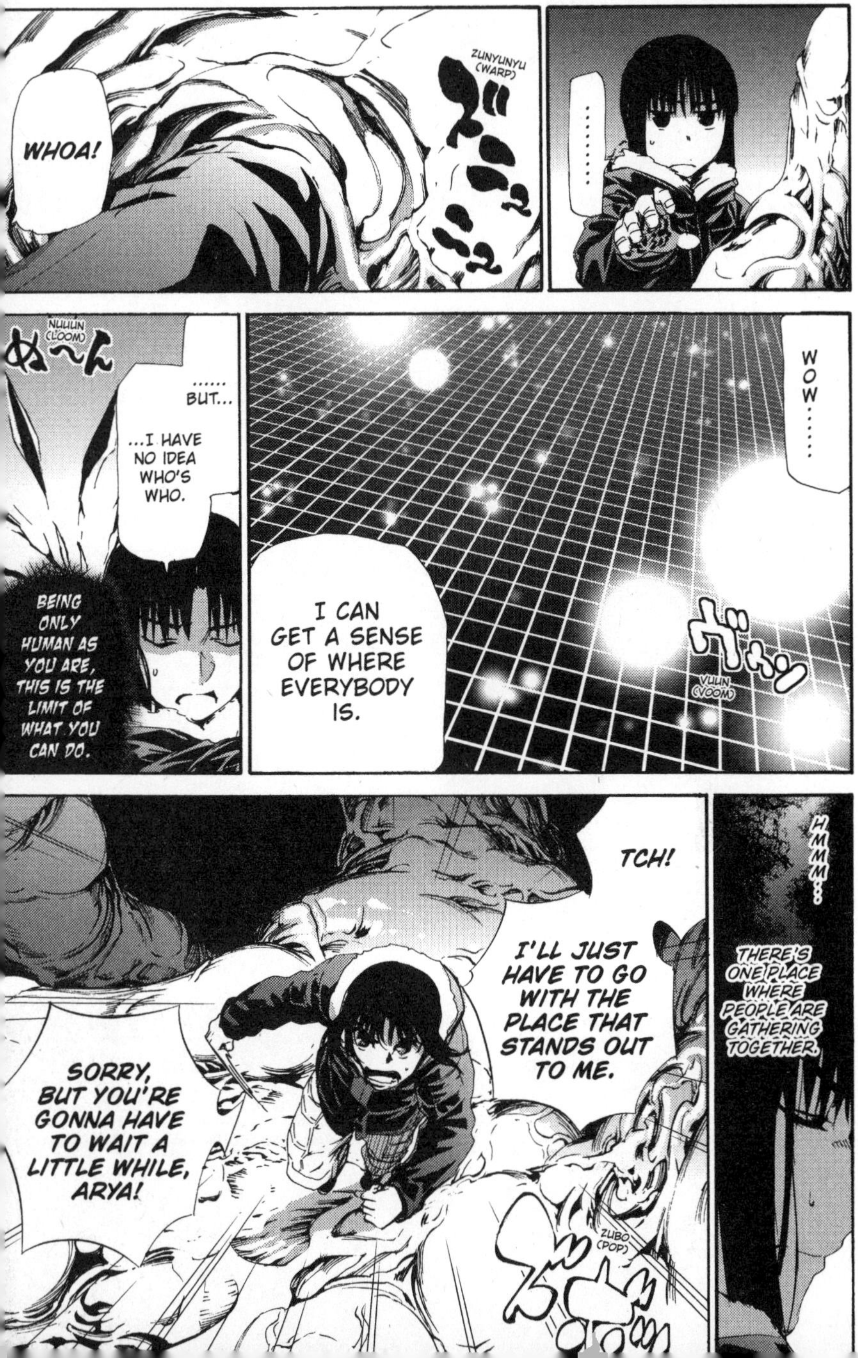
......
ZUNYUNYU (WARP)
ズニュニュ
WHOA!
WOW......
I CAN GET A SENSE OF WHERE EVERYBODY IS.
ヴゥン
VUUN (VOOM)
ぬ～ん
NUUUN (LOOM)
...... BUT...
...I HAVE NO IDEA WHO'S WHO.
BEING ONLY HUMAN AS YOU ARE, THIS IS THE LIMIT OF WHAT YOU CAN DO.
HMMM...
THERE'S ONE PLACE WHERE PEOPLE ARE GATHERING TOGETHER.
TCH!
I'LL JUST HAVE TO GO WITH THE PLACE THAT STANDS OUT TO ME.
SORRY, BUT YOU'RE GONNA HAVE TO WAIT A LITTLE WHILE, ARYA!
ZUBO (POP)

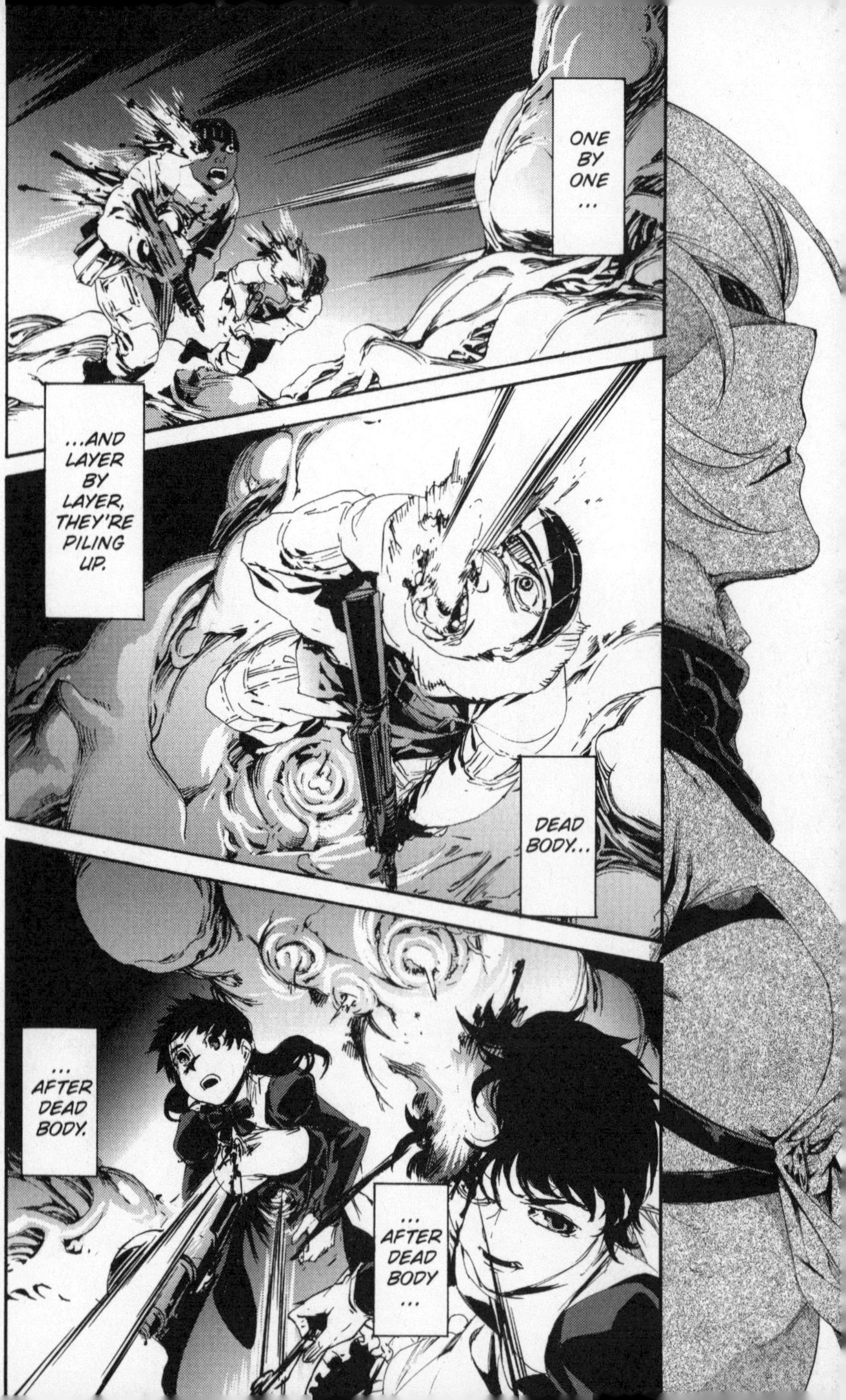

ONE BY ONE ...
...AND LAYER BY LAYER, THEY'RE PILING UP.
DEAD BODY...
... AFTER DEAD BODY ...
... AFTER DEAD BODY.

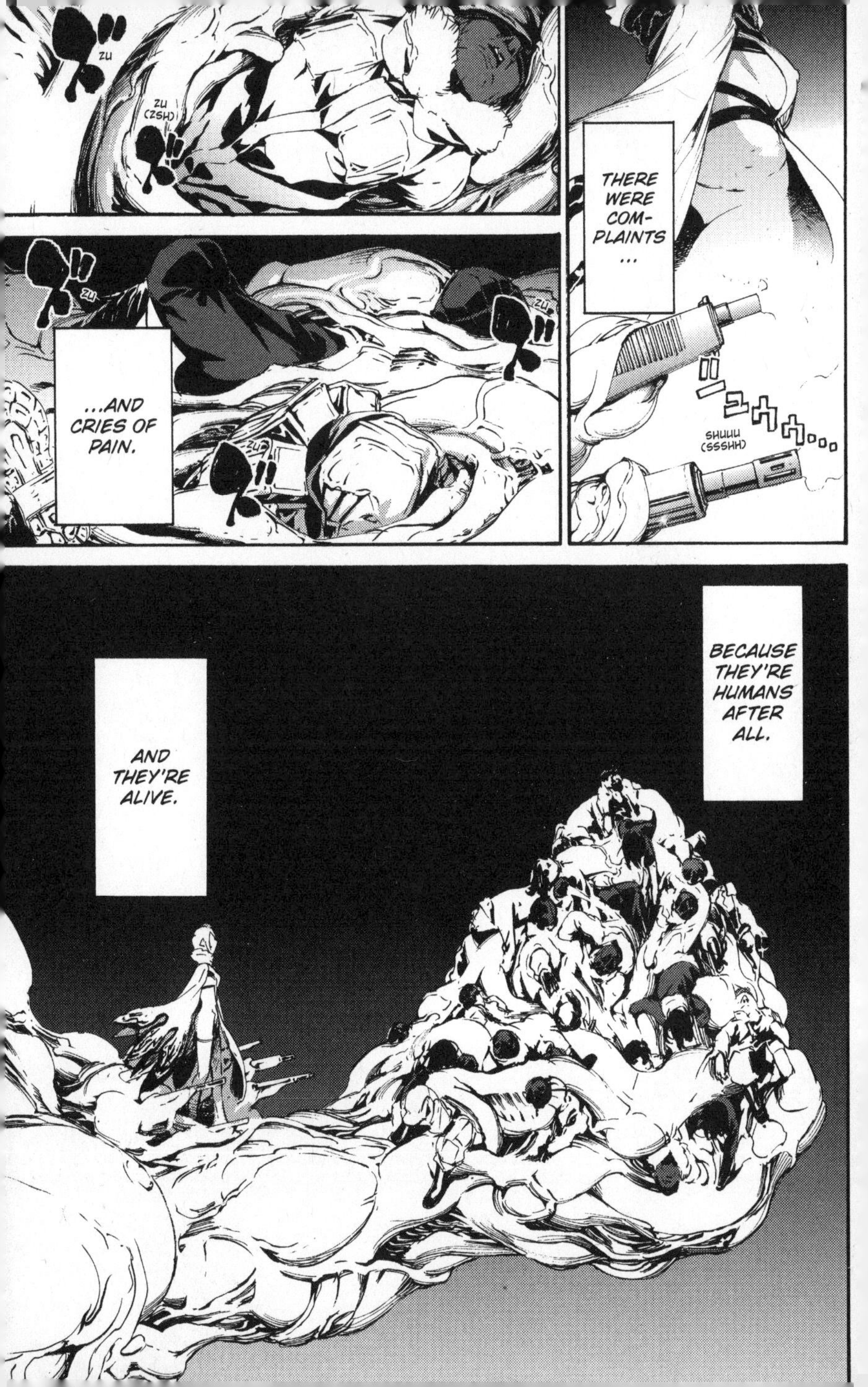
THERE WERE COM-PLAINTS...
SHUUU (SSSHH)
ZU
ZU (ZSH)
ZU
ZU
...AND CRIES OF PAIN.
ZU
BECAUSE THEY'RE HUMANS AFTER ALL.
AND THEY'RE ALIVE.

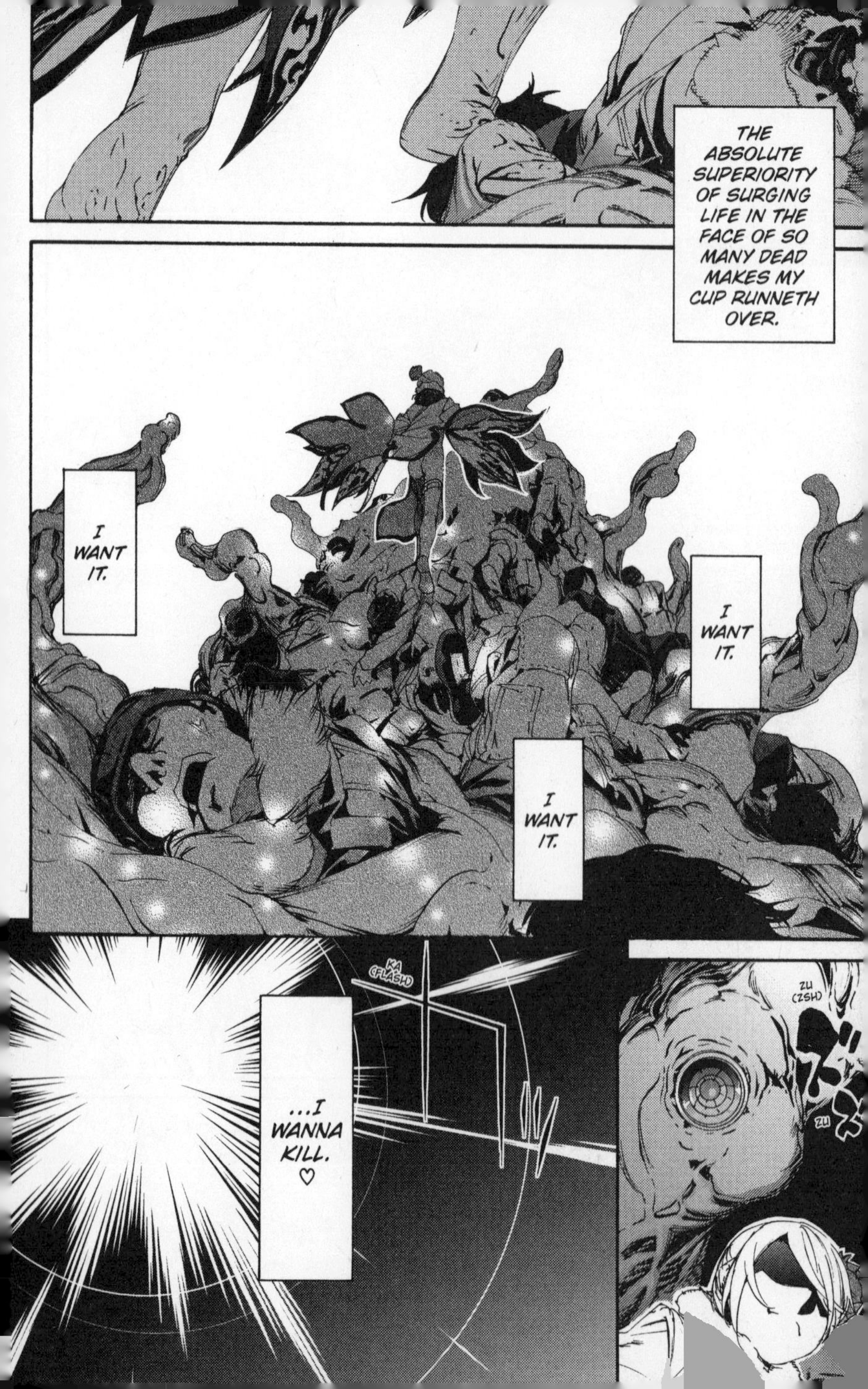
THE ABSOLUTE SUPERIORITY OF SURGING LIFE IN THE FACE OF SO MANY DEAD MAKES MY CUP RUNNETH OVER.
I WANT IT.
I WANT IT.
I WANT IT.
ZU (ZSH)
ZU
KA (FLASH)
...I WANNA KILL. ♡

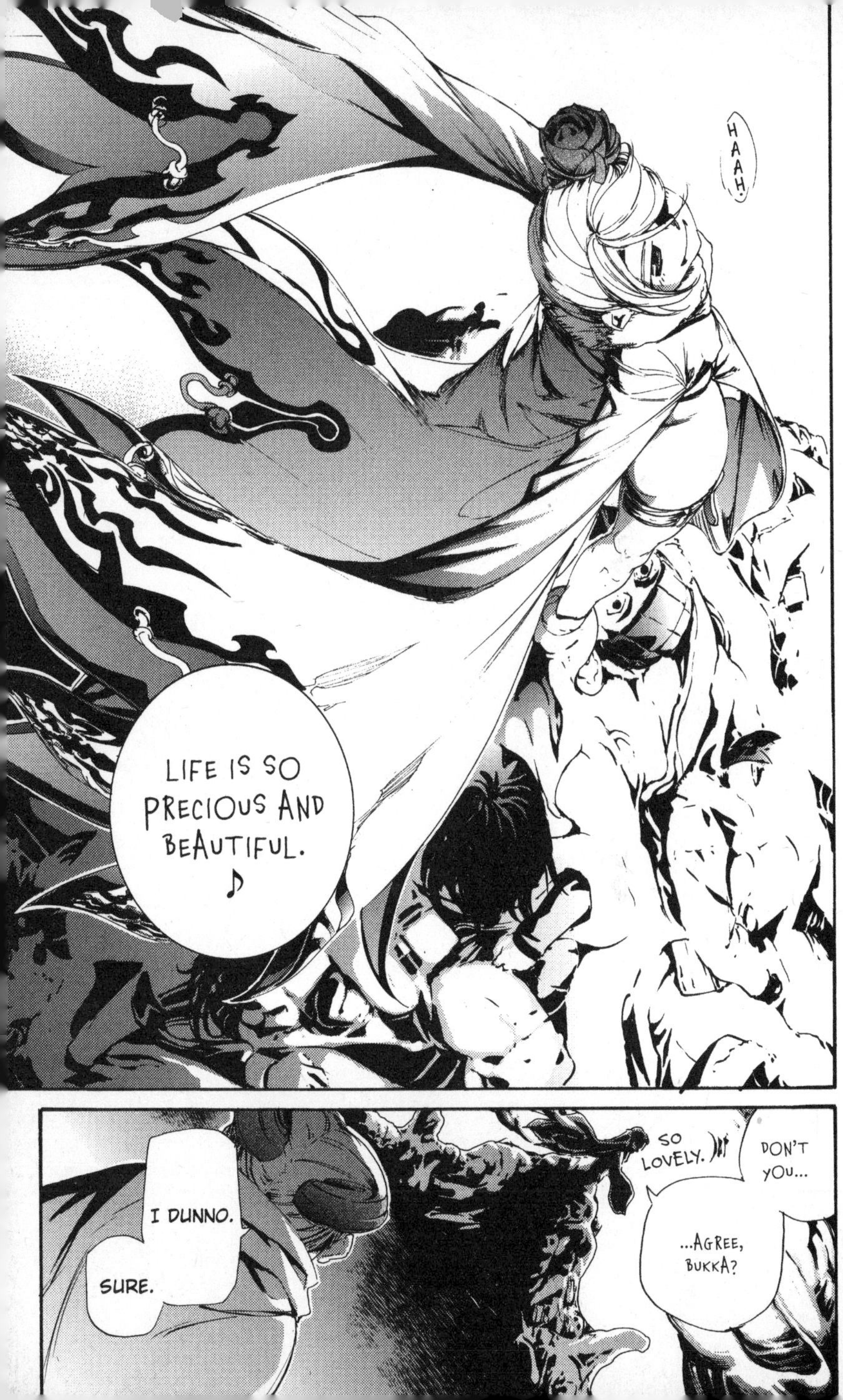
HAAAH.
LIFE IS SO PRECIOUS AND BEAUTIFUL. ♪
DON'T YOU...
SO LOVELY.
...AGREE, BUKKA?
I DUNNO.
SURE.

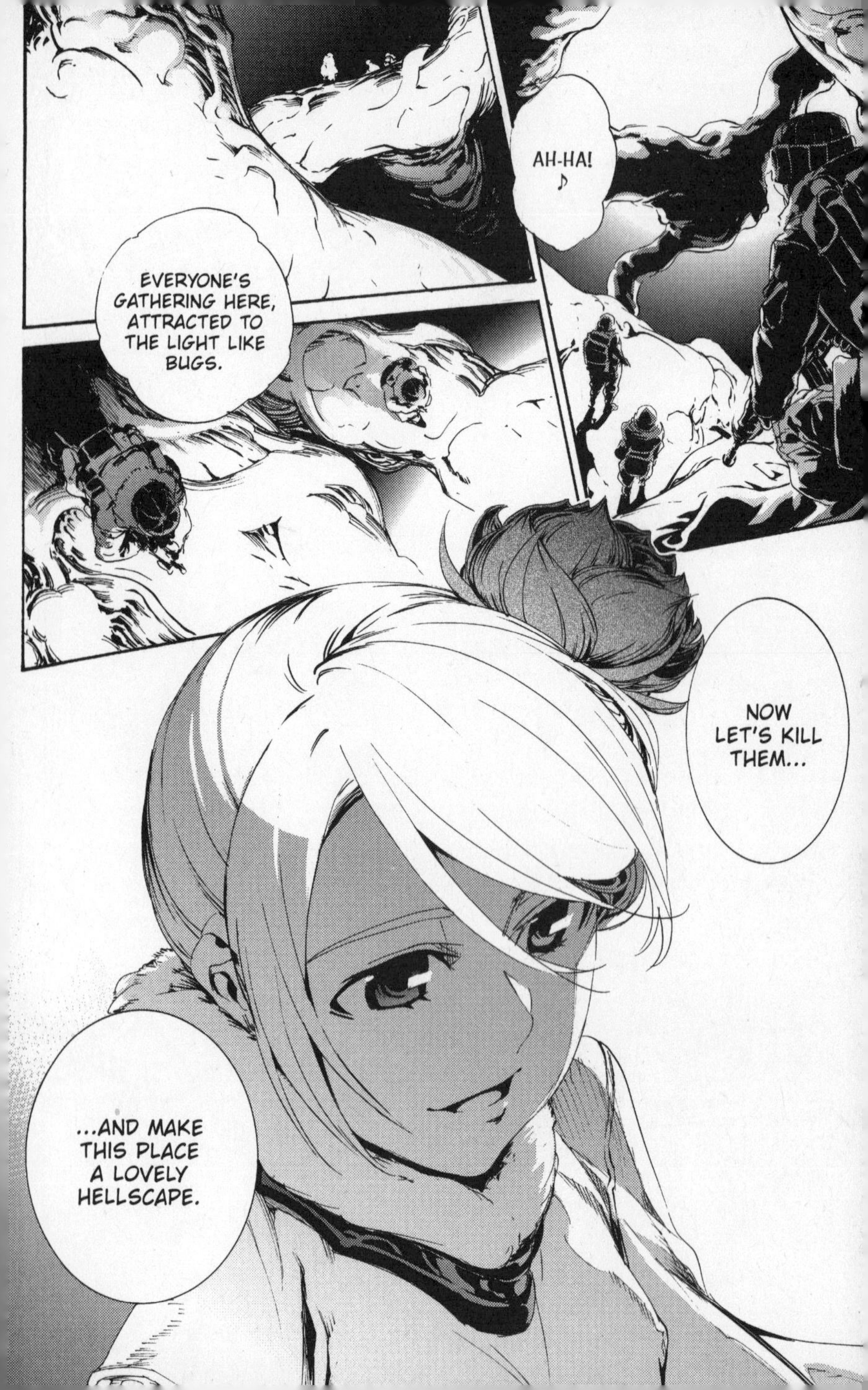
AH-HA! ♪
EVERYONE'S GATHERING HERE, ATTRACTED TO THE LIGHT LIKE BUGS.
NOW LET'S KILL THEM...
...AND MAKE THIS PLACE A LOVELY HELLSCAPE.

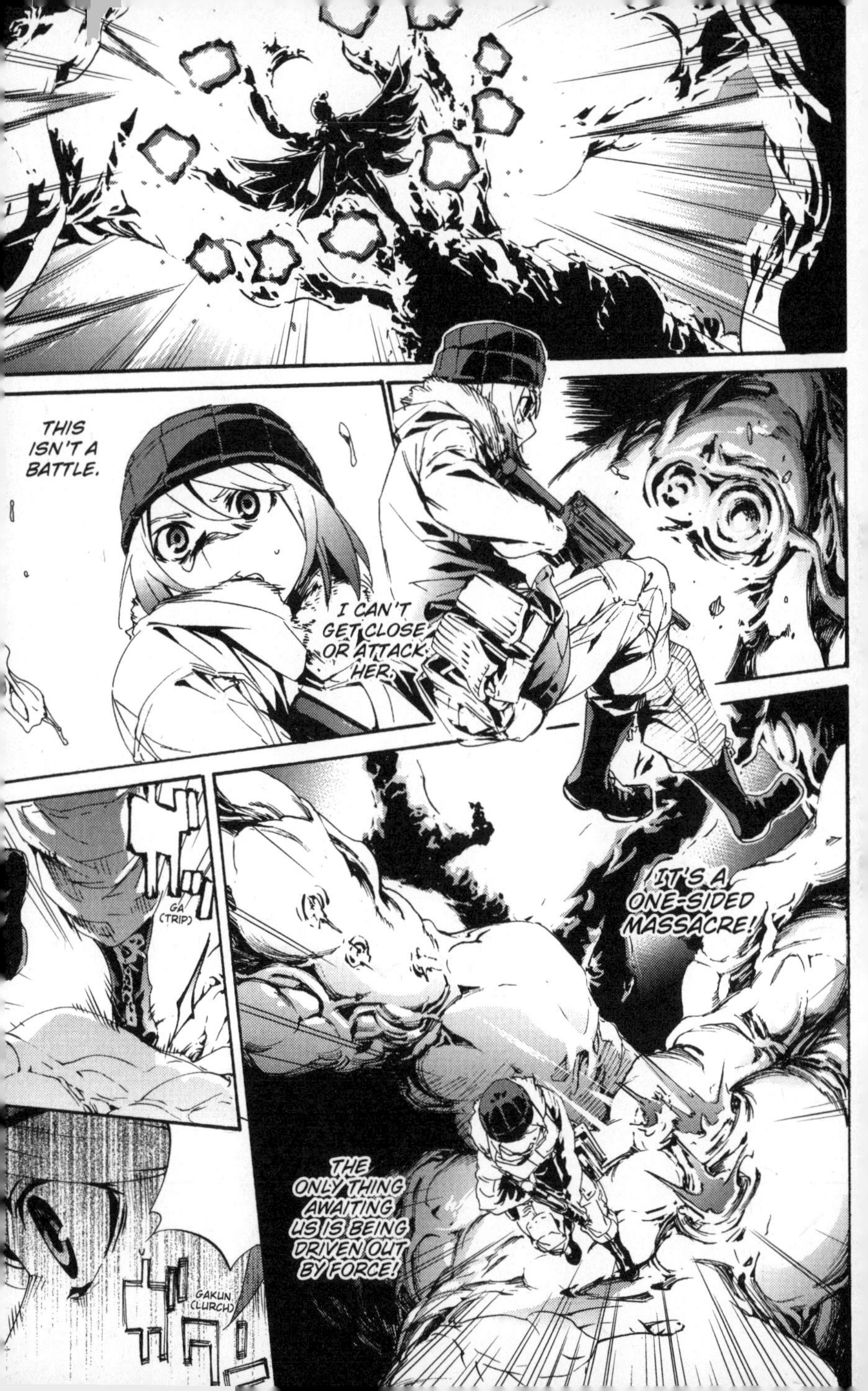
I CAN'T GET CLOSE OR ATTACK HER.
THIS ISN'T A BATTLE.
IT'S A ONE-SIDED MASSACRE!
GA (TRIP)
THE ONLY THING AWAITING US IS BEING DRIVEN OUT BY FORCE!
GAKUN (LURCH)

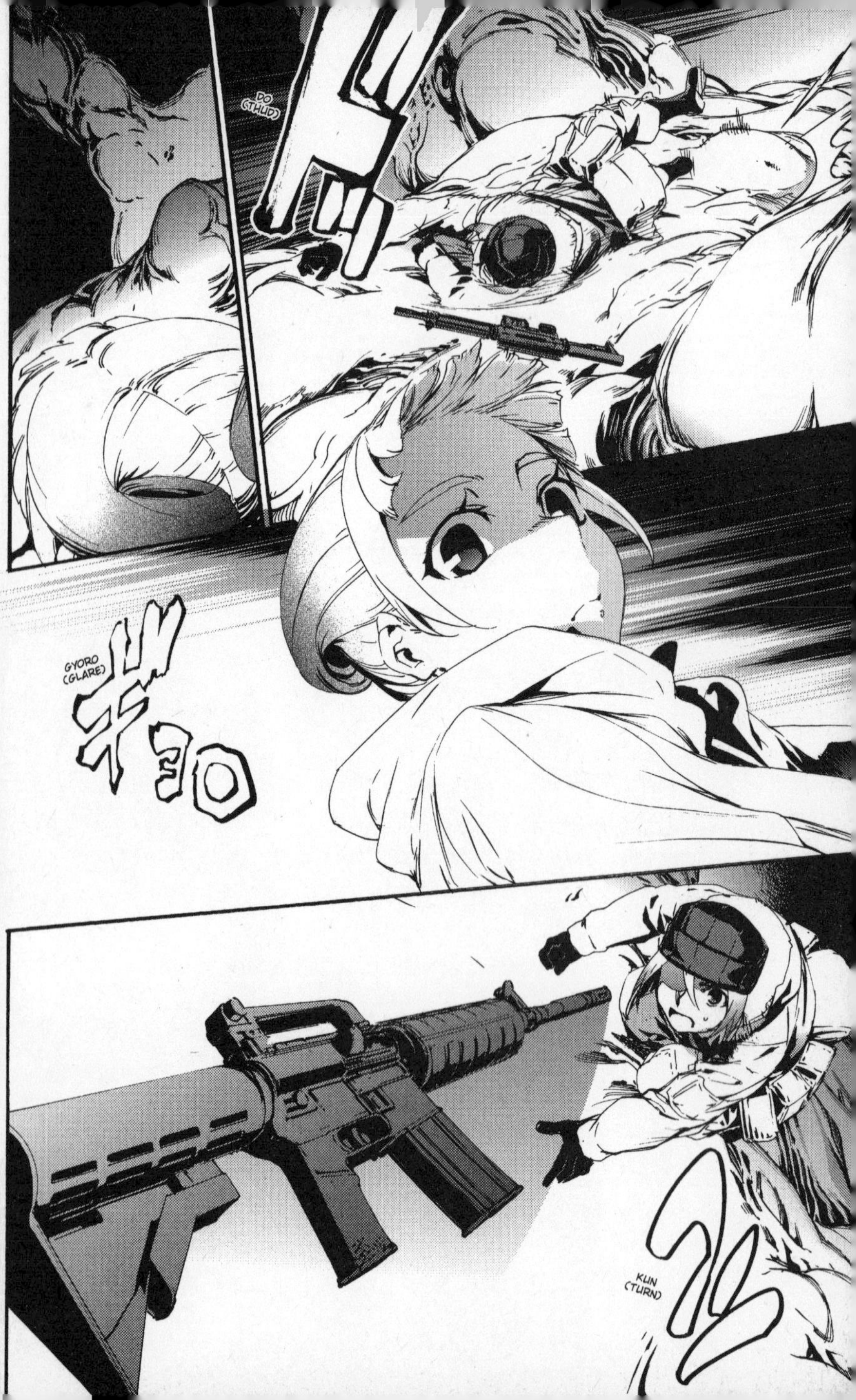
DO (THUD)
GYORO (GLARE)
KUN (TURN)

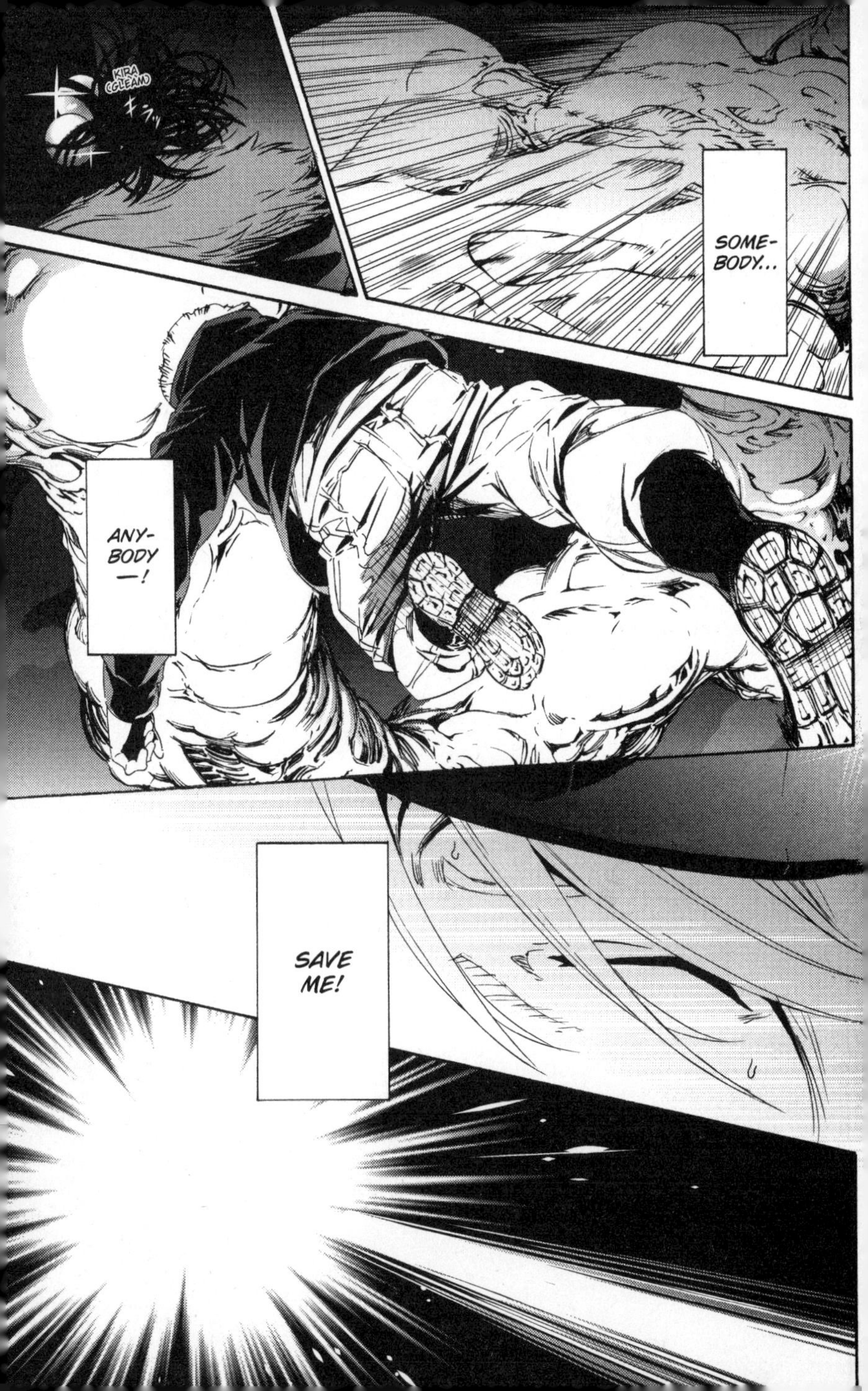
SOME-BODY...
KIRA (GLEAM)
キラッ
ANY-BODY—!
SAVE ME!

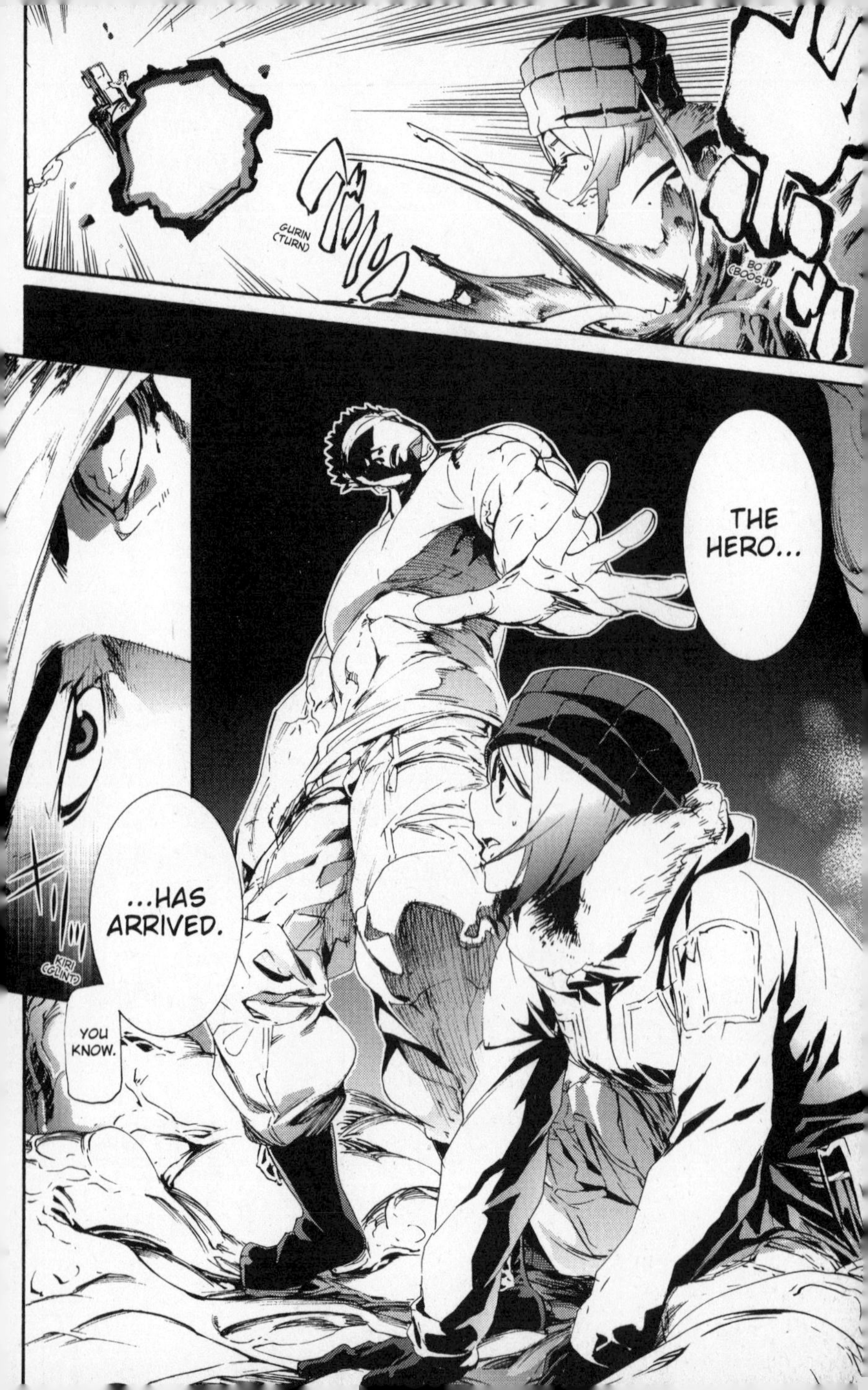
BO (BOOSH)
GURIN (TURN)
THE HERO...
...HAS ARRIVED.
KIRI (GLINT)
YOU KNOW.

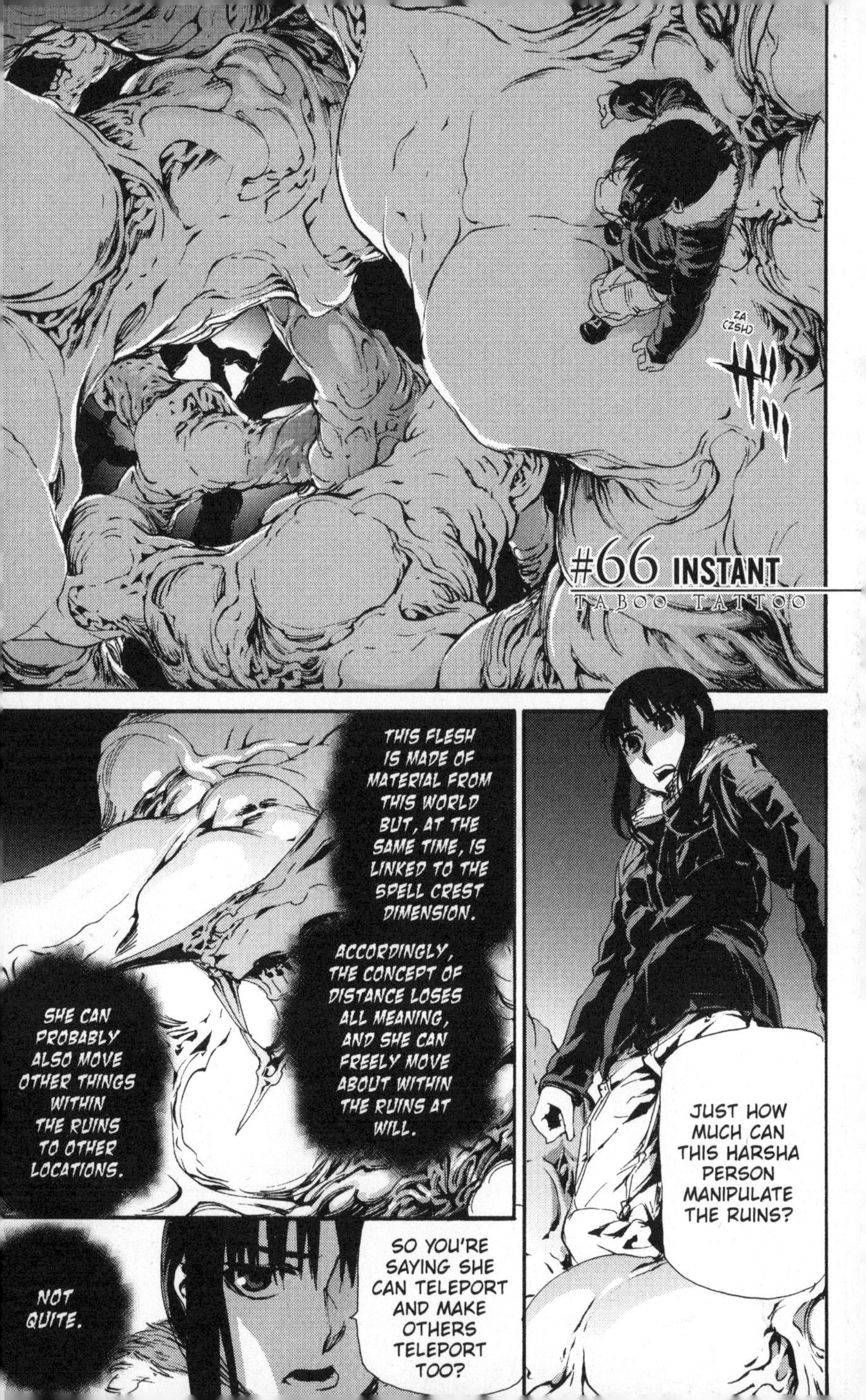
ZA (ZSH)
#66 INSTANT
TABOO TATTOO
JUST HOW MUCH CAN THIS HARSHA PERSON MANIPULATE THE RUINS?
THIS FLESH IS MADE OF MATERIAL FROM THIS WORLD BUT, AT THE SAME TIME, IS LINKED TO THE SPELL CREST DIMENSION.
ACCORDINGLY, THE CONCEPT OF DISTANCE LOSES ALL MEANING, AND SHE CAN FREELY MOVE ABOUT WITHIN THE RUINS AT WILL.
SHE CAN PROBABLY ALSO MOVE OTHER THINGS WITHIN THE RUINS TO OTHER LOCATIONS.
SO YOU'RE SAYING SHE CAN TELEPORT AND MAKE OTHERS TELEPORT TOO?
NOT QUITE.

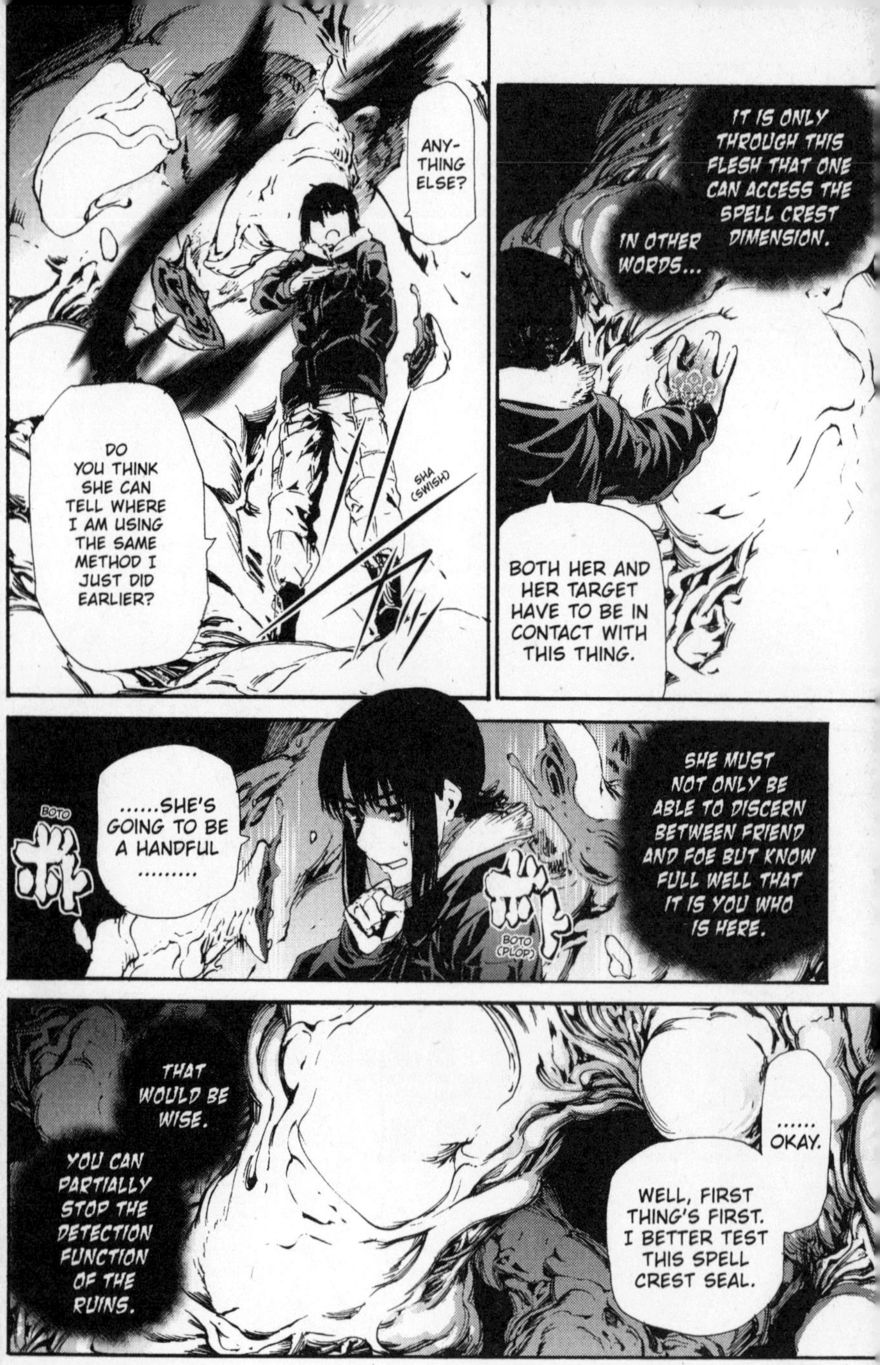
IT IS ONLY THROUGH THIS FLESH THAT ONE CAN ACCESS THE SPELL CREST DIMENSION.
IN OTHER WORDS...
BOTH HER AND HER TARGET HAVE TO BE IN CONTACT WITH THIS THING.
ANY-THING ELSE?
SHA (SWISH)
DO YOU THINK SHE CAN TELL WHERE I AM USING THE SAME METHOD I JUST DID EARLIER?
SHE MUST NOT ONLY BE ABLE TO DISCERN BETWEEN FRIEND AND FOE BUT KNOW FULL WELL THAT IT IS YOU WHO IS HERE.
BOTO (PLOP)
......SHE'S GOING TO BE A HANDFUL ....
BOTO
...... OKAY.
WELL, FIRST THING'S FIRST. I BETTER TEST THIS SPELL CREST SEAL.
THAT WOULD BE WISE.
YOU CAN PARTIALLY STOP THE DETECTION FUNCTION OF THE RUINS.

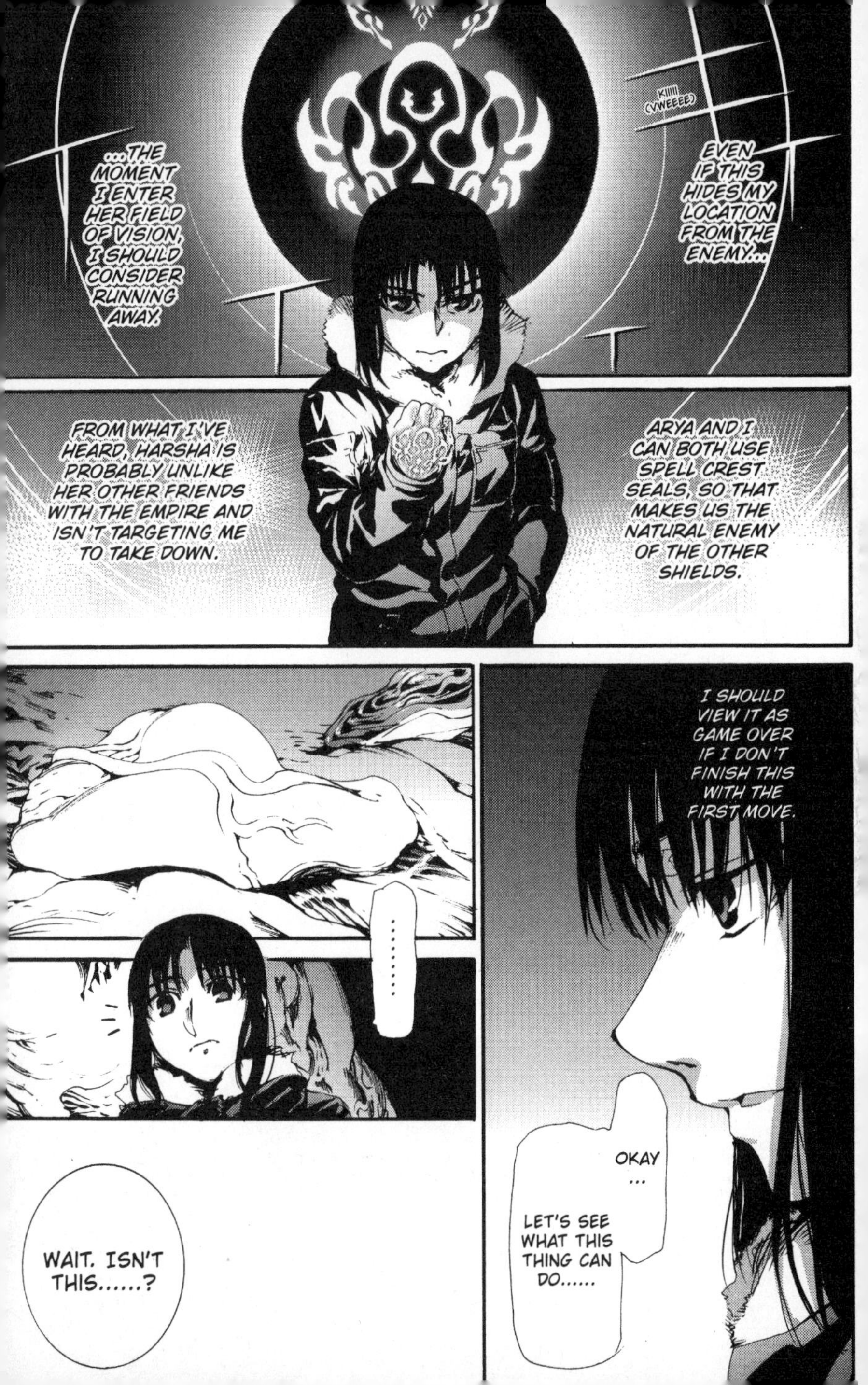
KIIIII (VWEEEE)
EVEN IF THIS HIDES MY LOCATION FROM THE ENEMY...
...THE MOMENT I ENTER HER FIELD OF VISION, I SHOULD CONSIDER RUNNING AWAY.
ARYA AND I CAN BOTH USE SPELL CREST SEALS, SO THAT MAKES US THE NATURAL ENEMY OF THE OTHER SHIELDS.
FROM WHAT I'VE HEARD, HARSHA IS PROBABLY UNLIKE HER OTHER FRIENDS WITH THE EMPIRE AND ISN'T TARGETING ME TO TAKE DOWN.
I SHOULD VIEW IT AS GAME OVER IF I DON'T FINISH THIS WITH THE FIRST MOVE.
OKAY ...
LET'S SEE WHAT THIS THING CAN DO......
......
WAIT. ISN'T THIS......?

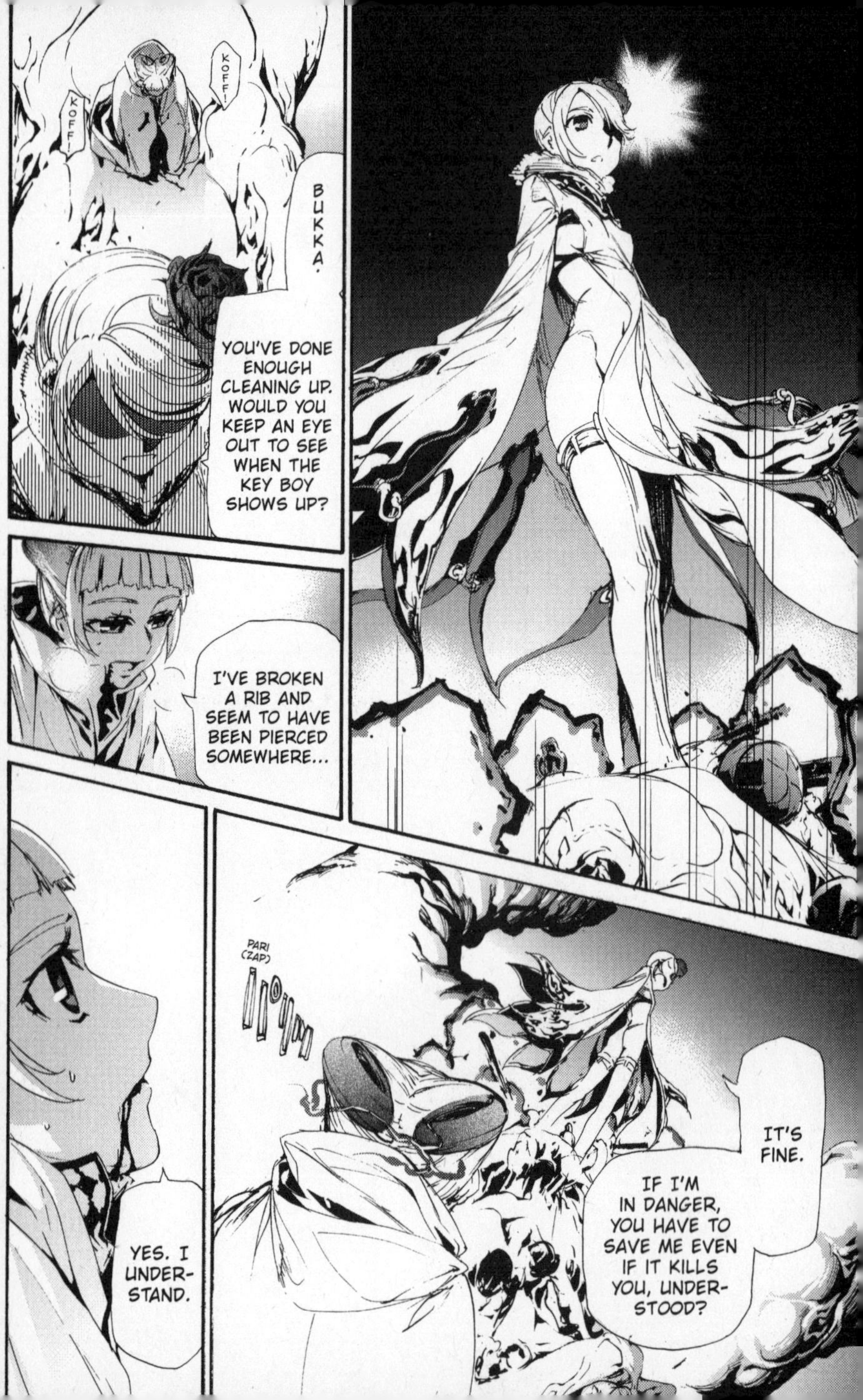
KOFF!
KOFF!
BUKKA.
YOU'VE DONE ENOUGH CLEANING UP. WOULD YOU KEEP AN EYE OUT TO SEE WHEN THE KEY BOY SHOWS UP?
I'VE BROKEN A RIB AND SEEM TO HAVE BEEN PIERCED SOMEWHERE...
PARI (ZAP)
IT'S FINE.
IF I'M IN DANGER, YOU HAVE TO SAVE ME EVEN IF IT KILLS YOU, UNDER-STOOD?
YES. I UNDER-STAND.

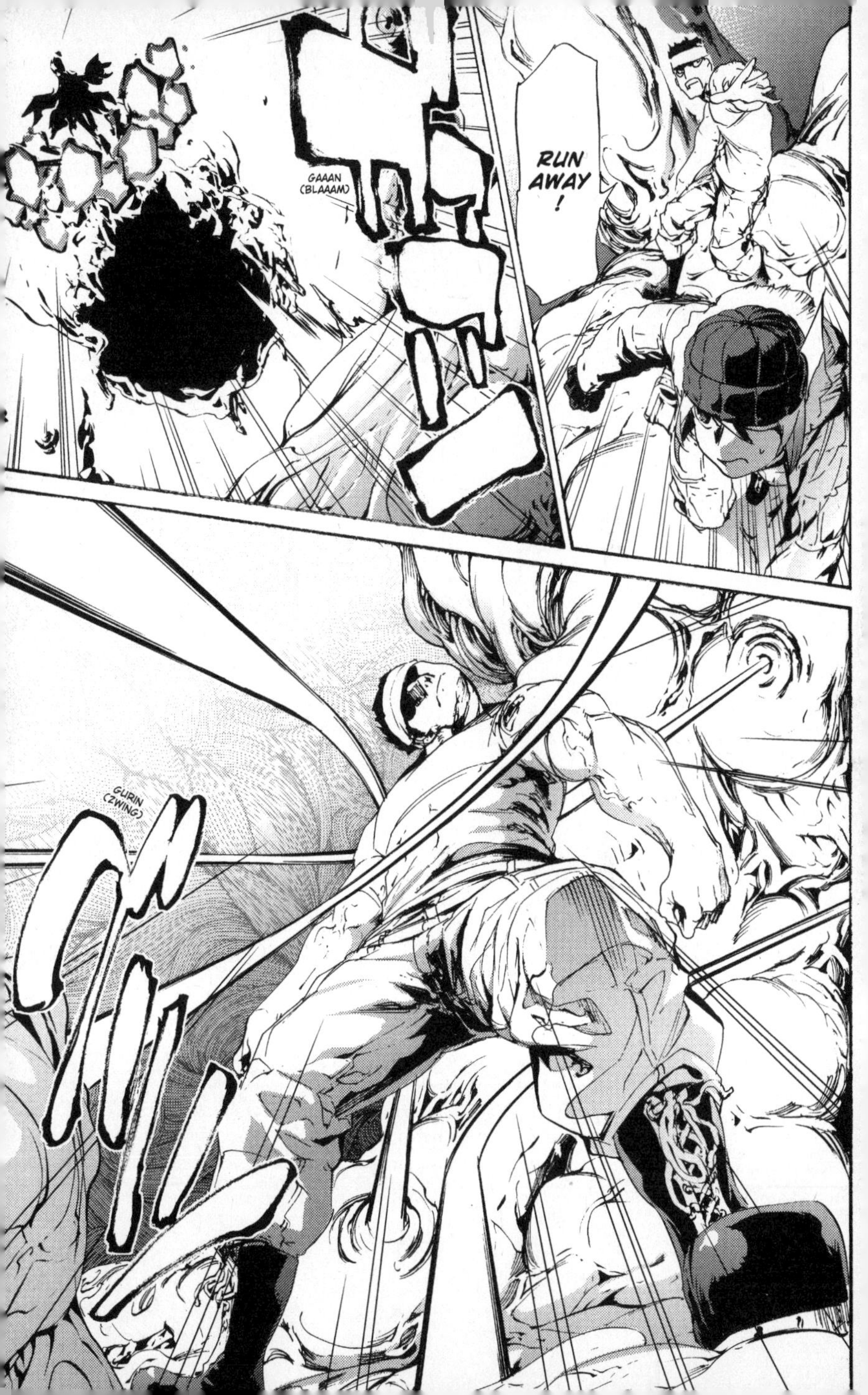
RUN AWAY!
GAAAN (BLAAAM)
GURIN (ZWING)

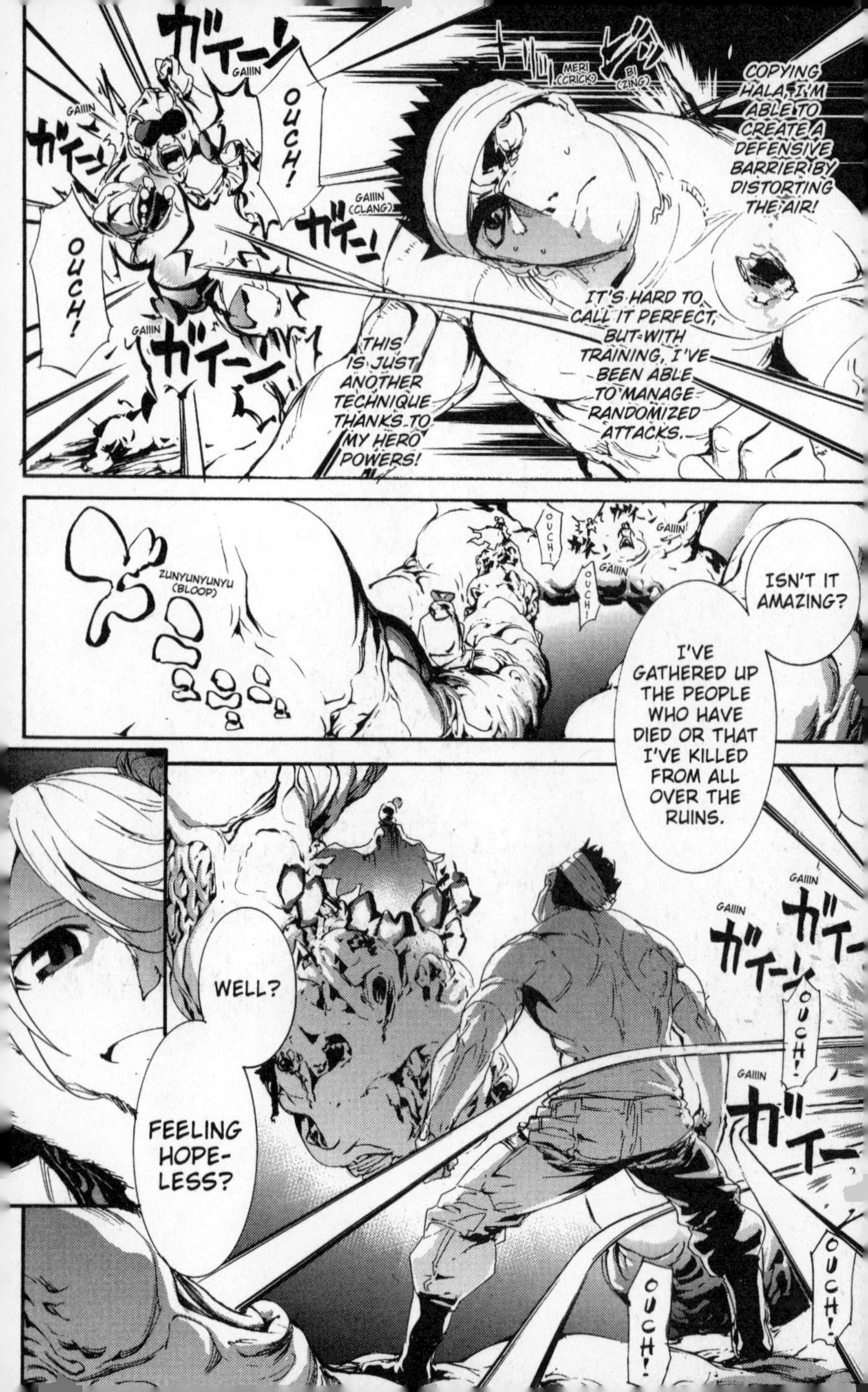
ビシ
BI (ZING)
メリ
MERI (CRICK)
COPYING HALA, I'M ABLE TO CREATE A DEFENSIVE BARRIER BY DISTORTING THE AIR!
IT'S HARD TO CALL IT PERFECT, BUT WITH TRAINING, I'VE BEEN ABLE TO MANAGE RANDOMIZED ATTACKS.
THIS IS JUST ANOTHER TECHNIQUE THANKS TO MY HERO POWERS!
ガイーン
GAIIIN
OUCH!
ガイーン
GAIIIN
ガイーン
GAIIIN (CLANG)
OUCH!
ガイーン
GAIIIN
ISN'T IT AMAZING?
I'VE GATHERED UP THE PEOPLE WHO HAVE DIED OR THAT I'VE KILLED FROM ALL OVER THE RUINS.
GAIIIN!
OUCH!
GAIIIN
OUCH!
ZUNYUNYUNYU (BLOOP)
ガイーン
GAIIIN
ガイーン
GAIIIN
OUCH!
GAIIIN
ガイー
OUCH!
OUCH!
WELL?
FEELING HOPE-LESS?

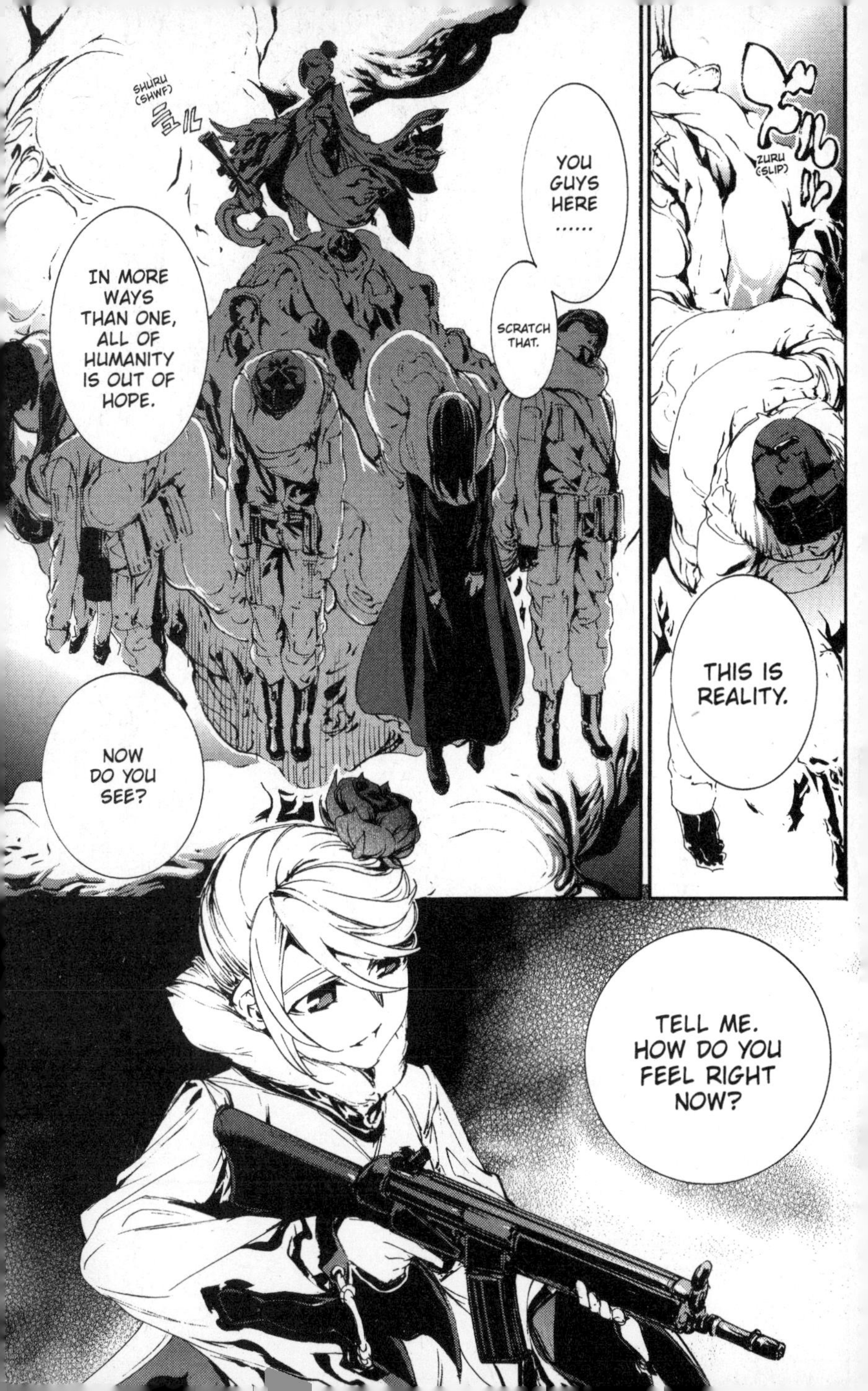
ズルル
ZURU (SLIP)
THIS IS REALITY.
YOU GUYS HERE ......
SCRATCH THAT.
シュル
SHURU (SHWF)
IN MORE WAYS THAN ONE, ALL OF HUMANITY IS OUT OF HOPE.
NOW DO YOU SEE?
TELL ME. HOW DO YOU FEEL RIGHT NOW?

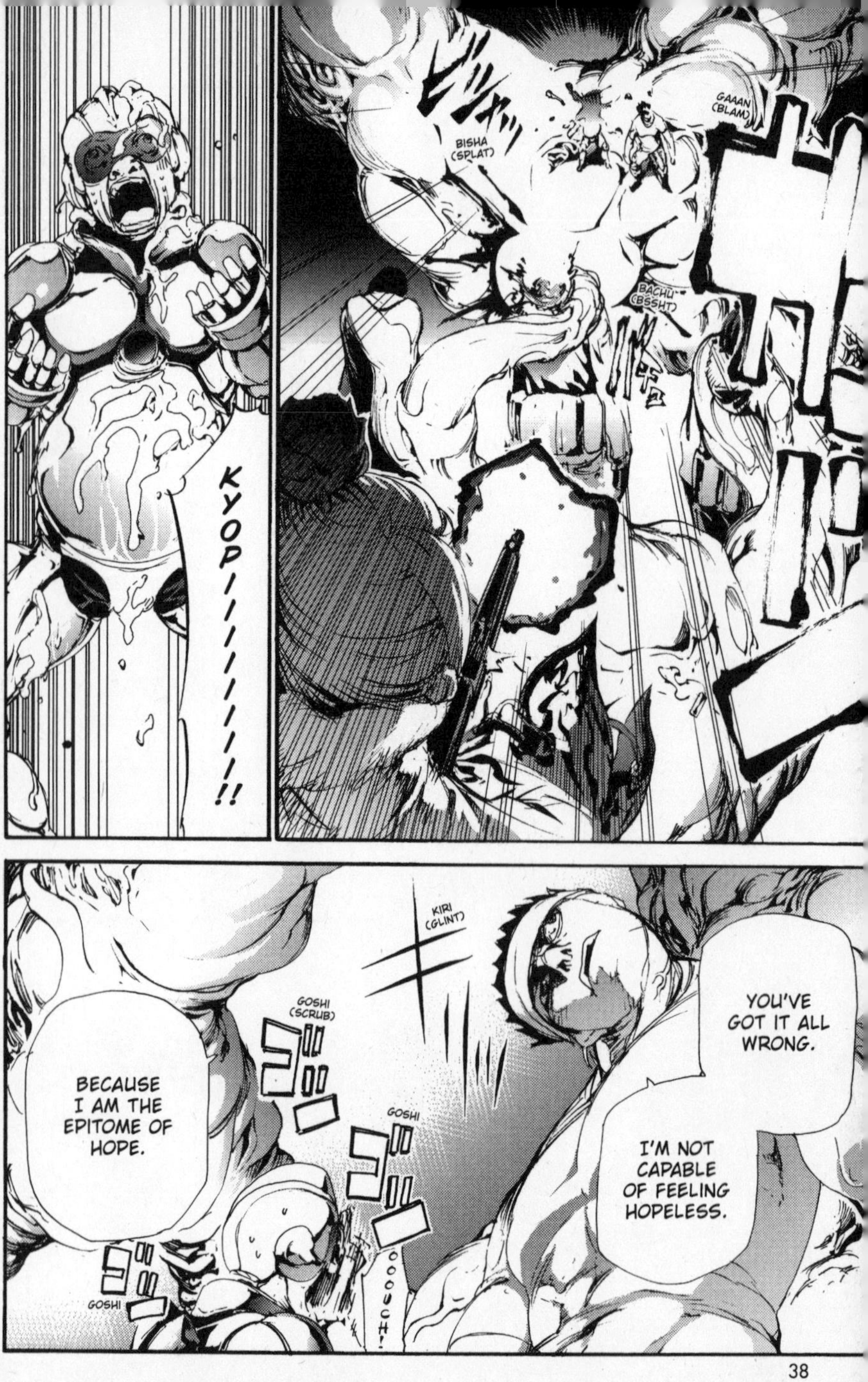
GAAAN (BLAM)
BISHA (SPLAT)
BACHU (BSSHT)
KYOPIIIIIIIIIII!!
YOU'VE GOT IT ALL WRONG.
I'M NOT CAPABLE OF FEELING HOPELESS.
KIRI (GLINT)
OOOUCH!
GOSHI
GOSHI (SCRUB)
BECAUSE I AM THE EPITOME OF HOPE.
GOSHI

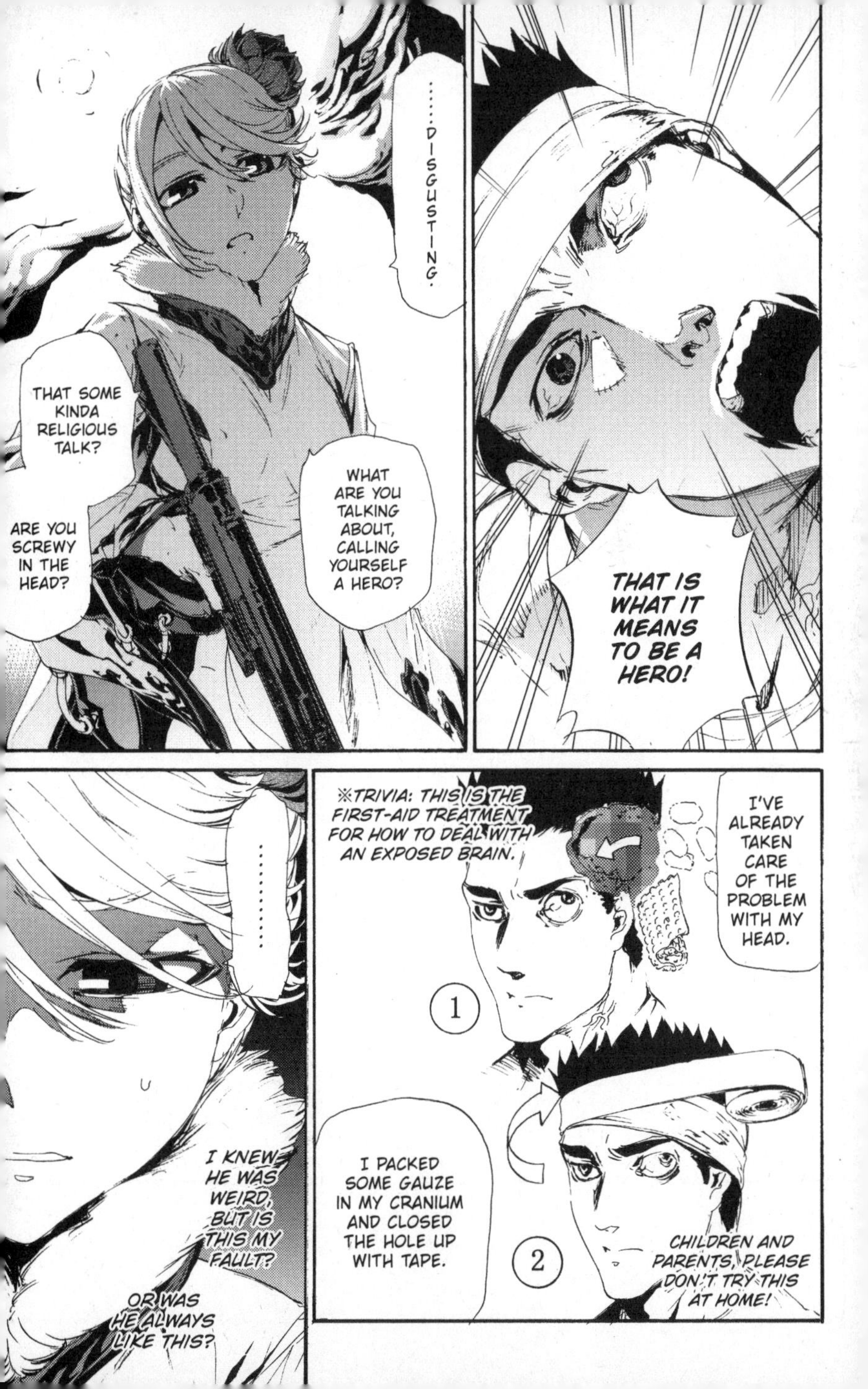
THAT IS WHAT IT MEANS TO BE A HERO!
.....DISGUSTING.
WHAT ARE YOU TALKING ABOUT, CALLING YOURSELF A HERO?
THAT SOME KINDA RELIGIOUS TALK?
ARE YOU SCREWY IN THE HEAD?
I'VE ALREADY TAKEN CARE OF THE PROBLEM WITH MY HEAD.
※TRIVIA: THIS IS THE FIRST-AID TREATMENT FOR HOW TO DEAL WITH AN EXPOSED BRAIN.
1
I PACKED SOME GAUZE IN MY CRANIUM AND CLOSED THE HOLE UP WITH TAPE.
2
CHILDREN AND PARENTS, PLEASE DON'T TRY THIS AT HOME!
....
I KNEW HE WAS WEIRD, BUT IS THIS MY FAULT?
OR WAS HE ALWAYS LIKE THIS?

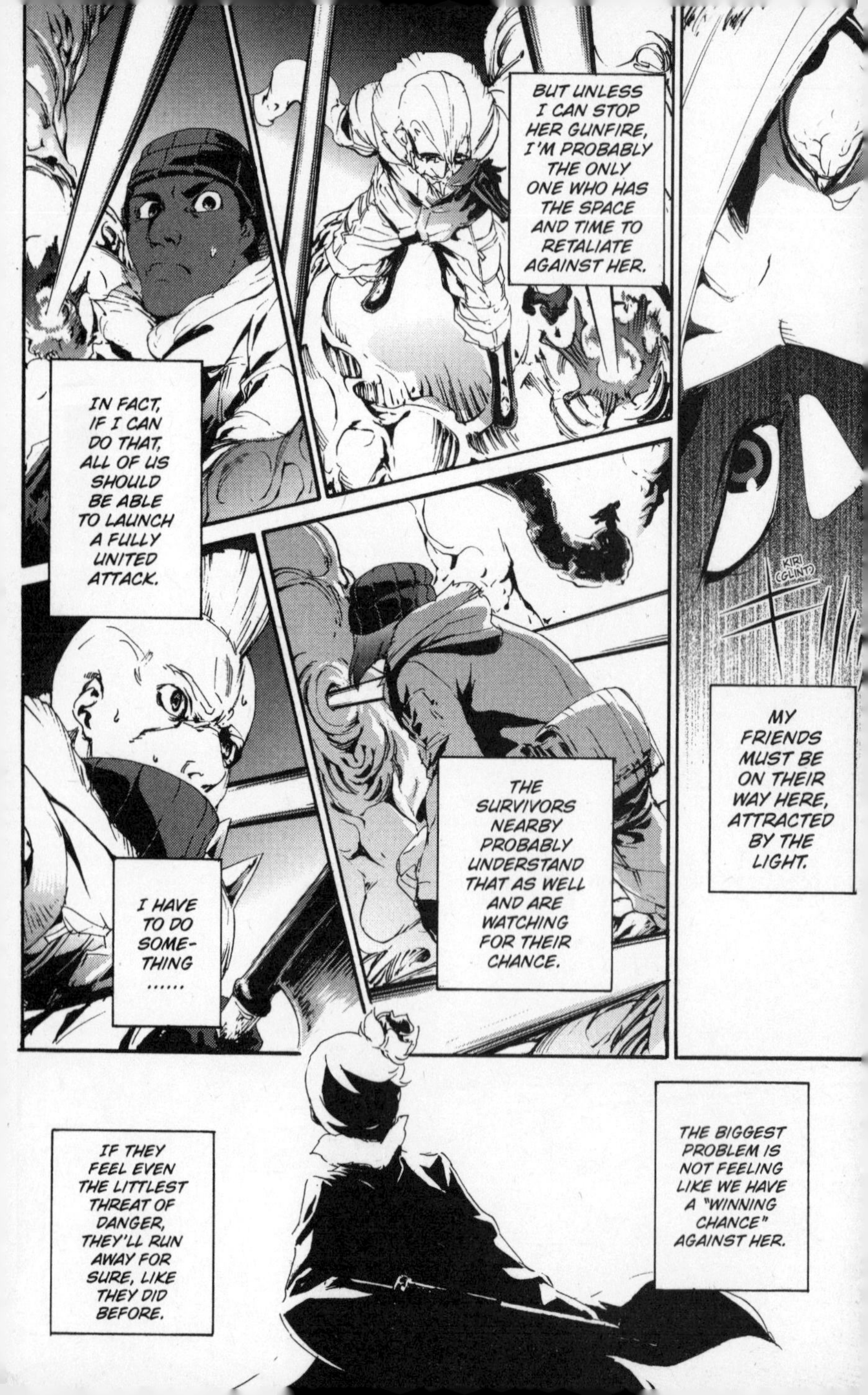
KIRI (GLINT)
MY FRIENDS MUST BE ON THEIR WAY HERE, ATTRACTED BY THE LIGHT.
BUT UNLESS I CAN STOP HER GUNFIRE, I'M PROBABLY THE ONLY ONE WHO HAS THE SPACE AND TIME TO RETALIATE AGAINST HER.
IN FACT, IF I CAN DO THAT, ALL OF US SHOULD BE ABLE TO LAUNCH A FULLY UNITED ATTACK.
THE SURVIVORS NEARBY PROBABLY UNDERSTAND THAT AS WELL AND ARE WATCHING FOR THEIR CHANCE.
I HAVE TO DO SOME-THING......
THE BIGGEST PROBLEM IS NOT FEELING LIKE WE HAVE A "WINNING CHANCE" AGAINST HER.
IF THEY FEEL EVEN THE LITTLEST THREAT OF DANGER, THEY'LL RUN AWAY FOR SURE, LIKE THEY DID BEFORE.

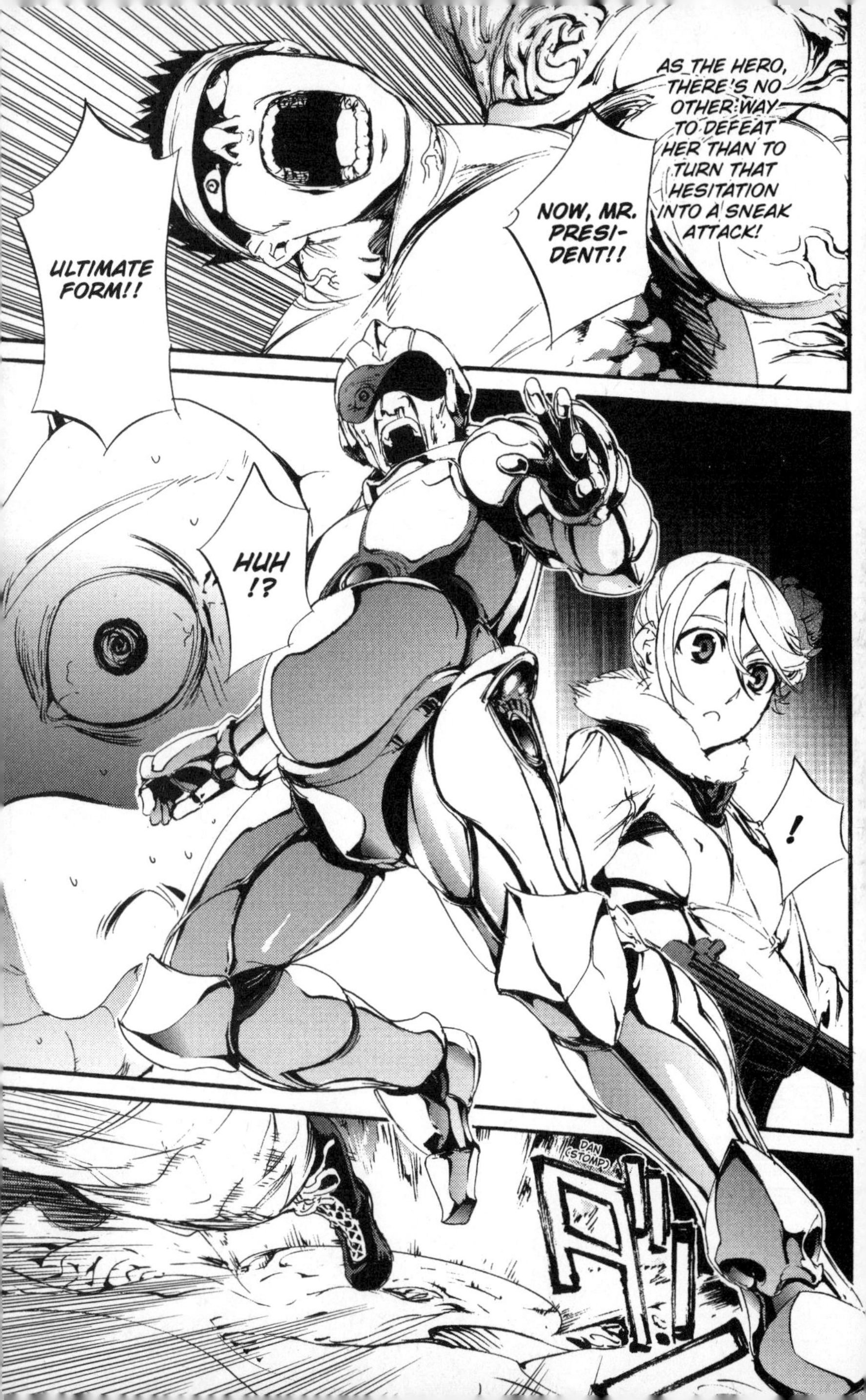
AS THE HERO, THERE'S NO OTHER WAY TO DEFEAT HER THAN TO TURN THAT HESITATION INTO A SNEAK ATTACK!
NOW, MR. PRESI-DENT!!
ULTIMATE FORM!!
!
HUH!?
DAN (STOMP)

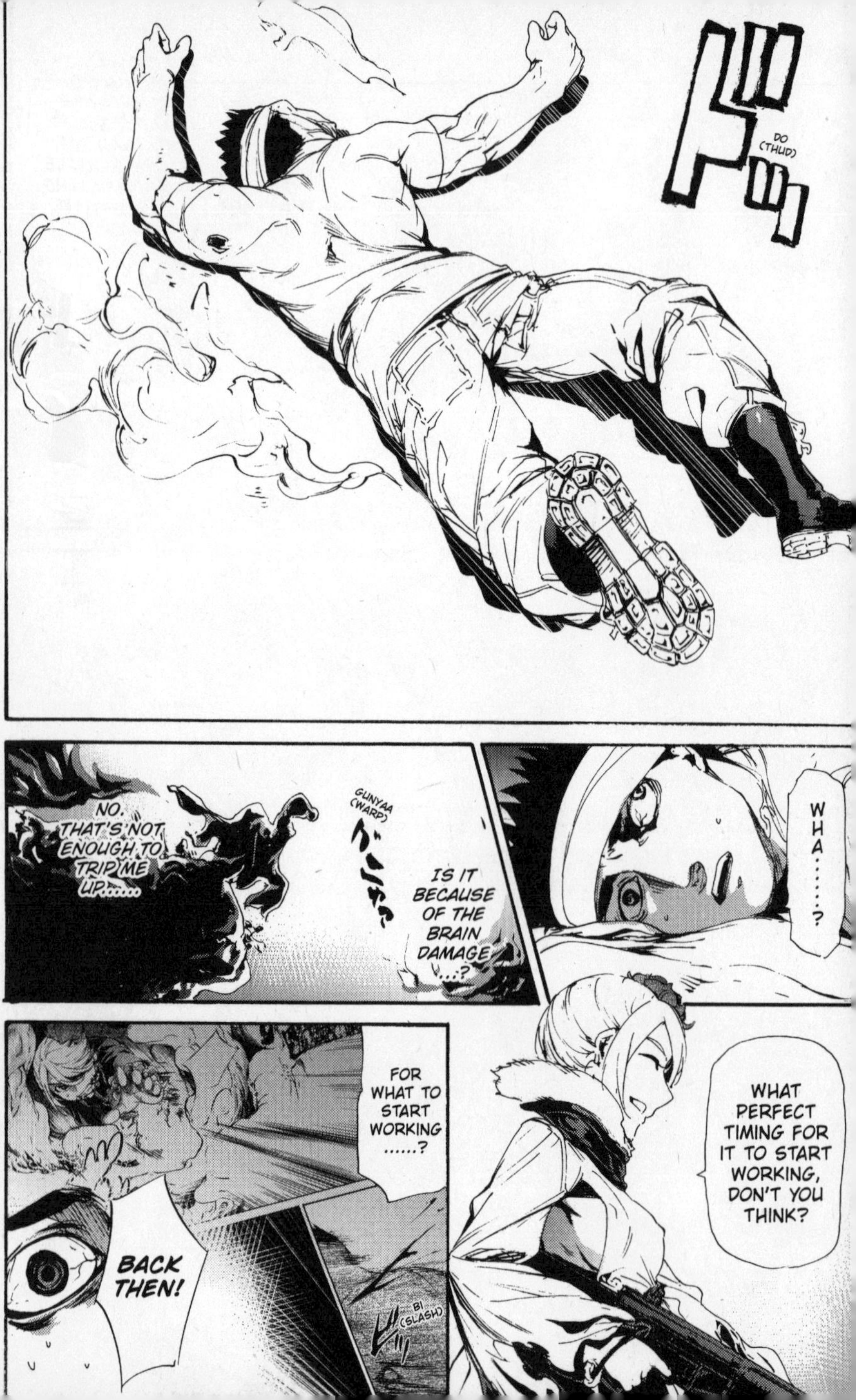
DO (THUD)
WHA......?
GUNYAA (WARP)
IS IT BECAUSE OF THE BRAIN DAMAGE...?
NO. THAT'S NOT ENOUGH TO TRIP ME UP......
WHAT PERFECT TIMING FOR IT TO START WORKING, DON'T YOU THINK?
FOR WHAT TO START WORKING......?
BACK THEN!
BI (SLASH)

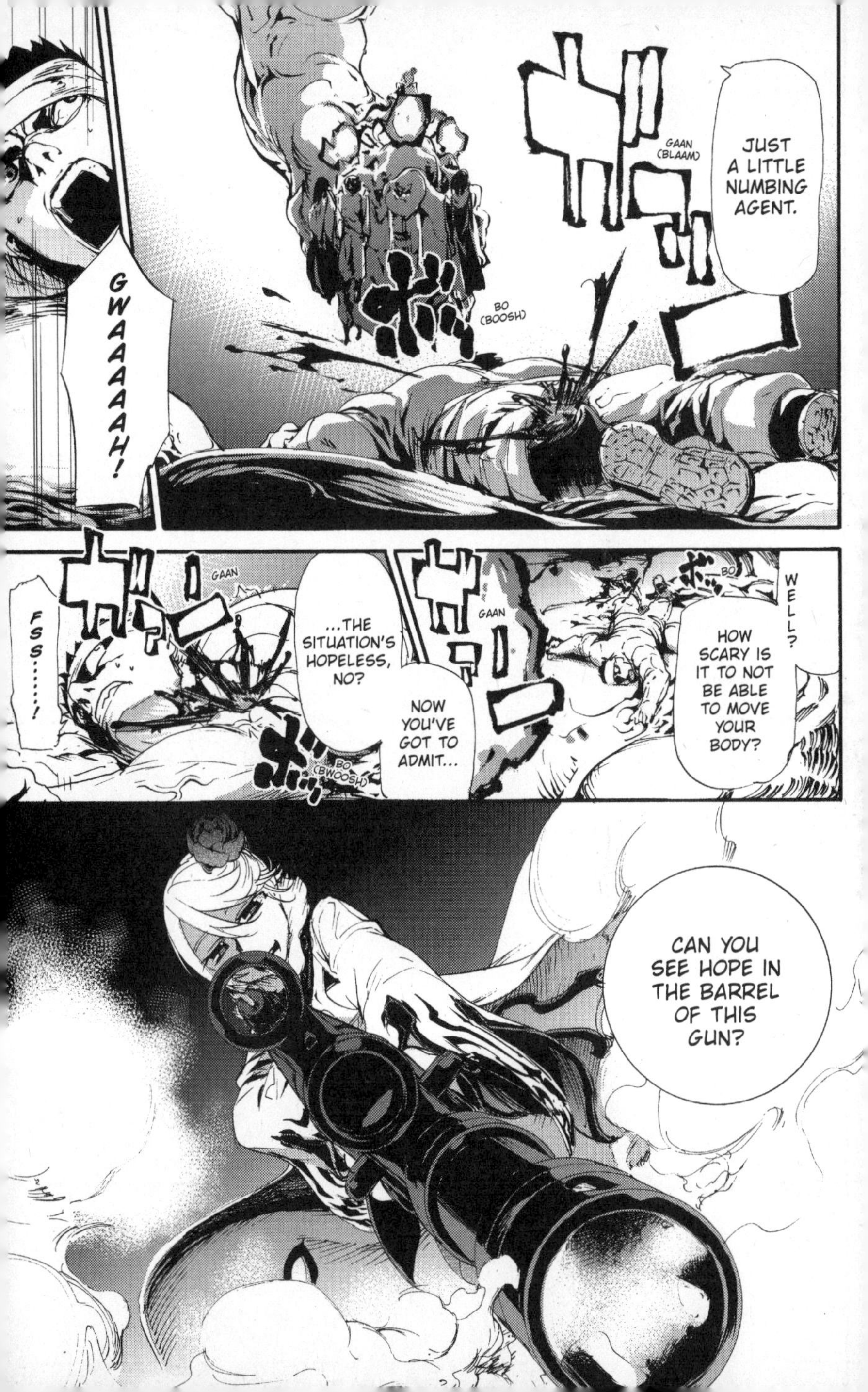
JUST A LITTLE NUMBING AGENT.
GAAN (BLAAM)
BO (BOOSH)
GWAAAAAAH!
WELL?
HOW SCARY IS IT TO NOT BE ABLE TO MOVE YOUR BODY?
BO
GAAN
NOW YOU'VE GOT TO ADMIT...
...THE SITUATION'S HOPELESS, NO?
BO (BWOOSH)
GAAN
FSS......!
CAN YOU SEE HOPE IN THE BARREL OF THIS GUN?

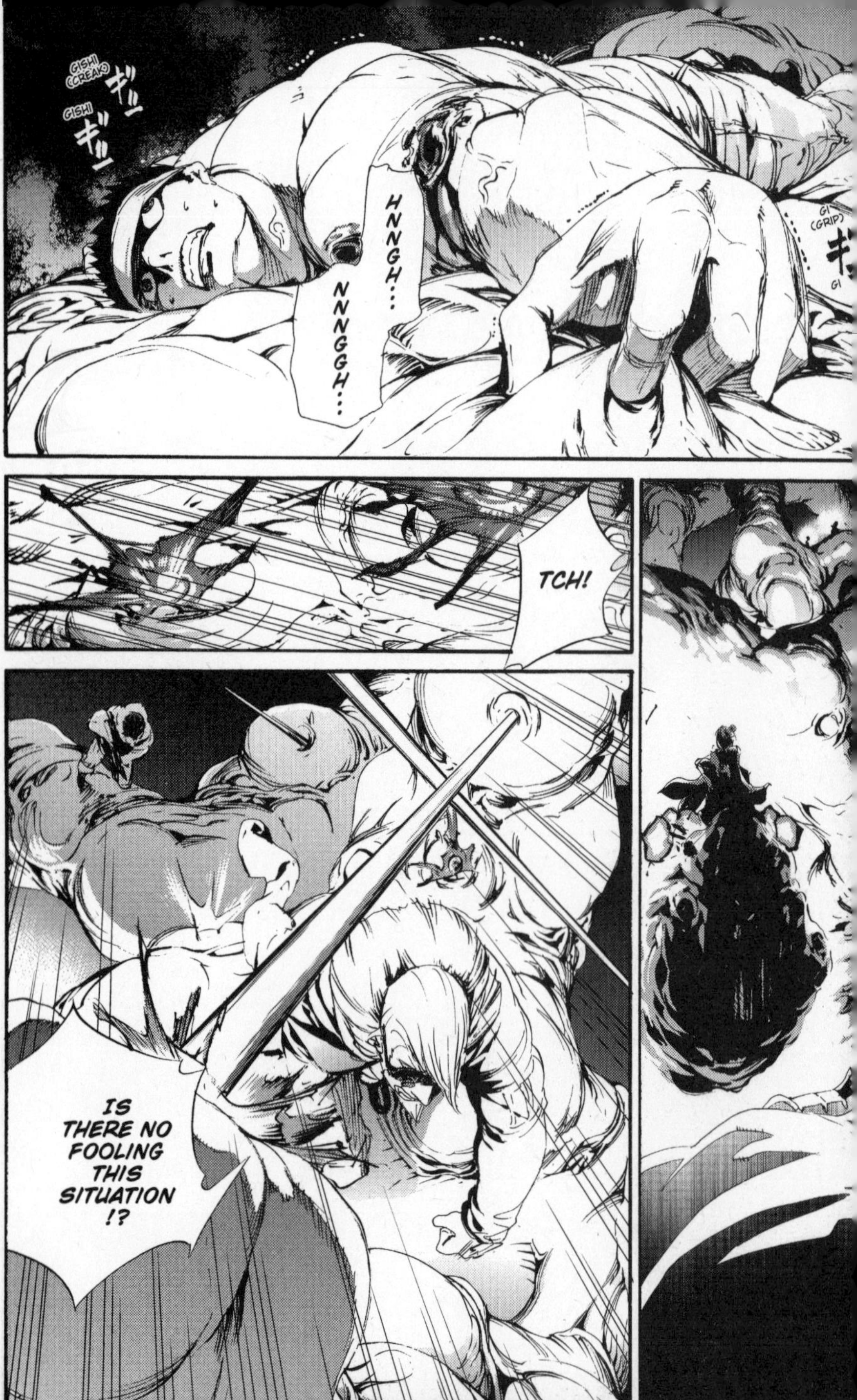
GISHI (CREAK)
GISHI
GI (GRIP)
GI
HNNGH...
NNNGGH...
TCH!
IS THERE NO FOOLING THIS SITUATION !?

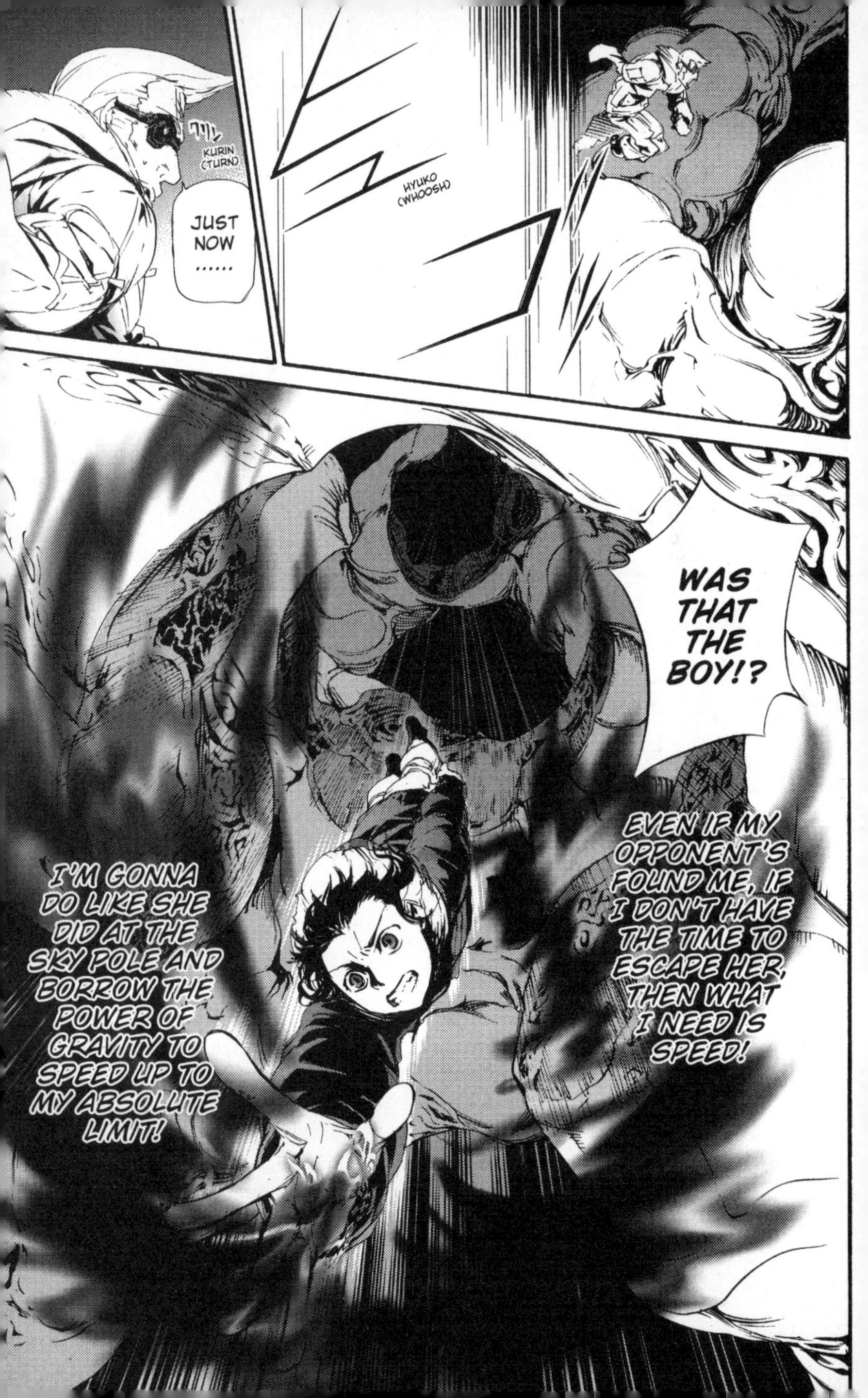
HYUKO (WHOOSH)
KURIN (TURN)
JUST NOW ......
WAS THAT THE BOY!?
EVEN IF MY OPPONENT'S FOUND ME, IF I DON'T HAVE THE TIME TO ESCAPE HER, THEN WHAT I NEED IS SPEED!
I'M GONNA DO LIKE SHE DID AT THE SKY POLE AND BORROW THE POWER OF GRAVITY TO SPEED UP TO MY ABSOLUTE LIMIT!

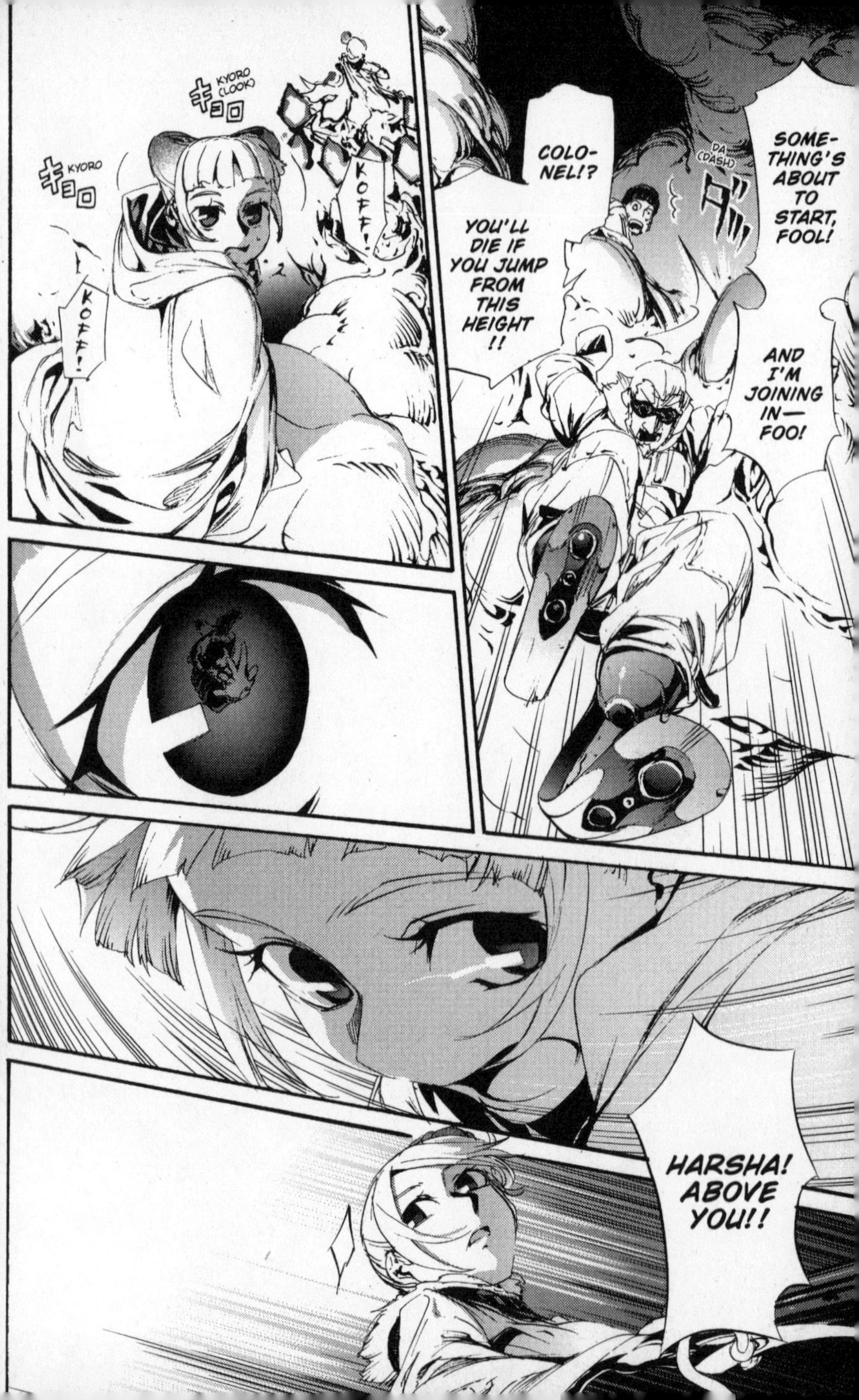
SOME-THING'S ABOUT TO START, FOOL!
COLO-NEL!?
DA (DASH)
YOU'LL DIE IF YOU JUMP FROM THIS HEIGHT!!
AND I'M JOINING IN—FOO!
KYORO (LOOK)
KOFF!
KYORO
KOFF!
HARSHA! ABOVE YOU!!

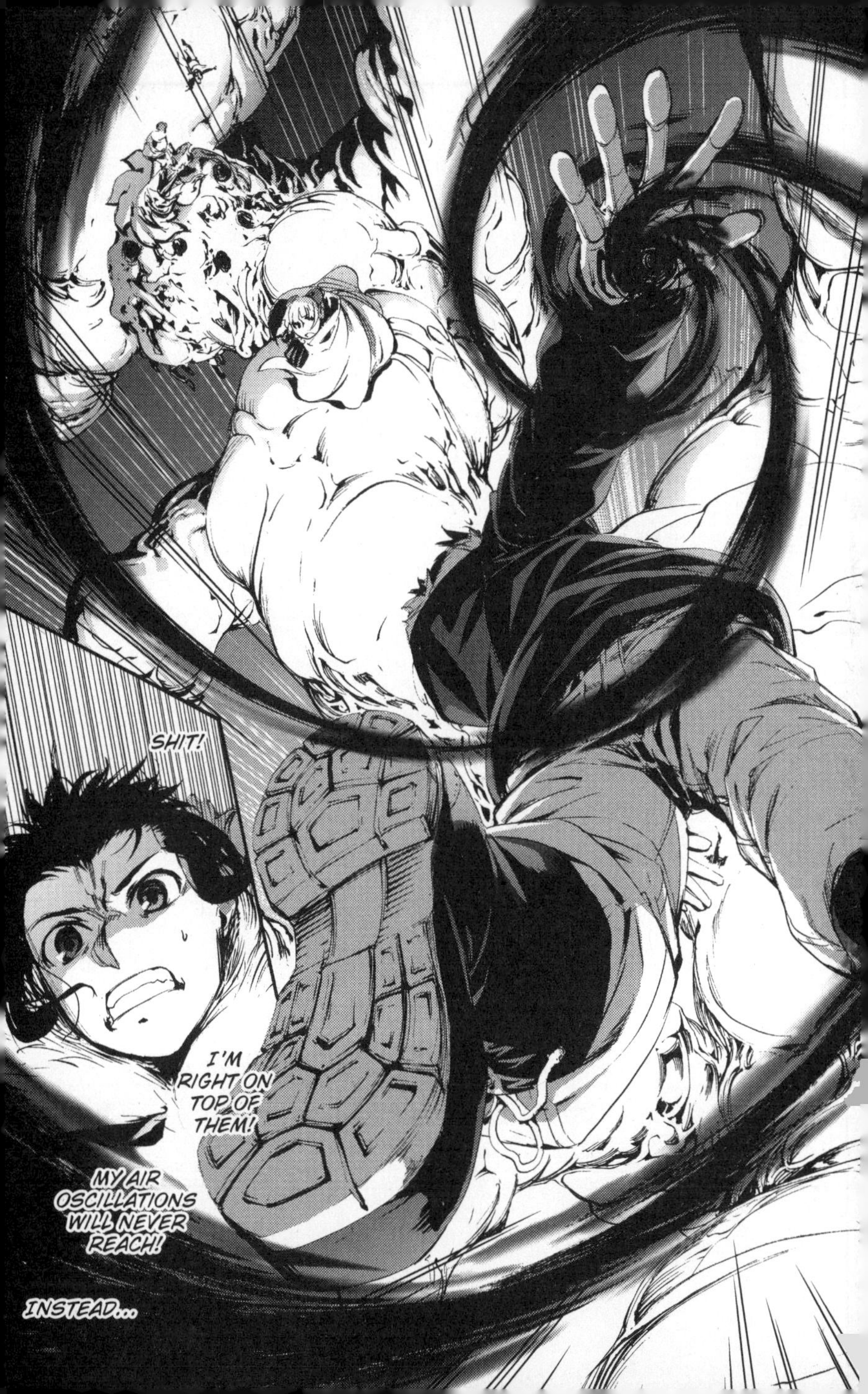
SHIT!
I'M RIGHT ON TOP OF THEM!
MY AIR OSCILLATIONS WILL NEVER REACH!
INSTEAD...

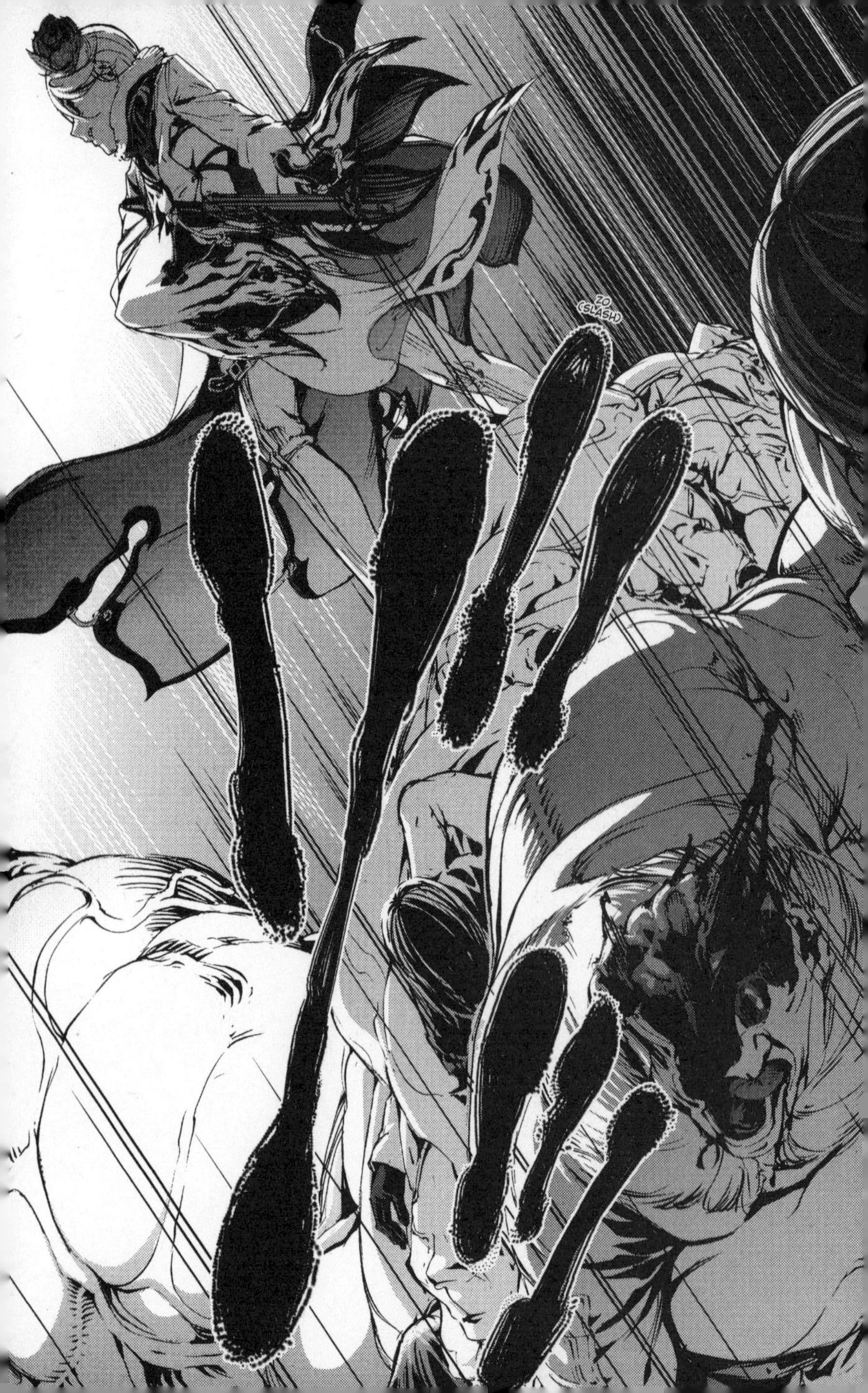
ZO
(SLASH)

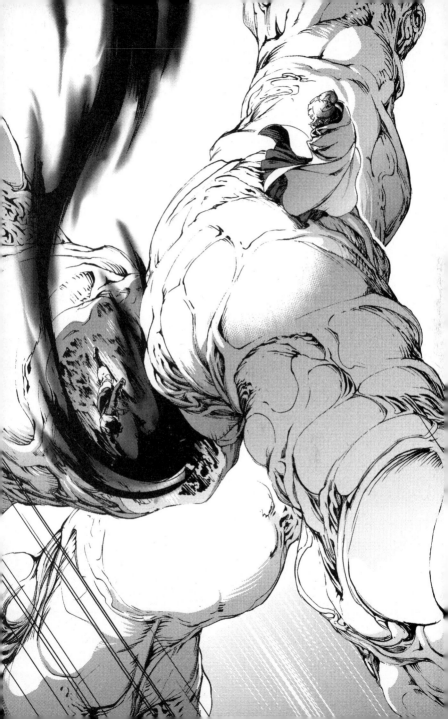

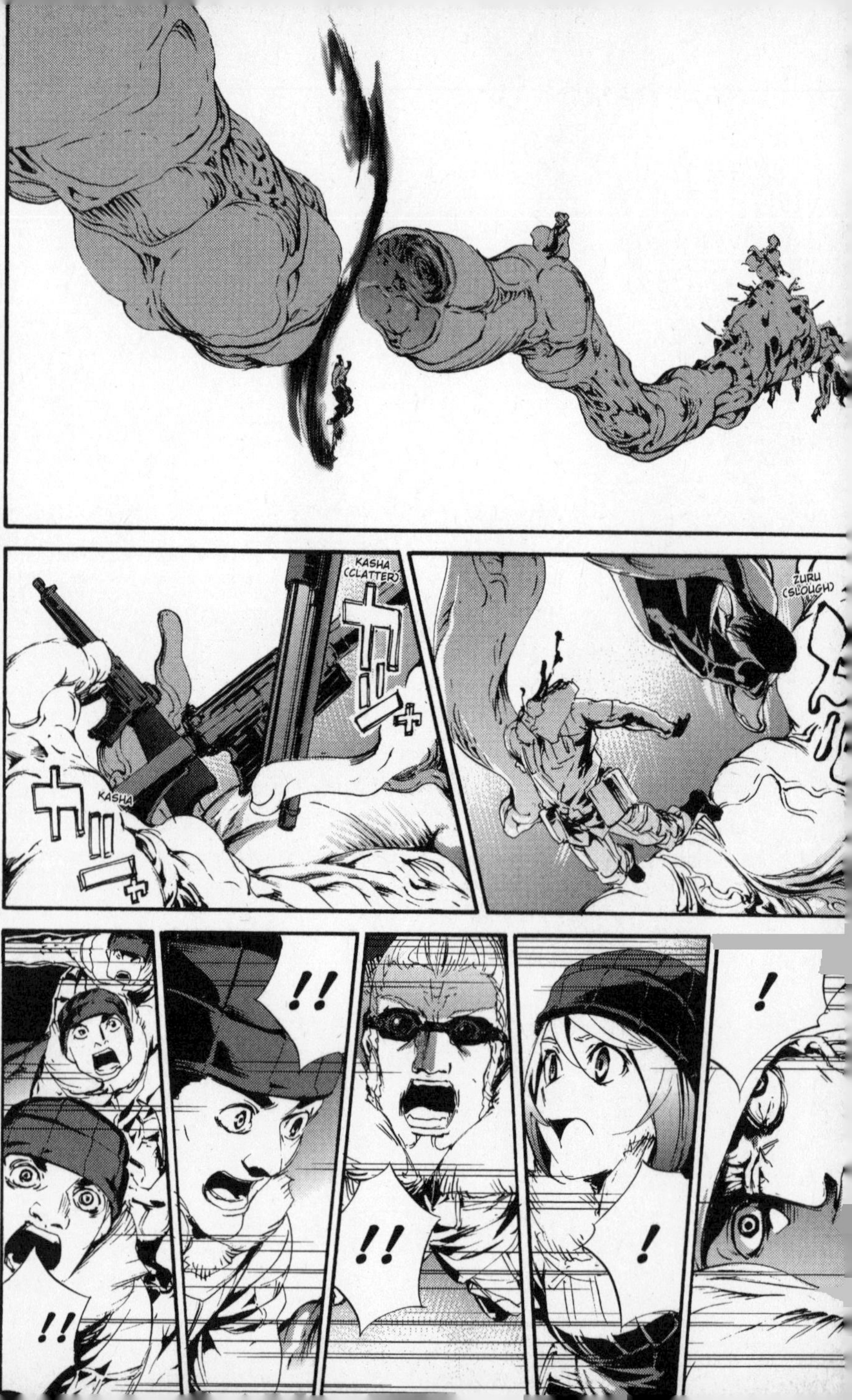
ZURU (SLOUGH)
KASHA (CLATTER)
KASHA
!
!
!!
!!
!!

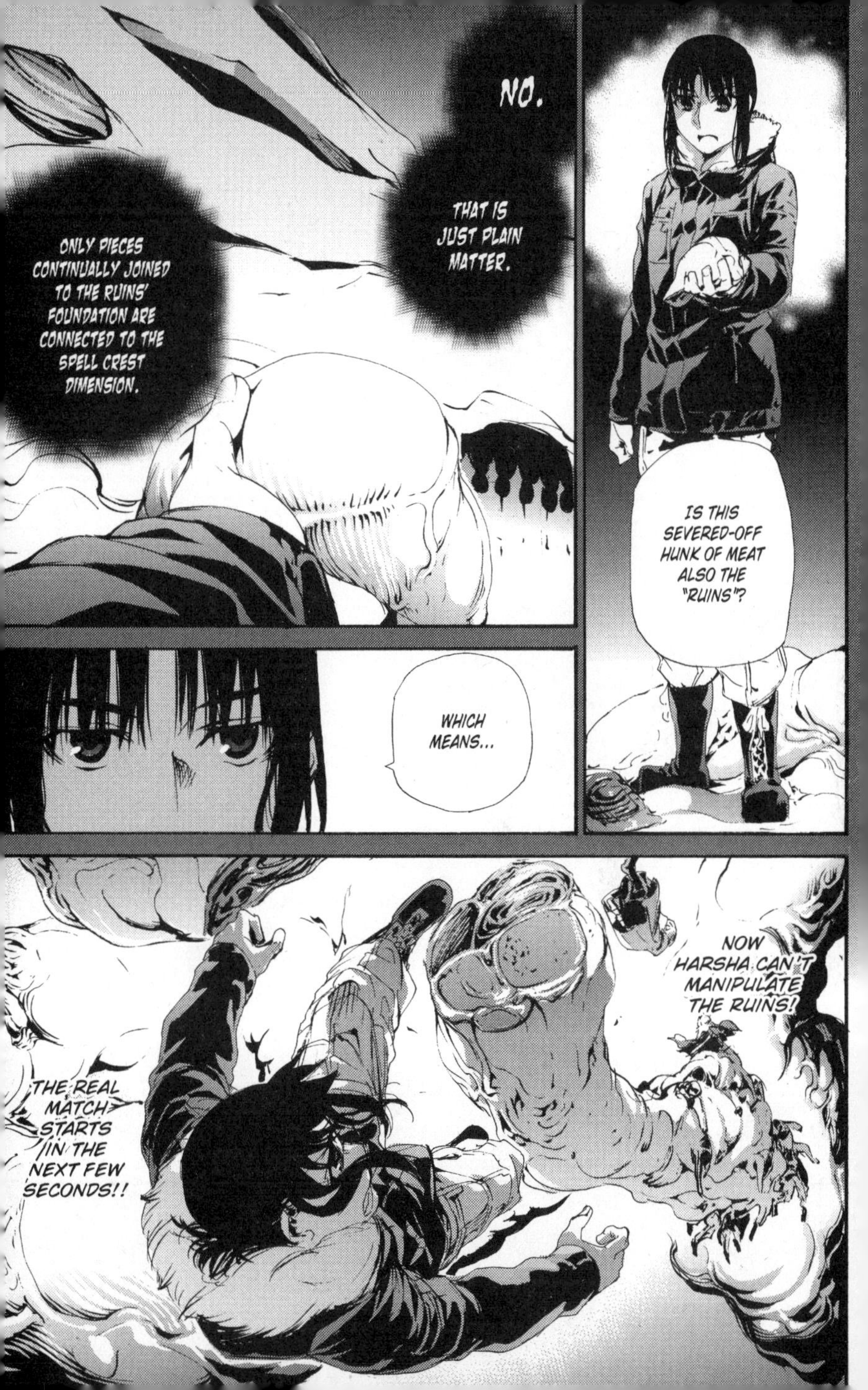
IS THIS SEVERED-OFF HUNK OF MEAT ALSO THE "RUINS"?
NO.
THAT IS JUST PLAIN MATTER.
ONLY PIECES CONTINUALLY JOINED TO THE RUINS' FOUNDATION ARE CONNECTED TO THE SPELL CREST DIMENSION.
WHICH MEANS...
NOW HARSHA CAN'T MANIPULATE THE RUINS!
THE REAL MATCH STARTS IN THE NEXT FEW SECONDS!!

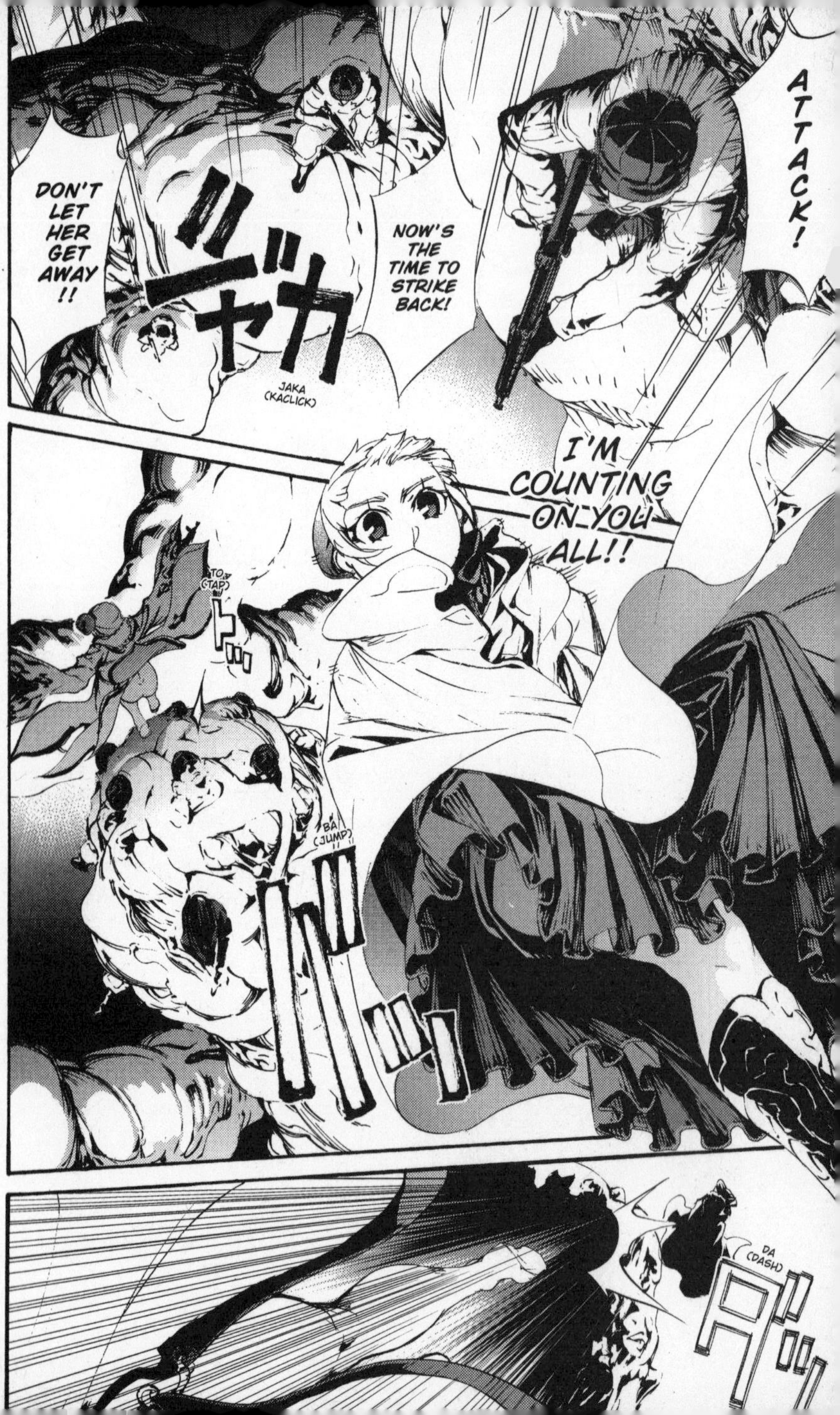
ATTACK!
NOW'S THE TIME TO STRIKE BACK!
JAKA (KACLICK)
DON'T LET HER GET AWAY!!
I'M COUNTING ON YOU ALL!!
TO (TAP)
BA (JUMP)
DA (DASH)

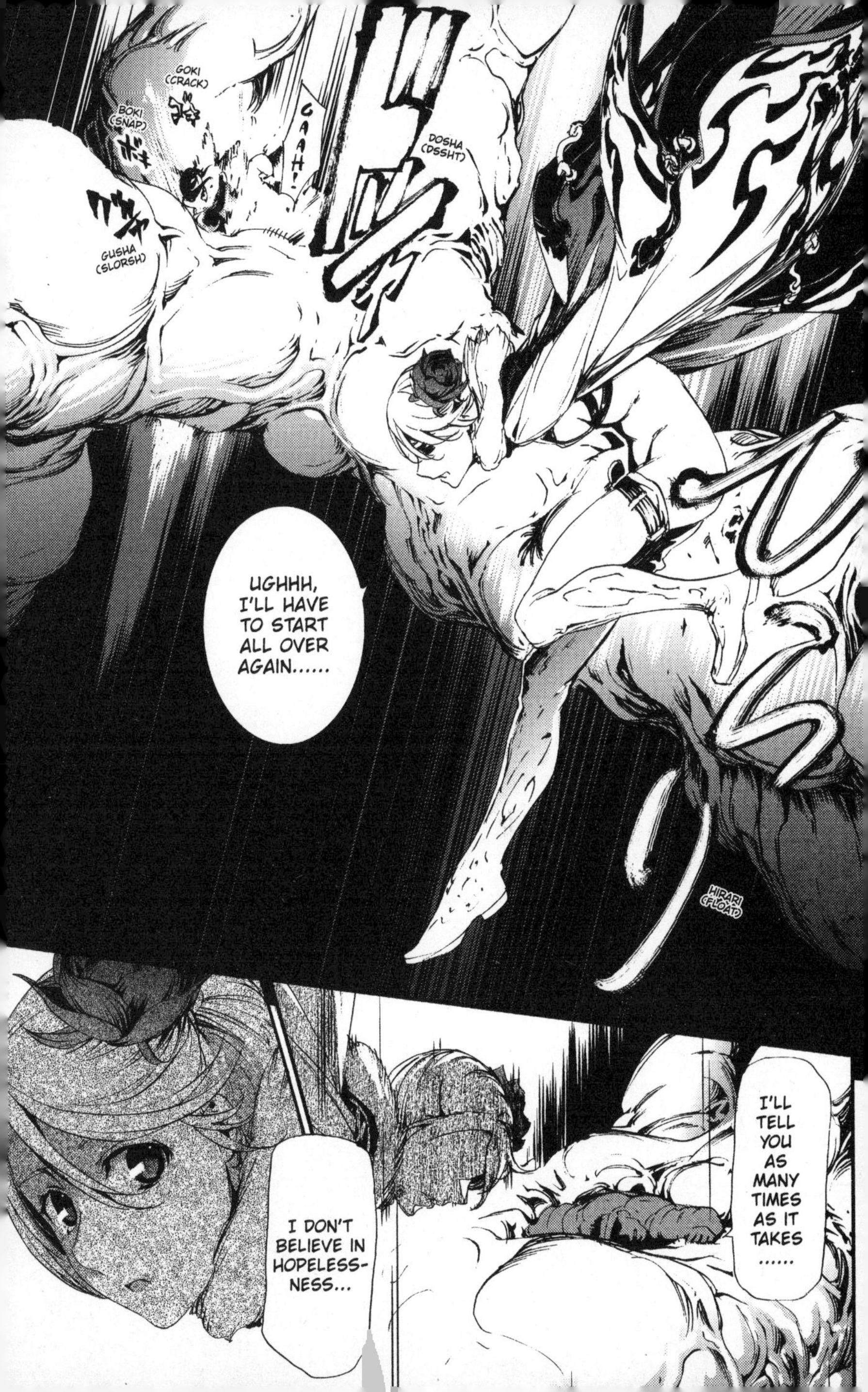
DOSHA (DSSHT)
GAAH!
GOKI (CRACK)
BOKI (SNAP)
GUSHA (SLORSH)
UGHHH, I'LL HAVE TO START ALL OVER AGAIN......
HIRARI (FLOAT)
I'LL TELL YOU AS MANY TIMES AS IT TAKES......
I DON'T BELIEVE IN HOPELESS-NESS...

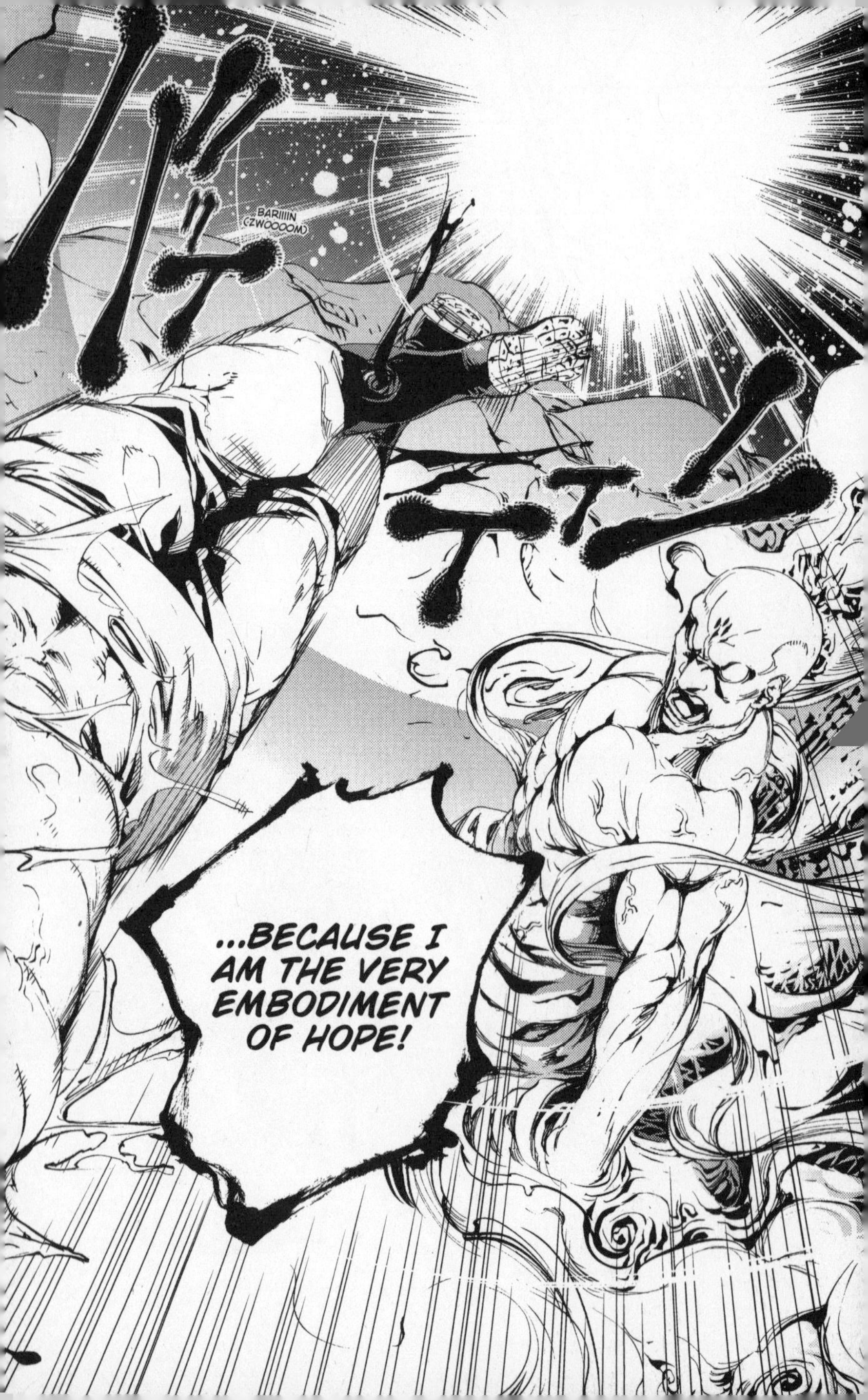
BARIIIIN (ZWOOOOM)
...BECAUSE I AM THE VERY EMBODIMENT OF HOPE!

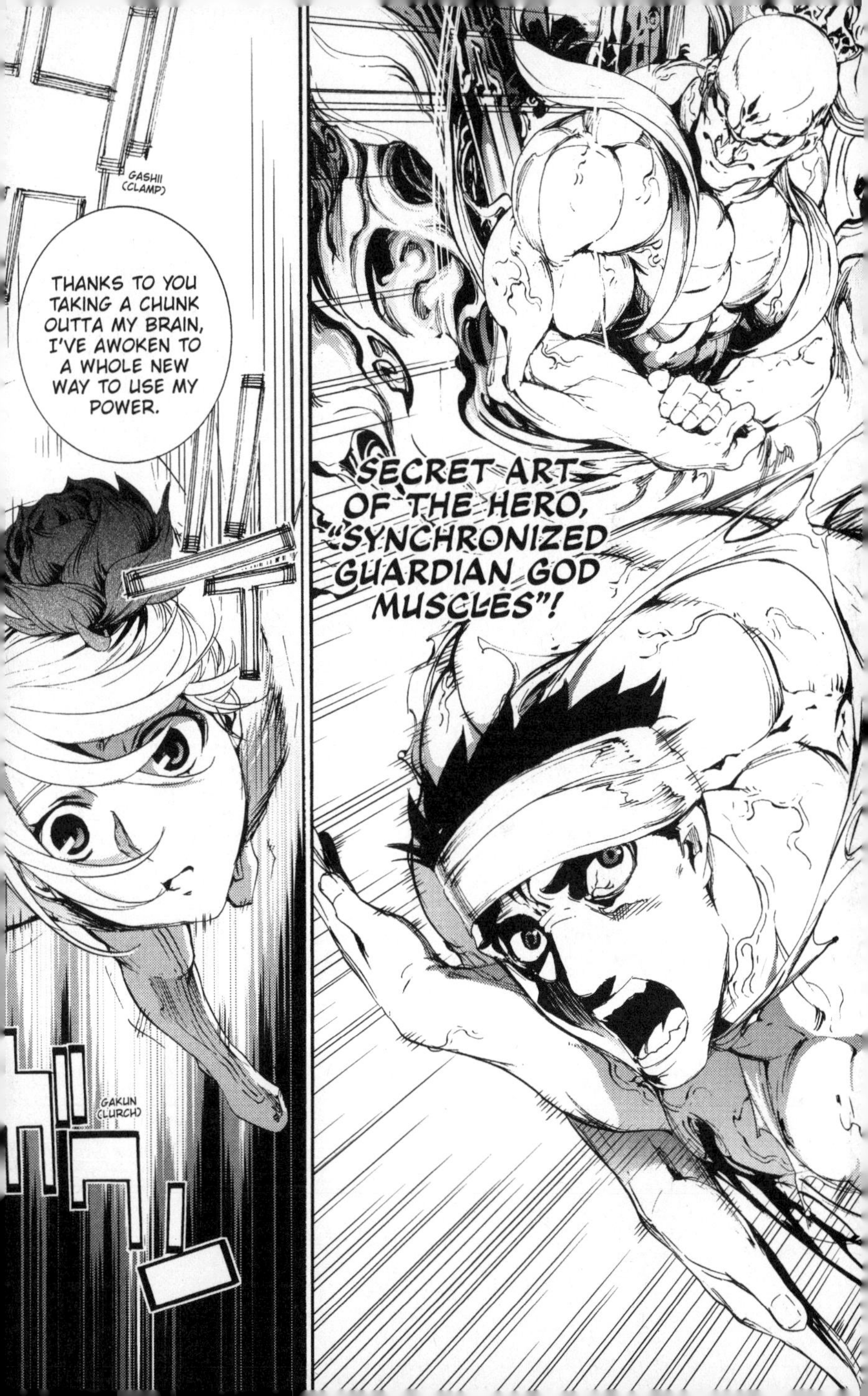
SECRET ART OF THE HERO, "SYNCHRONIZED GUARDIAN GOD MUSCLES"!
GASHII (CLAMP)
THANKS TO YOU TAKING A CHUNK OUTTA MY BRAIN, I'VE AWOKEN TO A WHOLE NEW WAY TO USE MY POWER.
GAKUN (LURCH)

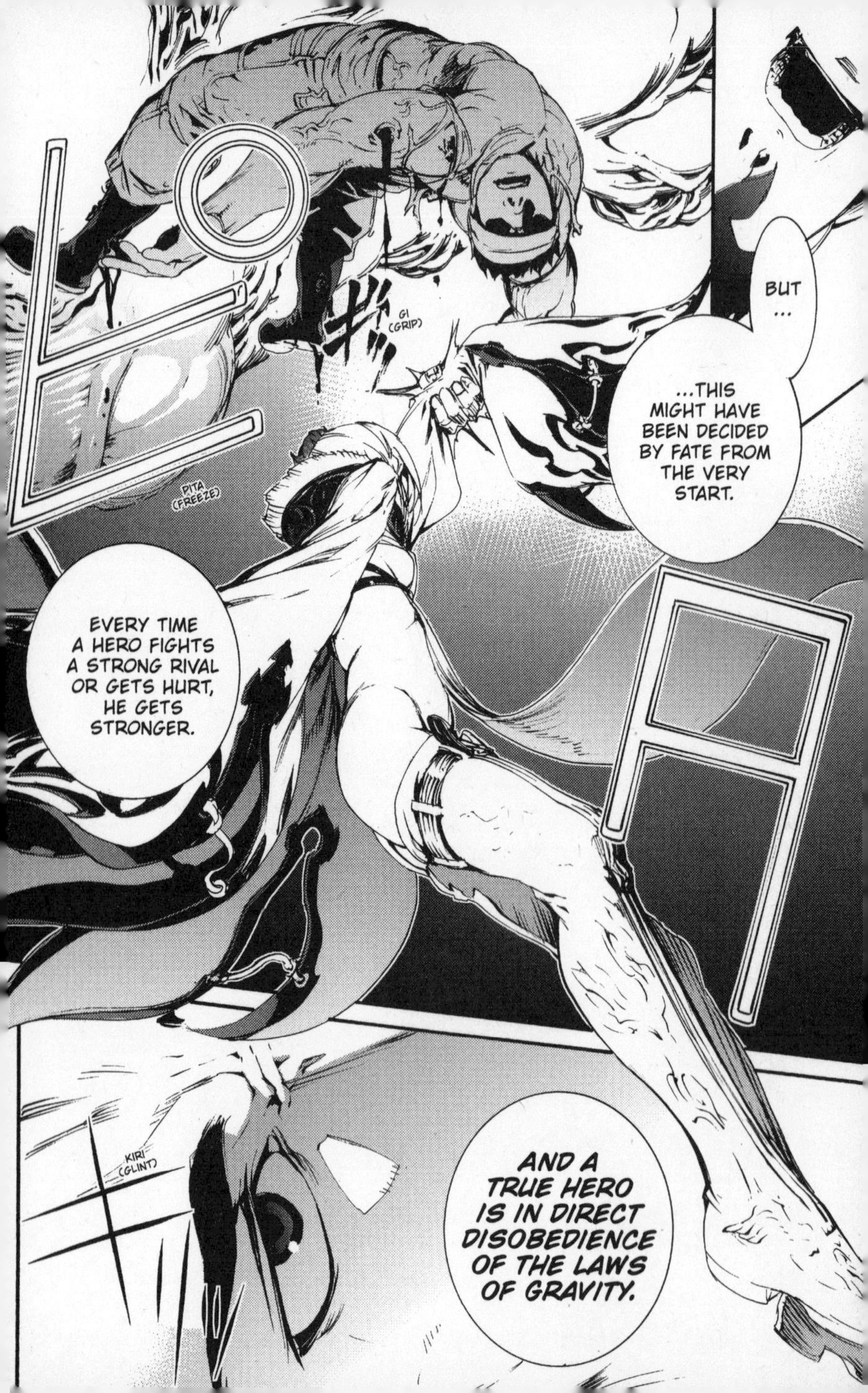
BUT ...
...THIS MIGHT HAVE BEEN DECIDED BY FATE FROM THE VERY START.
GI (GRIP)
PITA (FREEZE)
EVERY TIME A HERO FIGHTS A STRONG RIVAL OR GETS HURT, HE GETS STRONGER.
AND A TRUE HERO IS IN DIRECT DISOBEDIENCE OF THE LAWS OF GRAVITY.
KIRI (GLINT)

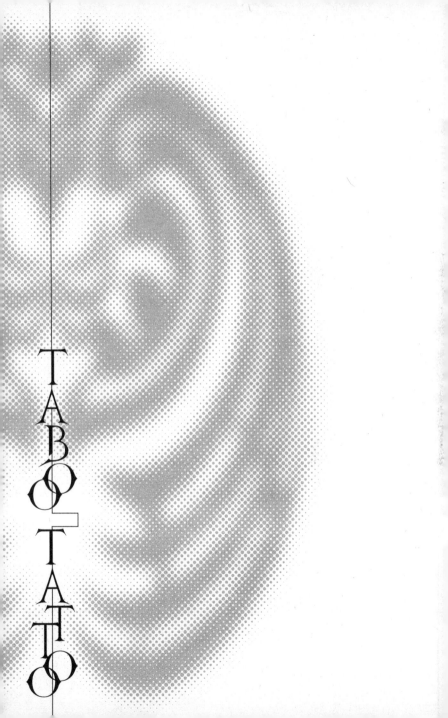

TABOO TATTOO

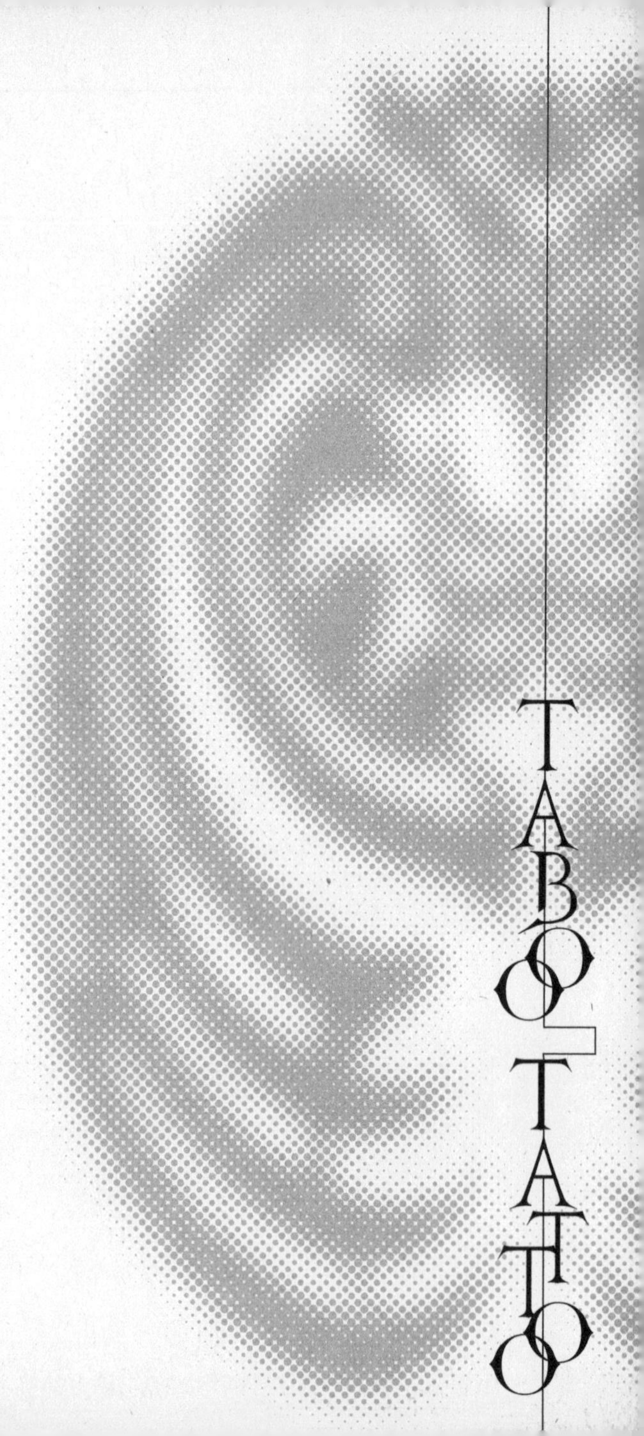

TABOO TATTOO

#67 IRRATIONAL

TABOO TATTOO

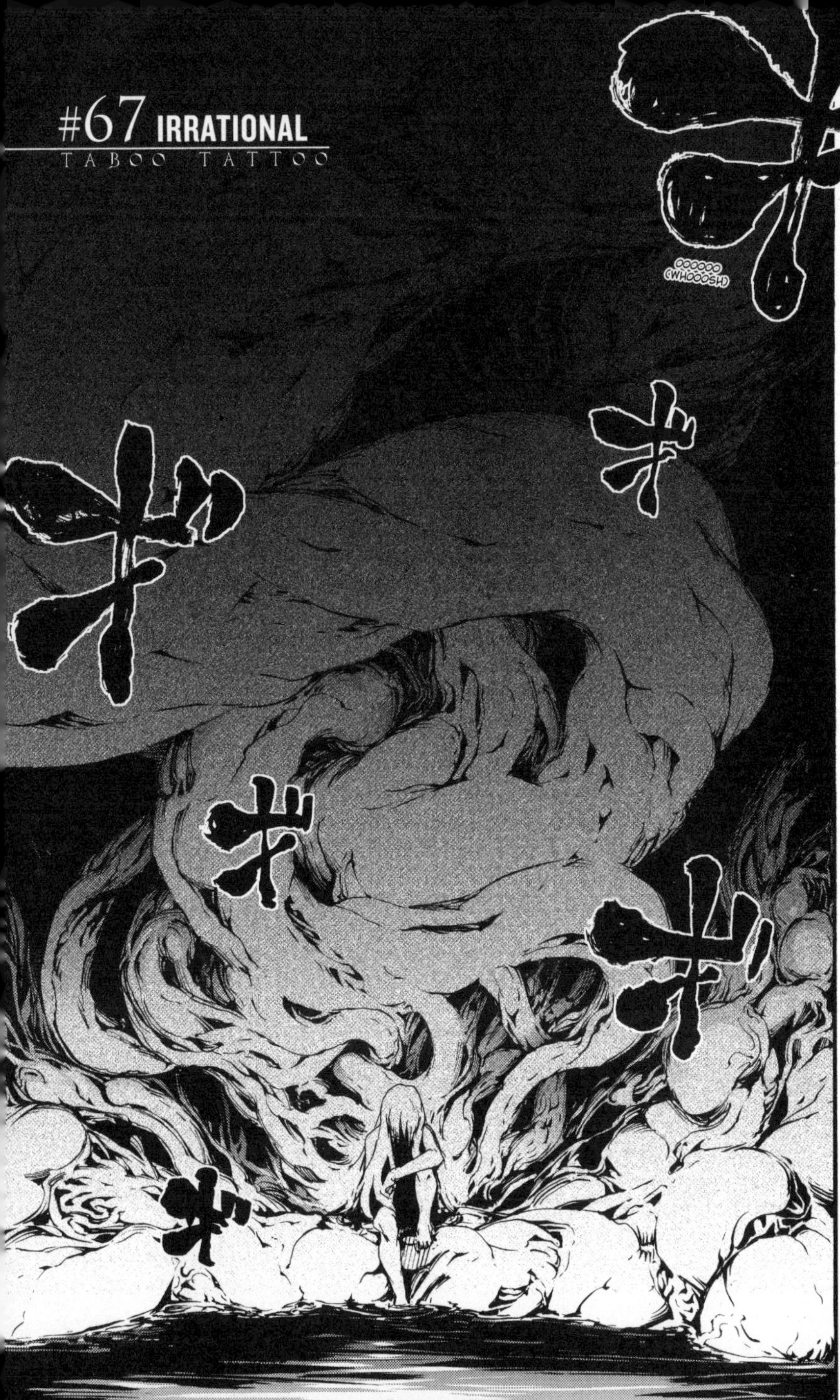
OOOOOO
(WHOOOSH)

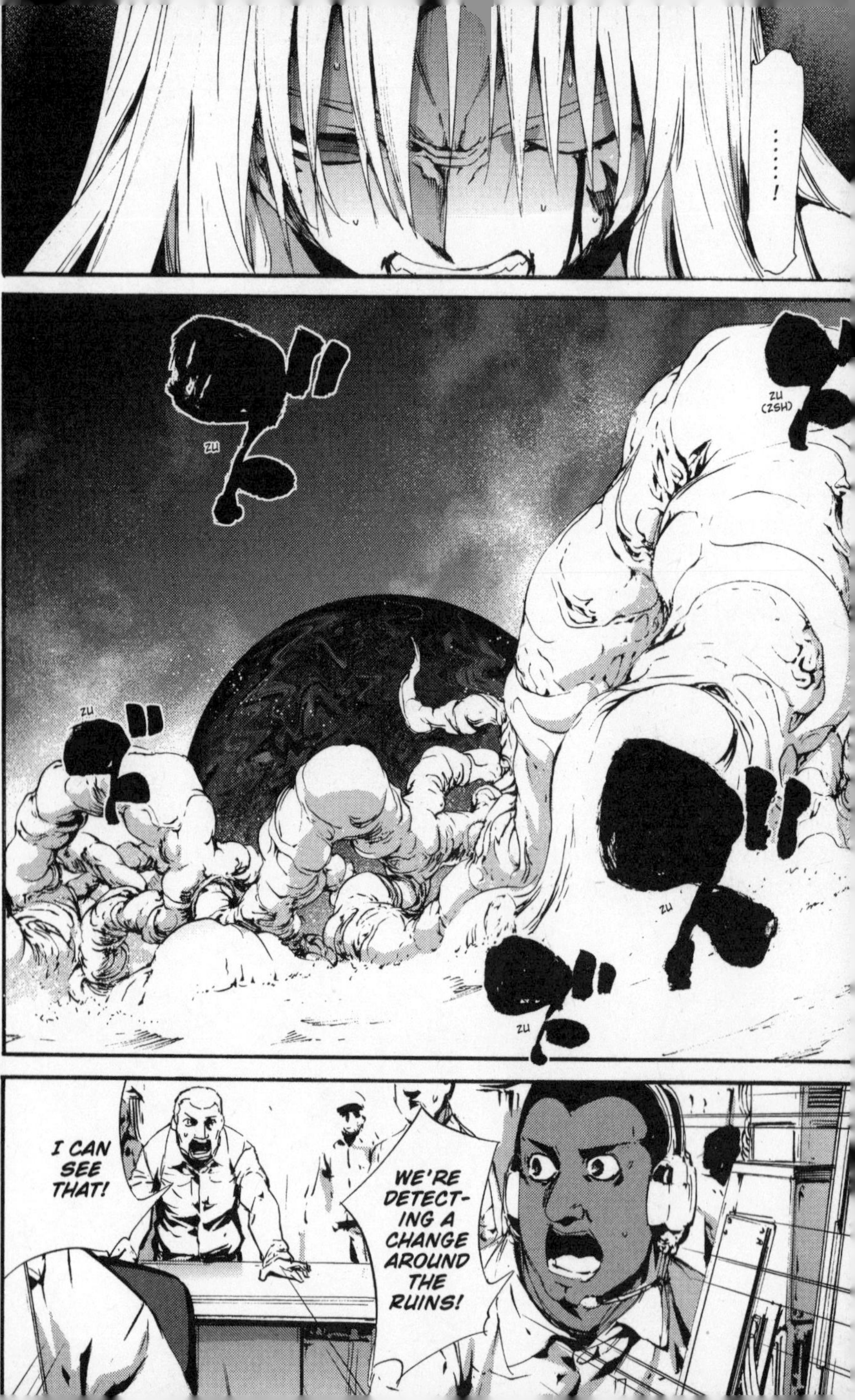
......!
ZU (ZSH)
ZU
ZU
ZU
ZU
WE'RE DETECT-ING A CHANGE AROUND THE RUINS!
I CAN SEE THAT!

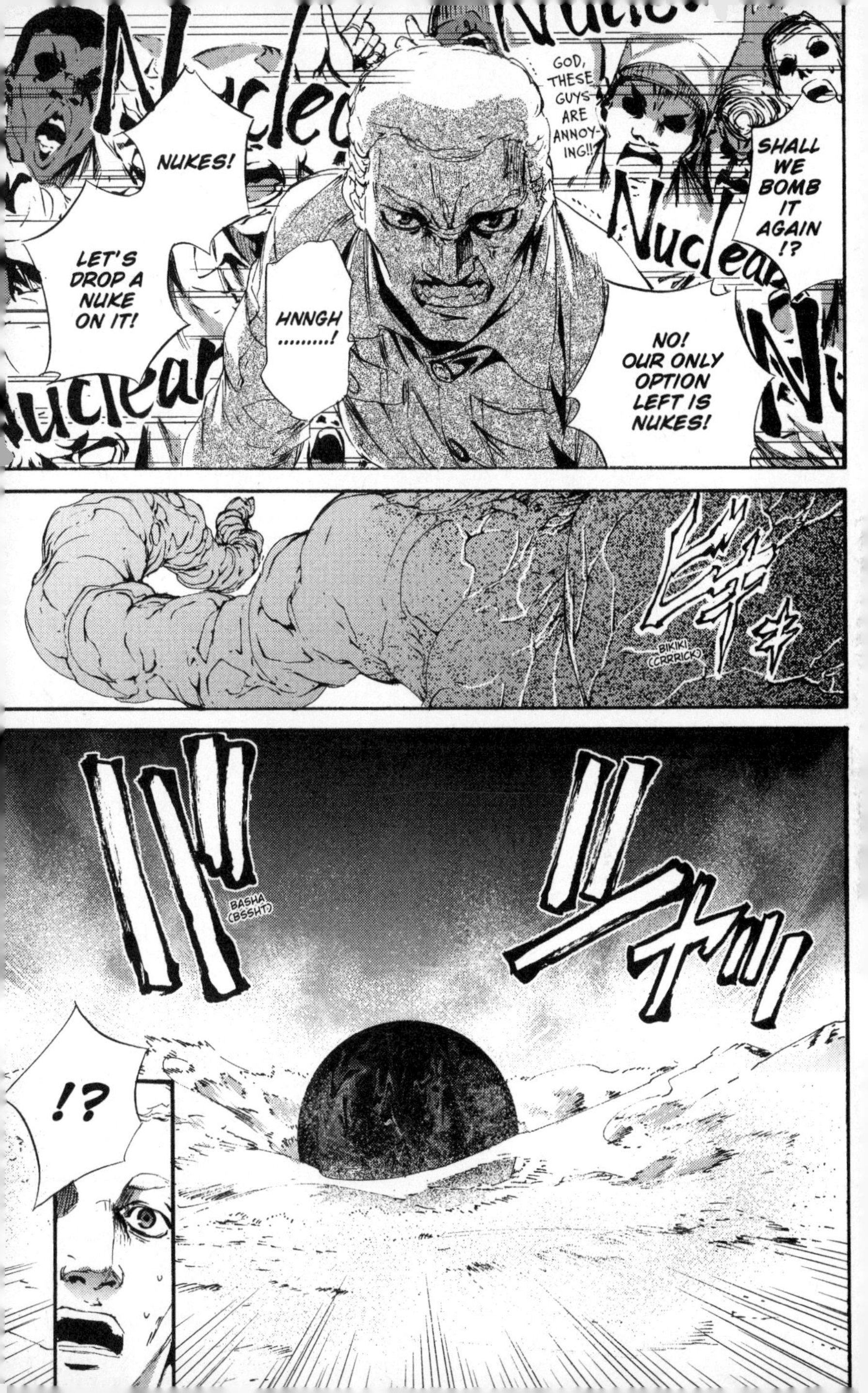
SHALL WE BOMB IT AGAIN!?
Nuclear
GOD, THESE GUYS ARE ANNOY-ING!!
NUKES!
NO! OUR ONLY OPTION LEFT IS NUKES!
HNNGH ....!
LET'S DROP A NUKE ON IT!
BIKIKI (CRRRICK)
BASHA (BSSHT)
!?

WHAT ON EARTH JUST HAPPENED ......?

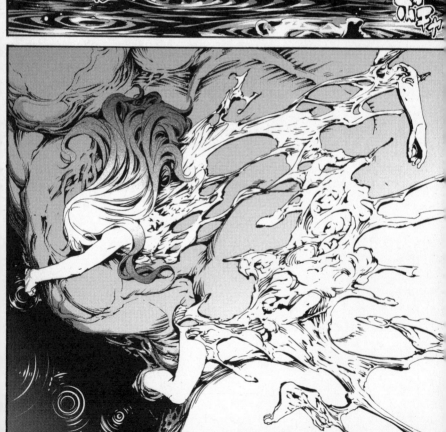

POCHAN (SPLASH)

BOCHA (SPLASH)

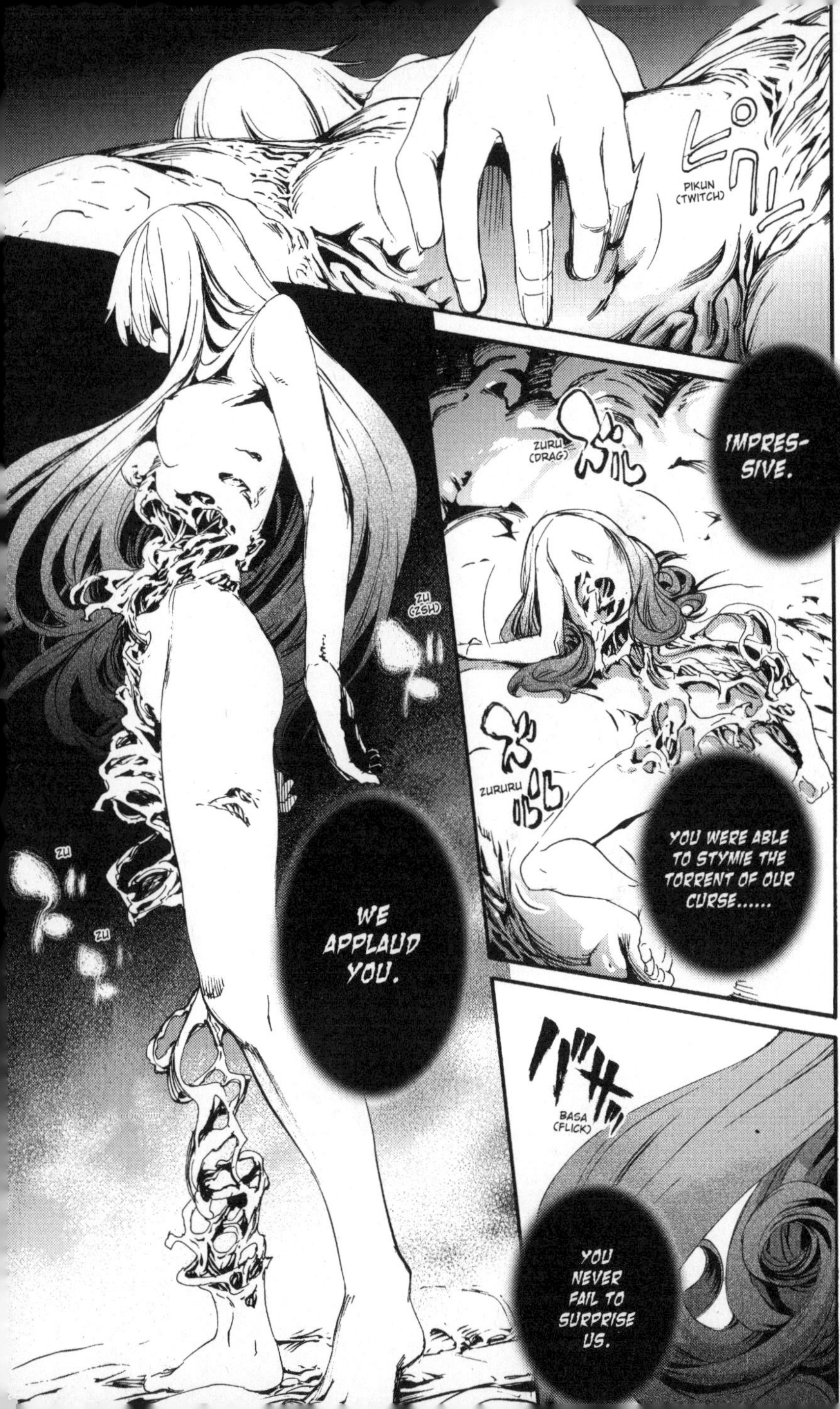
PIKUN (TWITCH)
IMPRES-SIVE.
ZURU (DRAG)
ZURURU
YOU WERE ABLE TO STYMIE THE TORRENT OF OUR CURSE......
BASA (FLICK)
YOU NEVER FAIL TO SURPRISE US.
ZU (ZSH)
WE APPLAUD YOU.
ZU
ZU

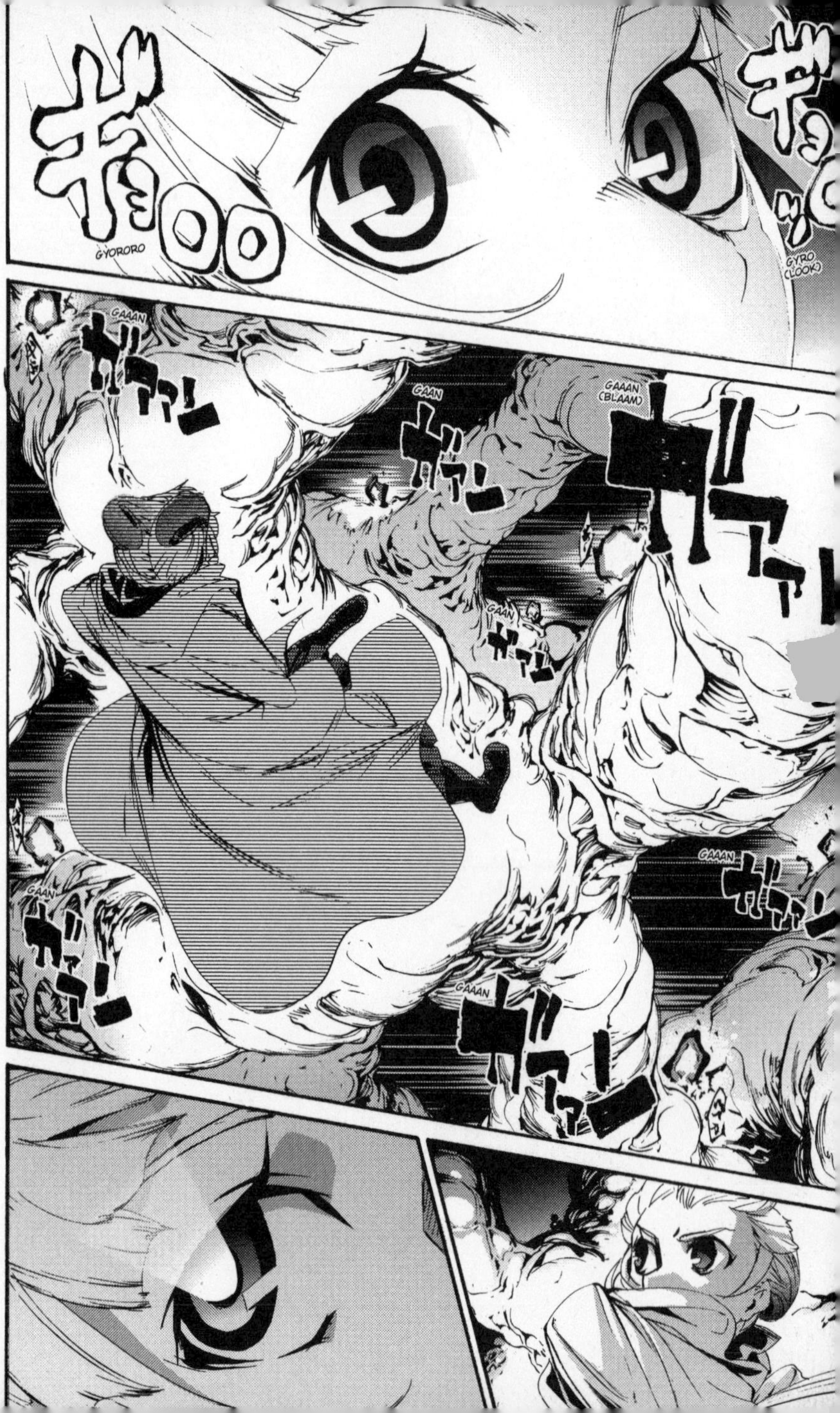
GYRO
(LOOK)
GYORORO
GAAAN
(BLAAM)
GAAN
GAAAN
GAAN
GAAAN
GAAN
GAAAN

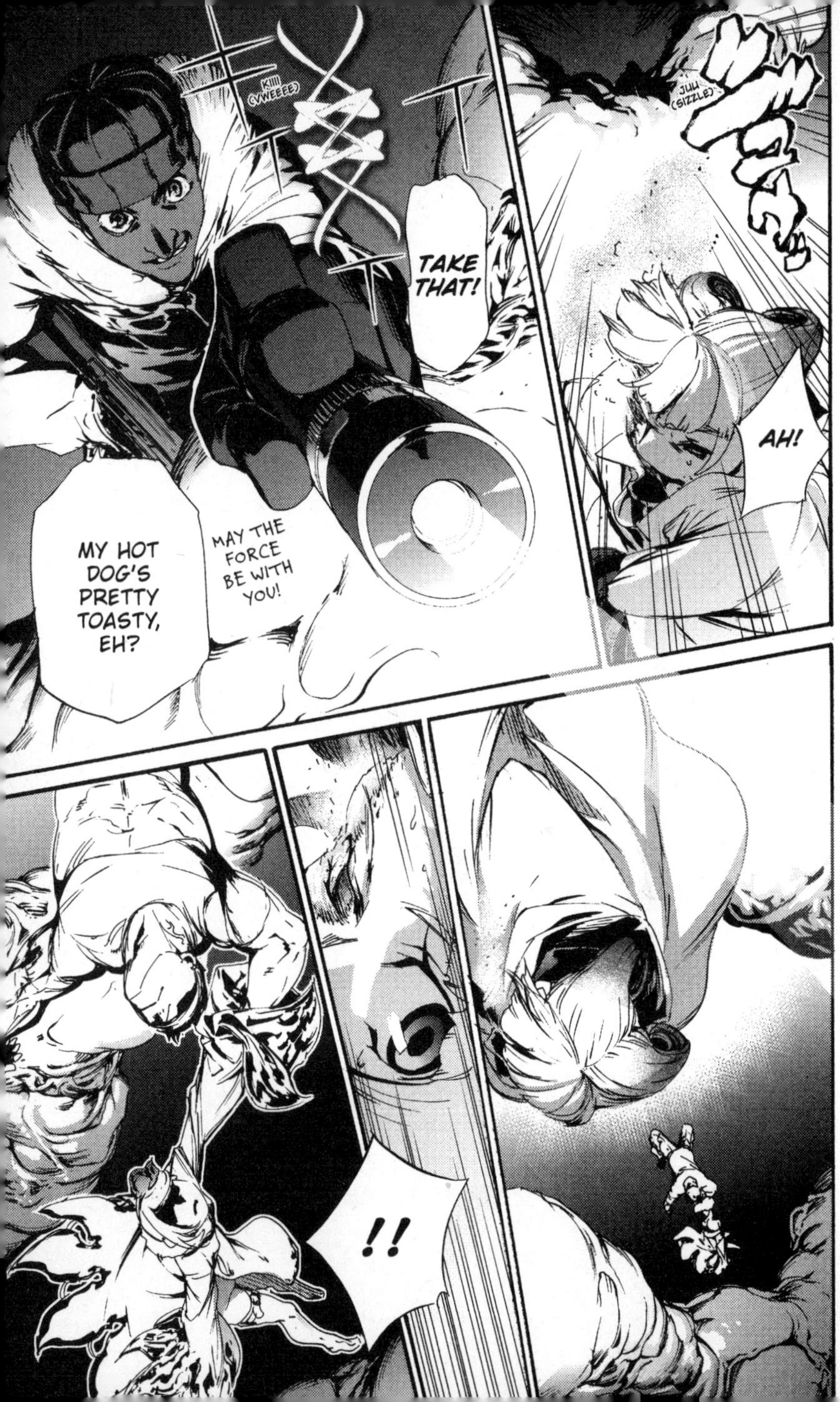
JUU (SIZZLE)
AH!
KIIII (VWEEEE)
TAKE THAT!
MAY THE FORCE BE WITH YOU!
MY HOT DOG'S PRETTY TOASTY, EH?
!!

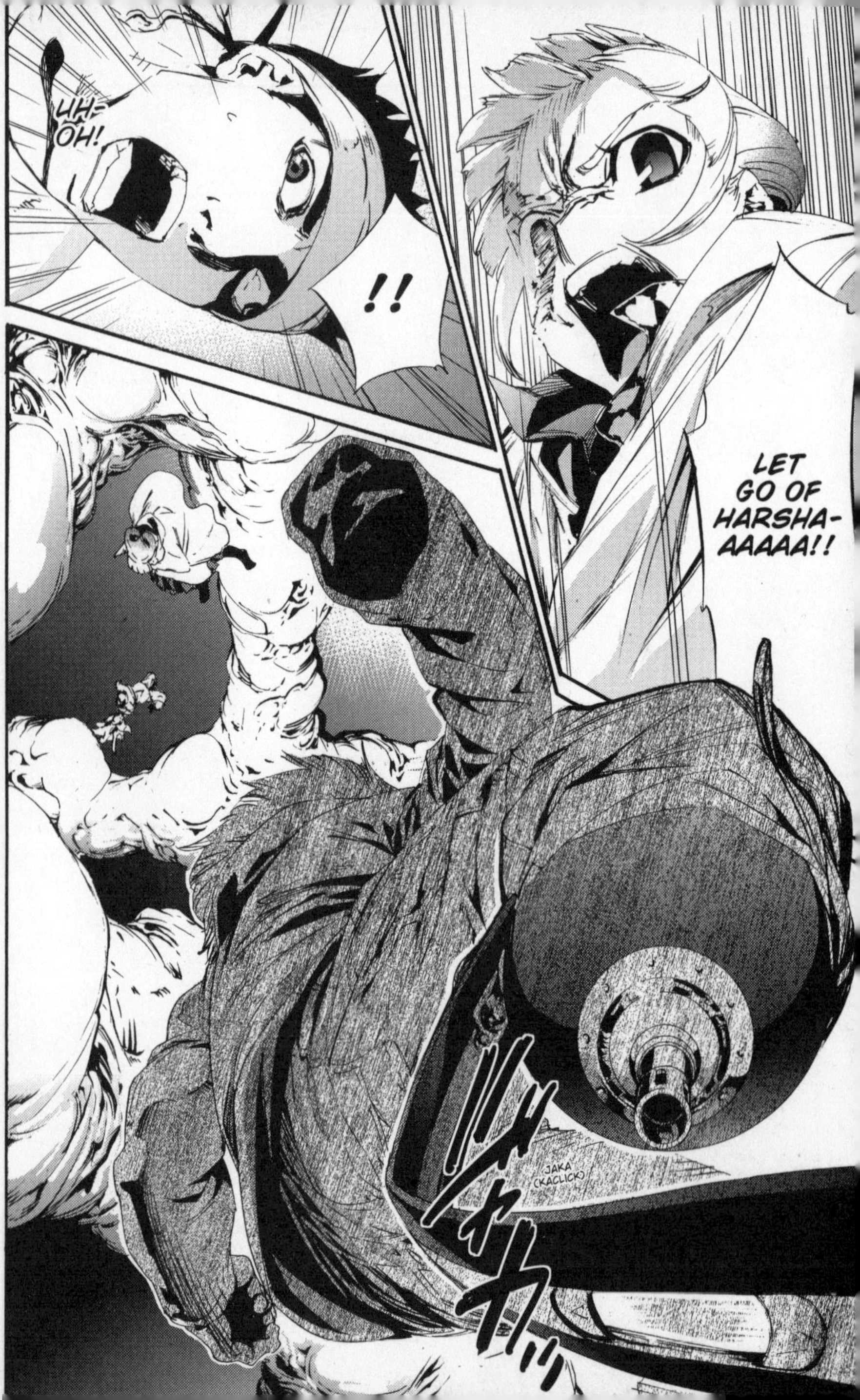

UH-OH!
!!
LET GO OF HARSHA-AAAAA!!
JAKA (KACLICK)

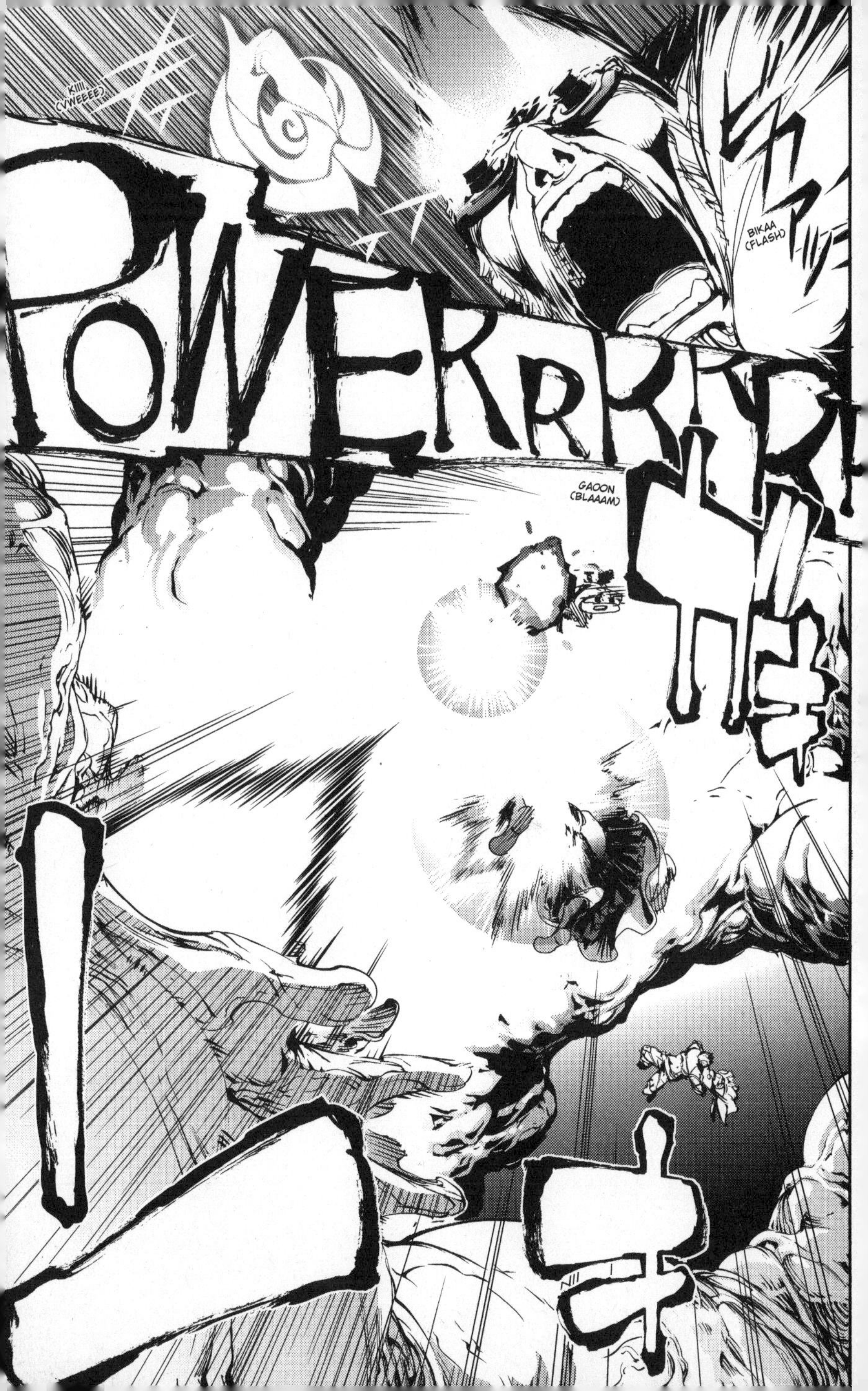
BIKAA
(FLASH)
KIIII
(VWEEEE)
POWERRR
GAOON
(BLAAAM)
NII

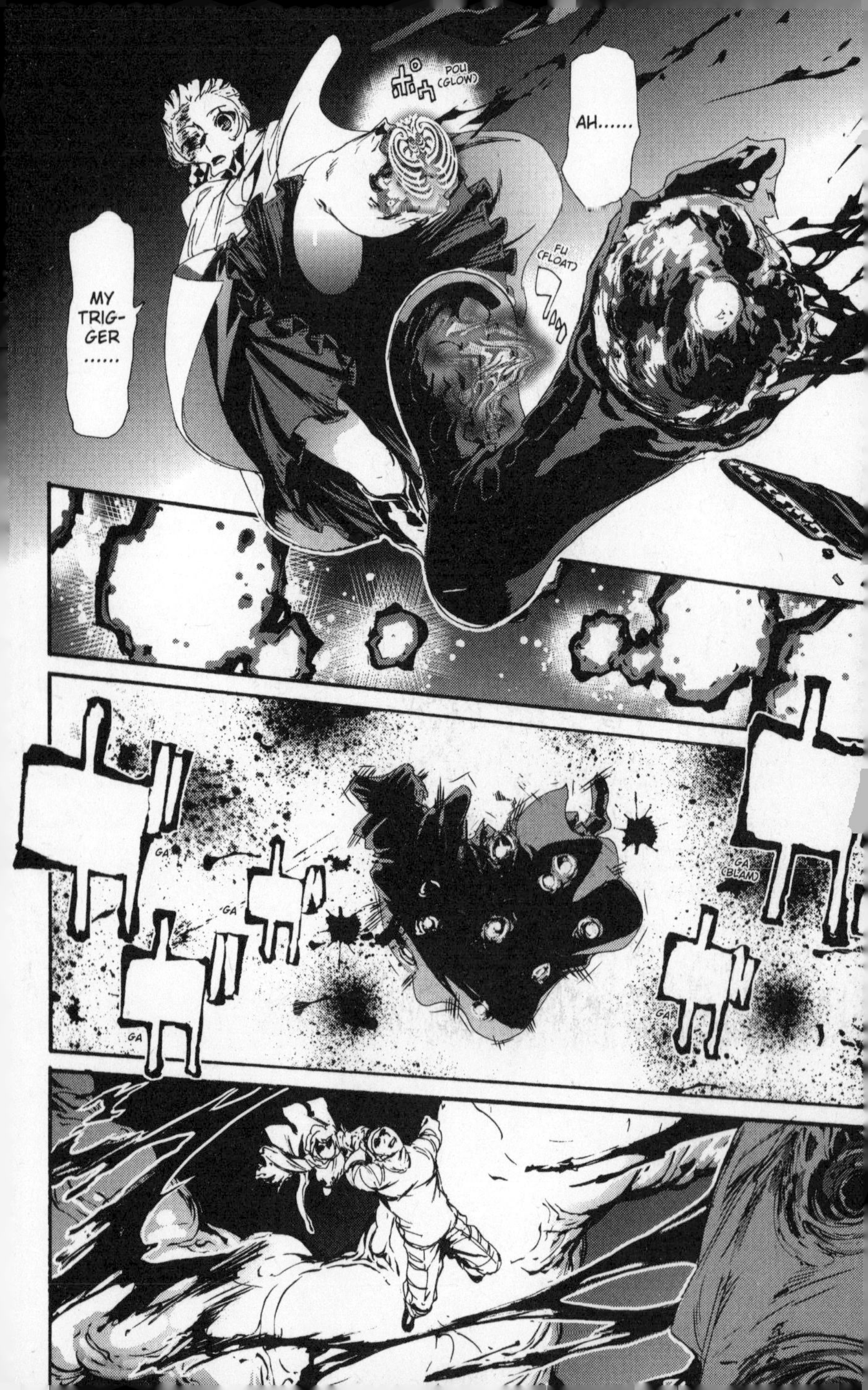
AH......
POU (GLOW)
MY TRIG-GER ......
FU (FLOAT)
GA (BLAM)
GA
GA
GA
GA

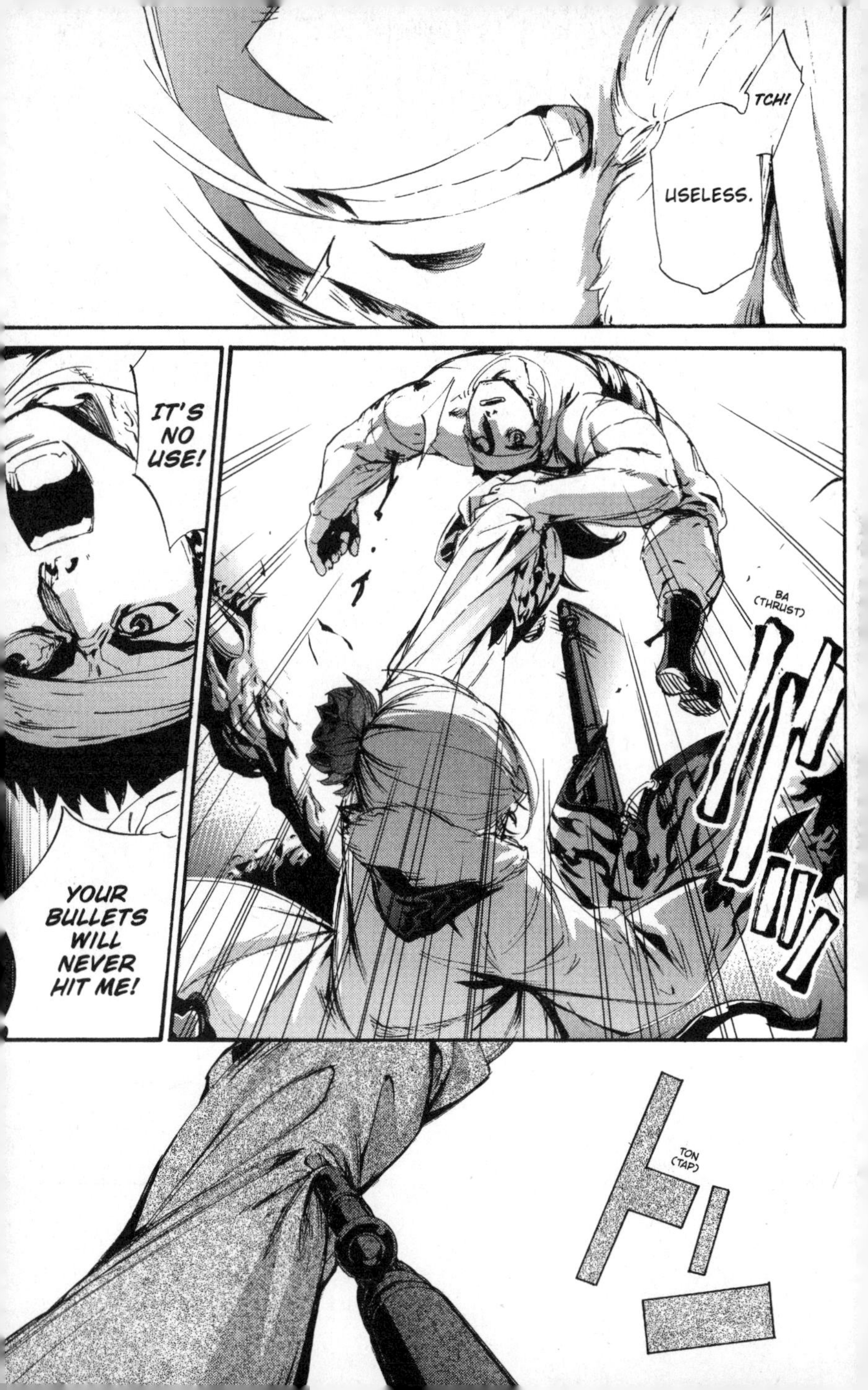
TCH!
USELESS.
BA (THRUST)
IT'S NO USE!
YOUR BULLETS WILL NEVER HIT ME!
TON (TAP)

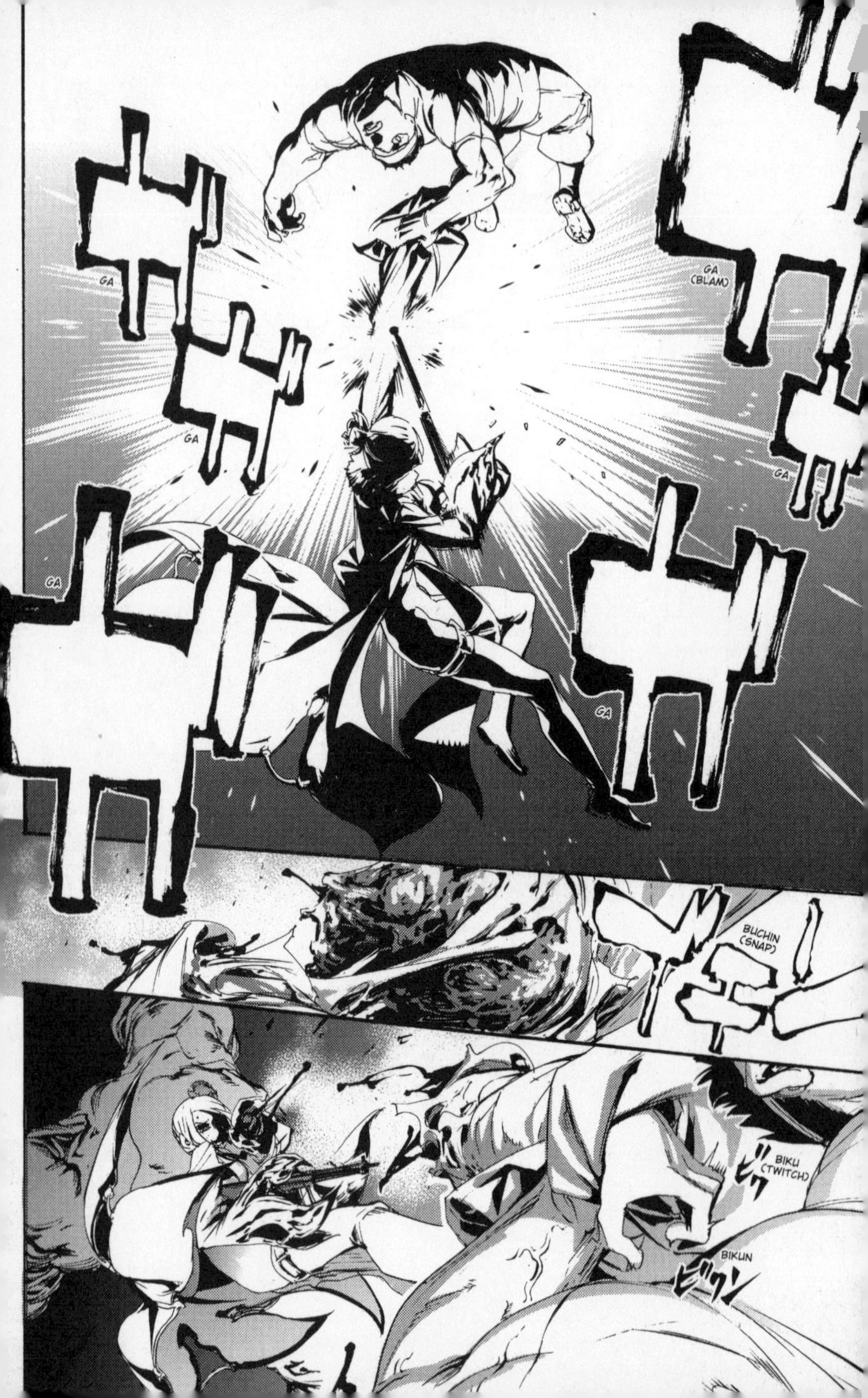
GA
(BLAM)
GA
GA
GA
GA
GA
BUCHIN
(SNAP)
BIKU
(TWITCH)
BIKUN

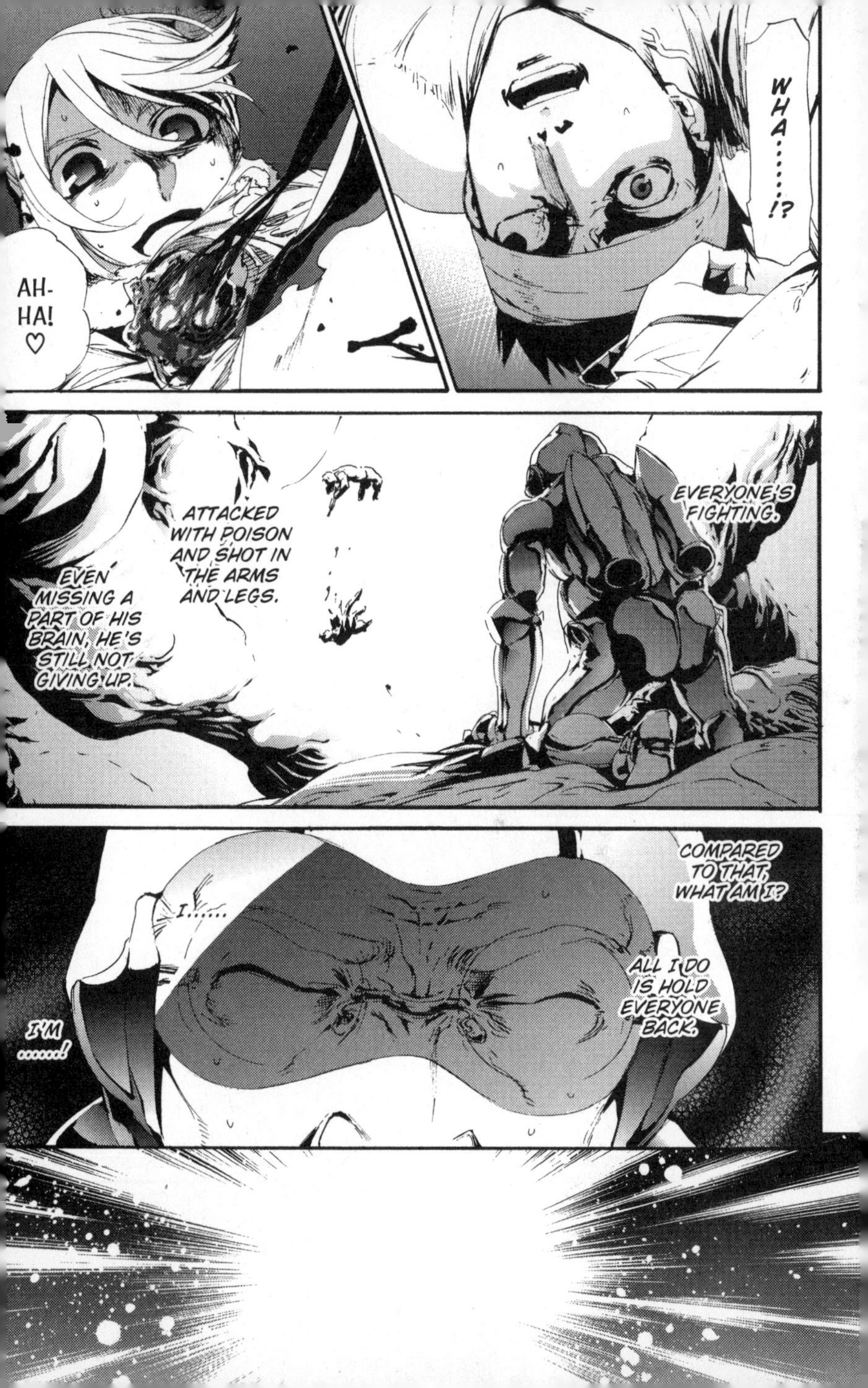
WHA......!?
AH-HA! ♡
EVERYONE'S FIGHTING.
ATTACKED WITH POISON AND SHOT IN THE ARMS AND LEGS.
EVEN MISSING A PART OF HIS BRAIN, HE'S STILL NOT GIVING UP.
COMPARED TO THAT, WHAT AM I?
I......
ALL I DO IS HOLD EVERYONE BACK.
I'M ......!

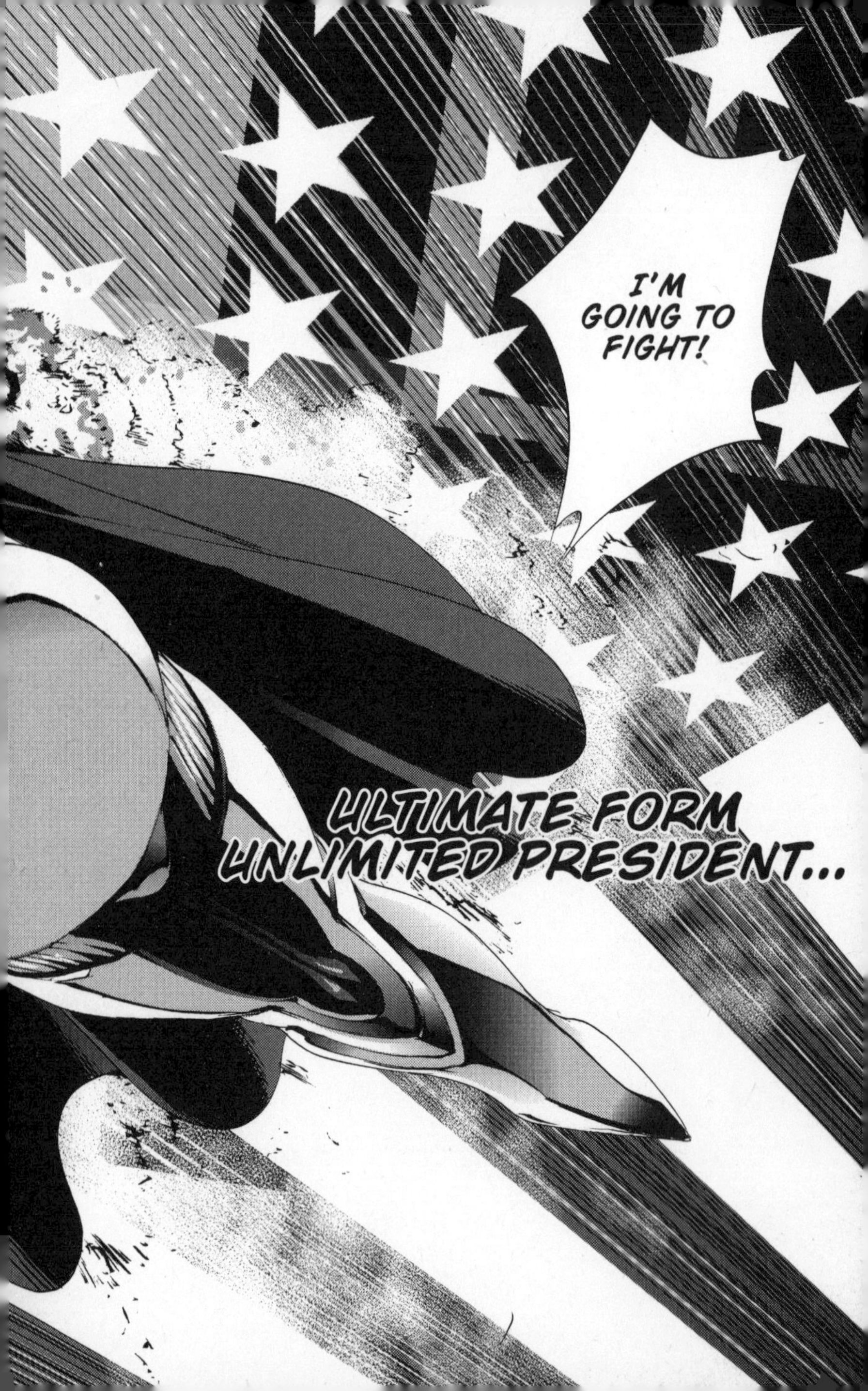
I'M GOING TO FIGHT!
ULTIMATE FORM UNLIMITED PRESIDENT...

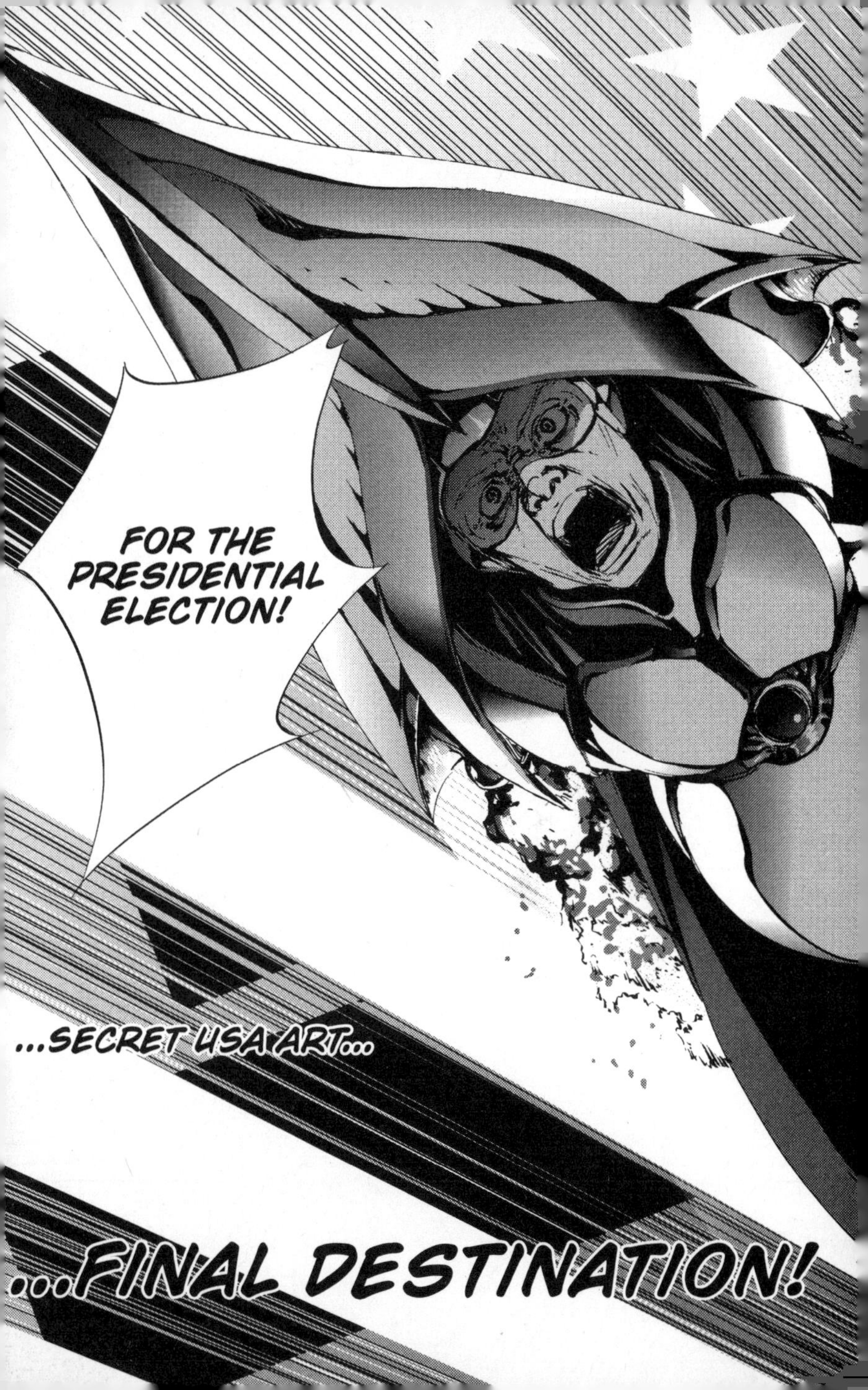
FOR THE PRESIDENTIAL ELECTION!
...SECRET USA ART...
...FINAL DESTINATION!

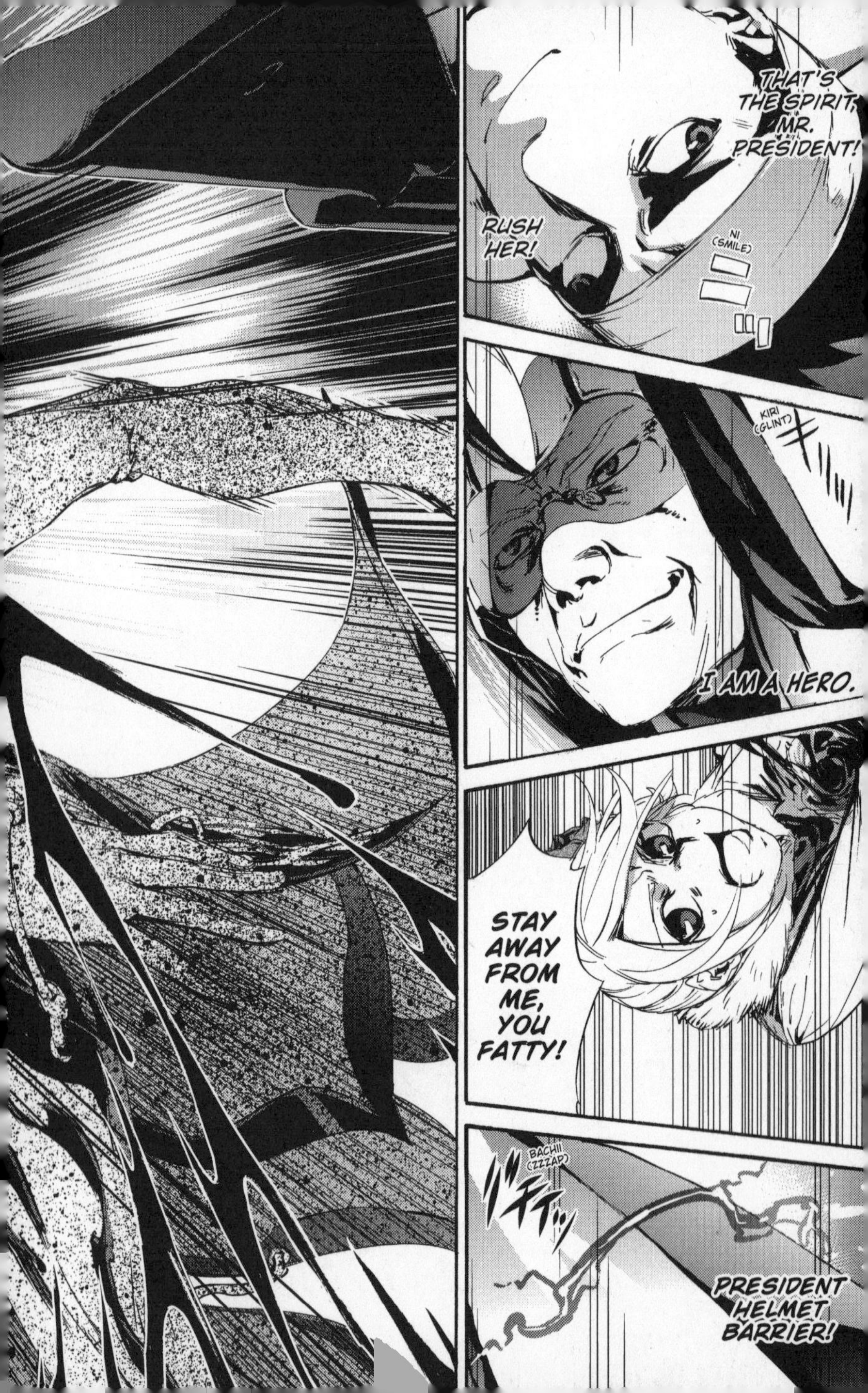
THAT'S THE SPIRIT, MR. PRESIDENT!
RUSH HER!
NI (SMILE)
KIRI (GLINT)
I AM A HERO.
STAY AWAY FROM ME, YOU FATTY!
BACHII (ZZZAP)
PRESIDENT HELMET BARRIER!

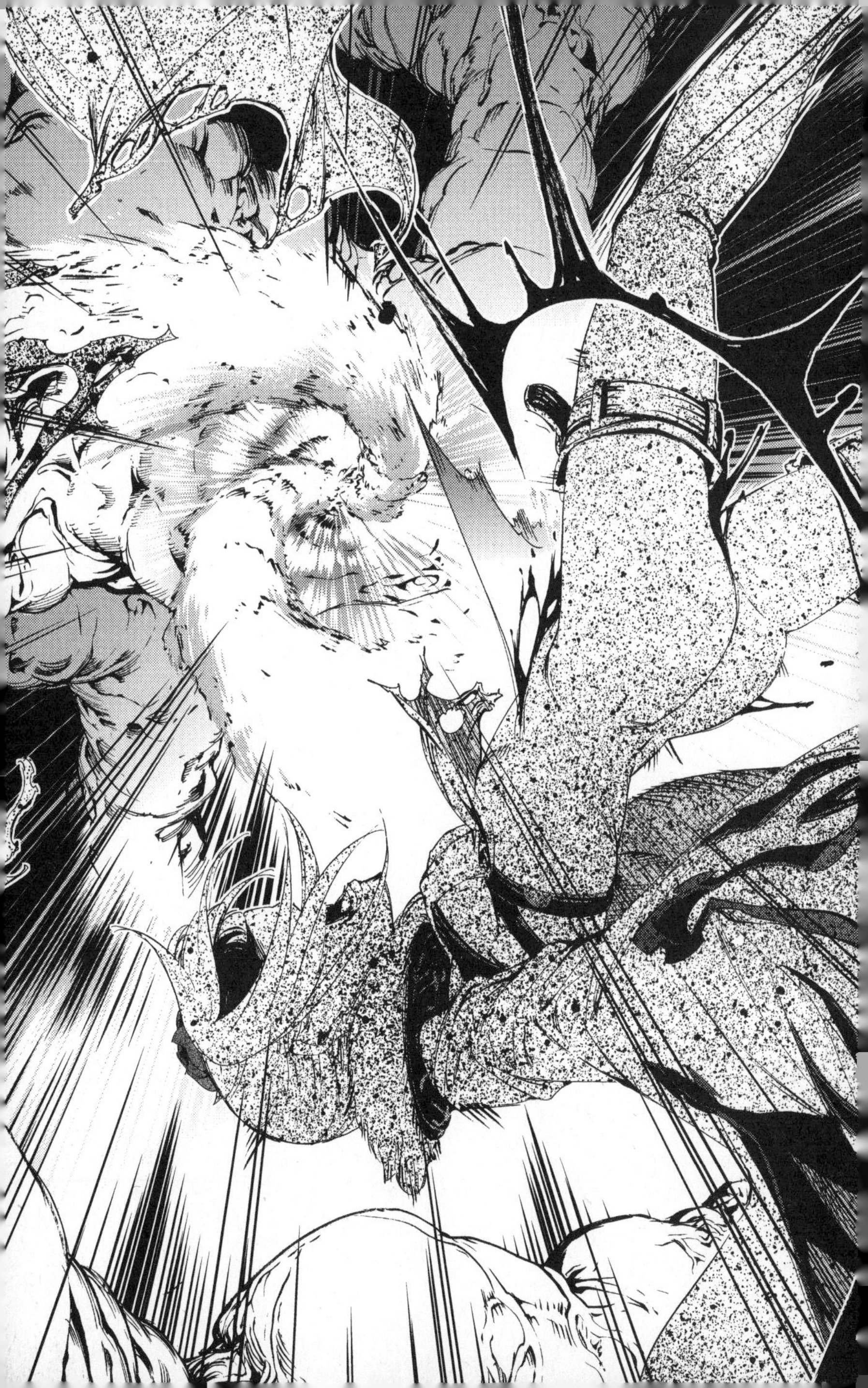

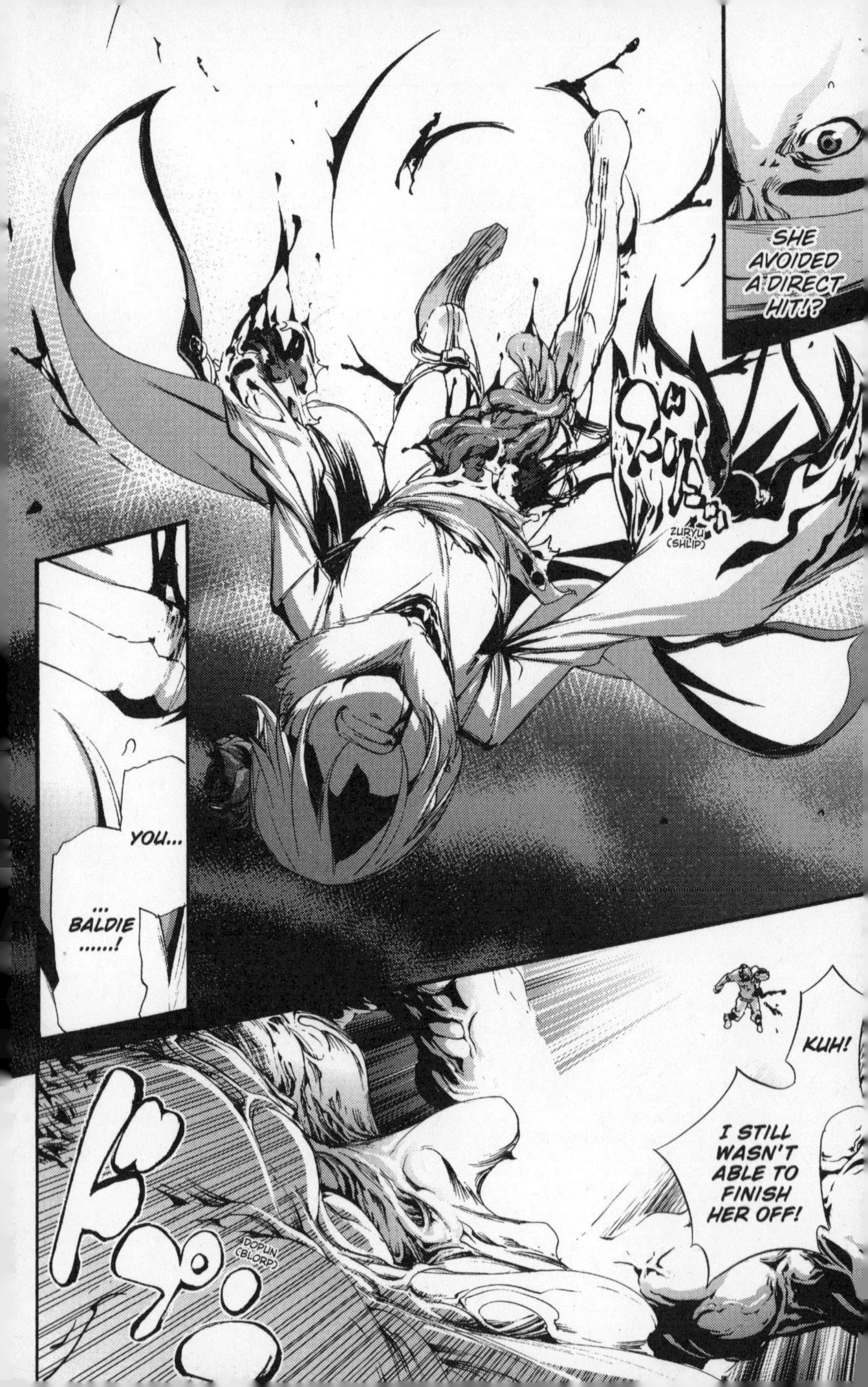
SHE AVOIDED A DIRECT HIT!?
ZURYU (SHLIP)
YOU...
...BALDIE ......!
KUH!
I STILL WASN'T ABLE TO FINISH HER OFF!
DOPUN (BLORP)

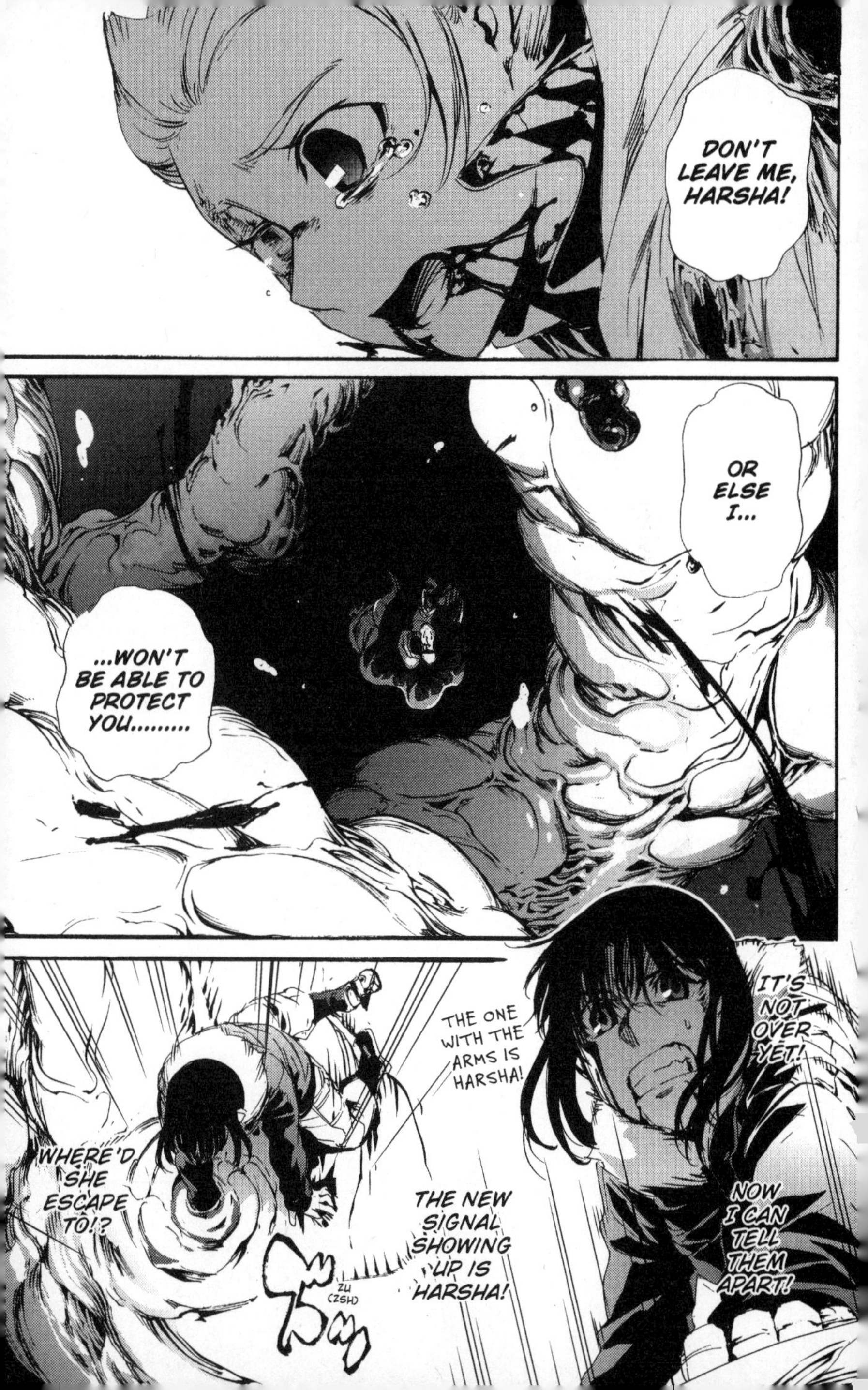
DON'T LEAVE ME, HARSHA!
OR ELSE I...
...WON'T BE ABLE TO PROTECT YOU.........
IT'S NOT OVER YET!
NOW I CAN TELL THEM APART!
THE ONE WITH THE ARMS IS HARSHA!
THE NEW SIGNAL SHOWING UP IS HARSHA!
WHERE'D SHE ESCAPE TO!?
ZU (ZSH)

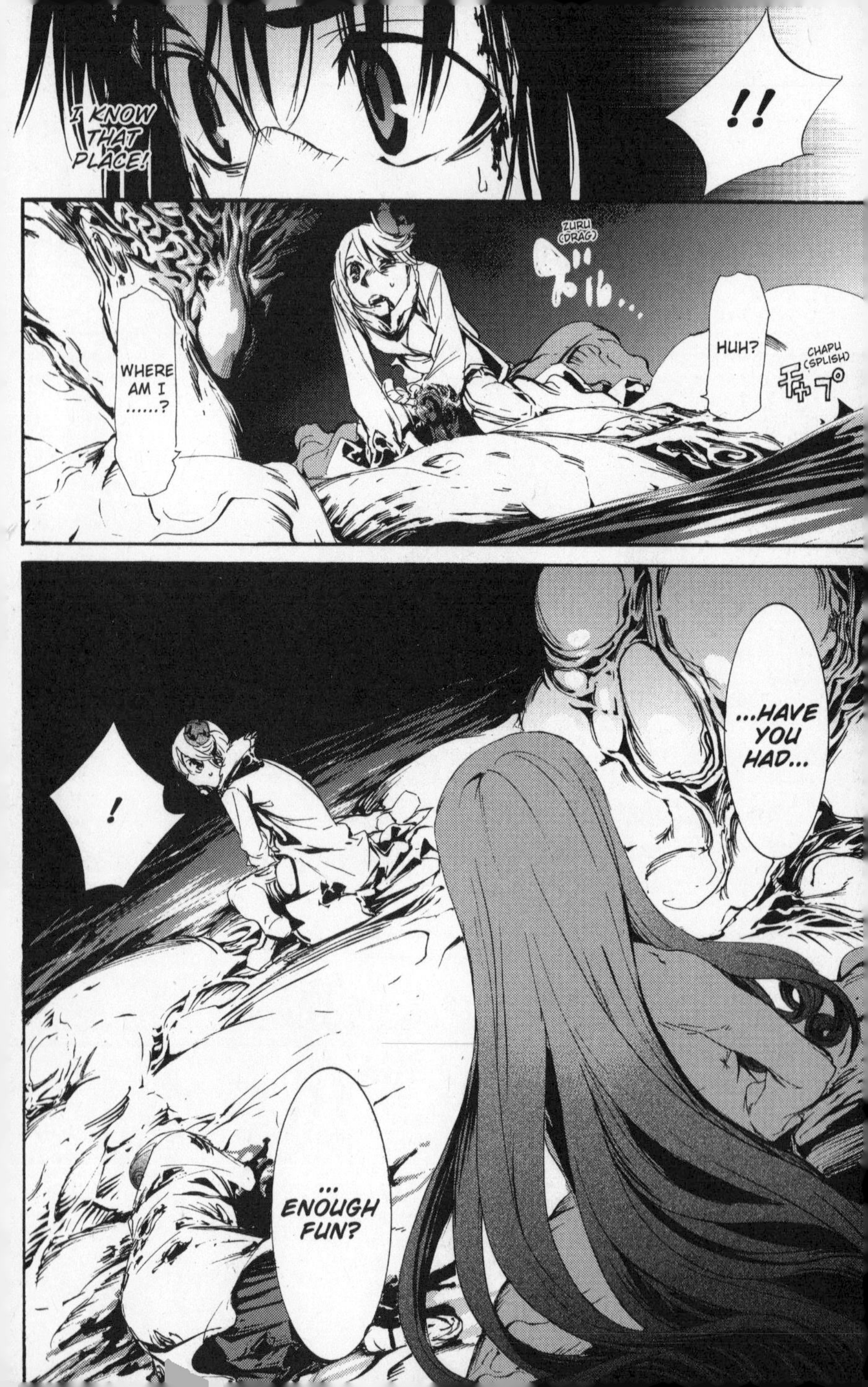
!!
I KNOW THAT PLACE!
CHAPU (SPLISH)
HUH?
ZURU (DRAG)
WHERE AM I ......?
...HAVE YOU HAD...
!
... ENOUGH FUN?

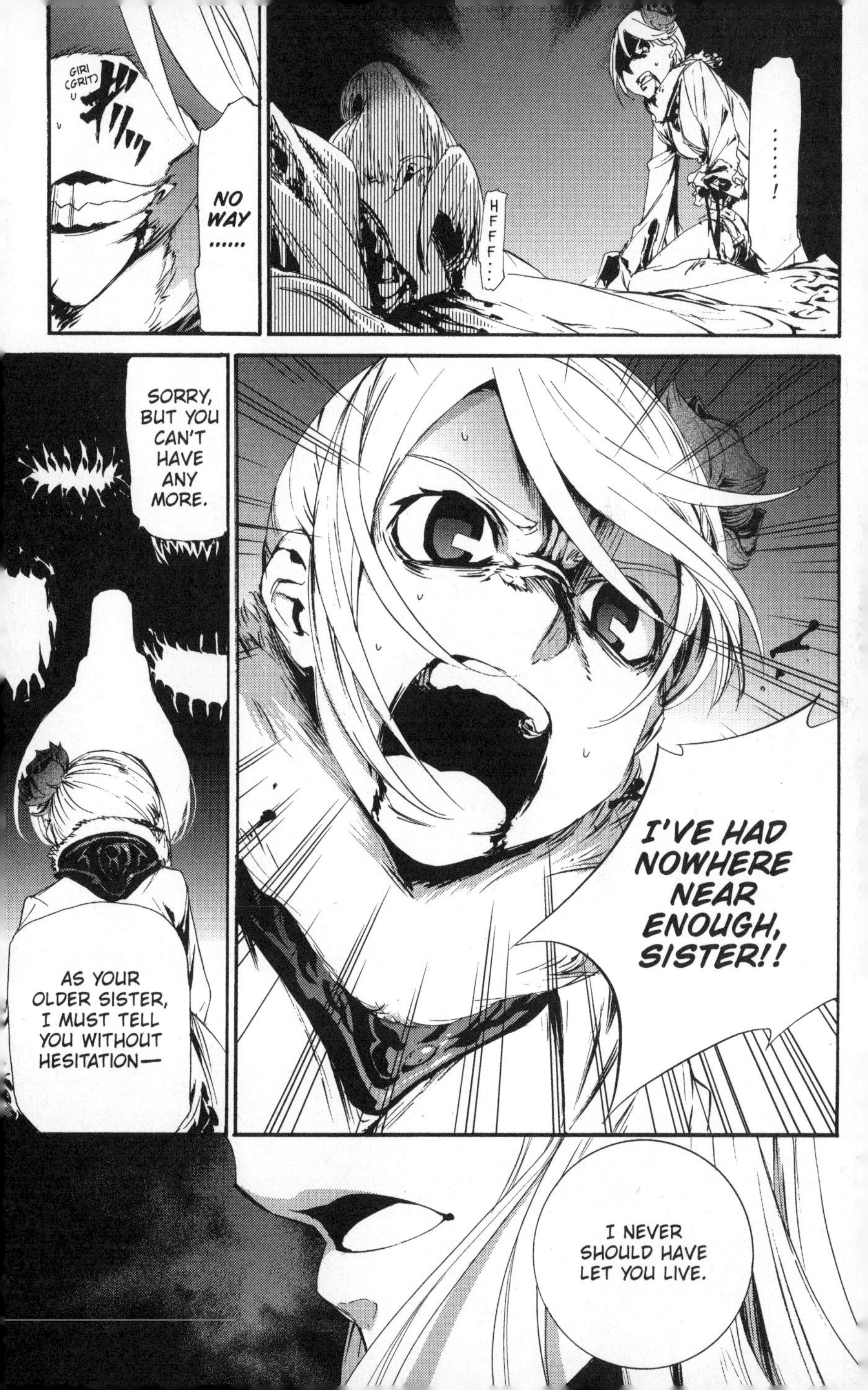
......!
HFFF...
GIRI (GRIT)
NO WAY ......
I'VE HAD NOWHERE NEAR ENOUGH, SISTER!!
SORRY, BUT YOU CAN'T HAVE ANY MORE.
AS YOUR OLDER SISTER, I MUST TELL YOU WITHOUT HESITATION—
I NEVER SHOULD HAVE LET YOU LIVE.

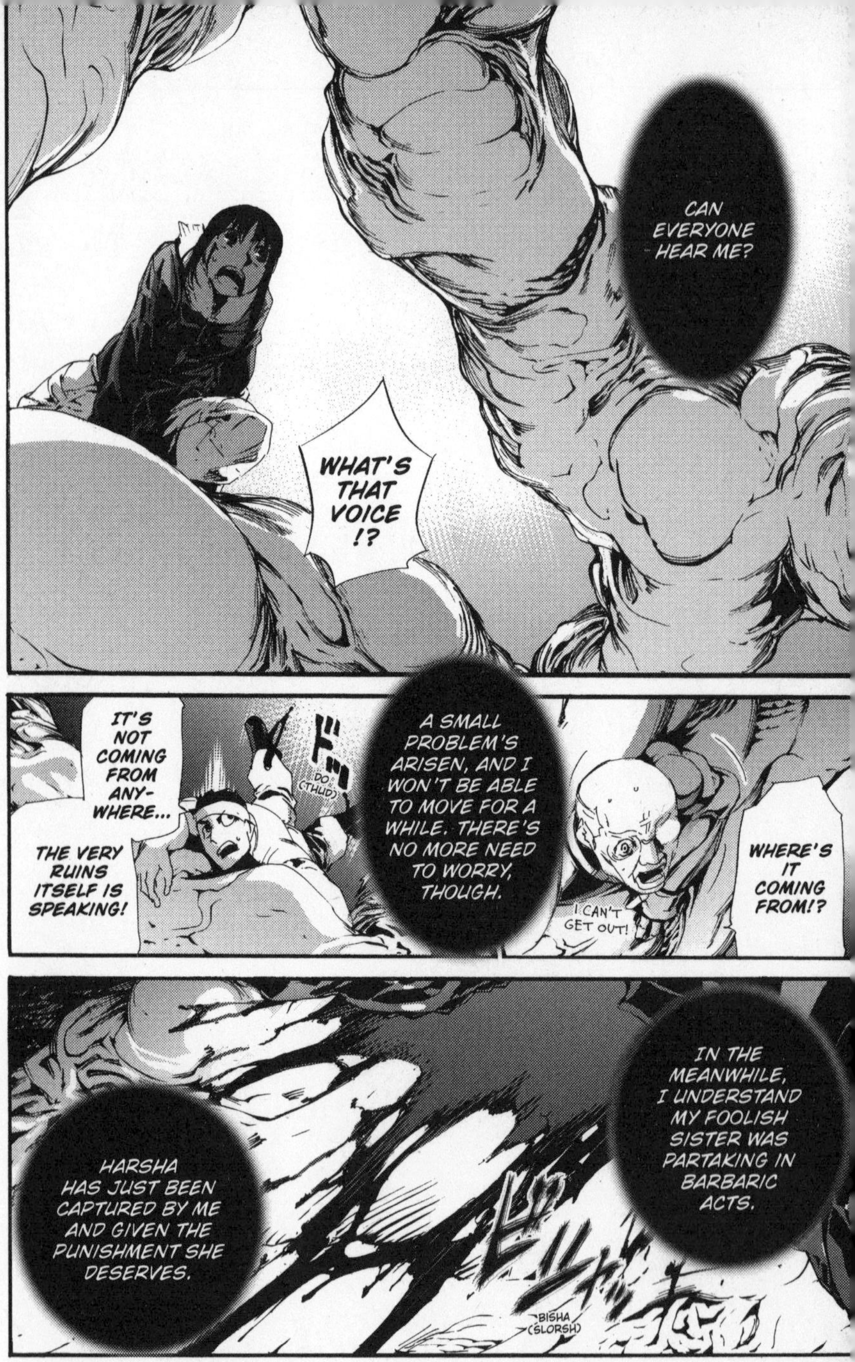
CAN EVERYONE HEAR ME?
WHAT'S THAT VOICE !?
WHERE'S IT COMING FROM!?
I CAN'T GET OUT!
A SMALL PROBLEM'S ARISEN, AND I WON'T BE ABLE TO MOVE FOR A WHILE. THERE'S NO MORE NEED TO WORRY, THOUGH.
DO (THUD)
IT'S NOT COMING FROM ANY-WHERE...
THE VERY RUINS ITSELF IS SPEAKING!
IN THE MEANWHILE, I UNDERSTAND MY FOOLISH SISTER WAS PARTAKING IN BARBARIC ACTS.
HARSHA HAS JUST BEEN CAPTURED BY ME AND GIVEN THE PUNISHMENT SHE DESERVES.
BISHA (SLORSH)

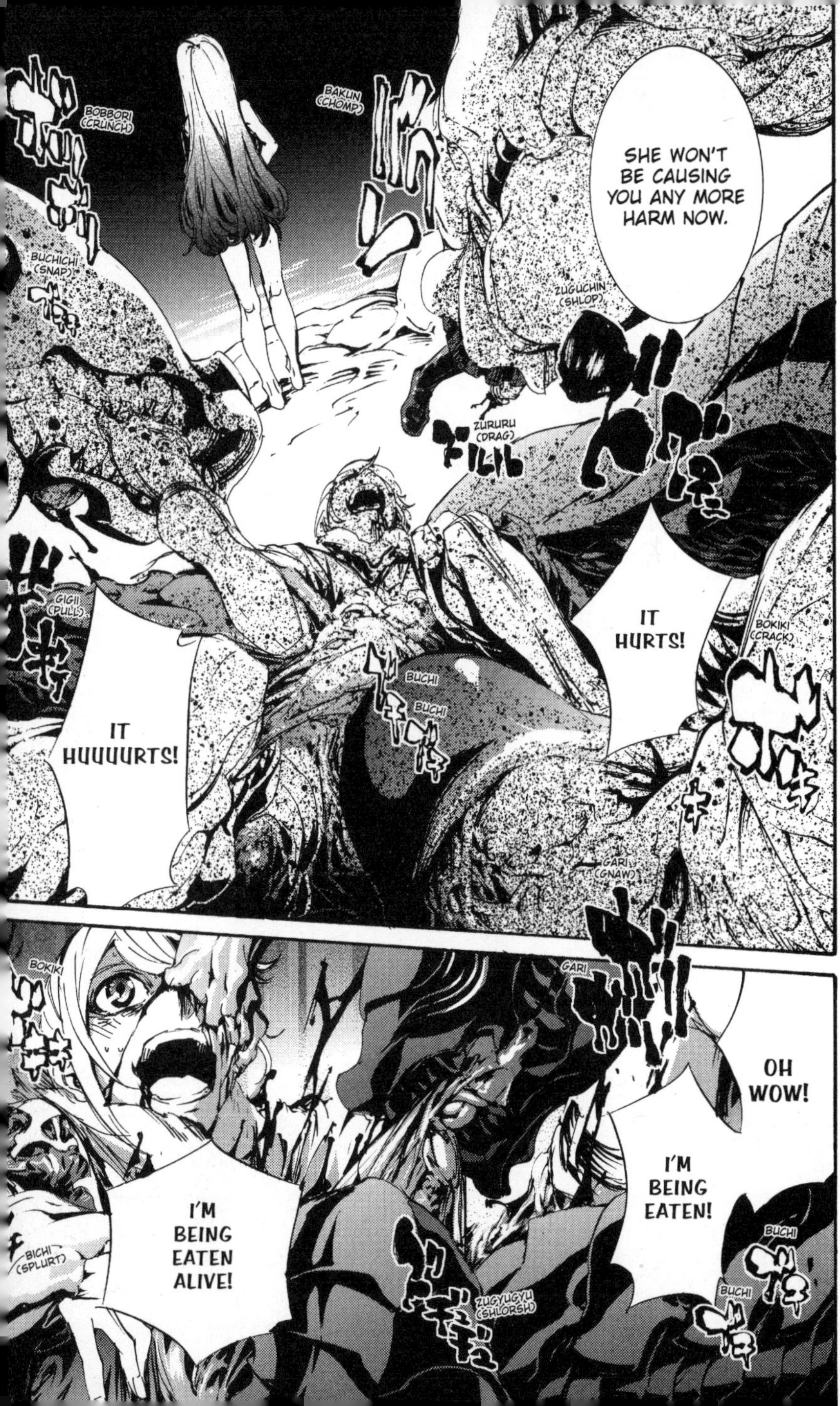
SHE WON'T BE CAUSING YOU ANY MORE HARM NOW.
ZUGUCHIN (SHLOP)
BAKUN (CHOMP)
BOBBORI (CRUNCH)
BUCHICHI (SNAP)
ZURURU (DRAG)
IT HURTS!
BOKIKI (CRACK)
BUCHI
BUCHI
GIGII (PULL)
IT HUUUURTS!
GARI (GNAW)
GARI
OH WOW!
I'M BEING EATEN!
BUCHI
BUCHI
ZUGYUGYU (SHLORSH)
I'M BEING EATEN ALIVE!
BOKIKI
BICHI (SPLURT)

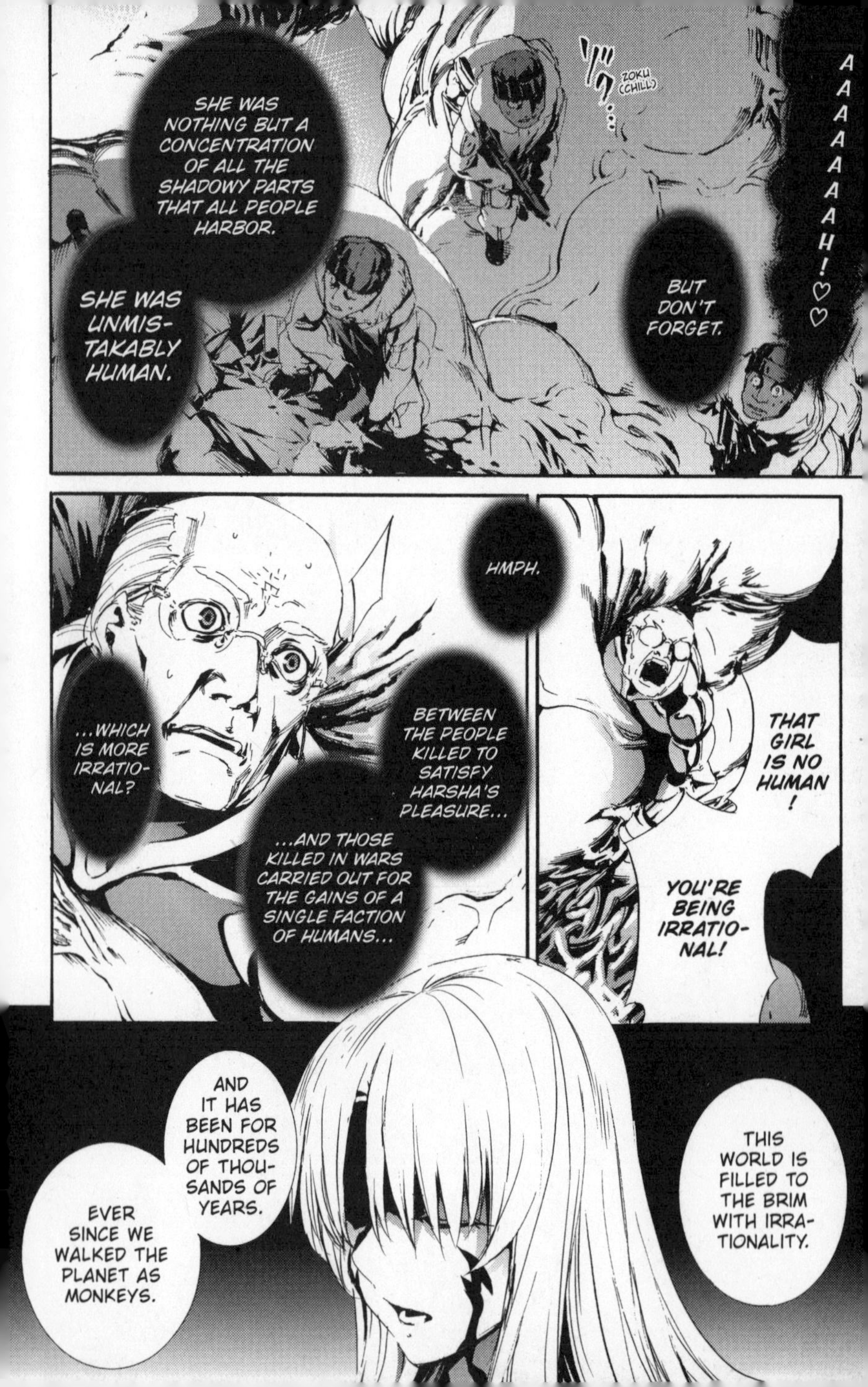
AAAAAAAAH! ♡ ♡
ZOKU (CHILL)
BUT DON'T FORGET.
SHE WAS NOTHING BUT A CONCENTRATION OF ALL THE SHADOWY PARTS THAT ALL PEOPLE HARBOR.
SHE WAS UNMISTAKABLY HUMAN.
THAT GIRL IS NO HUMAN!
YOU'RE BEING IRRATIONAL!
HMPH.
BETWEEN THE PEOPLE KILLED TO SATISFY HARSHA'S PLEASURE...
...AND THOSE KILLED IN WARS CARRIED OUT FOR THE GAINS OF A SINGLE FACTION OF HUMANS...
...WHICH IS MORE IRRATIONAL?
THIS WORLD IS FILLED TO THE BRIM WITH IRRATIONALITY.
AND IT HAS BEEN FOR HUNDREDS OF THOUSANDS OF YEARS.
EVER SINCE WE WALKED THE PLANET AS MONKEYS.

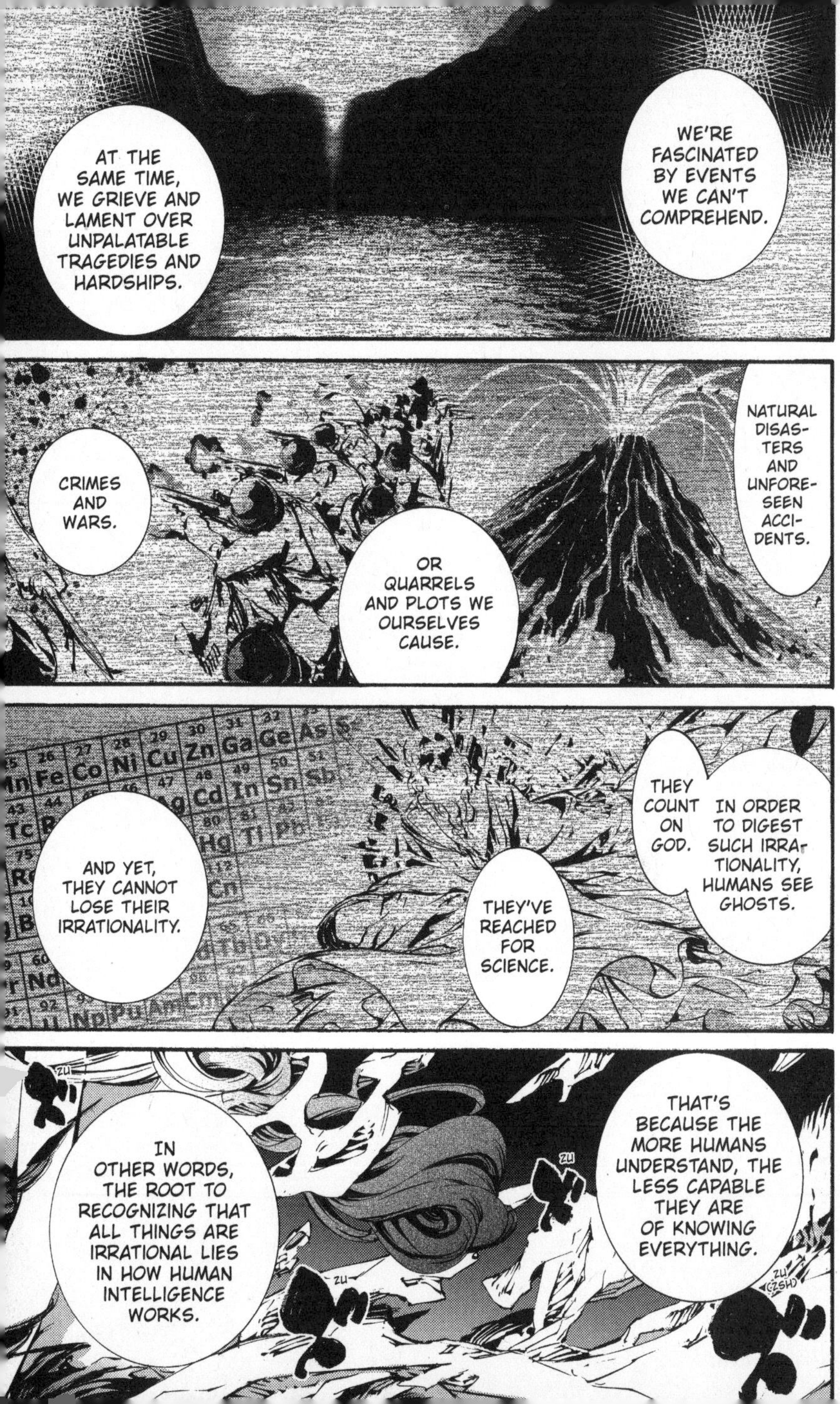
WE'RE FASCINATED BY EVENTS WE CAN'T COMPREHEND.
AT THE SAME TIME, WE GRIEVE AND LAMENT OVER UNPALATABLE TRAGEDIES AND HARDSHIPS.
NATURAL DISASTERS AND UNFORESEEN ACCIDENTS.
CRIMES AND WARS.
OR QUARRELS AND PLOTS WE OURSELVES CAUSE.
IN ORDER TO DIGEST SUCH IRRATIONALITY, HUMANS SEE GHOSTS.
THEY COUNT ON GOD.
THEY'VE REACHED FOR SCIENCE.
AND YET, THEY CANNOT LOSE THEIR IRRATIONALITY.
ZU
THAT'S BECAUSE THE MORE HUMANS UNDERSTAND, THE LESS CAPABLE THEY ARE OF KNOWING EVERYTHING.
ZU (CZSH)
ZU
ZU
IN OTHER WORDS, THE ROOT TO RECOGNIZING THAT ALL THINGS ARE IRRATIONAL LIES IN HOW HUMAN INTELLIGENCE WORKS.

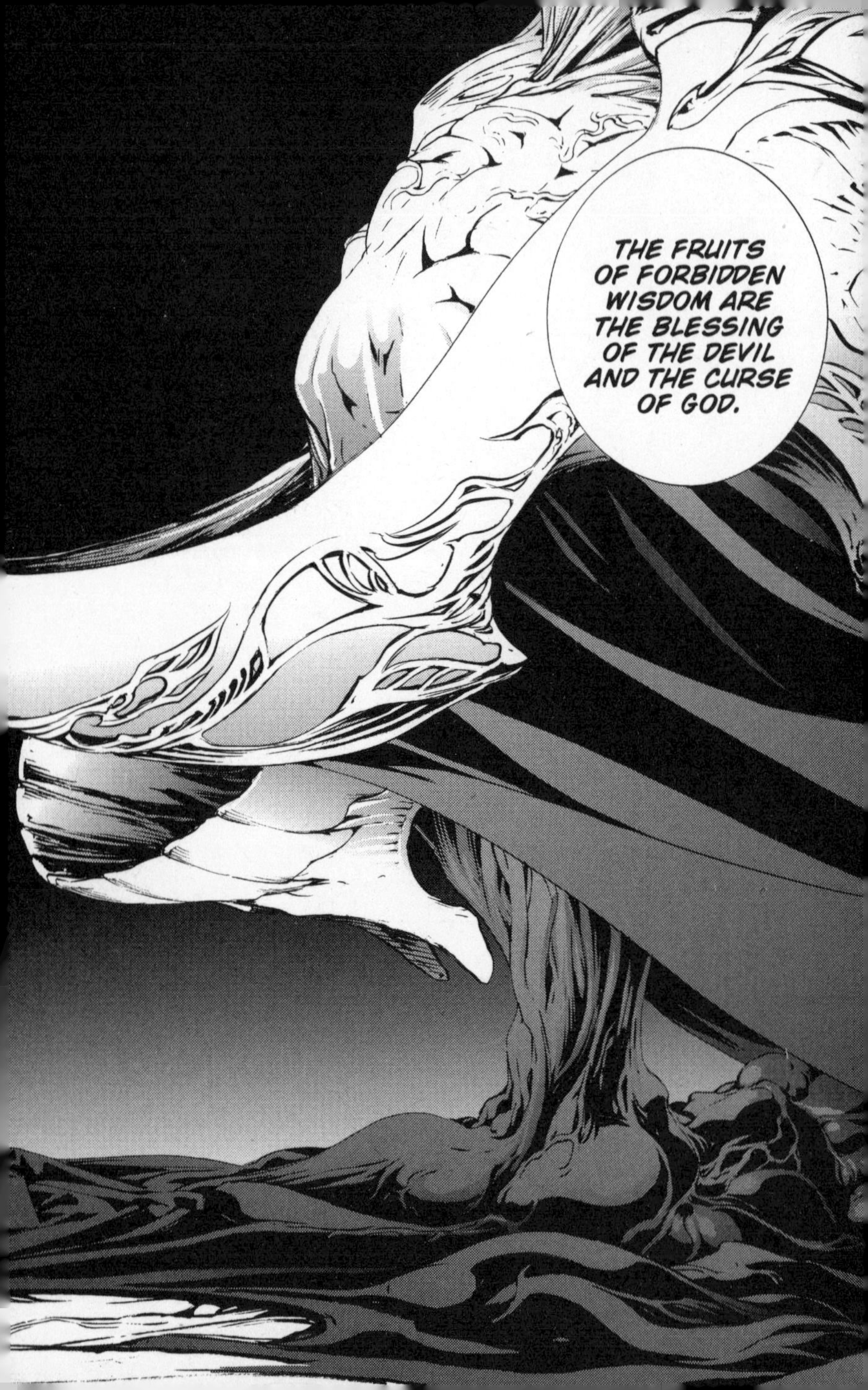
THE FRUITS OF FORBIDDEN WISDOM ARE THE BLESSING OF THE DEVIL AND THE CURSE OF GOD.

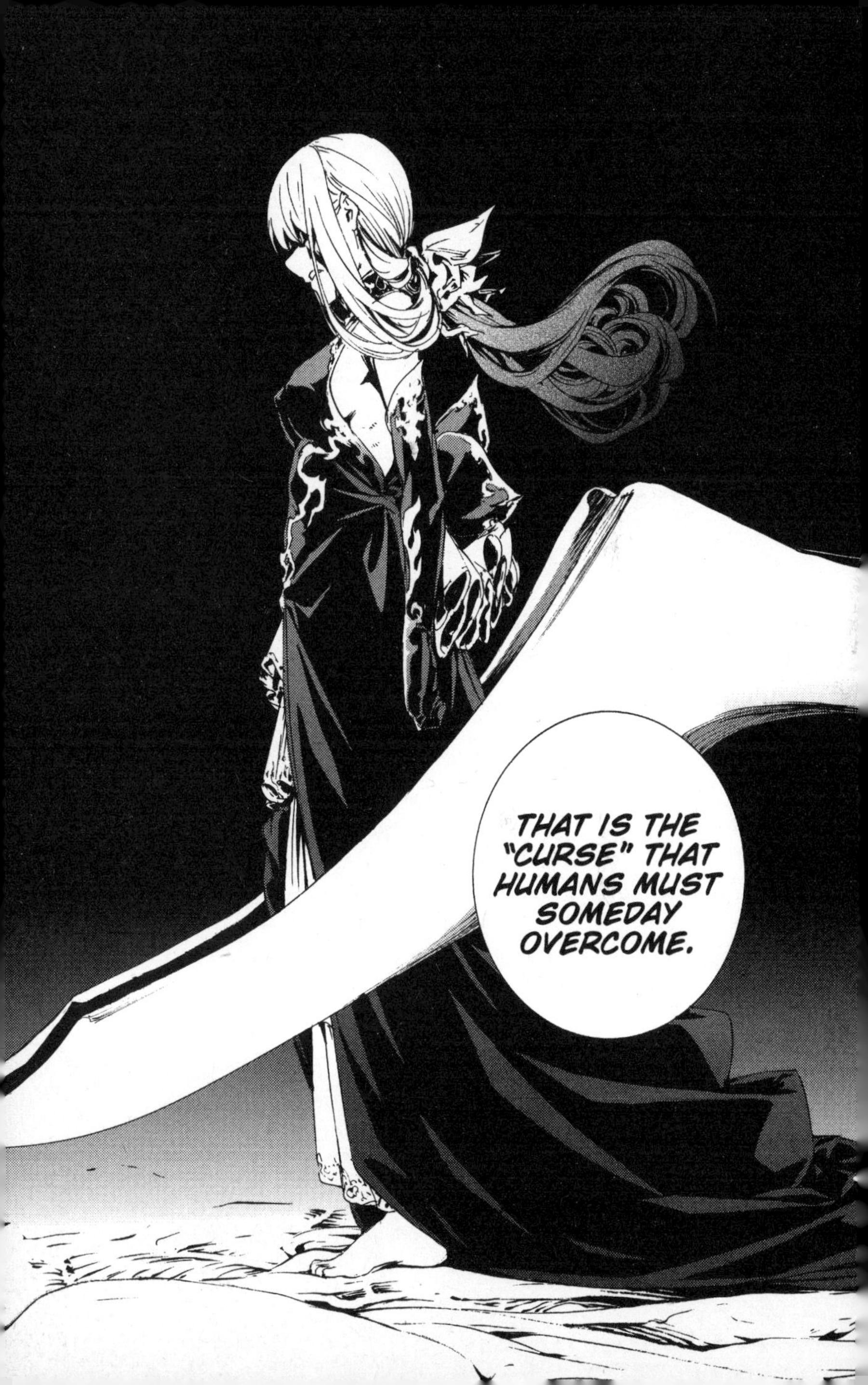
THAT IS THE "CURSE" THAT HUMANS MUST SOMEDAY OVERCOME.

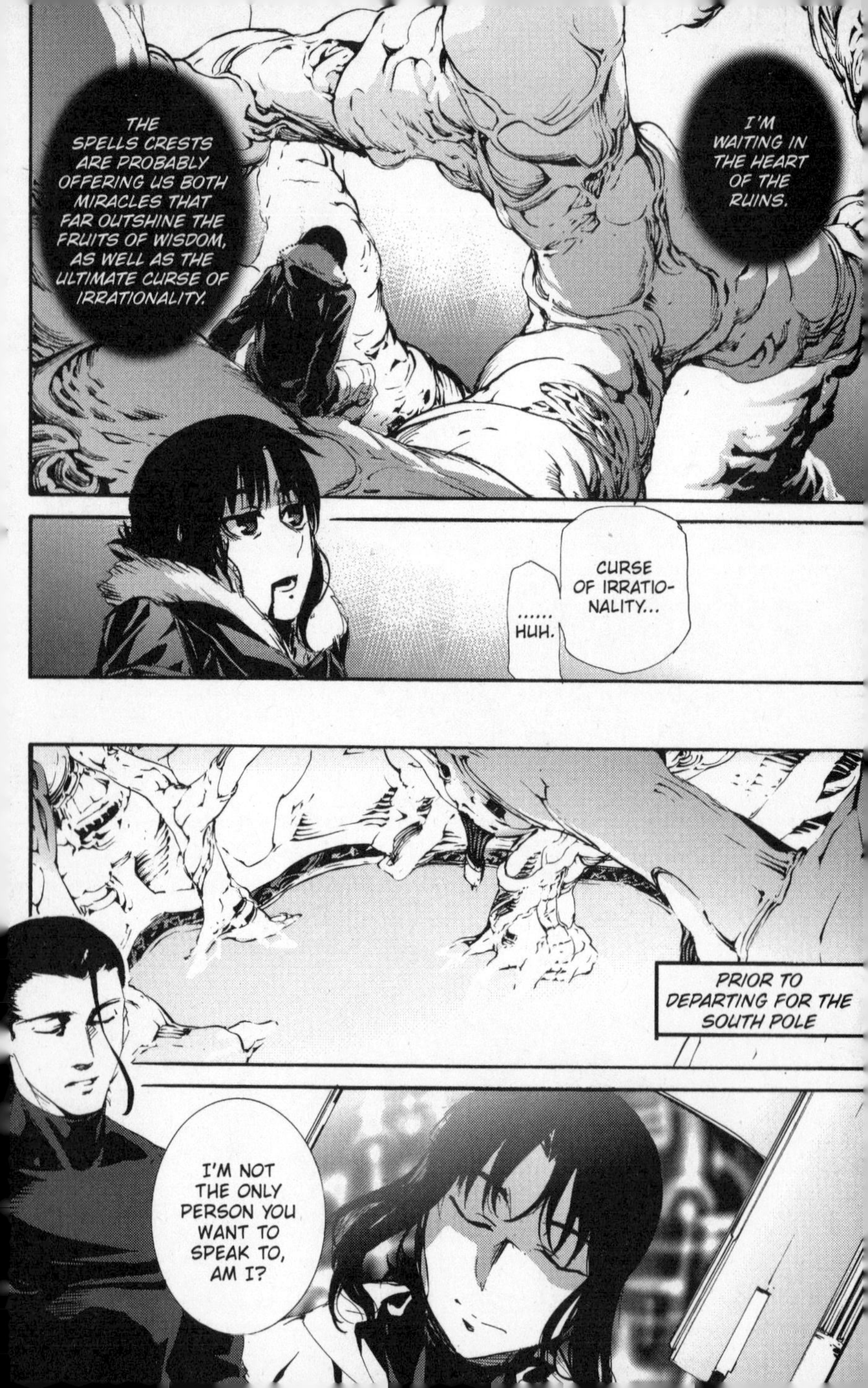
I'M WAITING IN THE HEART OF THE RUINS.
THE SPELLS CRESTS ARE PROBABLY OFFERING US BOTH MIRACLES THAT FAR OUTSHINE THE FRUITS OF WISDOM, AS WELL AS THE ULTIMATE CURSE OF IRRATIONALITY.
CURSE OF IRRATIONALITY...
......HUH.
PRIOR TO DEPARTING FOR THE SOUTH POLE
I'M NOT THE ONLY PERSON YOU WANT TO SPEAK TO, AM I?

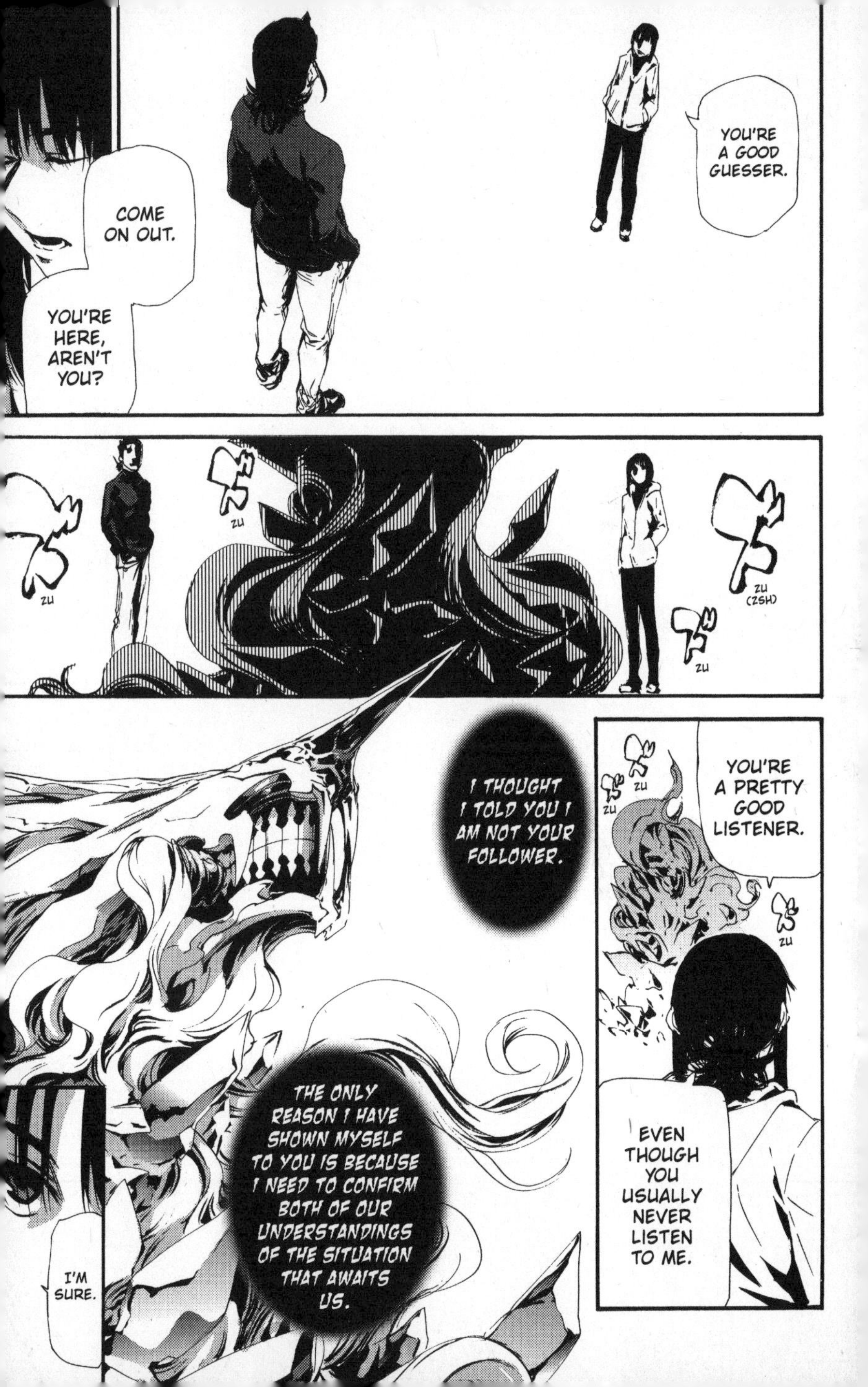
YOU'RE A GOOD GUESSER.
COME ON OUT.
YOU'RE HERE, AREN'T YOU?
ZU (ZSH)
ZU
ZU
ZU
YOU'RE A PRETTY GOOD LISTENER.
ZU
ZU
ZU
EVEN THOUGH YOU USUALLY NEVER LISTEN TO ME.
I THOUGHT I TOLD YOU I AM NOT YOUR FOLLOWER.
THE ONLY REASON I HAVE SHOWN MYSELF TO YOU IS BECAUSE I NEED TO CONFIRM BOTH OF OUR UNDERSTANDINGS OF THE SITUATION THAT AWAITS US.
I'M SURE.

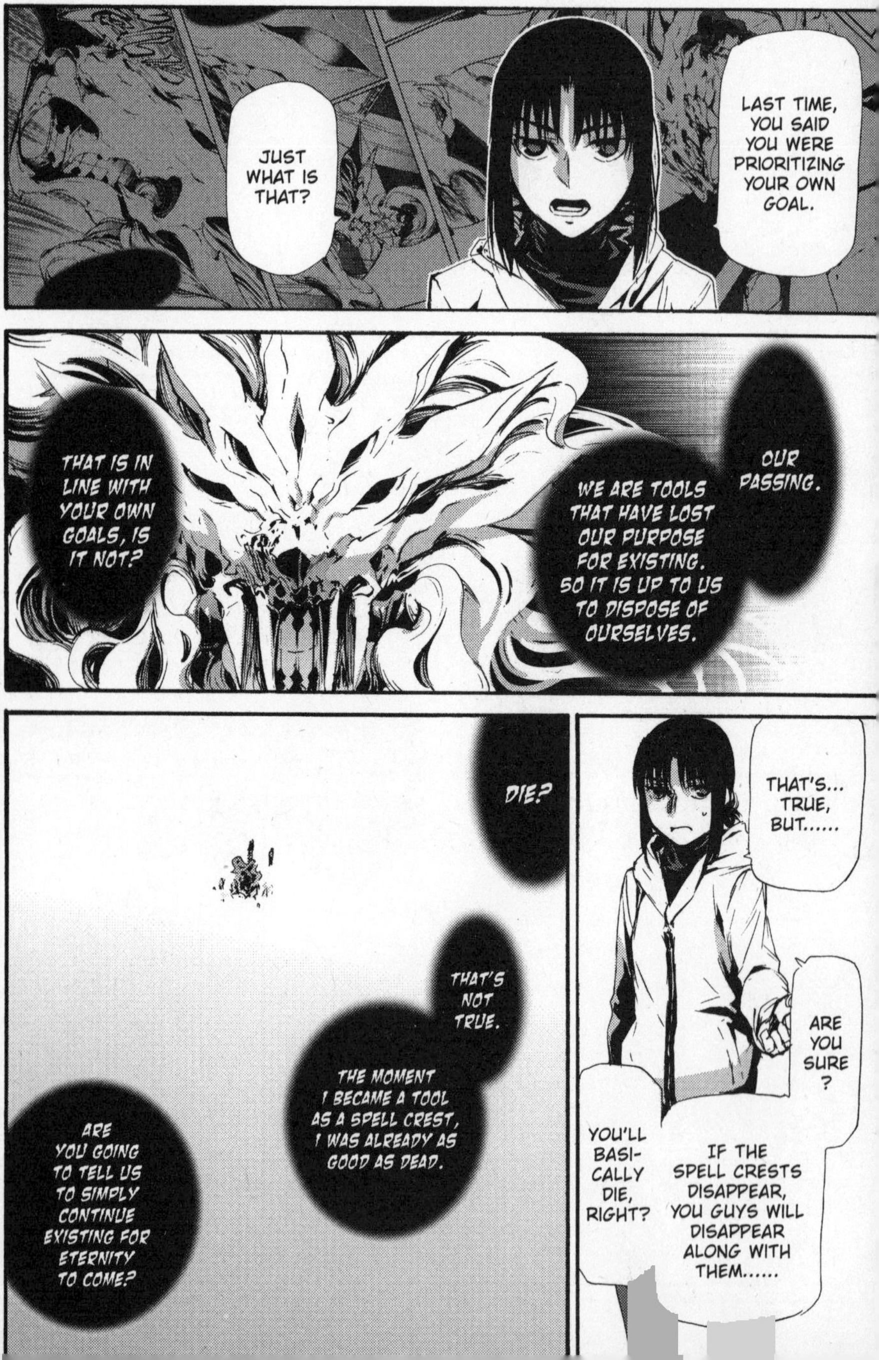
LAST TIME, YOU SAID YOU WERE PRIORITIZING YOUR OWN GOAL.
JUST WHAT IS THAT?
OUR PASSING.
WE ARE TOOLS THAT HAVE LOST OUR PURPOSE FOR EXISTING. SO IT IS UP TO US TO DISPOSE OF OURSELVES.
THAT IS IN LINE WITH YOUR OWN GOALS, IS IT NOT?
THAT'S... TRUE, BUT......
ARE YOU SURE?
IF THE SPELL CRESTS DISAPPEAR, YOU GUYS WILL DISAPPEAR ALONG WITH THEM......
YOU'LL BASI-CALLY DIE, RIGHT?
DIE?
THAT'S NOT TRUE.
THE MOMENT I BECAME A TOOL AS A SPELL CREST, I WAS ALREADY AS GOOD AS DEAD.
ARE YOU GOING TO TELL US TO SIMPLY CONTINUE EXISTING FOR ETERNITY TO COME?

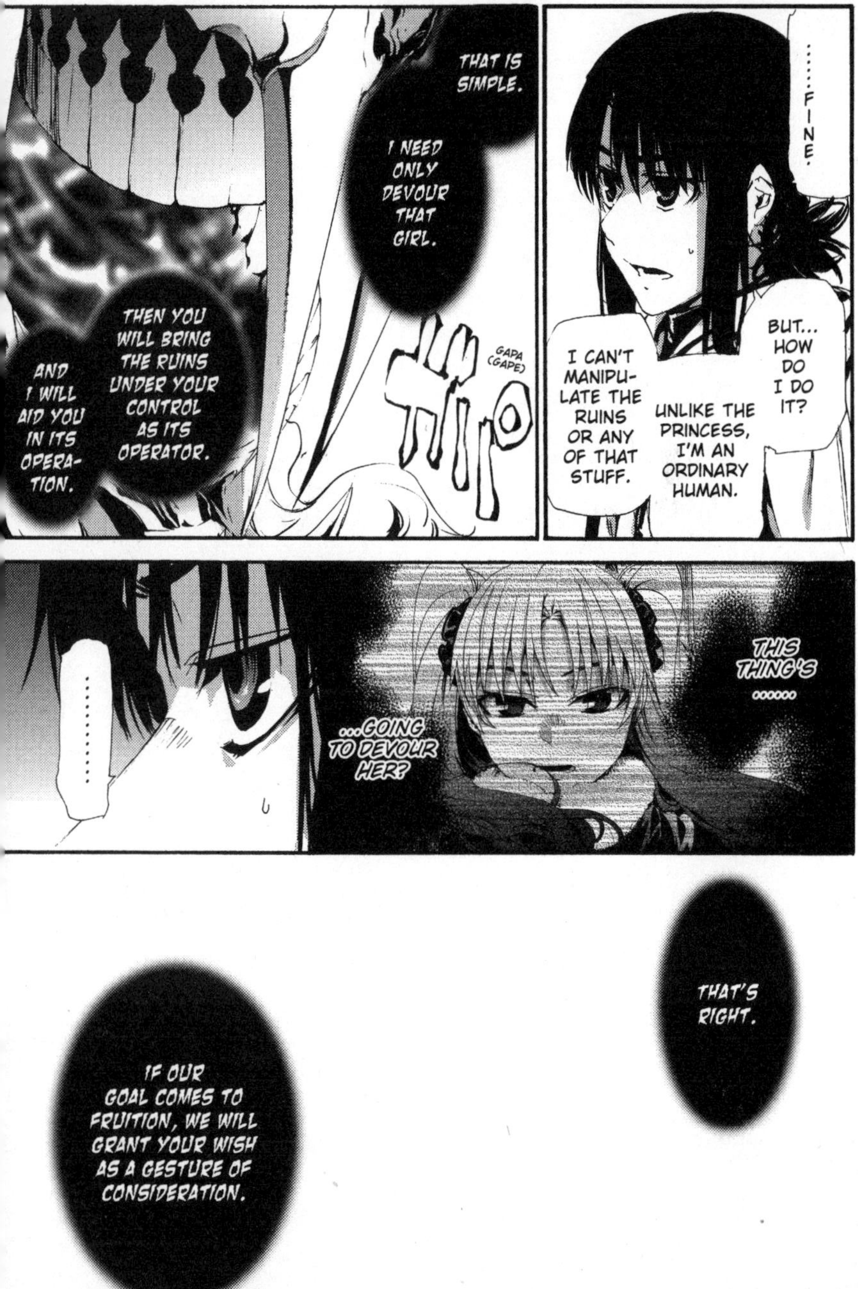

....FINE.
BUT... HOW DO I DO IT?
UNLIKE THE PRINCESS, I'M AN ORDINARY HUMAN.
I CAN'T MANIPU-LATE THE RUINS OR ANY OF THAT STUFF.
THAT IS SIMPLE.
I NEED ONLY DEVOUR THAT GIRL.
GAPA (GAPE)
THEN YOU WILL BRING THE RUINS UNDER YOUR CONTROL AS ITS OPERATOR.
AND I WILL AID YOU IN ITS OPERA-TION.
THIS THING'S ......
...GOING TO DEVOUR HER?
....
THAT'S RIGHT.
IF OUR GOAL COMES TO FRUITION, WE WILL GRANT YOUR WISH AS A GESTURE OF CONSIDERATION.

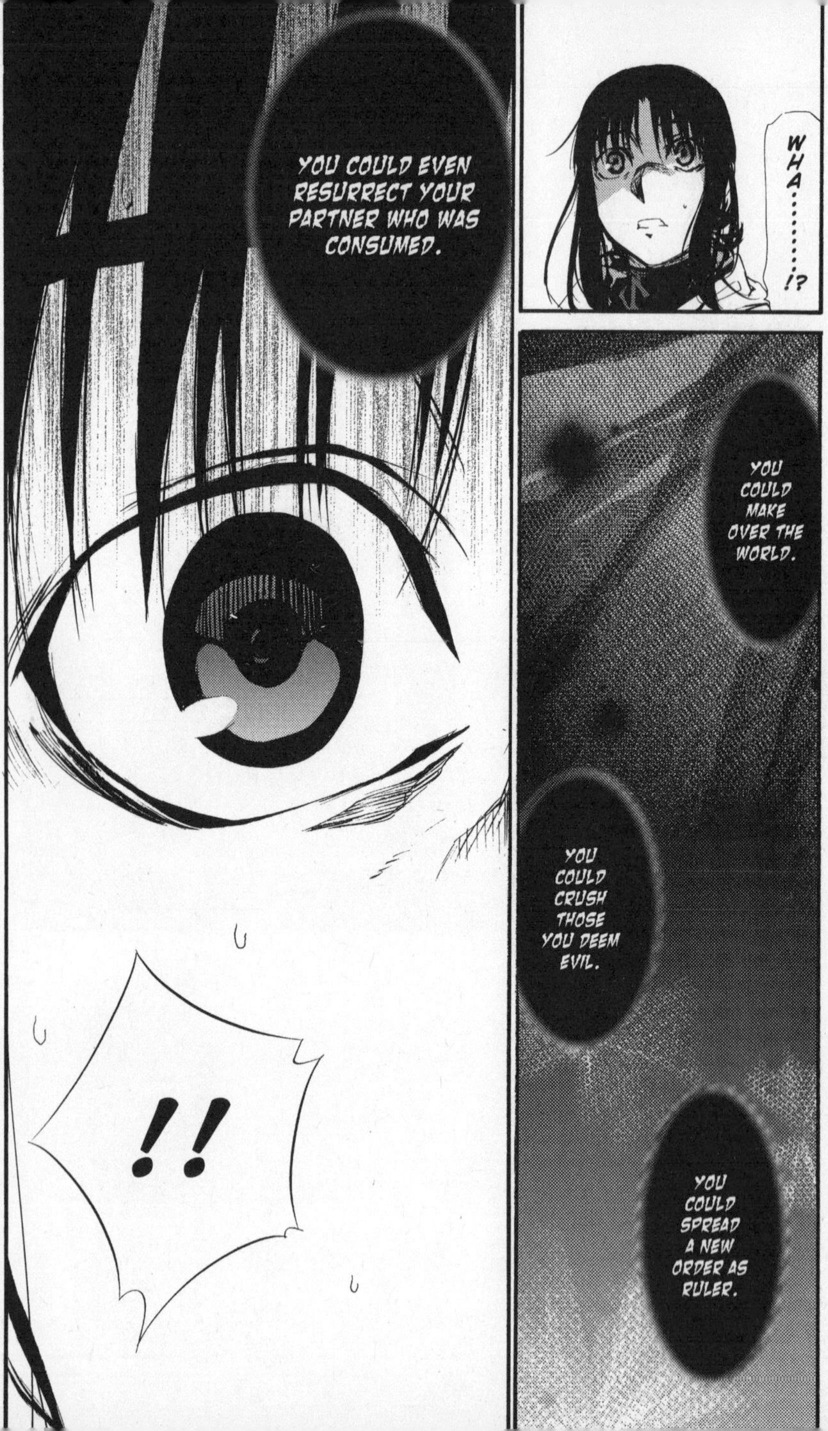
WHA......!?
YOU COULD MAKE OVER THE WORLD.
YOU COULD CRUSH THOSE YOU DEEM EVIL.
YOU COULD SPREAD A NEW ORDER AS RULER.
YOU COULD EVEN RESURRECT YOUR PARTNER WHO WAS CONSUMED.
!!

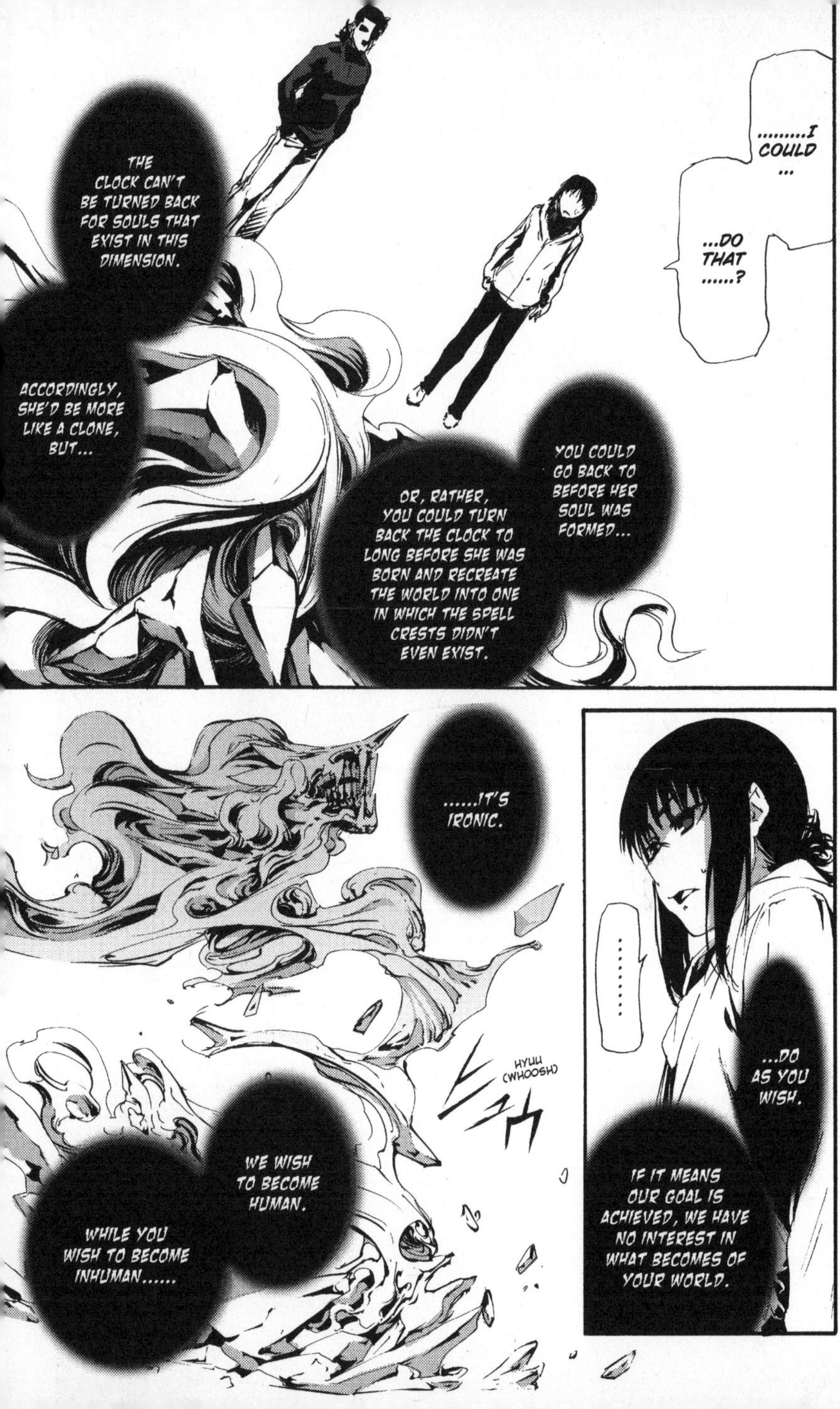
........I COULD ...
...DO THAT ......?
THE CLOCK CAN'T BE TURNED BACK FOR SOULS THAT EXIST IN THIS DIMENSION.
ACCORDINGLY, SHE'D BE MORE LIKE A CLONE, BUT...
YOU COULD GO BACK TO BEFORE HER SOUL WAS FORMED...
OR, RATHER, YOU COULD TURN BACK THE CLOCK TO LONG BEFORE SHE WAS BORN AND RECREATE THE WORLD INTO ONE IN WHICH THE SPELL CRESTS DIDN'T EVEN EXIST.
....
...DO AS YOU WISH.
IF IT MEANS OUR GOAL IS ACHIEVED, WE HAVE NO INTEREST IN WHAT BECOMES OF YOUR WORLD.
......IT'S IRONIC.
HYUU (WHOOSH)
WE WISH TO BECOME HUMAN.
WHILE YOU WISH TO BECOME INHUMAN......

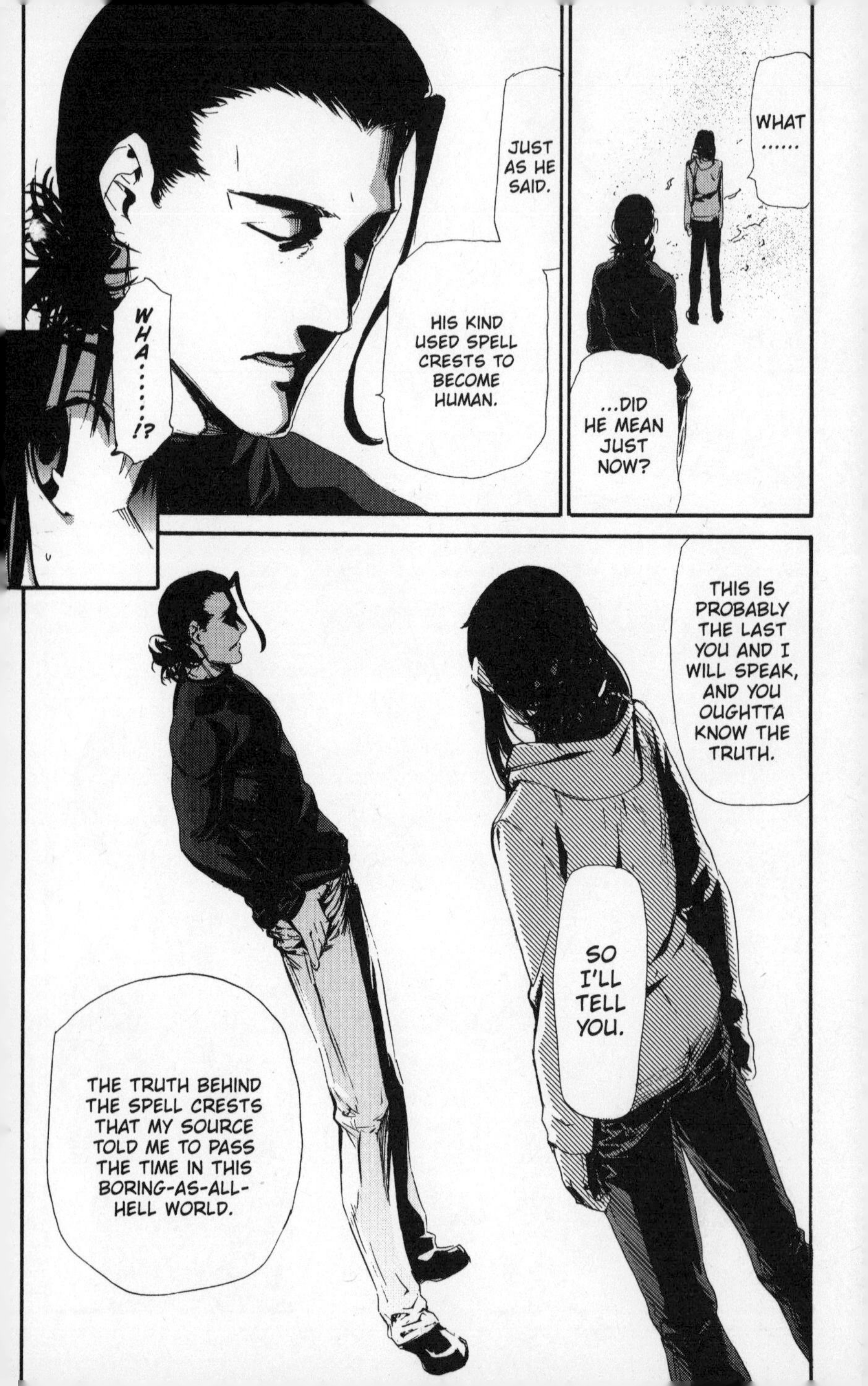
WHAT ......
...DID HE MEAN JUST NOW?
JUST AS HE SAID.
HIS KIND USED SPELL CRESTS TO BECOME HUMAN.
WHA......!?
THIS IS PROBABLY THE LAST YOU AND I WILL SPEAK, AND YOU OUGHTTA KNOW THE TRUTH.
SO I'LL TELL YOU.
THE TRUTH BEHIND THE SPELL CRESTS THAT MY SOURCE TOLD ME TO PASS THE TIME IN THIS BORING-AS-ALL-HELL WORLD.

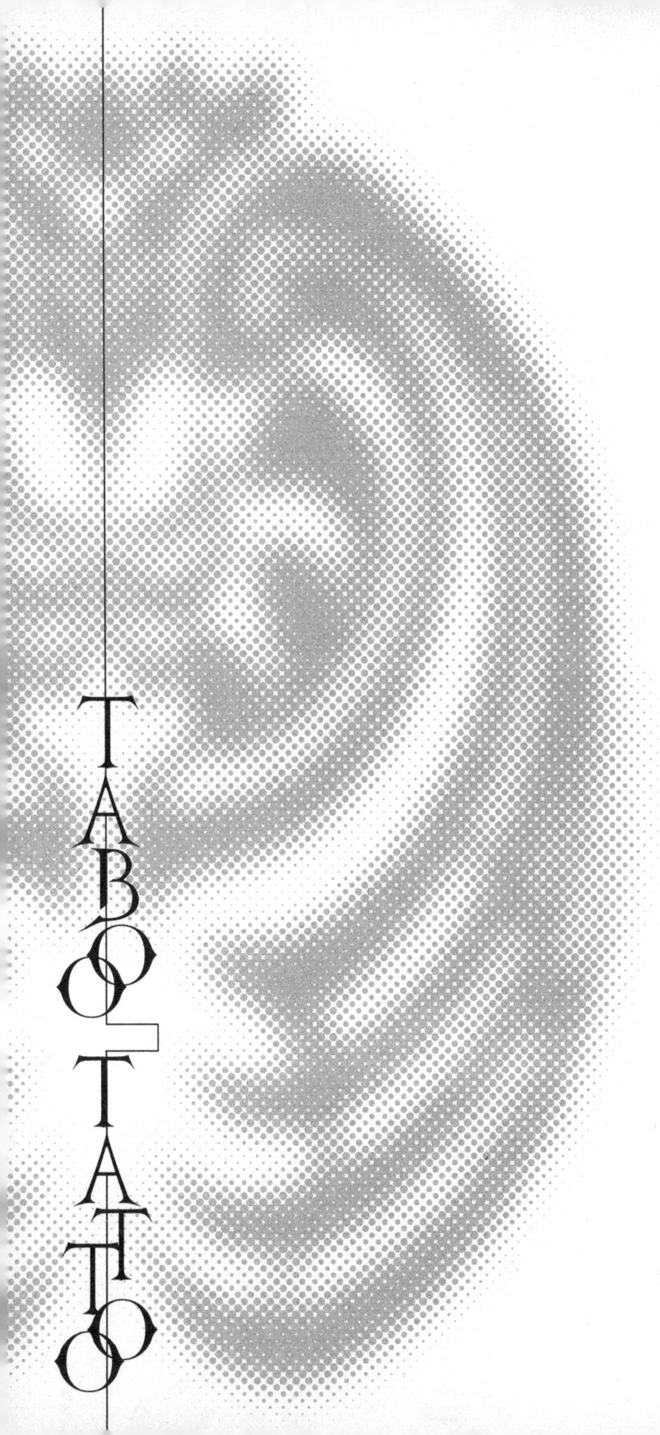

TABOO TATTOO

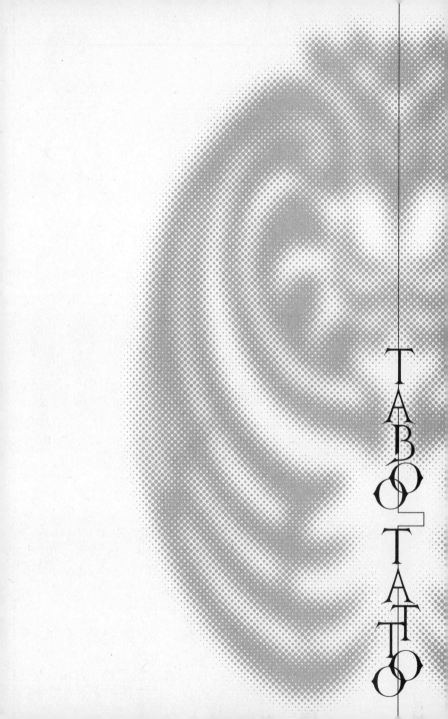

TABOO TATTOO

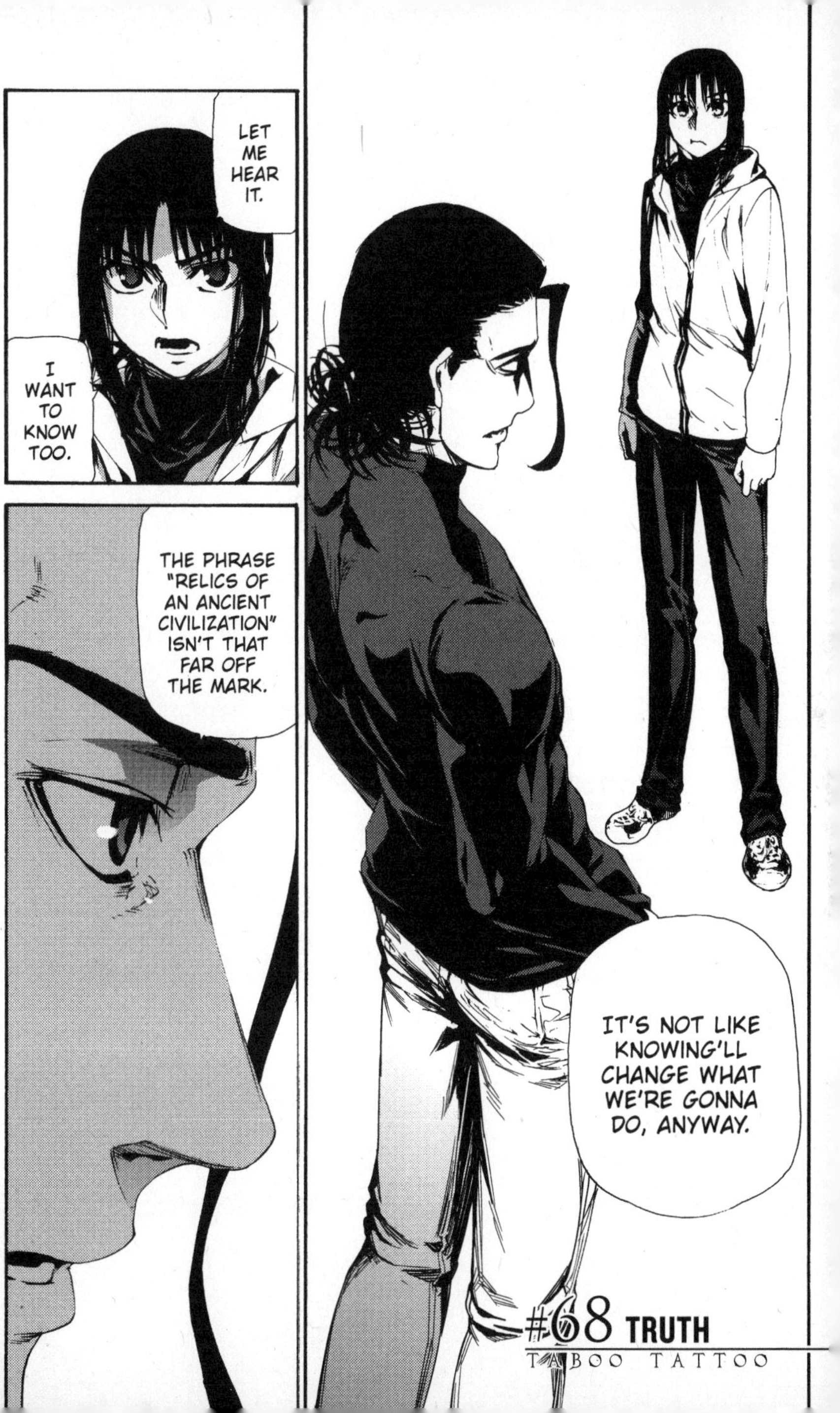
IT'S NOT LIKE KNOWING'LL CHANGE WHAT WE'RE GONNA DO, ANYWAY.
#68 TRUTH
TABOO TATTOO
LET ME HEAR IT.
I WANT TO KNOW TOO.
THE PHRASE "RELICS OF AN ANCIENT CIVILIZATION" ISN'T THAT FAR OFF THE MARK.

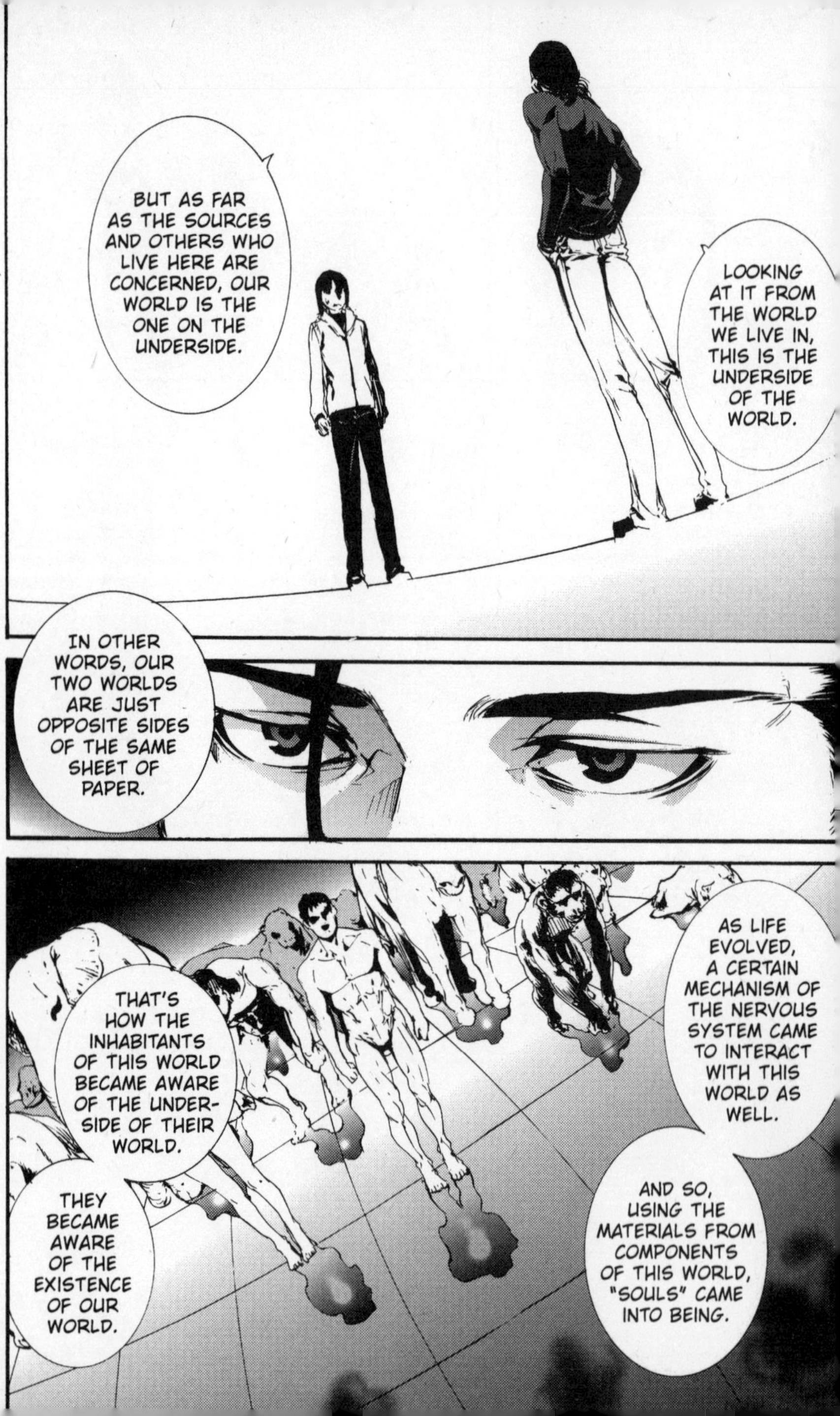
LOOKING AT IT FROM THE WORLD WE LIVE IN, THIS IS THE UNDERSIDE OF THE WORLD.
BUT AS FAR AS THE SOURCES AND OTHERS WHO LIVE HERE ARE CONCERNED, OUR WORLD IS THE ONE ON THE UNDERSIDE.
IN OTHER WORDS, OUR TWO WORLDS ARE JUST OPPOSITE SIDES OF THE SAME SHEET OF PAPER.
AS LIFE EVOLVED, A CERTAIN MECHANISM OF THE NERVOUS SYSTEM CAME TO INTERACT WITH THIS WORLD AS WELL.
AND SO, USING THE MATERIALS FROM COMPONENTS OF THIS WORLD, "SOULS" CAME INTO BEING.
THAT'S HOW THE INHABITANTS OF THIS WORLD BECAME AWARE OF THE UNDER-SIDE OF THEIR WORLD.
THEY BECAME AWARE OF THE EXISTENCE OF OUR WORLD.

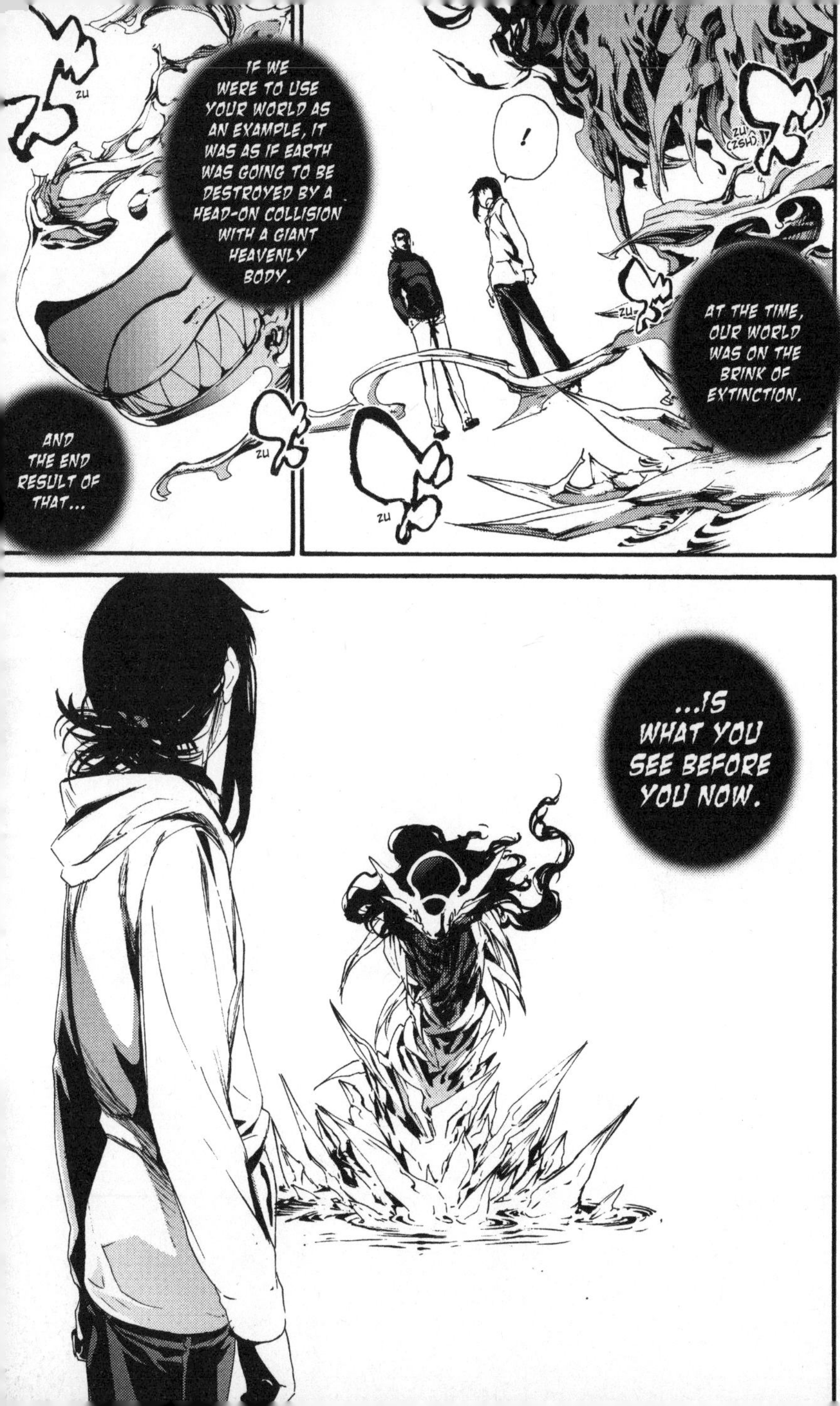
ZU (ZSH)
!
ZU
AT THE TIME, OUR WORLD WAS ON THE BRINK OF EXTINCTION.
ZU
ZU
IF WE WERE TO USE YOUR WORLD AS AN EXAMPLE, IT WAS AS IF EARTH WAS GOING TO BE DESTROYED BY A HEAD-ON COLLISION WITH A GIANT HEAVENLY BODY.
ZU
AND THE END RESULT OF THAT...
...IS WHAT YOU SEE BEFORE YOU NOW.

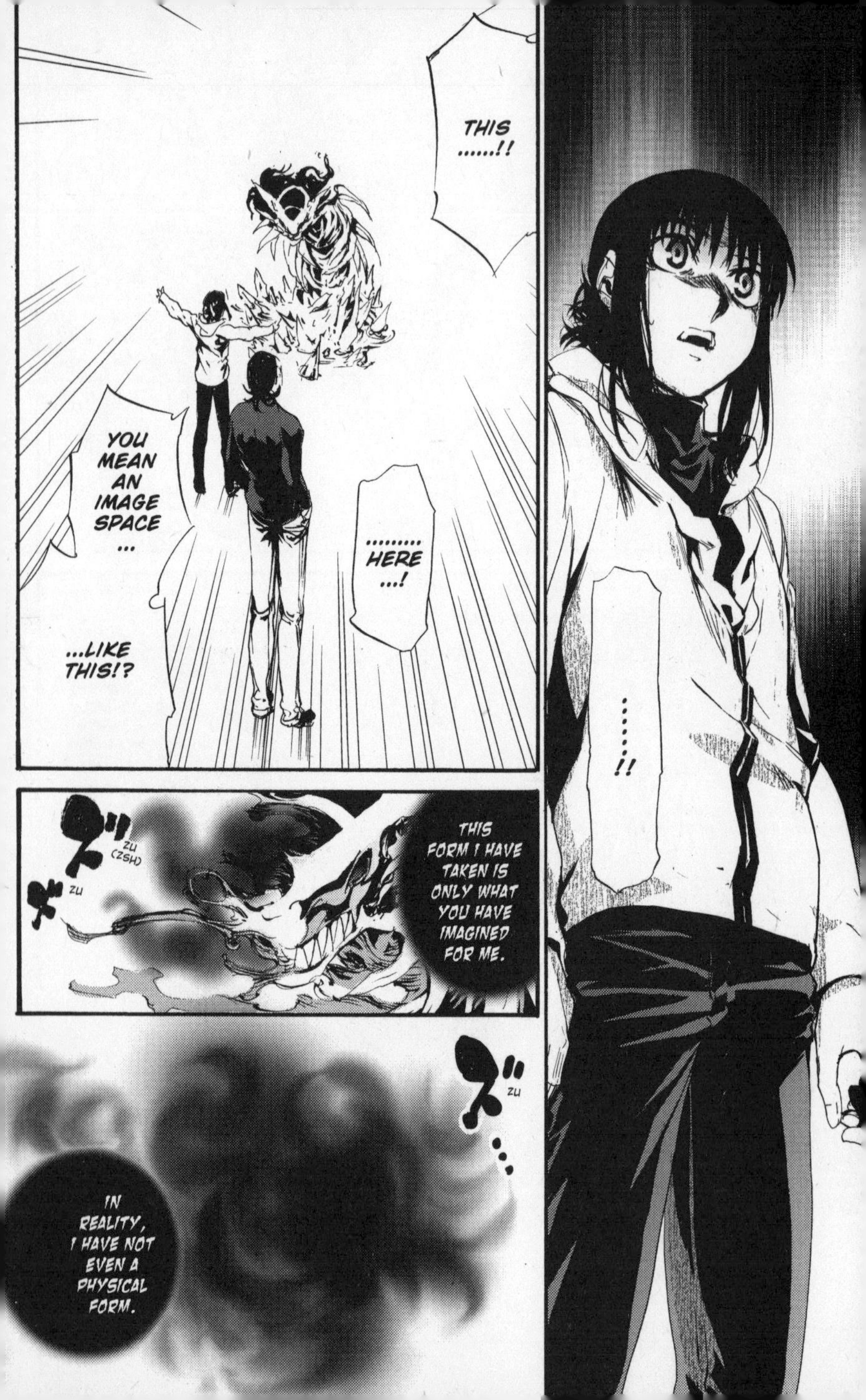
......!!
THIS ......!!
.... HERE ...!
YOU MEAN AN IMAGE SPACE ...
...LIKE THIS!?
ZU (ZSH)
ZU
THIS FORM I HAVE TAKEN IS ONLY WHAT YOU HAVE IMAGINED FOR ME.
ZU
...
IN REALITY, I HAVE NOT EVEN A PHYSICAL FORM.

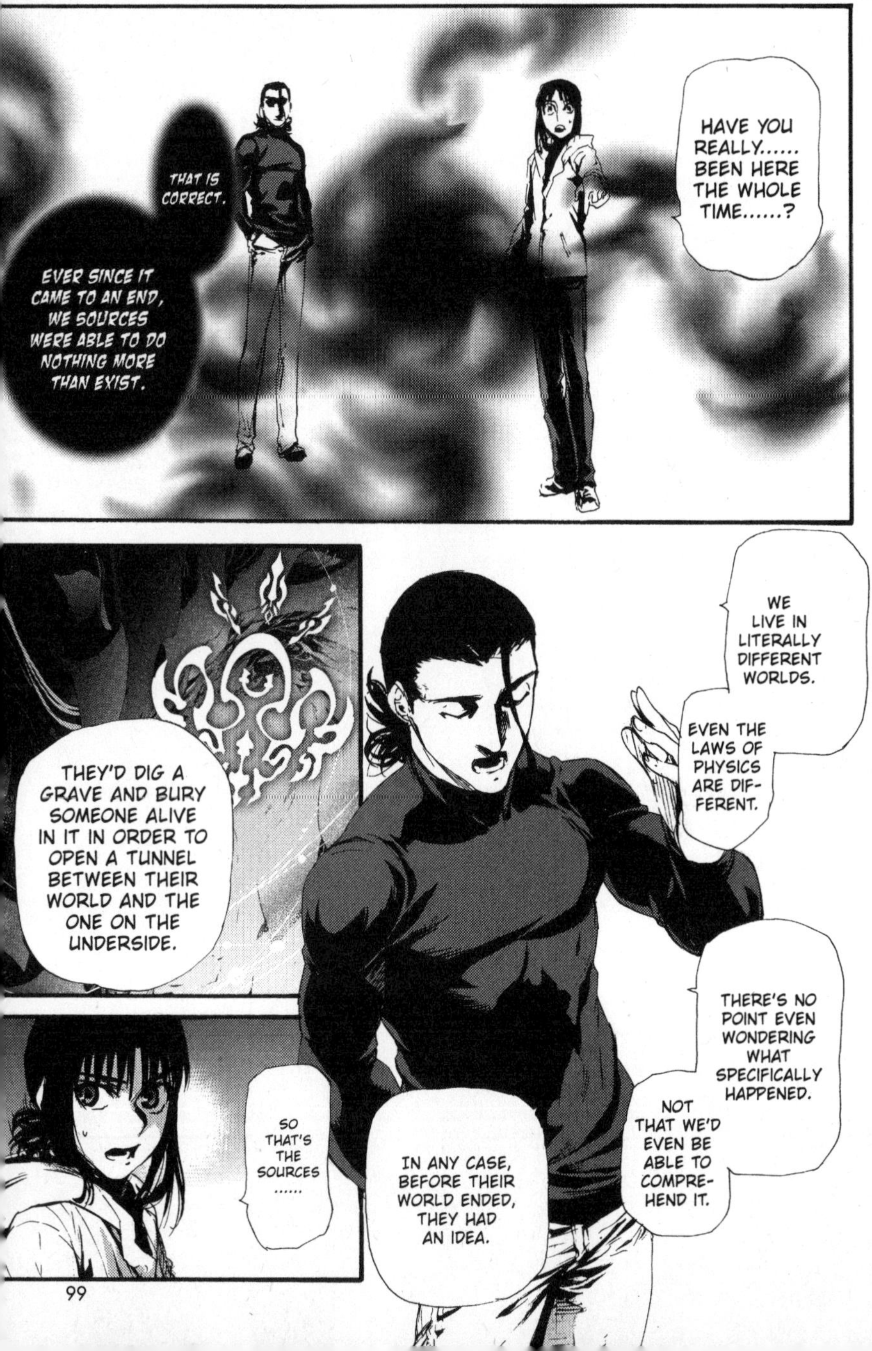
HAVE YOU REALLY...... BEEN HERE THE WHOLE TIME......?
THAT IS CORRECT.
EVER SINCE IT CAME TO AN END, WE SOURCES WERE ABLE TO DO NOTHING MORE THAN EXIST.
WE LIVE IN LITERALLY DIFFERENT WORLDS.
EVEN THE LAWS OF PHYSICS ARE DIF-FERENT.
THERE'S NO POINT EVEN WONDERING WHAT SPECIFICALLY HAPPENED.
NOT THAT WE'D EVEN BE ABLE TO COMPRE-HEND IT.
IN ANY CASE, BEFORE THEIR WORLD ENDED, THEY HAD AN IDEA.
THEY'D DIG A GRAVE AND BURY SOMEONE ALIVE IN IT IN ORDER TO OPEN A TUNNEL BETWEEN THEIR WORLD AND THE ONE ON THE UNDERSIDE.
SO THAT'S THE SOURCES......

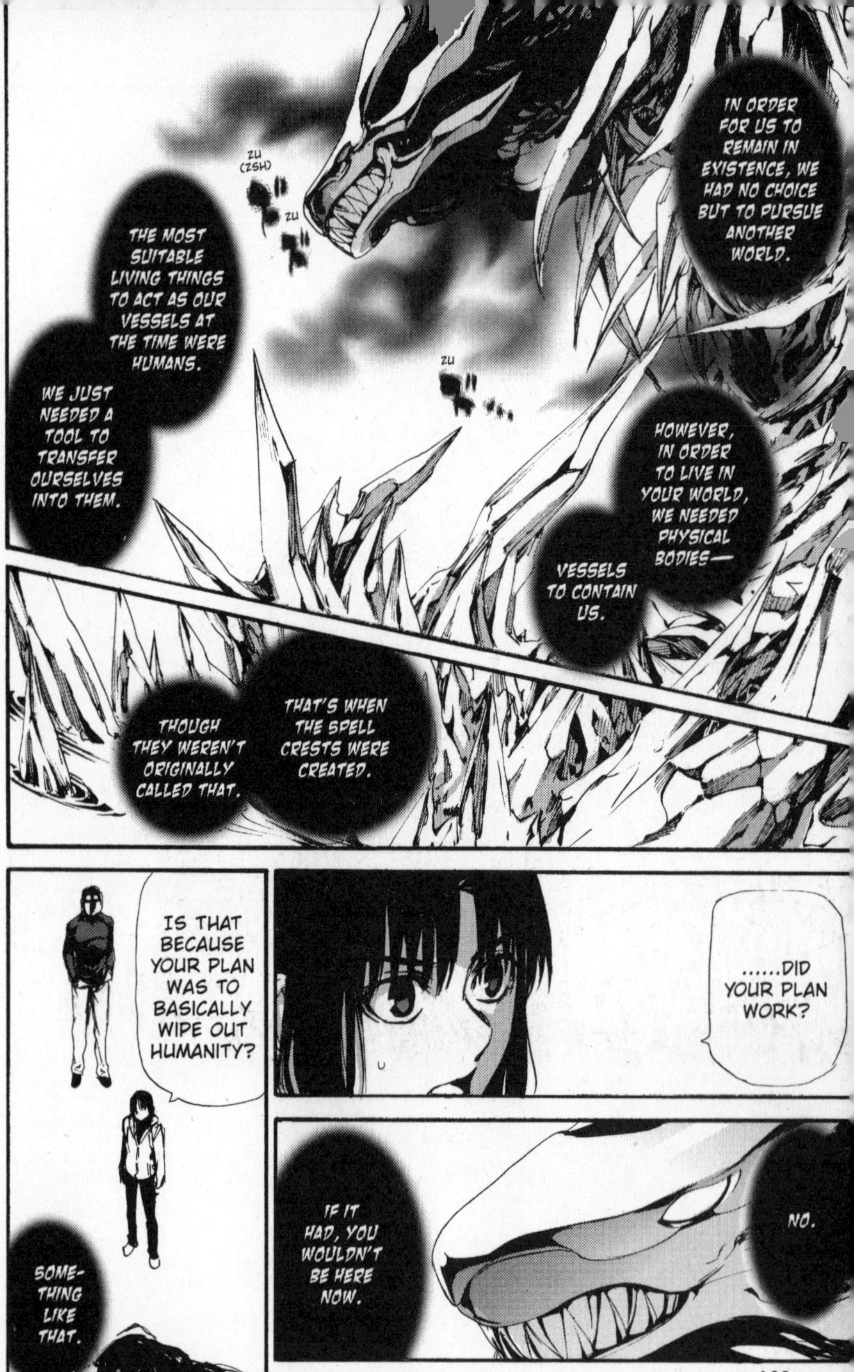
IN ORDER FOR US TO REMAIN IN EXISTENCE, WE HAD NO CHOICE BUT TO PURSUE ANOTHER WORLD.
ZU (ZSH)
ZU
ZU
HOWEVER, IN ORDER TO LIVE IN YOUR WORLD, WE NEEDED PHYSICAL BODIES—
VESSELS TO CONTAIN US.
THE MOST SUITABLE LIVING THINGS TO ACT AS OUR VESSELS AT THE TIME WERE HUMANS.
WE JUST NEEDED A TOOL TO TRANSFER OURSELVES INTO THEM.
THAT'S WHEN THE SPELL CRESTS WERE CREATED.
THOUGH THEY WEREN'T ORIGINALLY CALLED THAT.
......DID YOUR PLAN WORK?
NO.
IF IT HAD, YOU WOULDN'T BE HERE NOW.
IS THAT BECAUSE YOUR PLAN WAS TO BASICALLY WIPE OUT HUMANITY?
SOME-THING LIKE THAT.

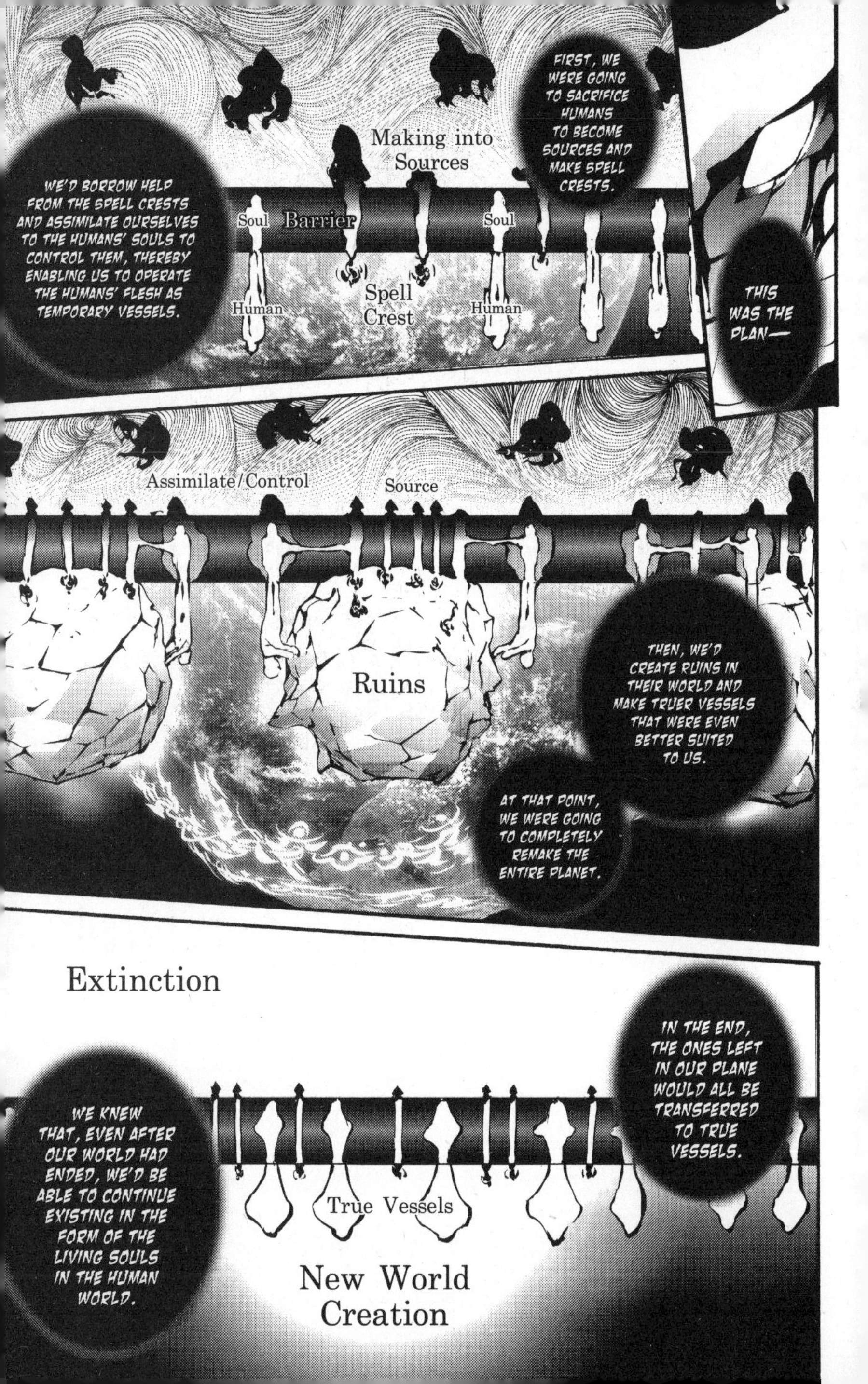
THIS WAS THE PLAN—
FIRST, WE WERE GOING TO SACRIFICE HUMANS TO BECOME SOURCES AND MAKE SPELL CRESTS.
Making into Sources
Soul
Barrier
Soul
Human
Spell Crest
Human
WE'D BORROW HELP FROM THE SPELL CRESTS AND ASSIMILATE OURSELVES TO THE HUMANS' SOULS TO CONTROL THEM, THEREBY ENABLING US TO OPERATE THE HUMANS' FLESH AS TEMPORARY VESSELS.
Source
Assimilate/Control
THEN, WE'D CREATE RUINS IN THEIR WORLD AND MAKE TRUER VESSELS THAT WERE EVEN BETTER SUITED TO US.
Ruins
AT THAT POINT, WE WERE GOING TO COMPLETELY REMAKE THE ENTIRE PLANET.
IN THE END, THE ONES LEFT IN OUR PLANE WOULD ALL BE TRANSFERRED TO TRUE VESSELS.
Extinction
WE KNEW THAT, EVEN AFTER OUR WORLD HAD ENDED, WE'D BE ABLE TO CONTINUE EXISTING IN THE FORM OF THE LIVING SOULS IN THE HUMAN WORLD.
True Vessels
New World Creation

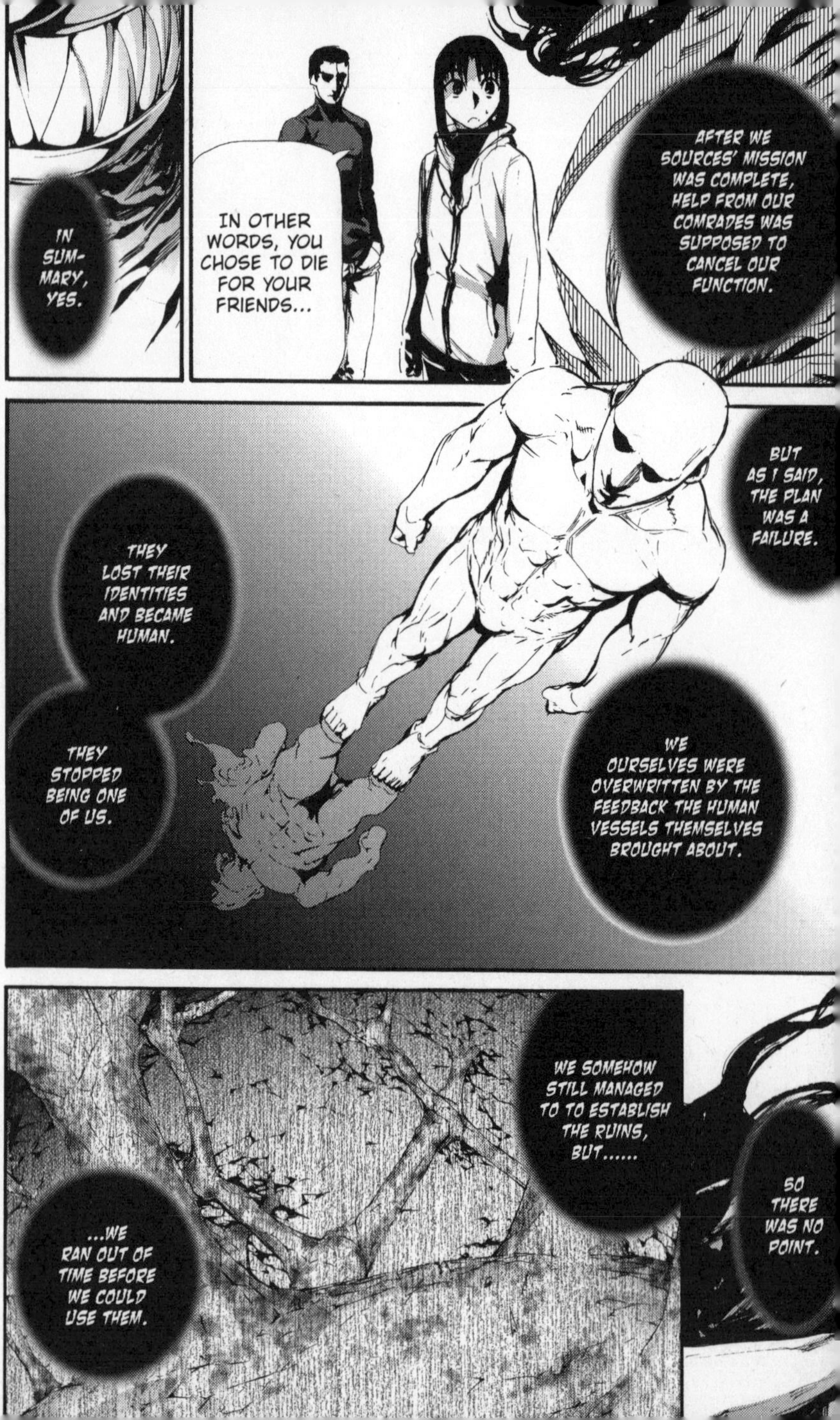
AFTER WE SOURCES' MISSION WAS COMPLETE, HELP FROM OUR COMRADES WAS SUPPOSED TO CANCEL OUR FUNCTION.
IN OTHER WORDS, YOU CHOSE TO DIE FOR YOUR FRIENDS...
IN SUM-MARY, YES.
BUT AS I SAID, THE PLAN WAS A FAILURE.
WE OURSELVES WERE OVERWRITTEN BY THE FEEDBACK THE HUMAN VESSELS THEMSELVES BROUGHT ABOUT.
THEY LOST THEIR IDENTITIES AND BECAME HUMAN.
THEY STOPPED BEING ONE OF US.
WE SOMEHOW STILL MANAGED TO TO ESTABLISH THE RUINS, BUT......
...WE RAN OUT OF TIME BEFORE WE COULD USE THEM.
SO THERE WAS NO POINT.

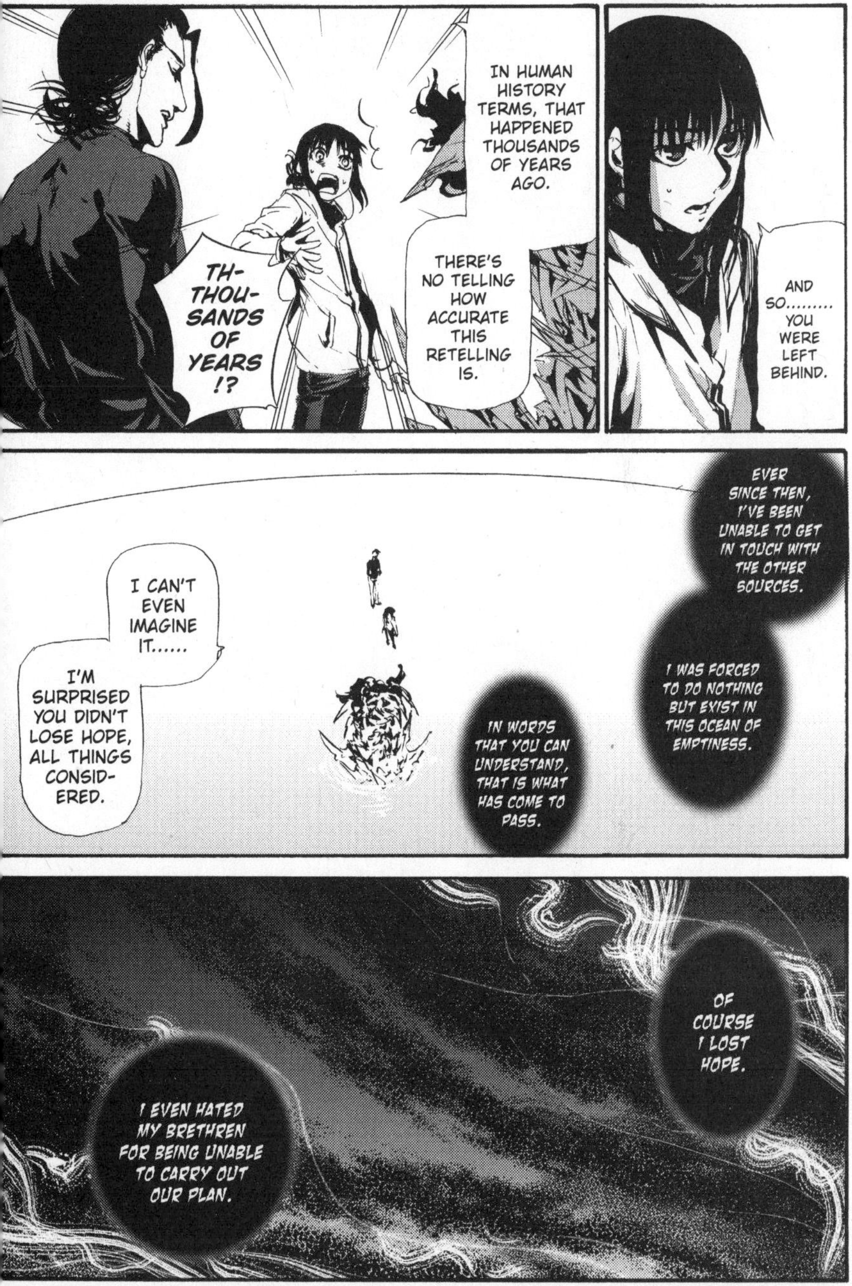
AND SO......... YOU WERE LEFT BEHIND.
IN HUMAN HISTORY TERMS, THAT HAPPENED THOUSANDS OF YEARS AGO.
THERE'S NO TELLING HOW ACCURATE THIS RETELLING IS.
TH-THOUSANDS OF YEARS!?
EVER SINCE THEN, I'VE BEEN UNABLE TO GET IN TOUCH WITH THE OTHER SOURCES.
I WAS FORCED TO DO NOTHING BUT EXIST IN THIS OCEAN OF EMPTINESS.
IN WORDS THAT YOU CAN UNDERSTAND, THAT IS WHAT HAS COME TO PASS.
I CAN'T EVEN IMAGINE IT......
I'M SURPRISED YOU DIDN'T LOSE HOPE, ALL THINGS CONSIDERED.
OF COURSE I LOST HOPE.
I EVEN HATED MY BRETHREN FOR BEING UNABLE TO CARRY OUT OUR PLAN.

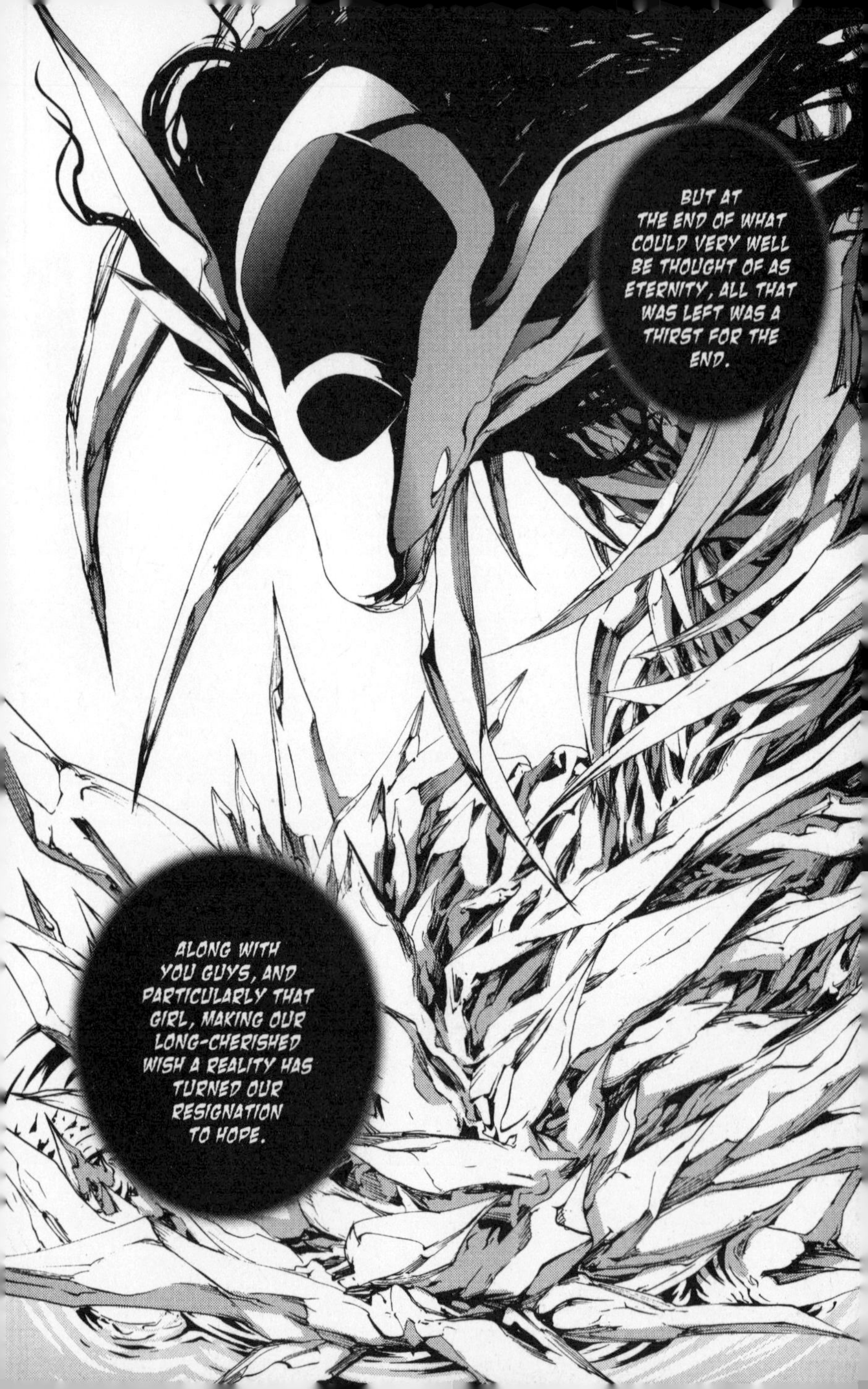
BUT AT THE END OF WHAT COULD VERY WELL BE THOUGHT OF AS ETERNITY, ALL THAT WAS LEFT WAS A THIRST FOR THE END.
ALONG WITH YOU GUYS, AND PARTICULARLY THAT GIRL, MAKING OUR LONG-CHERISHED WISH A REALITY HAS TURNED OUR RESIGNATION TO HOPE.

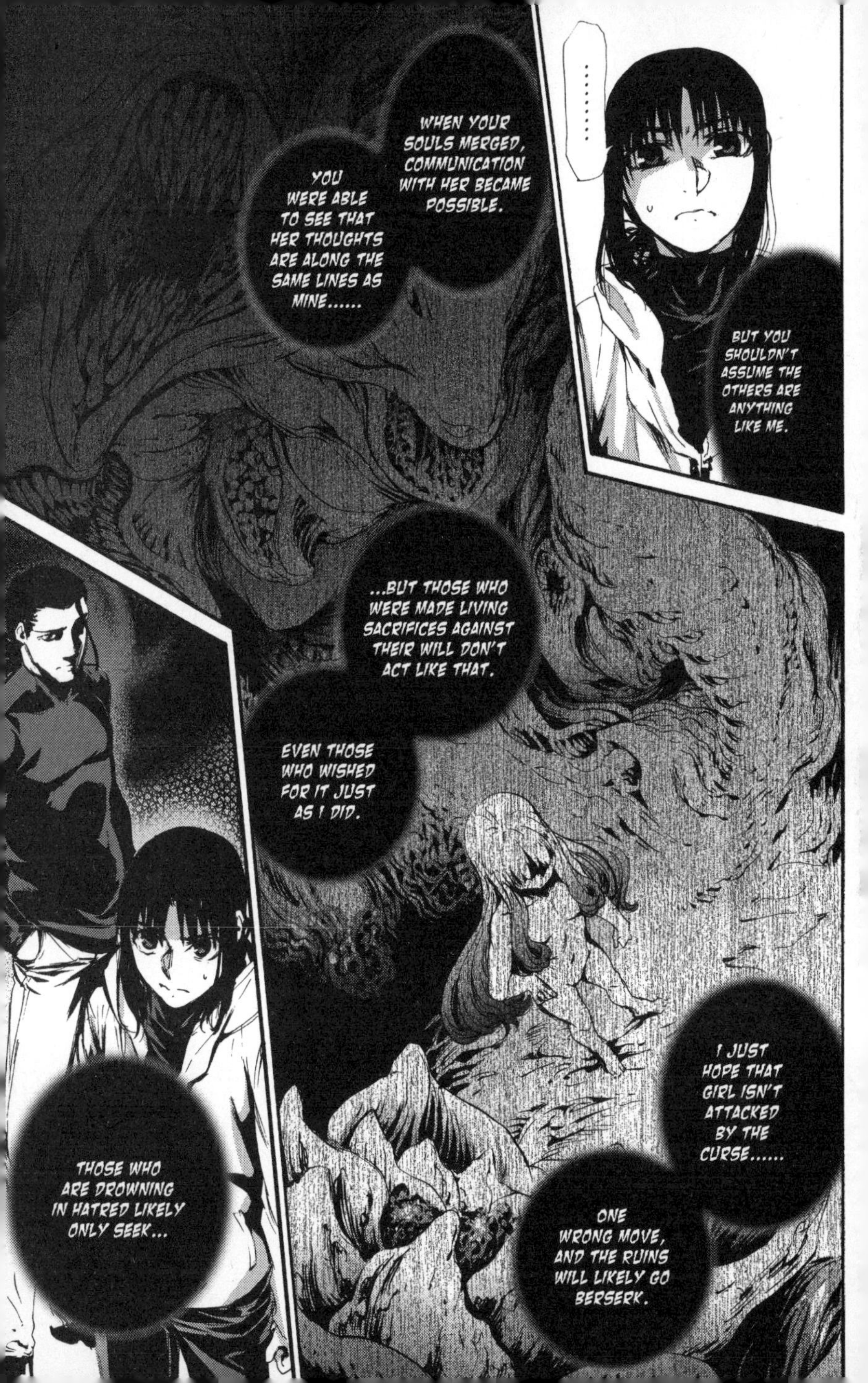
WHEN YOUR SOULS MERGED, COMMUNICATION WITH HER BECAME POSSIBLE.
YOU WERE ABLE TO SEE THAT HER THOUGHTS ARE ALONG THE SAME LINES AS MINE......
......
BUT YOU SHOULDN'T ASSUME THE OTHERS ARE ANYTHING LIKE ME.
...BUT THOSE WHO WERE MADE LIVING SACRIFICES AGAINST THEIR WILL DON'T ACT LIKE THAT.
EVEN THOSE WHO WISHED FOR IT JUST AS I DID.
I JUST HOPE THAT GIRL ISN'T ATTACKED BY THE CURSE......
ONE WRONG MOVE, AND THE RUINS WILL LIKELY GO BERSERK.
THOSE WHO ARE DROWNING IN HATRED LIKELY ONLY SEEK...

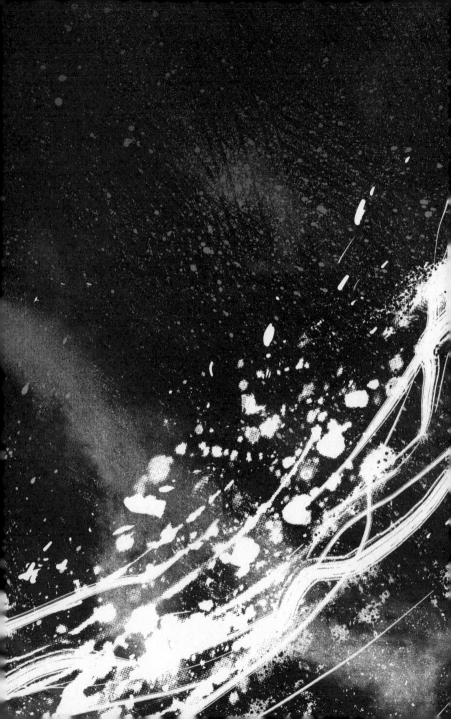

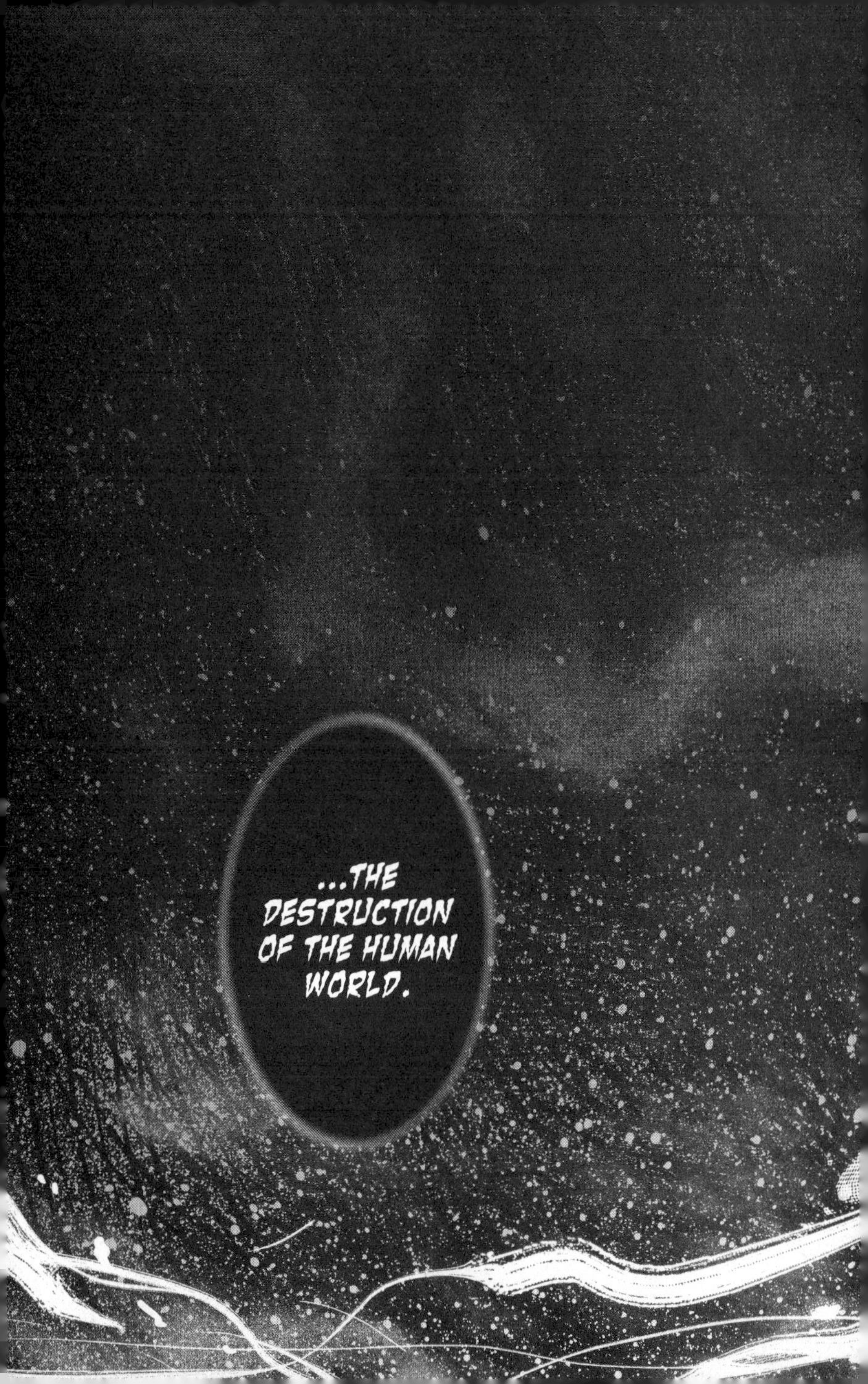
...THE DESTRUCTION OF THE HUMAN WORLD.

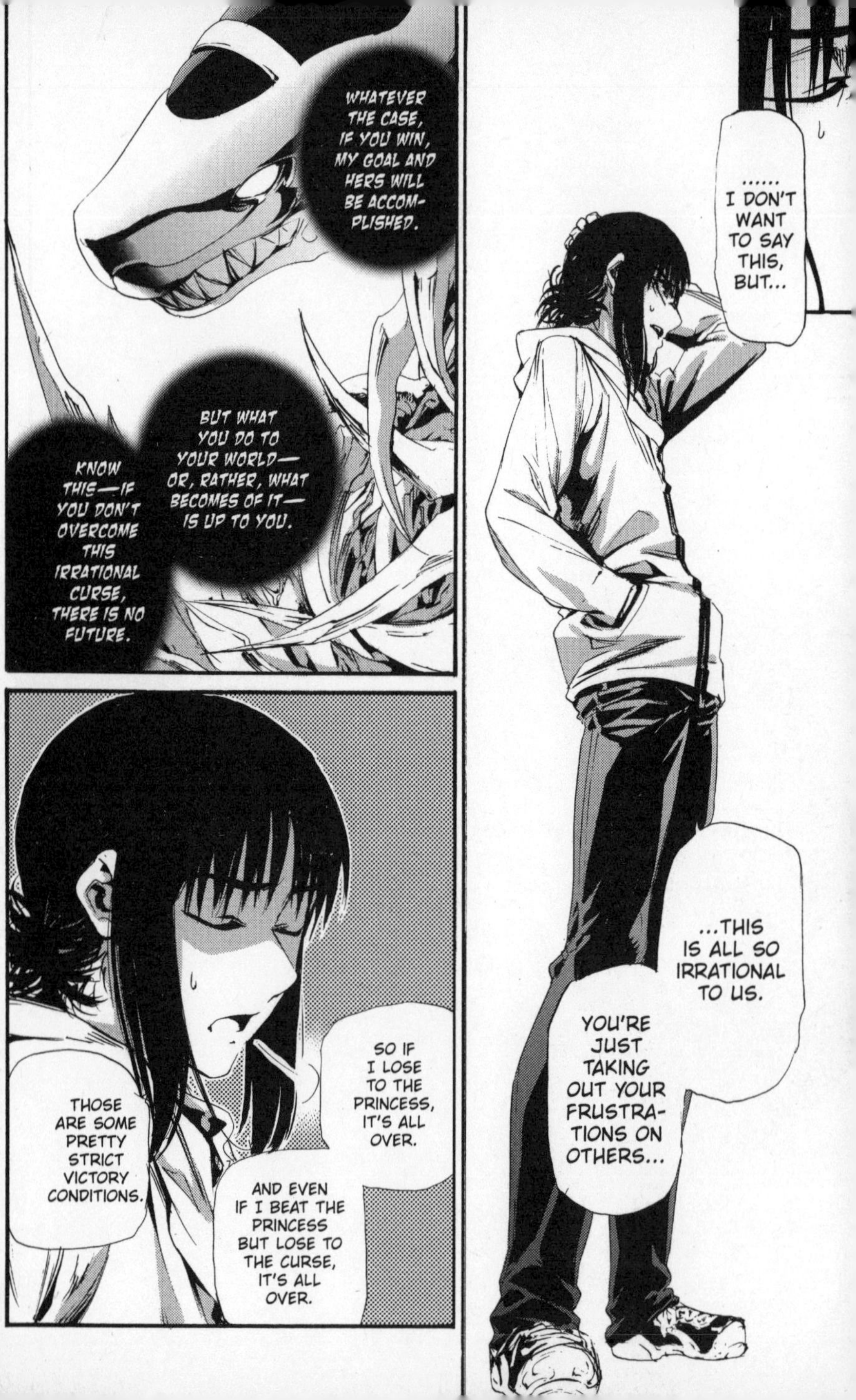
......
I DON'T WANT TO SAY THIS, BUT...
...THIS IS ALL SO IRRATIONAL TO US.
YOU'RE JUST TAKING OUT YOUR FRUSTRATIONS ON OTHERS...
WHATEVER THE CASE, IF YOU WIN, MY GOAL AND HERS WILL BE ACCOMPLISHED.
BUT WHAT YOU DO TO YOUR WORLD—OR, RATHER, WHAT BECOMES OF IT—IS UP TO YOU.
KNOW THIS—IF YOU DON'T OVERCOME THIS IRRATIONAL CURSE, THERE IS NO FUTURE.
SO IF I LOSE TO THE PRINCESS, IT'S ALL OVER.
AND EVEN IF I BEAT THE PRINCESS BUT LOSE TO THE CURSE, IT'S ALL OVER.
THOSE ARE SOME PRETTY STRICT VICTORY CONDITIONS.

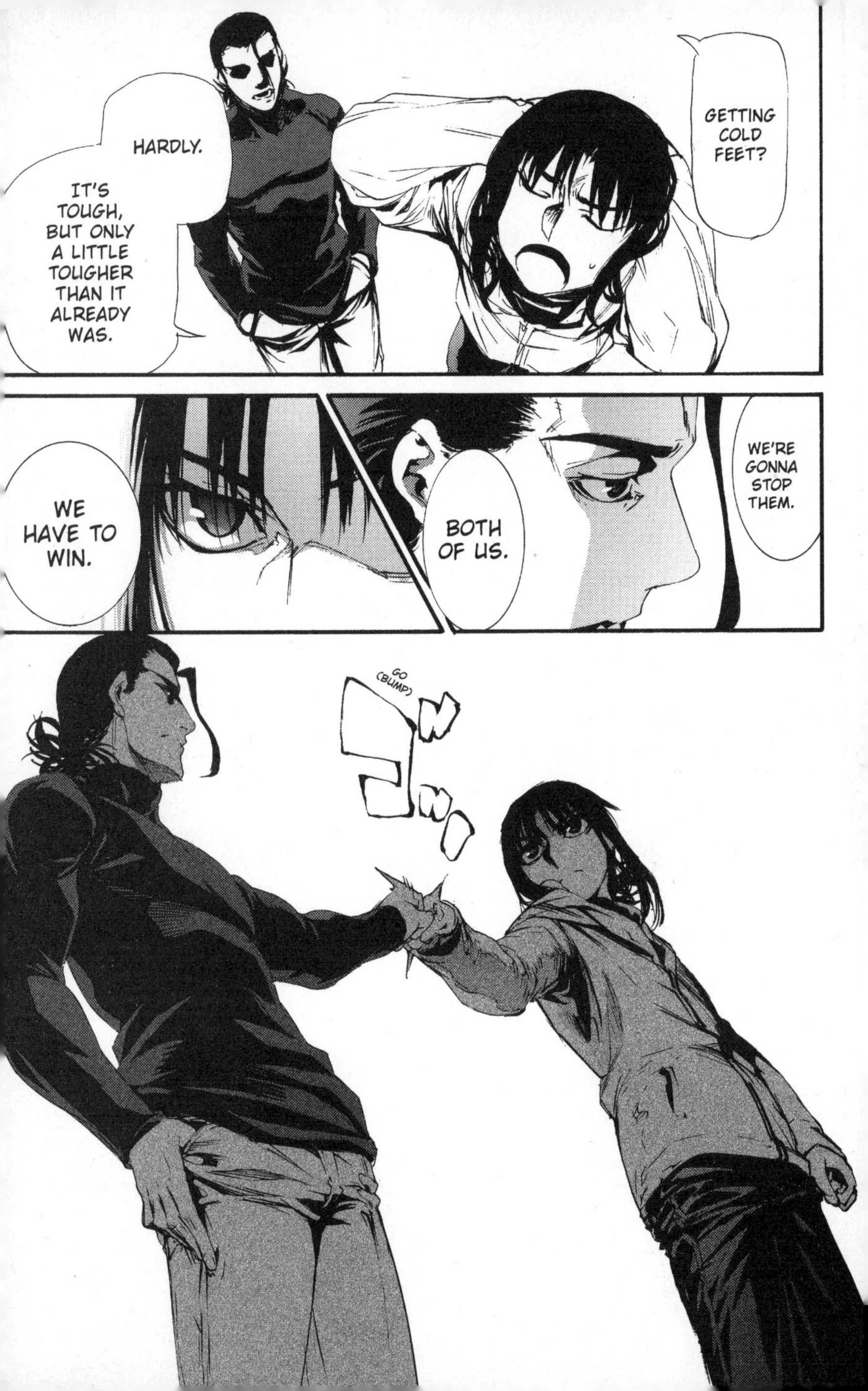
GETTING COLD FEET?
HARDLY.
IT'S TOUGH, BUT ONLY A LITTLE TOUGHER THAN IT ALREADY WAS.
WE'RE GONNA STOP THEM.
BOTH OF US.
WE HAVE TO WIN.
GO (BUMP)

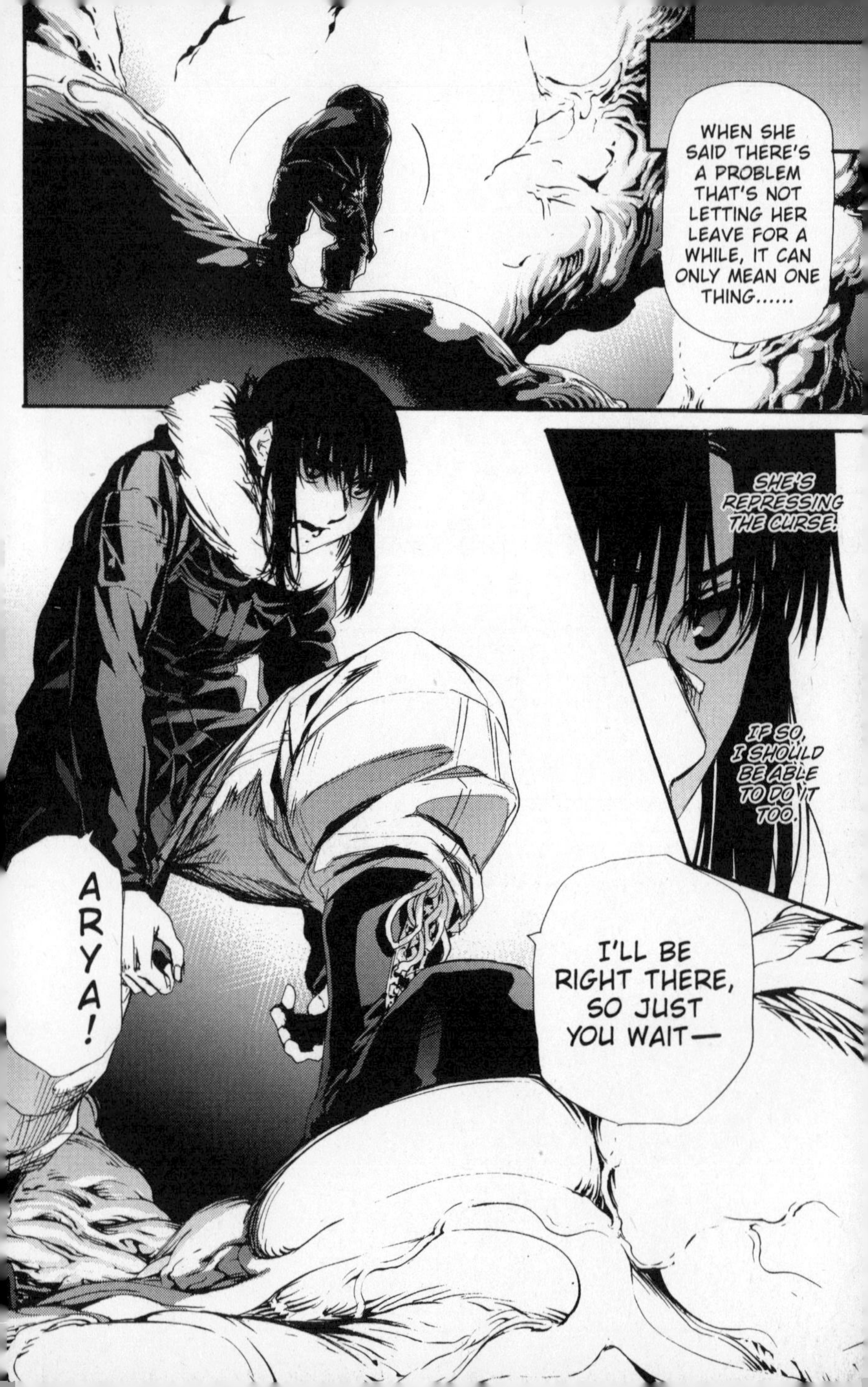
WHEN SHE SAID THERE'S A PROBLEM THAT'S NOT LETTING HER LEAVE FOR A WHILE, IT CAN ONLY MEAN ONE THING......
SHE'S REPRESSING THE CURSE.
IF SO, I SHOULD BE ABLE TO DO IT TOO.
I'LL BE RIGHT THERE, SO JUST YOU WAIT—
ARYA!

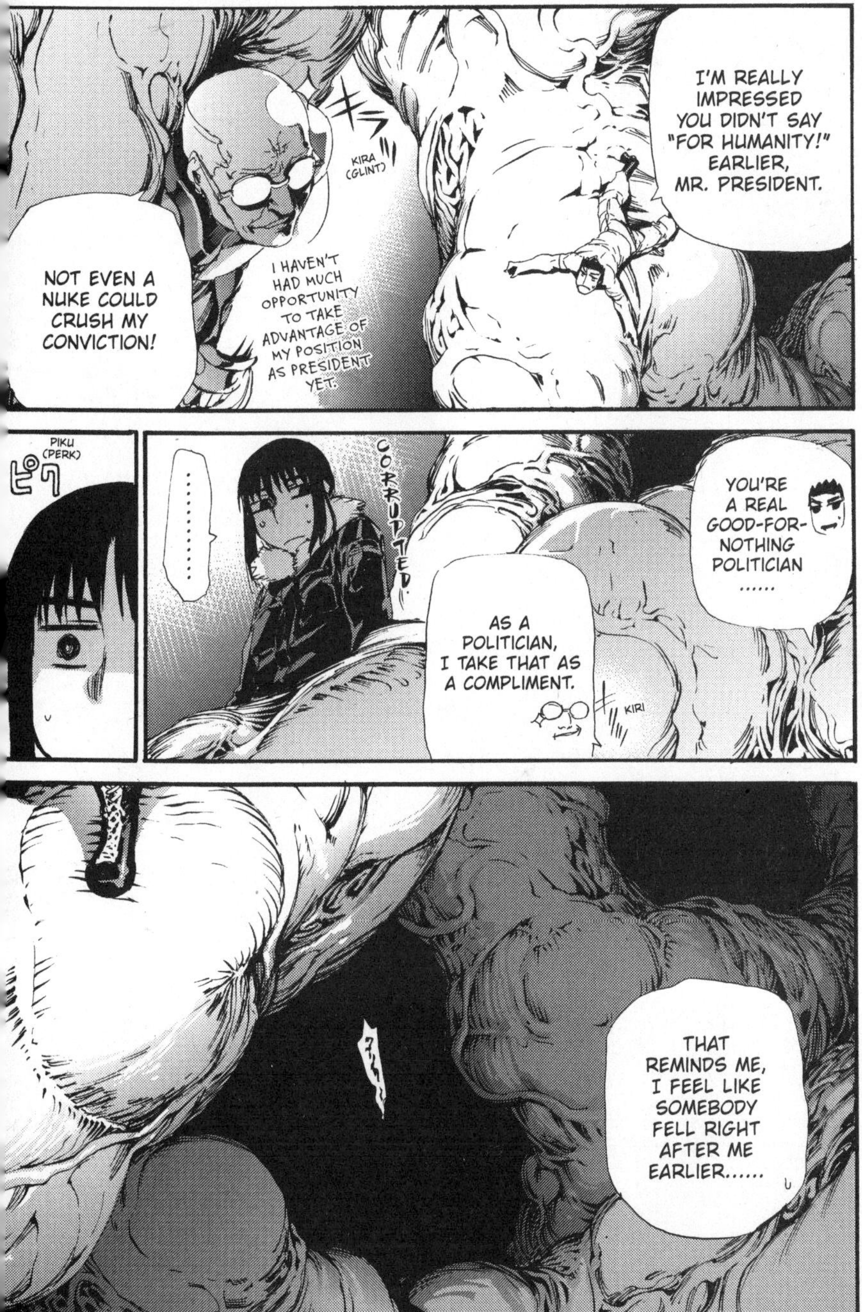
I'M REALLY IMPRESSED YOU DIDN'T SAY "FOR HUMANITY!" EARLIER, MR. PRESIDENT.
KIRA (GLINT)
I HAVEN'T HAD MUCH OPPORTUNITY TO TAKE ADVANTAGE OF MY POSITION AS PRESIDENT YET.
NOT EVEN A NUKE COULD CRUSH MY CONVICTION!
YOU'RE A REAL GOOD-FOR-NOTHING POLITICIAN ......
AS A POLITICIAN, I TAKE THAT AS A COMPLIMENT.
KIRI
CORRUPTED.
......
PIKU (PERK)
THAT REMINDS ME, I FEEL LIKE SOMEBODY FELL RIGHT AFTER ME EARLIER......

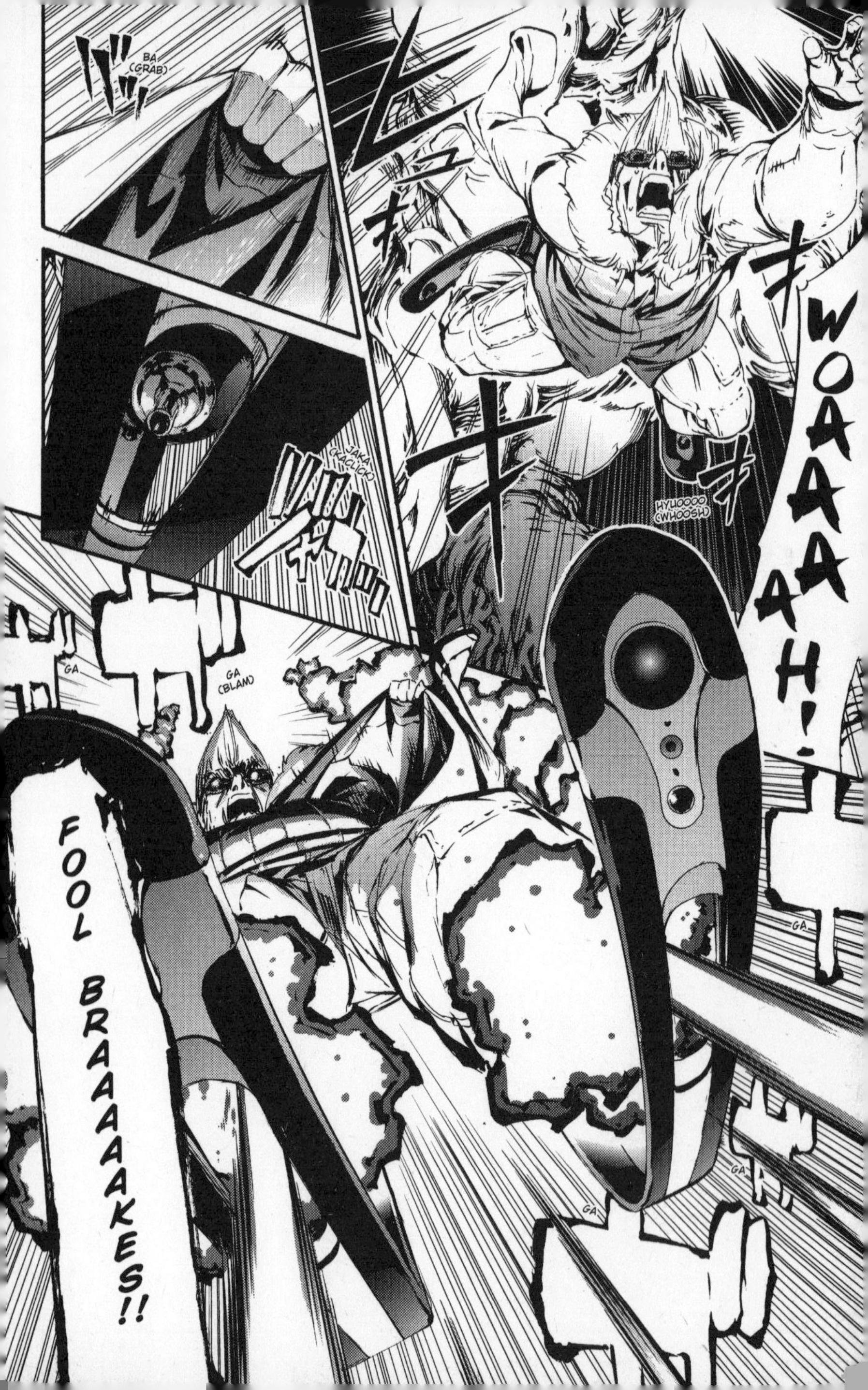

WOAAAAH!
HYUOOOO (WHOOSH)
BA (GRAB)
JAKA (KACLICK)
GA
GA
GA
GA (BLAM)
GA
FOOL BRAAAAAKES!!

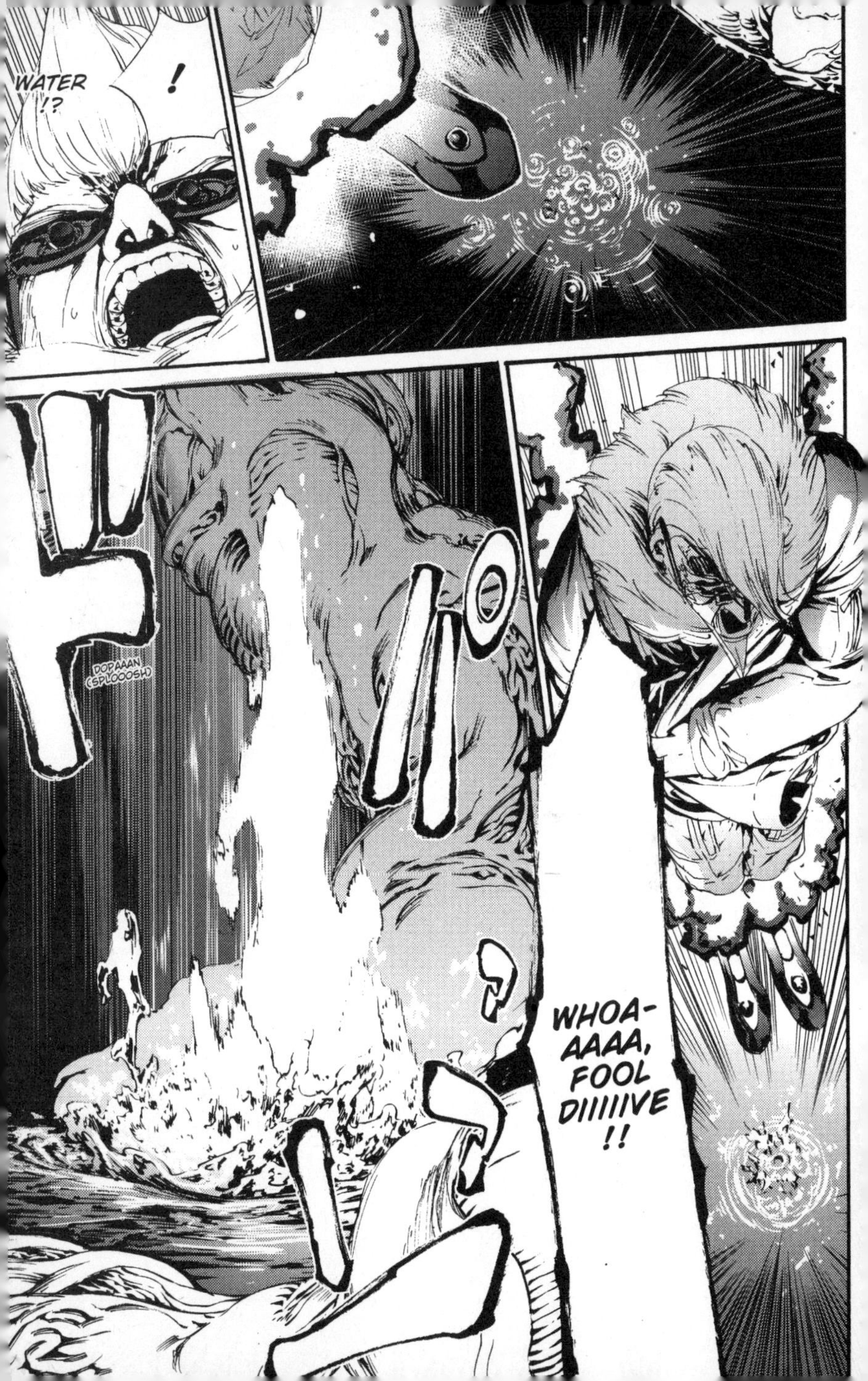
!
WATER !?
WHOA-AAAA, FOOL DIIIIIVE !!
DOPAAAN (SPLOOOSH)

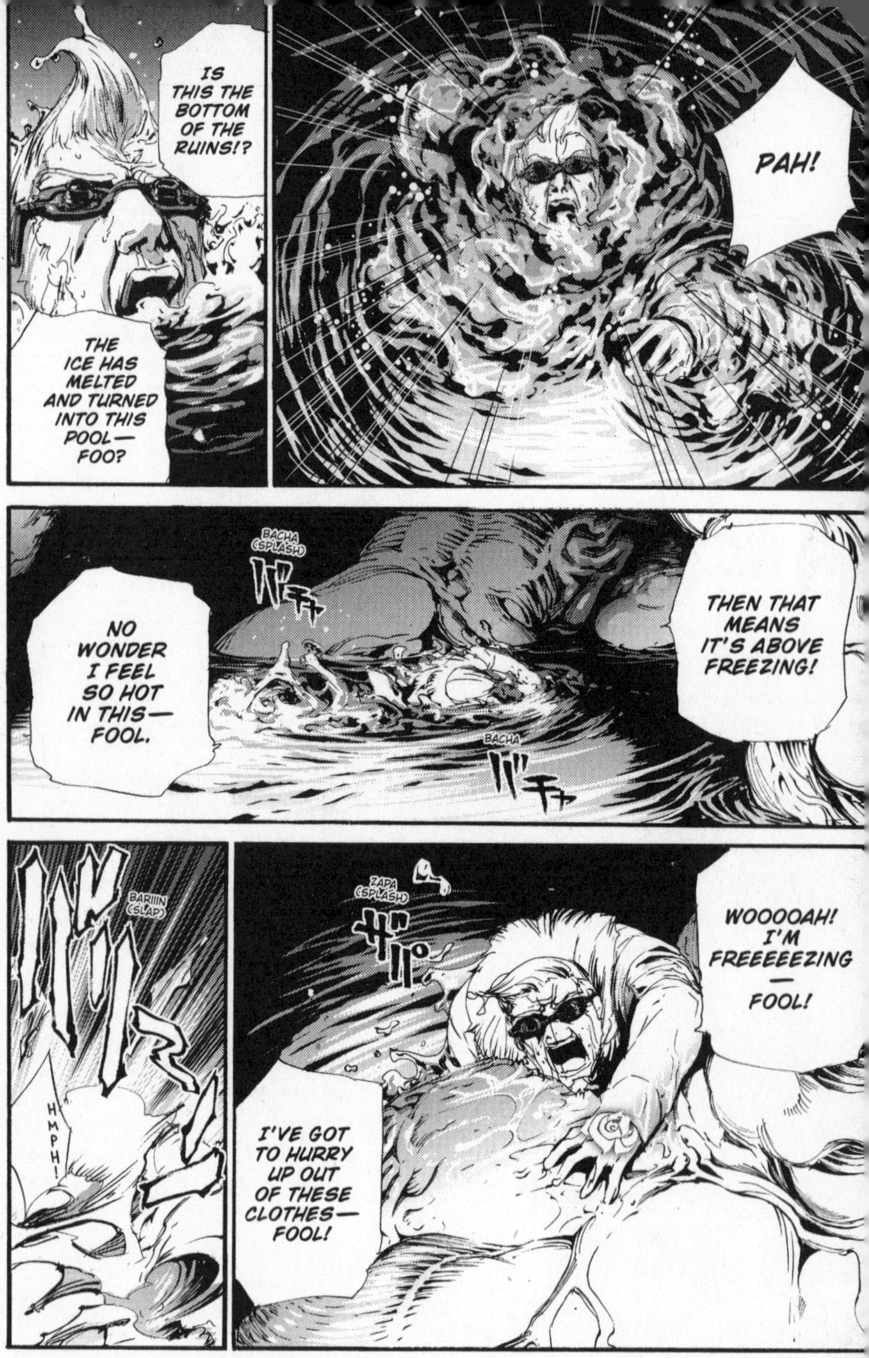
PAH!
IS THIS THE BOTTOM OF THE RUINS!?
THE ICE HAS MELTED AND TURNED INTO THIS POOL—FOO?
THEN THAT MEANS IT'S ABOVE FREEZING!
BACHA (SPLASH)
NO WONDER I FEEL SO HOT IN THIS—FOOL.
BACHA
WOOOOAH! I'M FREEEEEZING—FOOL!
ZAPA (SPLASH)
I'VE GOT TO HURRY UP OUT OF THESE CLOTHES—FOOL!
BARIIN (SLAP)
HMPH!

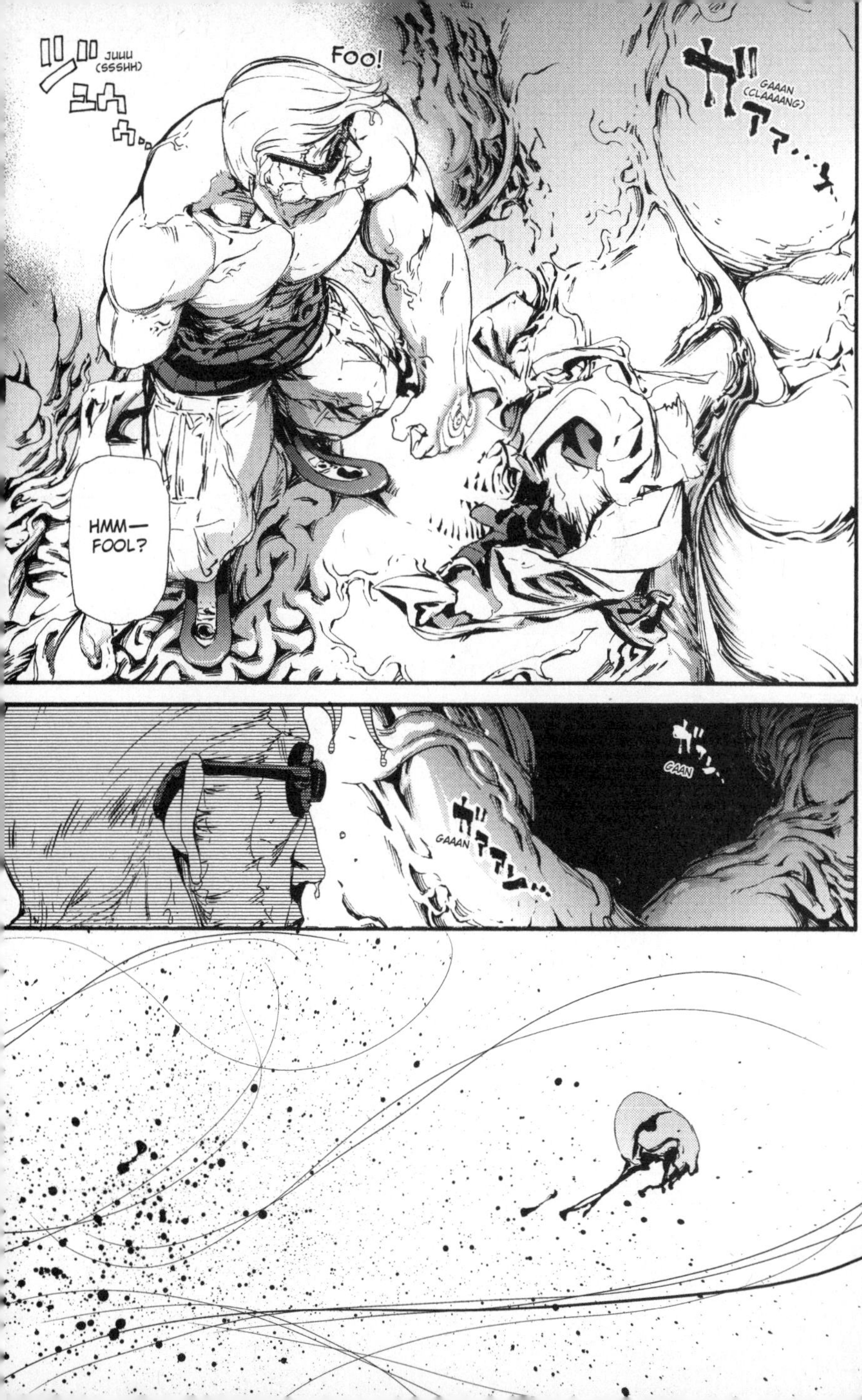
GAAAN
(CLAAAANG)
FOO!
JUUU
(SSSHH)
HMM—
FOOL?
GAAN
GAAAN

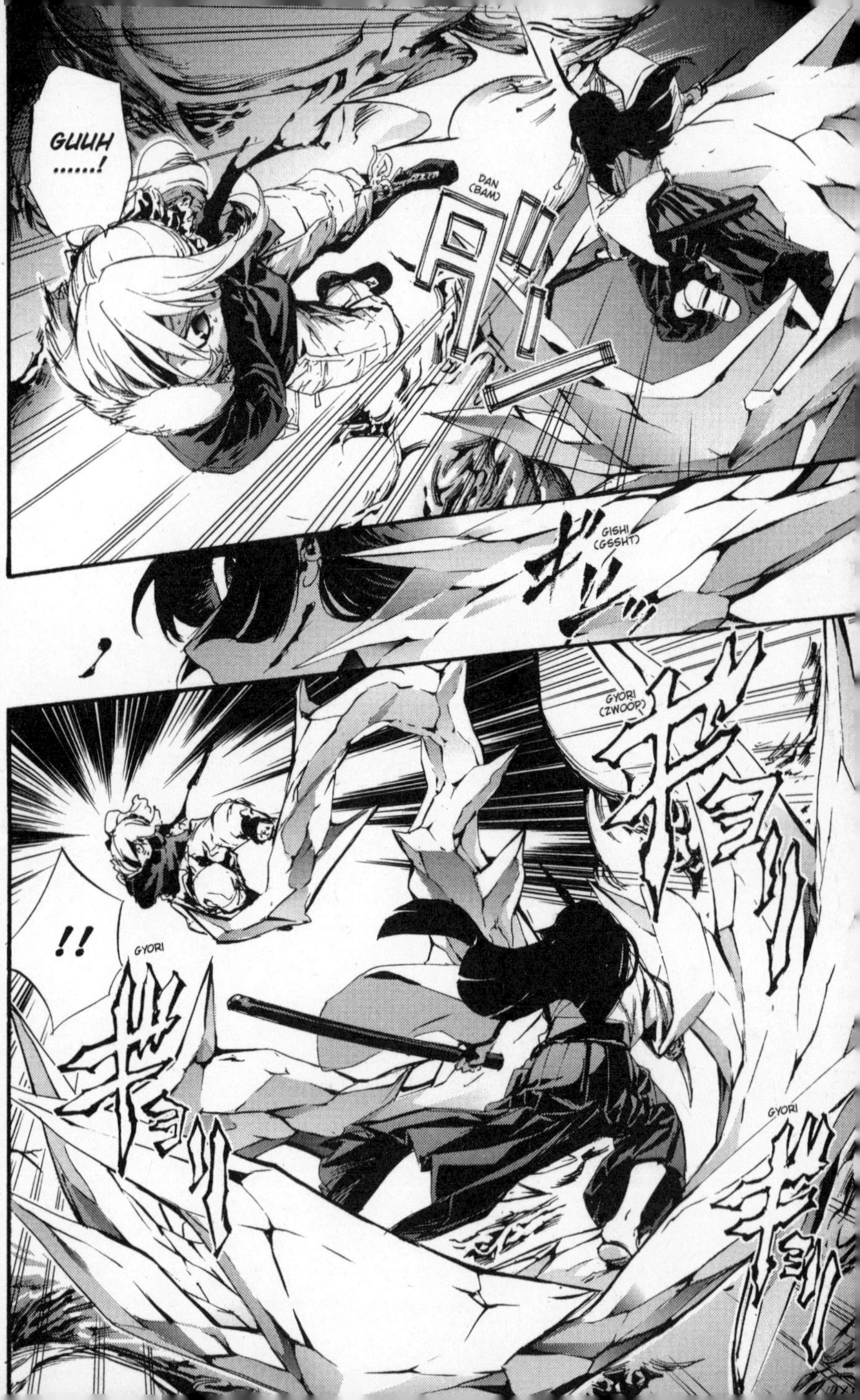
DAN (BAM)
GUUH ......!
GISHI (GSSHT)
GYORI (ZWOOP)
!!
GYORI
GYORI

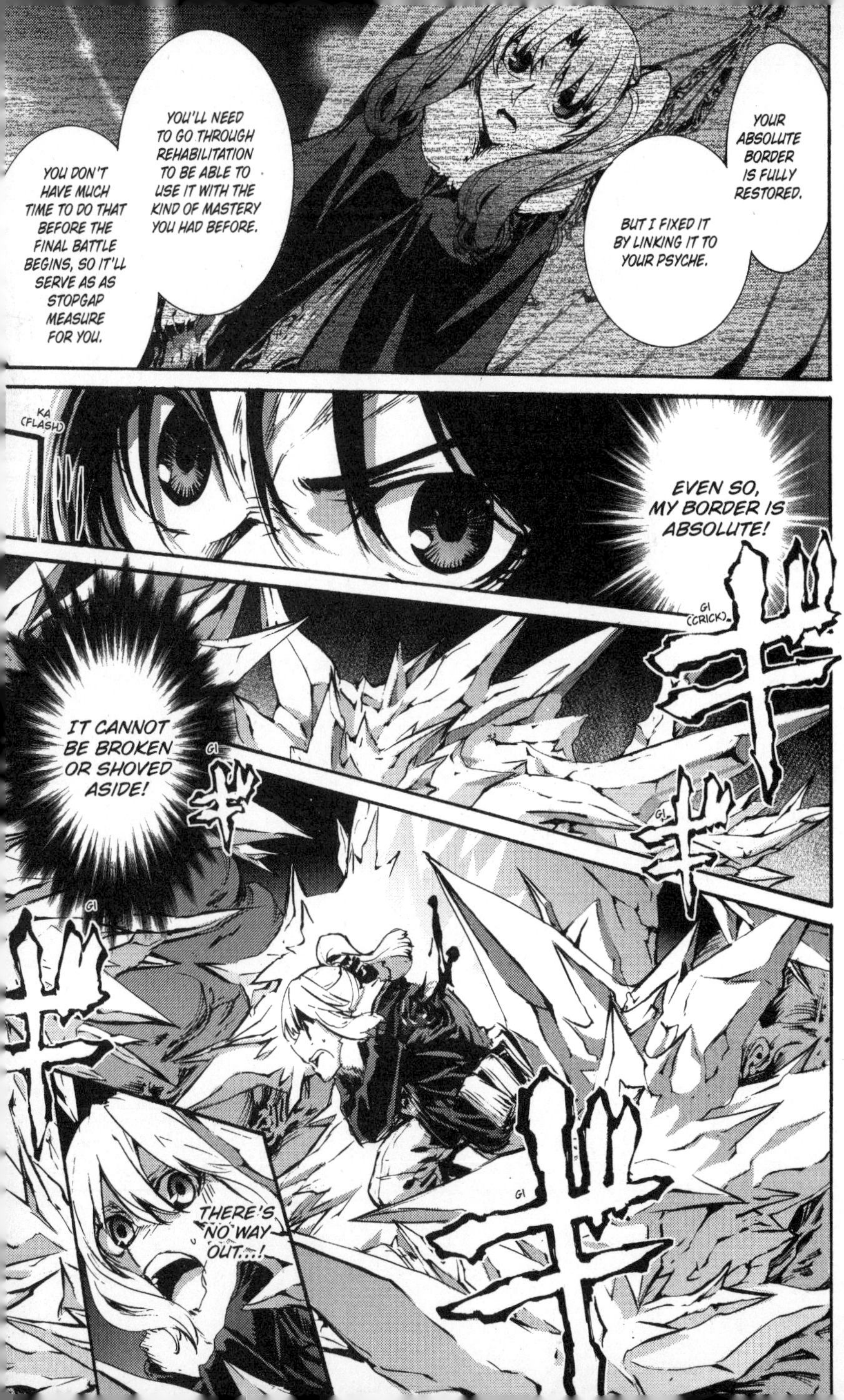
YOUR ABSOLUTE BORDER IS FULLY RESTORED.
BUT I FIXED IT BY LINKING IT TO YOUR PSYCHE.
YOU'LL NEED TO GO THROUGH REHABILITATION TO BE ABLE TO USE IT WITH THE KIND OF MASTERY YOU HAD BEFORE.
YOU DON'T HAVE MUCH TIME TO DO THAT BEFORE THE FINAL BATTLE BEGINS, SO IT'LL SERVE AS AS STOPGAP MEASURE FOR YOU.
KA (FLASH)
EVEN SO, MY BORDER IS ABSOLUTE!
GI (CRICK)
GI
IT CANNOT BE BROKEN OR SHOVED ASIDE!
GI
GI
GI
THERE'S NO WAY OUT...!

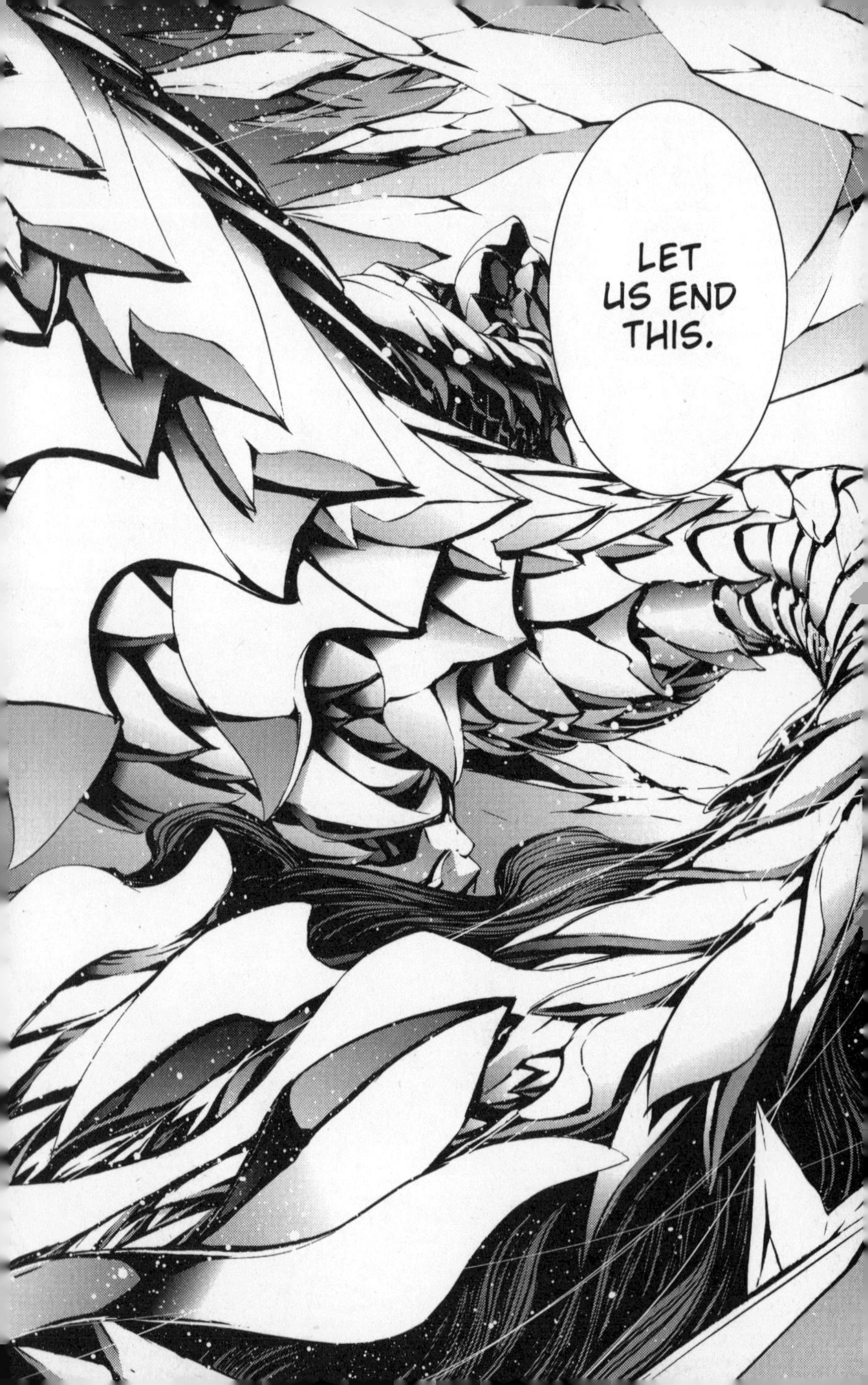
LET US END THIS.

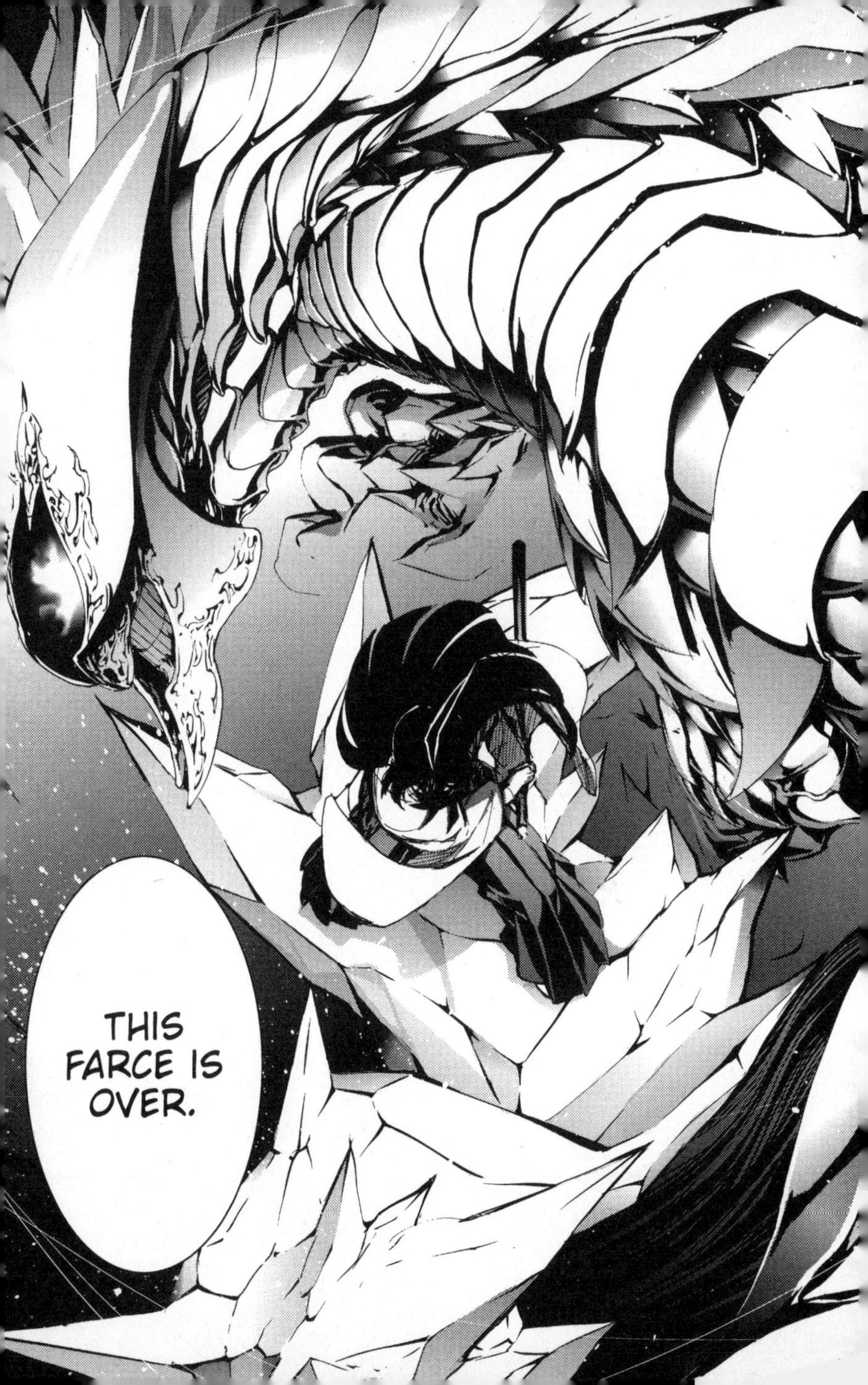
THIS FARCE IS OVER.

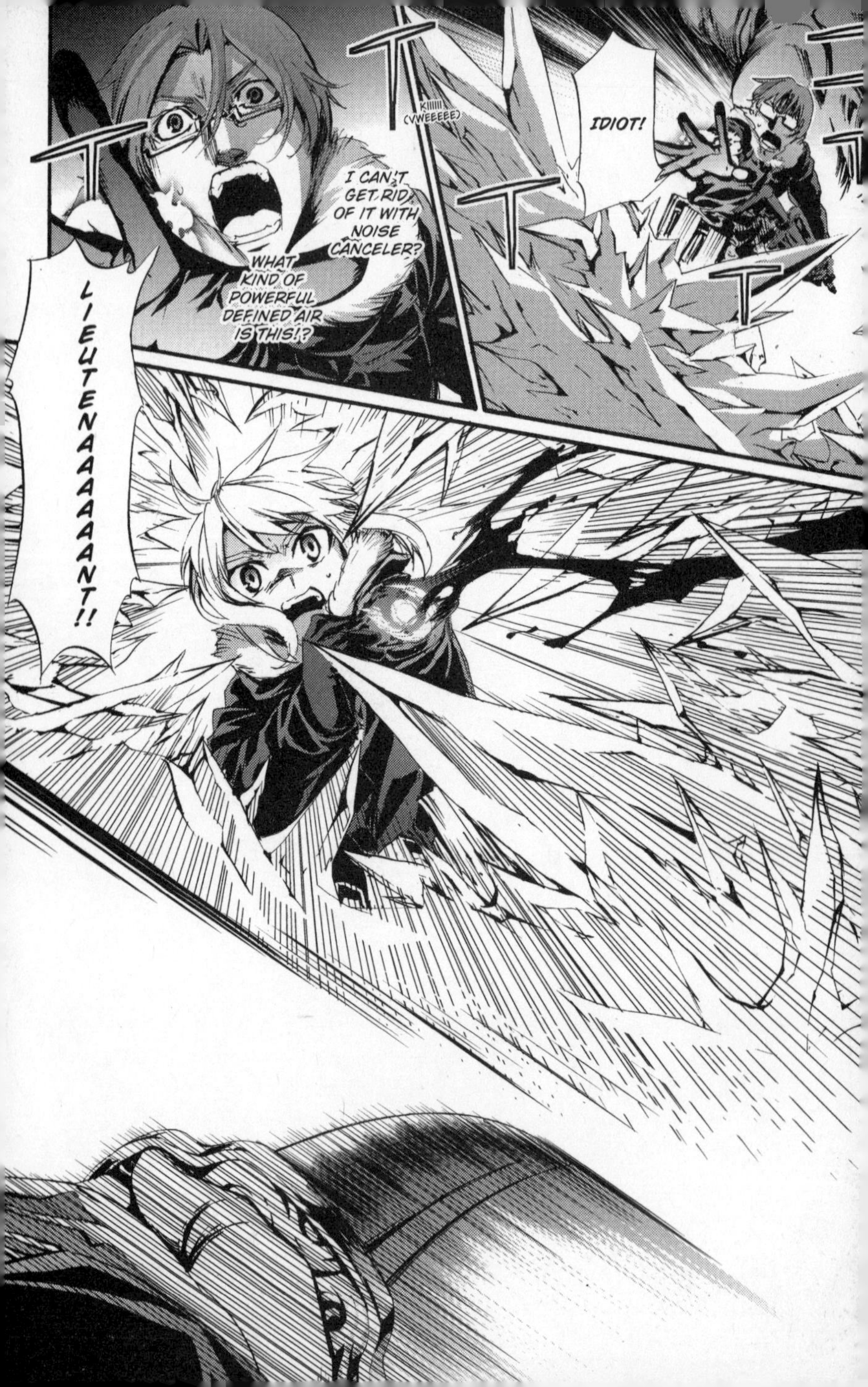
IDIOT!
KIIIII (VWEEEEE)
I CAN'T GET RID OF IT WITH NOISE CANCELER?
WHAT KIND OF POWERFUL DEFINED AIR IS THIS!?
LIEUTENAAAAAAANT!!

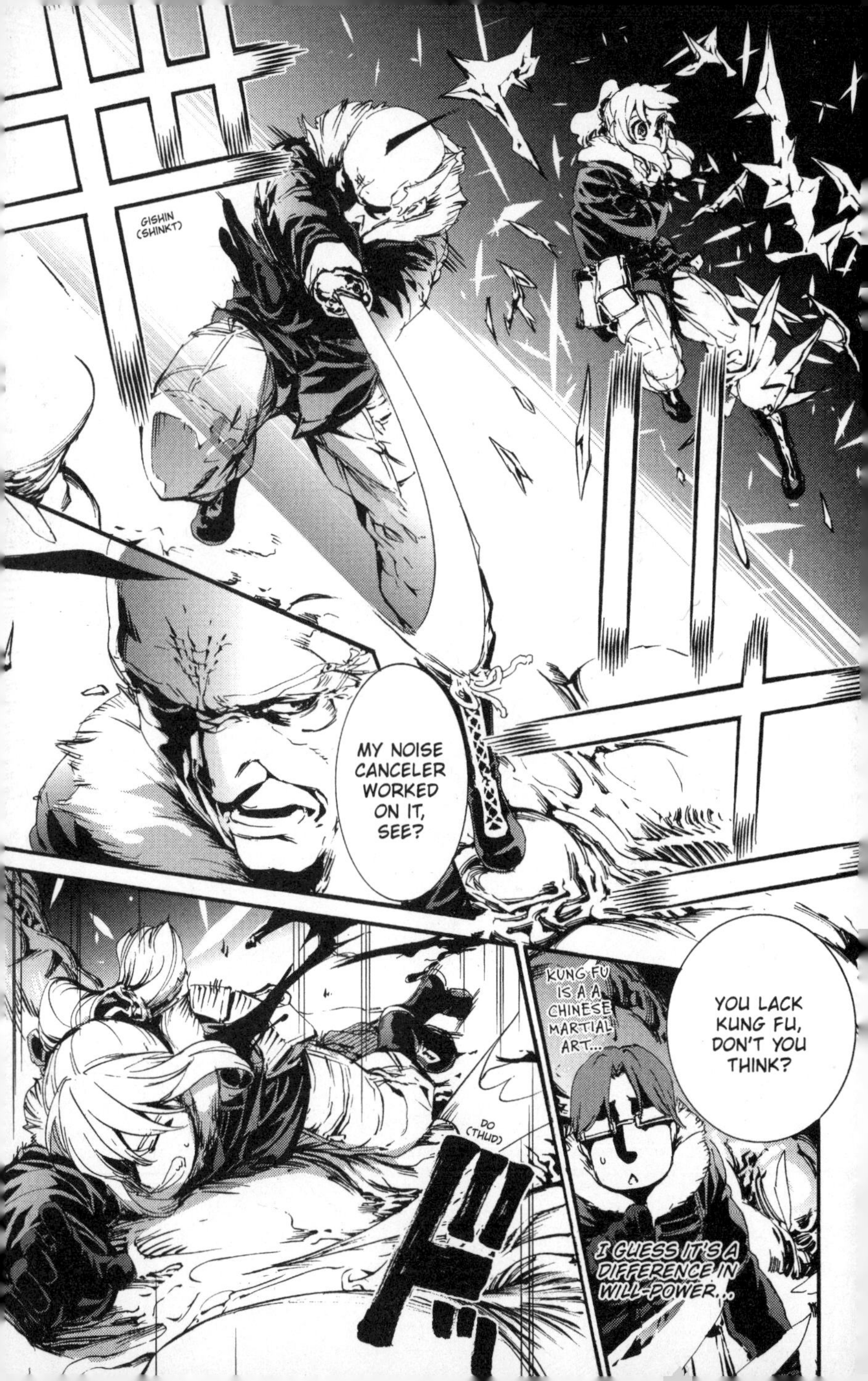
GISHIN (SHINKT)
MY NOISE CANCELER WORKED ON IT, SEE?
YOU LACK KUNG FU, DON'T YOU THINK?
KUNG FU IS A A CHINESE MARTIAL ART...
I GUESS IT'S A DIFFERENCE IN WILL-POWER...
DO (THUD)

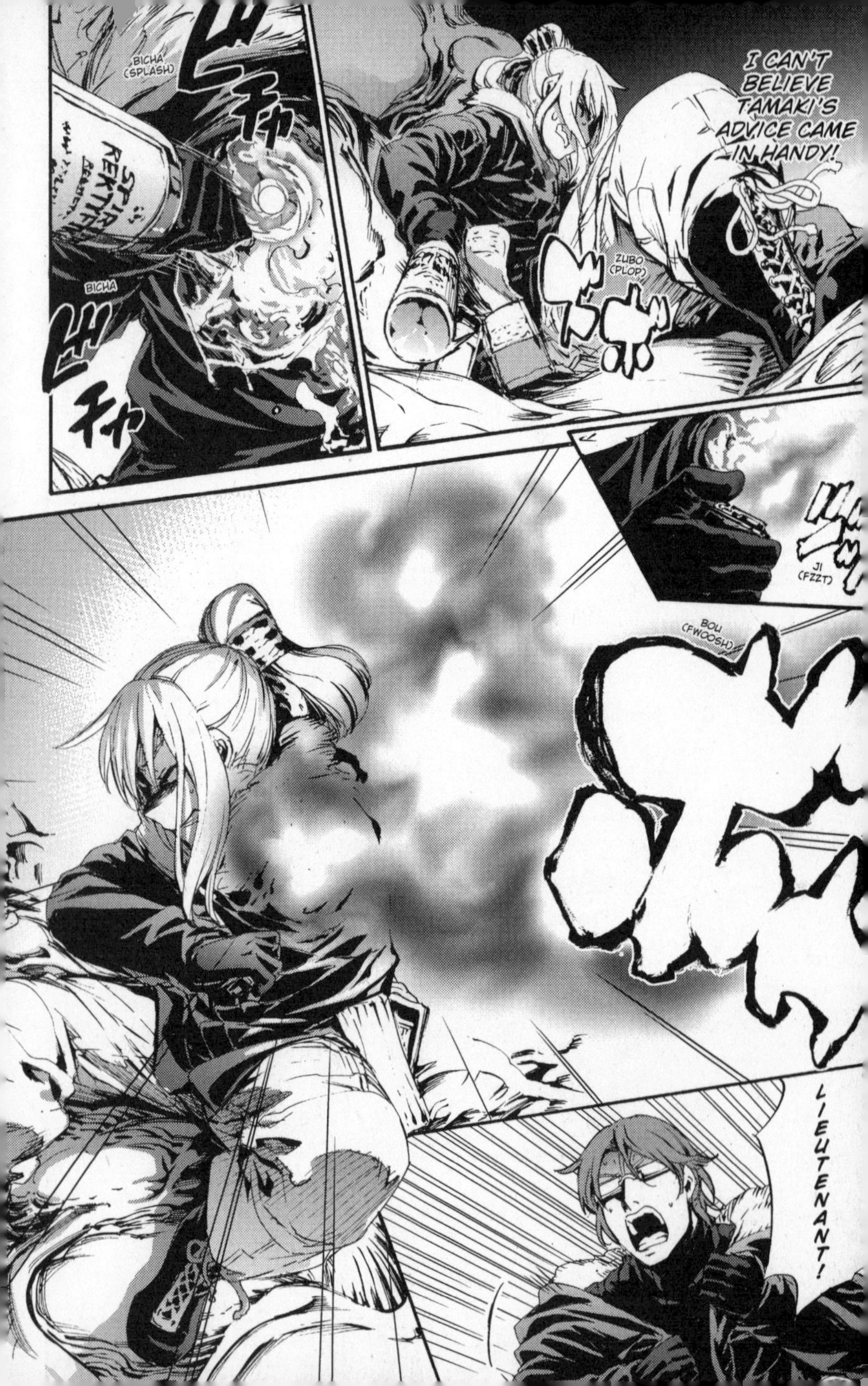
I CAN'T BELIEVE TAMAKI'S ADVICE CAME IN HANDY!
ZUBO (PLOP)
BICHA (SPLASH)
BICHA
JI (FZZT)
BOU (FWOOSH)
LIEUTENANT!

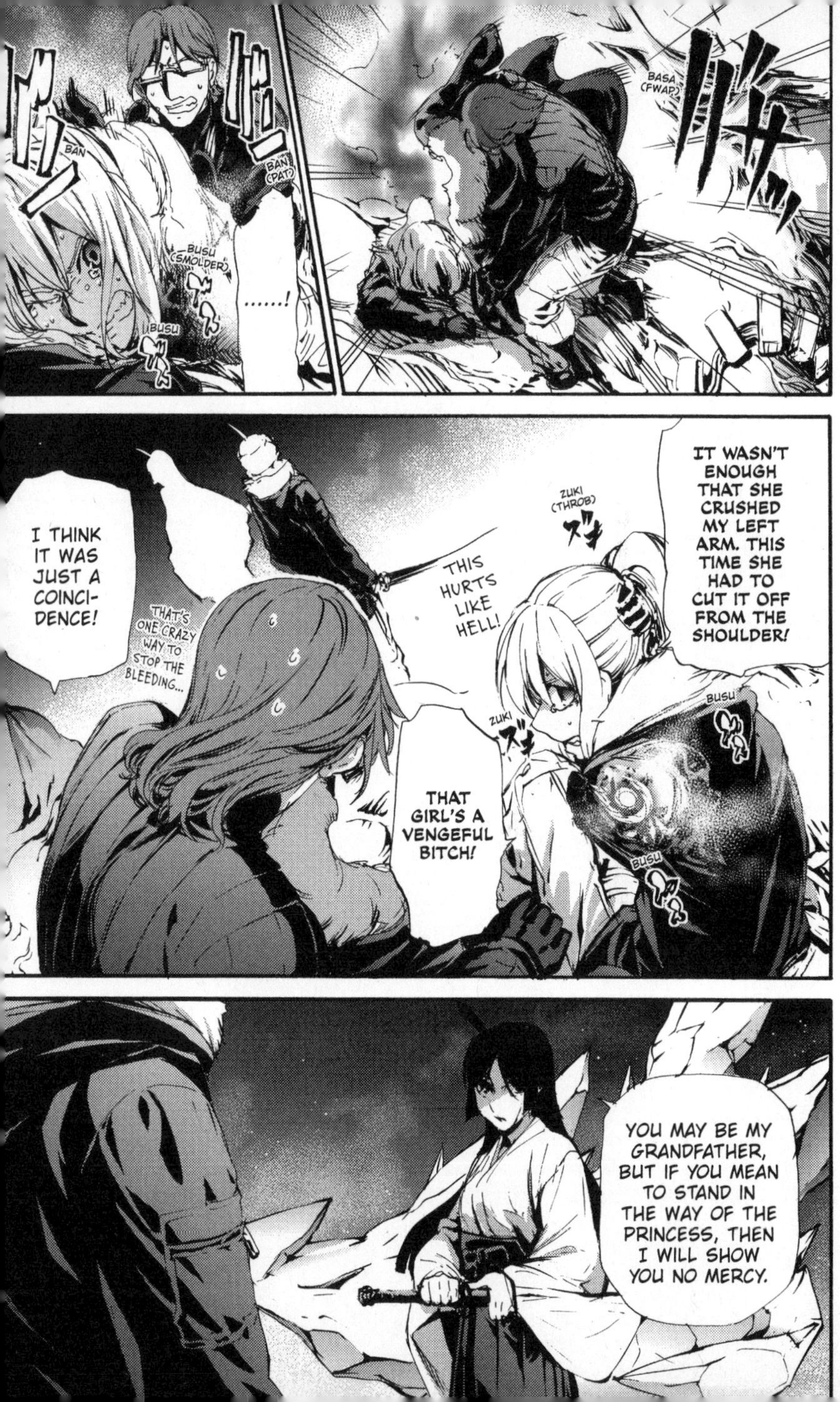
BASA (FWAP)
BAN (PAT)
BAN
BUSU (SMOLDER)
......!
BUSU
IT WASN'T ENOUGH THAT SHE CRUSHED MY LEFT ARM. THIS TIME SHE HAD TO CUT IT OFF FROM THE SHOULDER!
ZUKI (THROB)
THIS HURTS LIKE HELL!
BUSU
ZUKI
THAT GIRL'S A VENGEFUL BITCH!
BUSU
I THINK IT WAS JUST A COINCIDENCE!
THAT'S ONE CRAZY WAY TO STOP THE BLEEDING...
YOU MAY BE MY GRANDFATHER, BUT IF YOU MEAN TO STAND IN THE WAY OF THE PRINCESS, THEN I WILL SHOW YOU NO MERCY.

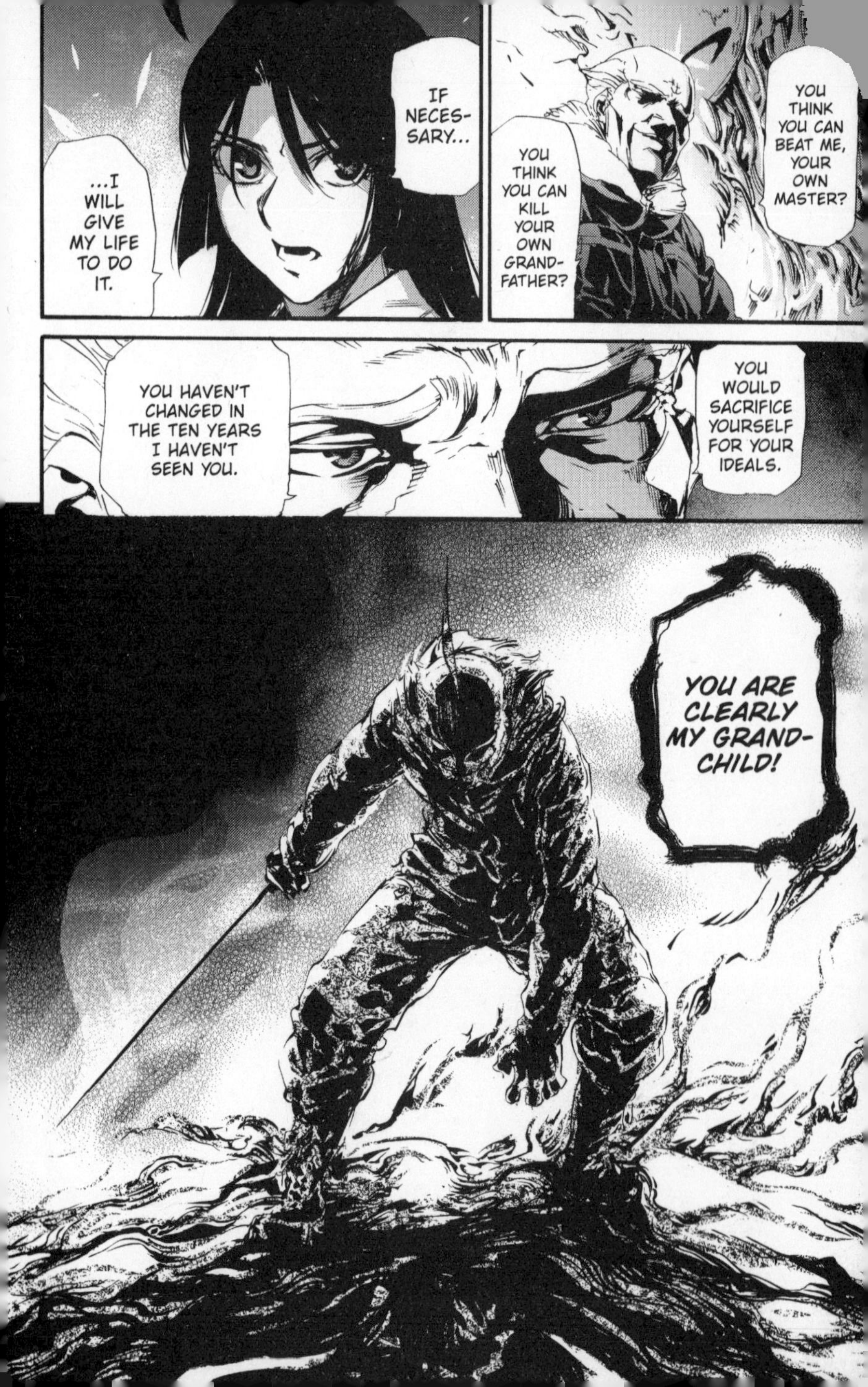
YOU THINK YOU CAN BEAT ME, YOUR OWN MASTER?
YOU THINK YOU CAN KILL YOUR OWN GRAND-FATHER?
IF NECES-SARY...
...I WILL GIVE MY LIFE TO DO IT.
YOU WOULD SACRIFICE YOURSELF FOR YOUR IDEALS.
YOU HAVEN'T CHANGED IN THE TEN YEARS I HAVEN'T SEEN YOU.
YOU ARE CLEARLY MY GRAND-CHILD!

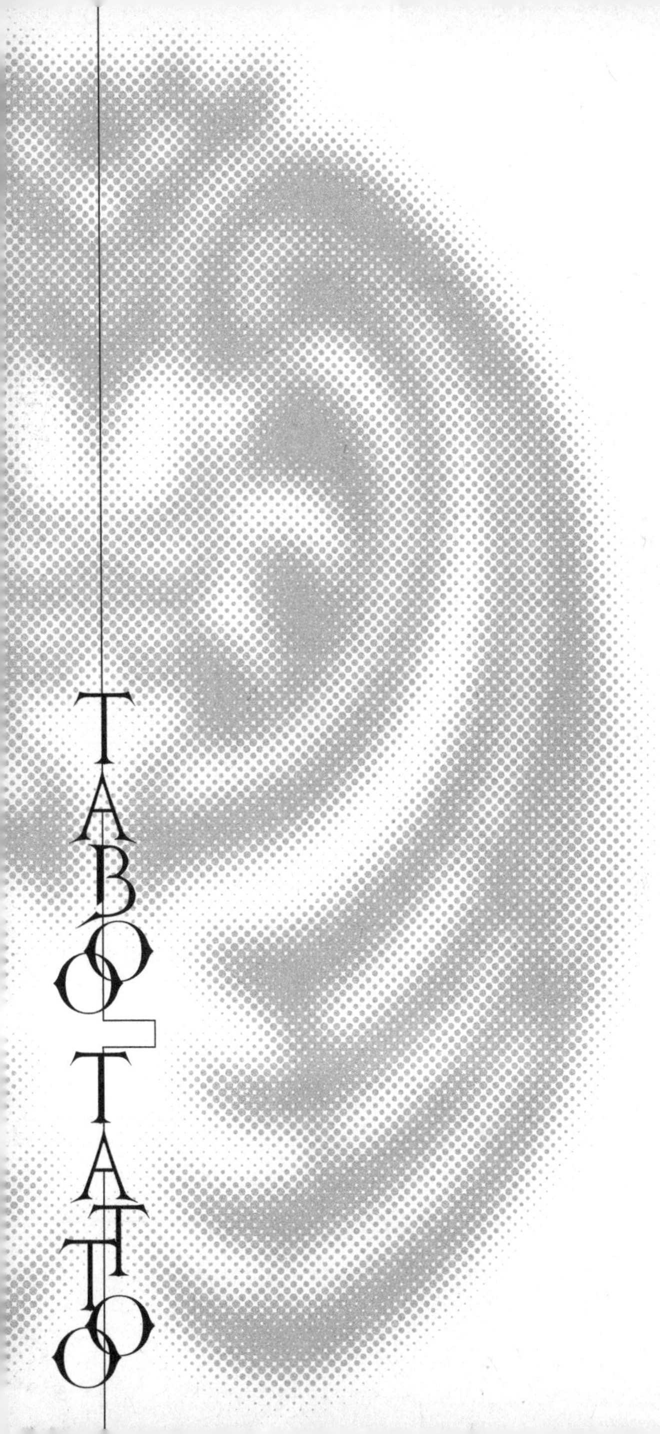

TABOO TATTOO

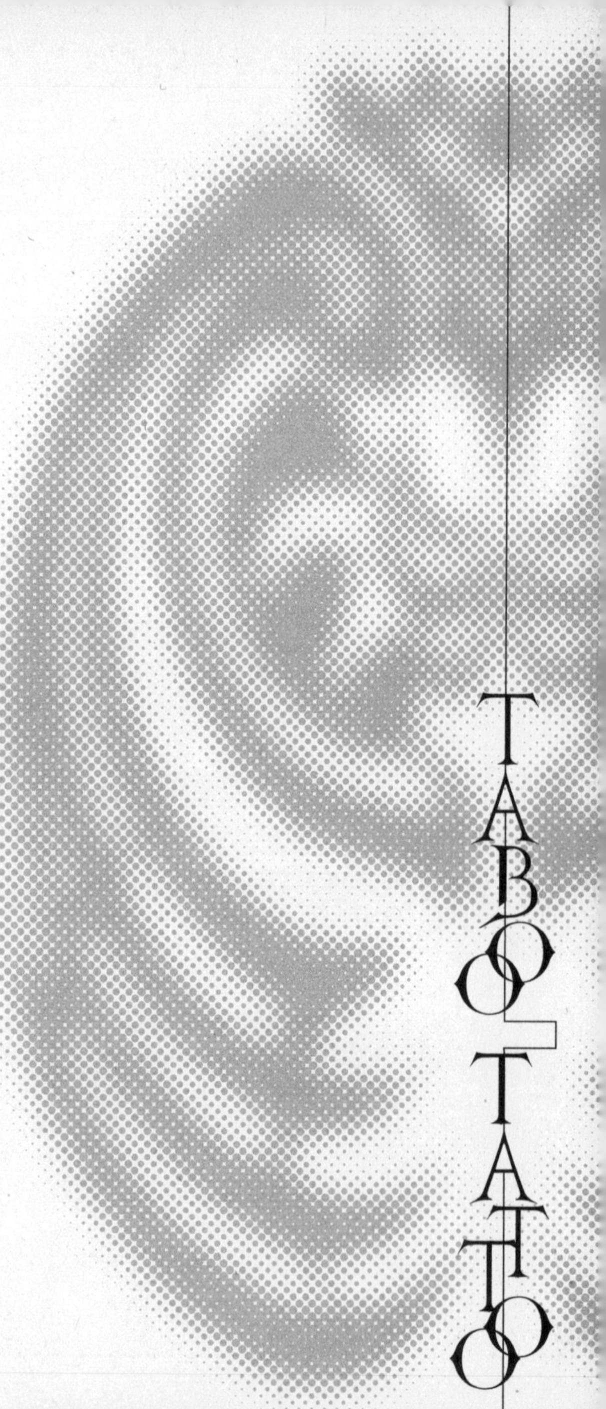

TABOO TATTOO

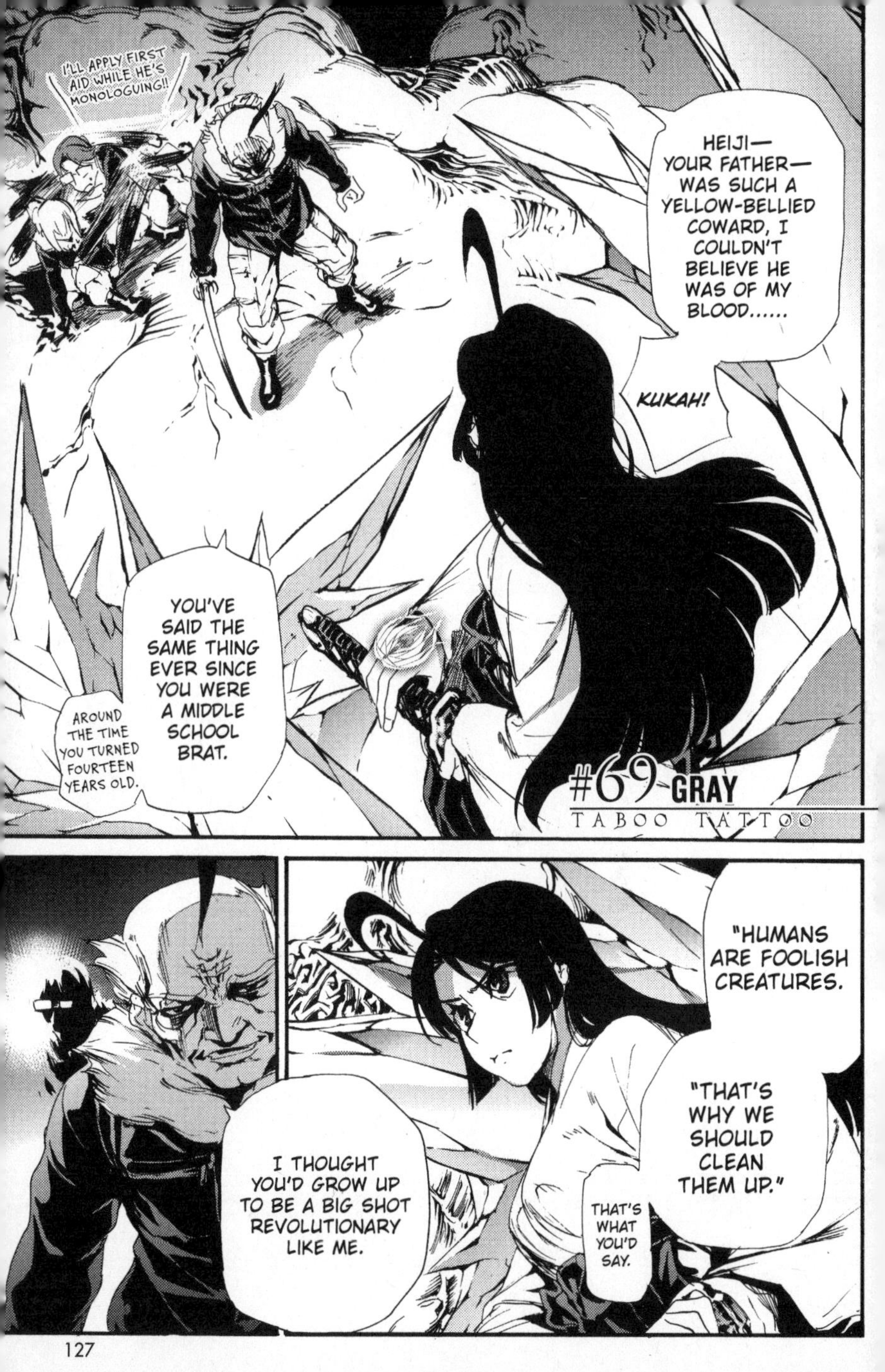
HEIJI— YOUR FATHER— WAS SUCH A YELLOW-BELLIED COWARD, I COULDN'T BELIEVE HE WAS OF MY BLOOD......
I'LL APPLY FIRST AID WHILE HE'S MONOLOGUING!!
KUKAH!
YOU'VE SAID THE SAME THING EVER SINCE YOU WERE A MIDDLE SCHOOL BRAT.
AROUND THE TIME YOU TURNED FOURTEEN YEARS OLD.
#69 GRAY
TABOO TATTOO
"HUMANS ARE FOOLISH CREATURES.
"THAT'S WHY WE SHOULD CLEAN THEM UP."
THAT'S WHAT YOU'D SAY.
I THOUGHT YOU'D GROW UP TO BE A BIG SHOT REVOLUTIONARY LIKE ME.

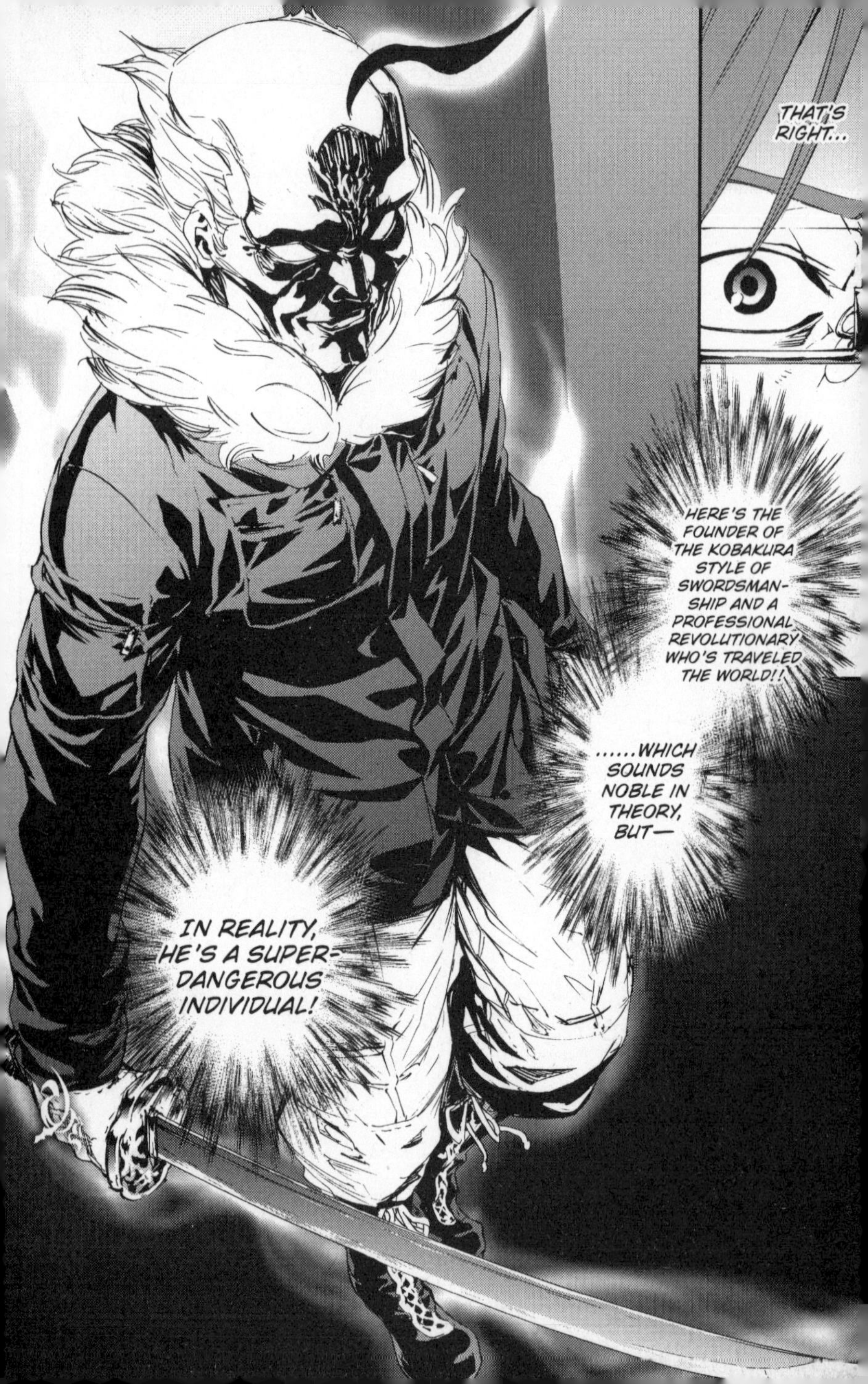
THAT'S RIGHT...
HERE'S THE FOUNDER OF THE KOBAKURA STYLE OF SWORDSMAN-SHIP AND A PROFESSIONAL REVOLUTIONARY WHO'S TRAVELED THE WORLD!!
......WHICH SOUNDS NOBLE IN THEORY, BUT—
IN REALITY, HE'S A SUPER-DANGEROUS INDIVIDUAL!

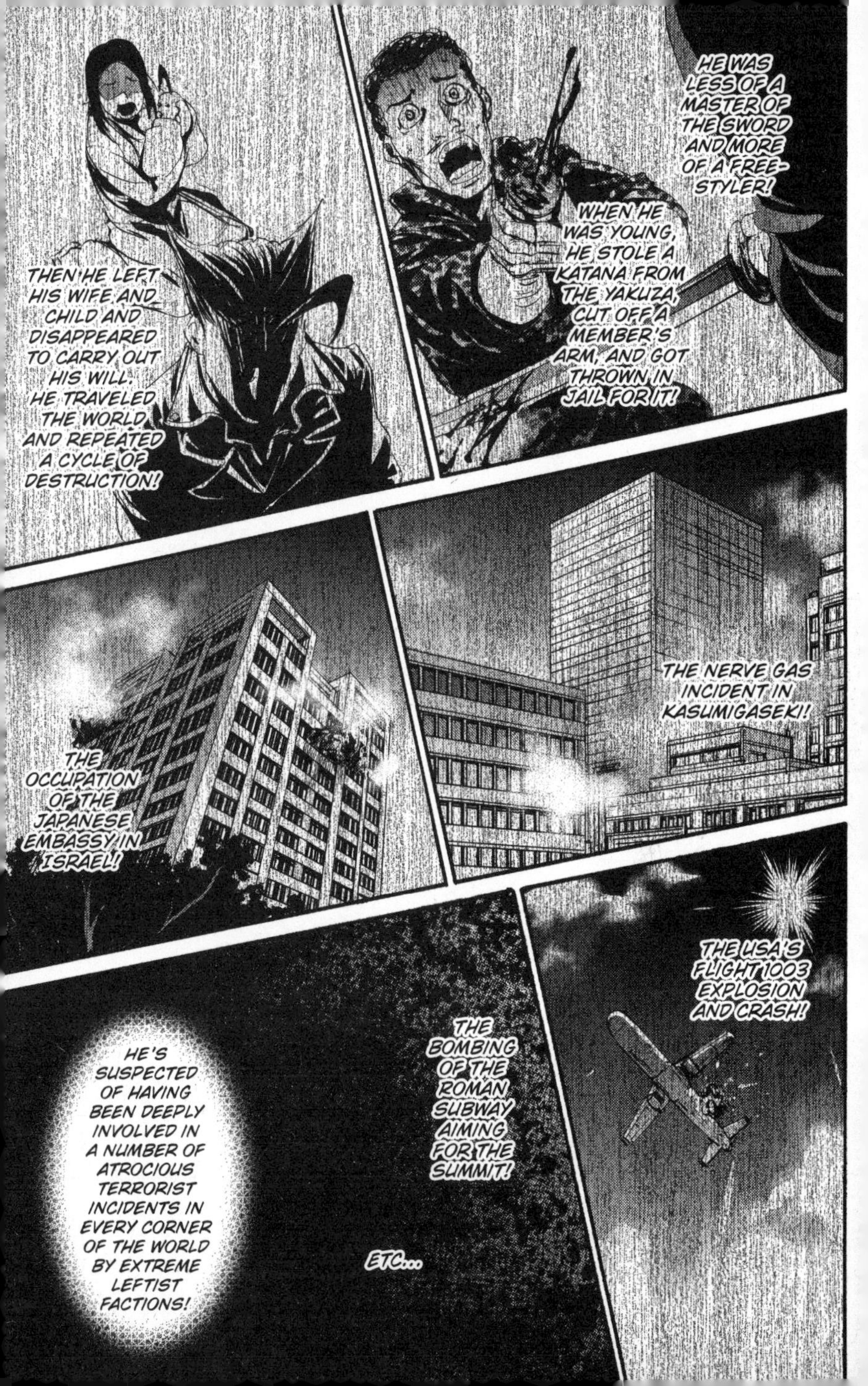
HE WAS LESS OF A MASTER OF THE SWORD AND MORE OF A FREE-STYLER!
WHEN HE WAS YOUNG, HE STOLE A KATANA FROM THE YAKUZA, CUT OFF A MEMBER'S ARM, AND GOT THROWN IN JAIL FOR IT!
THEN HE LEFT HIS WIFE AND CHILD AND DISAPPEARED TO CARRY OUT HIS WILL. HE TRAVELED THE WORLD AND REPEATED A CYCLE OF DESTRUCTION!
THE NERVE GAS INCIDENT IN KASUMIGASEKI!
THE OCCUPATION OF THE JAPANESE EMBASSY IN ISRAEL!
THE USA'S FLIGHT 1003 EXPLOSION AND CRASH!
THE BOMBING OF THE ROMAN SUBWAY AIMING FOR THE SUMMIT!
HE'S SUSPECTED OF HAVING BEEN DEEPLY INVOLVED IN A NUMBER OF ATROCIOUS TERRORIST INCIDENTS IN EVERY CORNER OF THE WORLD BY EXTREME LEFTIST FACTIONS!
ETC...

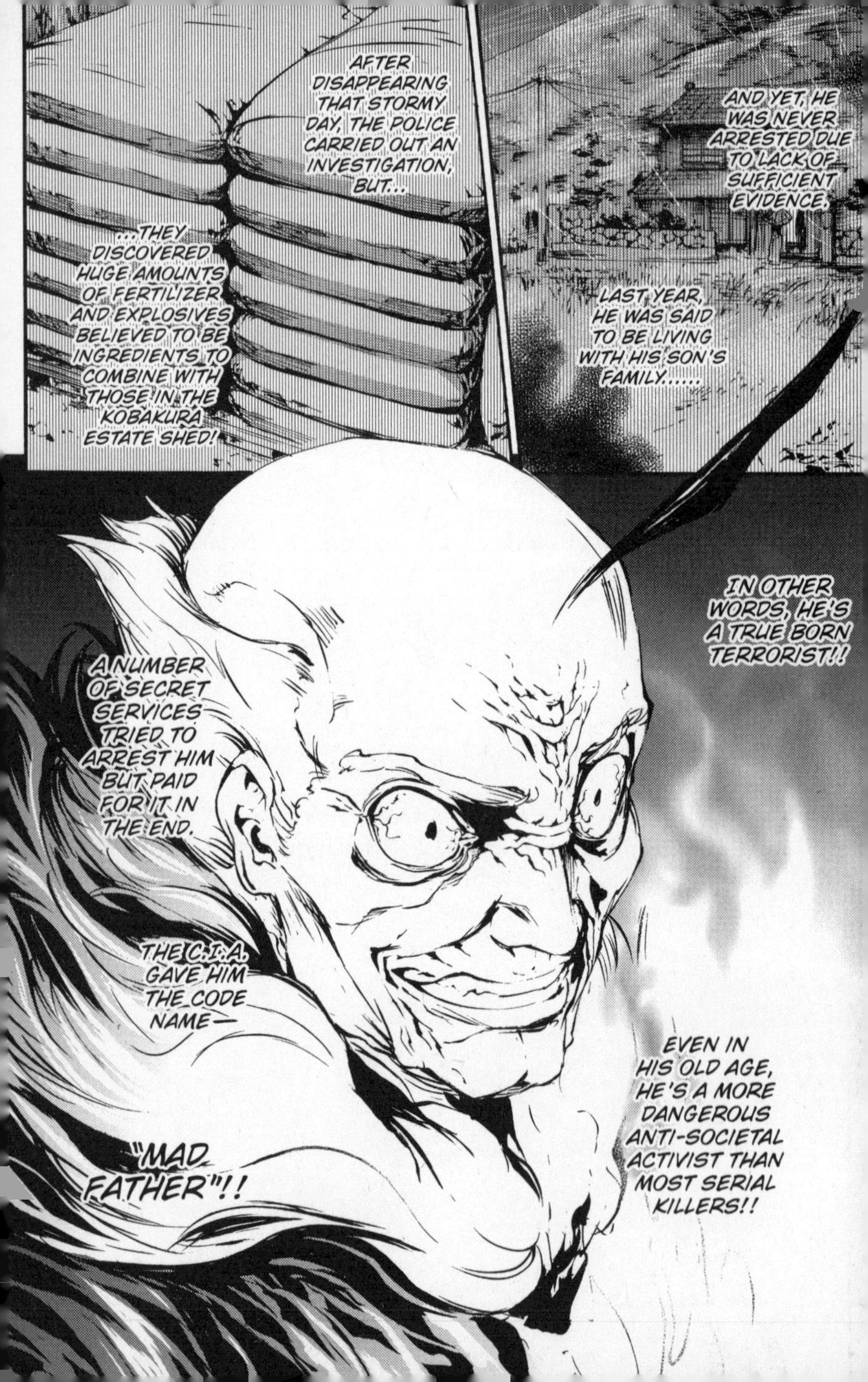
AFTER DISAPPEARING THAT STORMY DAY, THE POLICE CARRIED OUT AN INVESTIGATION, BUT...
...THEY DISCOVERED HUGE AMOUNTS OF FERTILIZER AND EXPLOSIVES BELIEVED TO BE INGREDIENTS TO COMBINE WITH THOSE IN THE KOBAKURA ESTATE SHED!
AND YET, HE WAS NEVER ARRESTED DUE TO LACK OF SUFFICIENT EVIDENCE.
LAST YEAR, HE WAS SAID TO BE LIVING WITH HIS SON'S FAMILY......
IN OTHER WORDS, HE'S A TRUE BORN TERRORIST!!
A NUMBER OF SECRET SERVICES TRIED TO ARREST HIM BUT PAID FOR IT IN THE END.
THE C.I.A. GAVE HIM THE CODE NAME—
EVEN IN HIS OLD AGE, HE'S A MORE DANGEROUS ANTI-SOCIETAL ACTIVIST THAN MOST SERIAL KILLERS!!
"MAD FATHER"!!

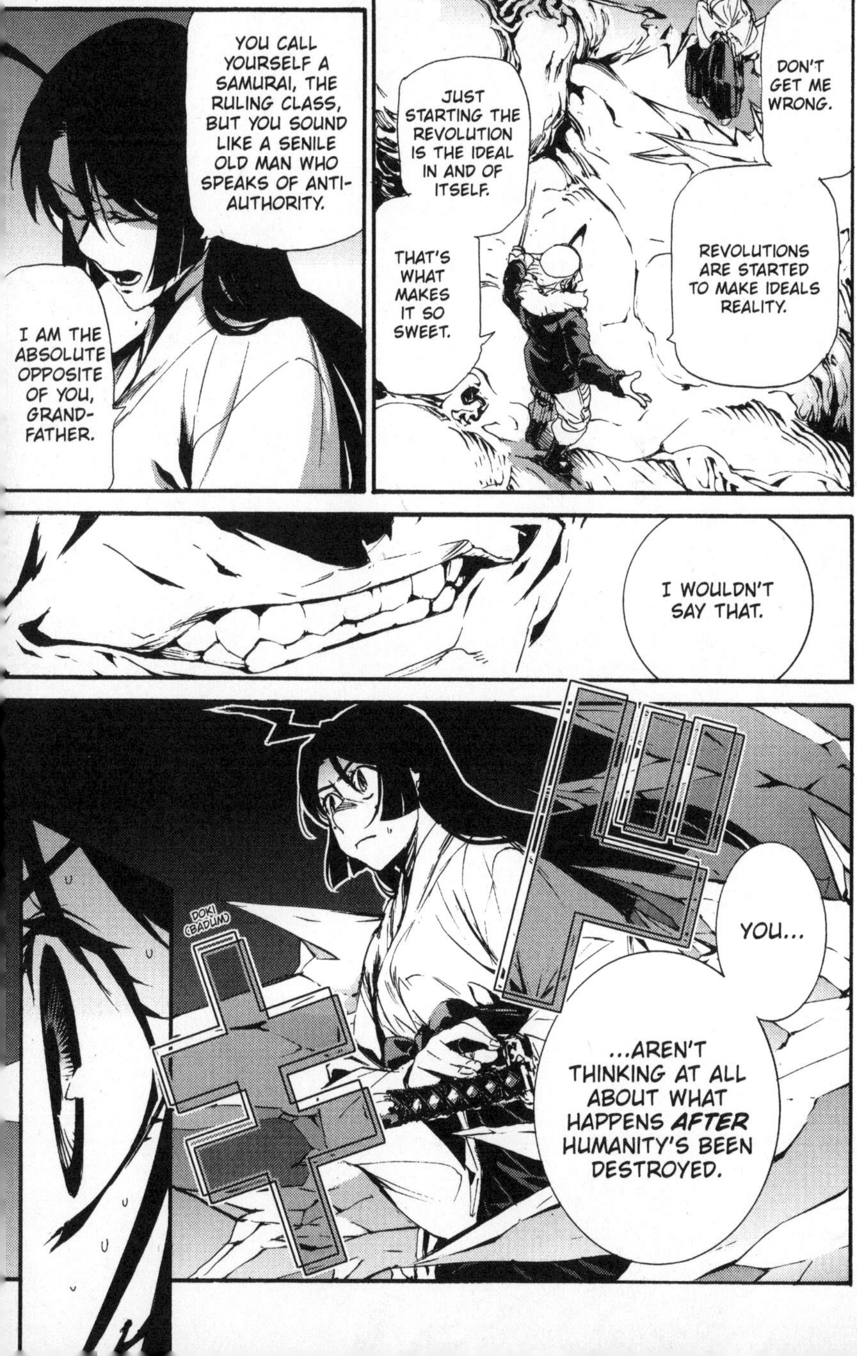
DON'T GET ME WRONG.
REVOLUTIONS ARE STARTED TO MAKE IDEALS REALITY.
JUST STARTING THE REVOLUTION IS THE IDEAL IN AND OF ITSELF.
THAT'S WHAT MAKES IT SO SWEET.
YOU CALL YOURSELF A SAMURAI, THE RULING CLASS, BUT YOU SOUND LIKE A SENILE OLD MAN WHO SPEAKS OF ANTI-AUTHORITY.
I AM THE ABSOLUTE OPPOSITE OF YOU, GRANDFATHER.
I WOULDN'T SAY THAT.
YOU...
...AREN'T THINKING AT ALL ABOUT WHAT HAPPENS **AFTER** HUMANITY'S BEEN DESTROYED.
DOKI (BADUM)

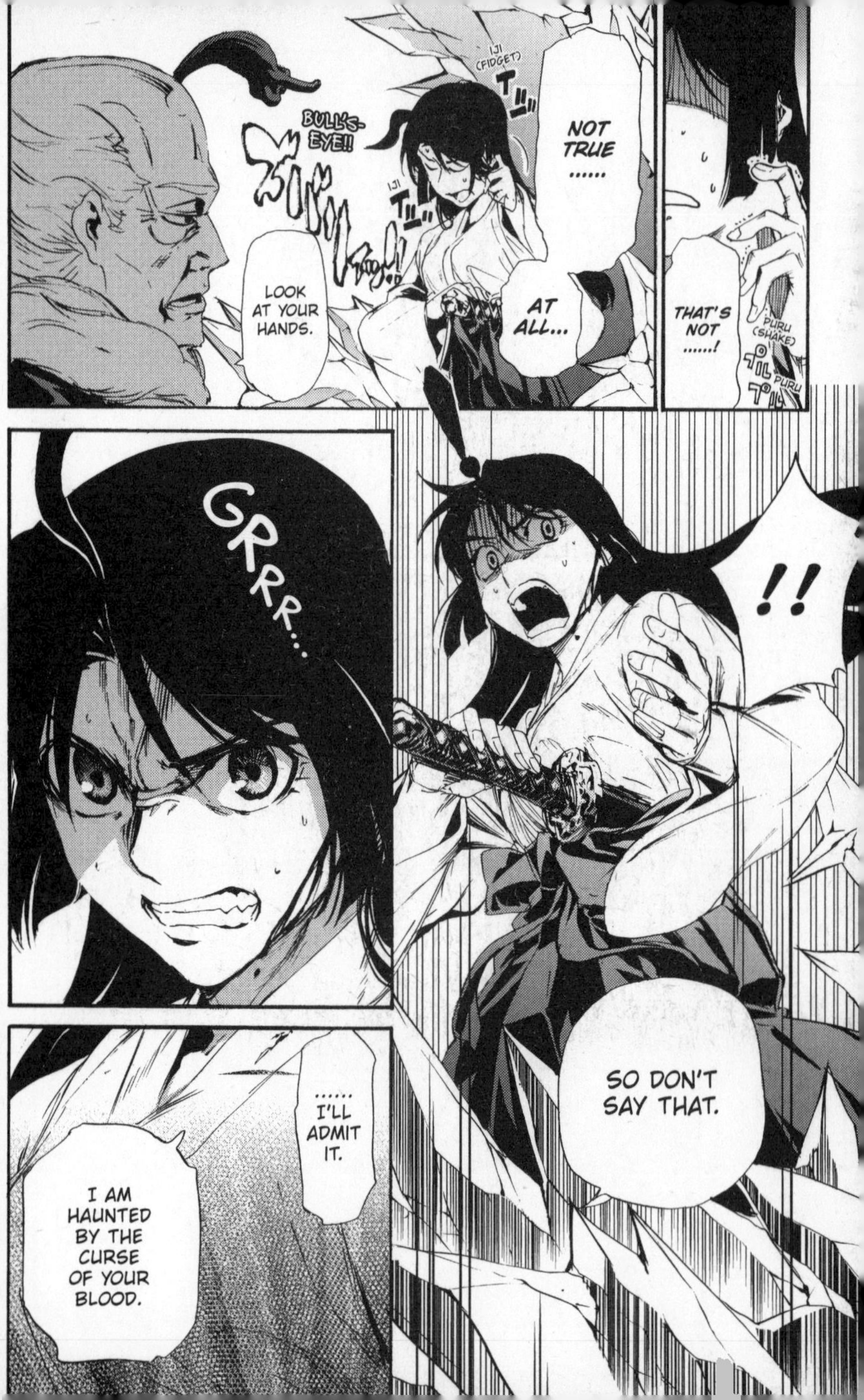
THAT'S NOT ......!
PURU (SHAKE)
PURU
IJI (FIDGET)
NOT TRUE ......
AT ALL...
IJI
BULL'S-EYE!!
LOOK AT YOUR HANDS.
!!
SO DON'T SAY THAT.
GRRR...
......I'LL ADMIT IT.
I AM HAUNTED BY THE CURSE OF YOUR BLOOD.

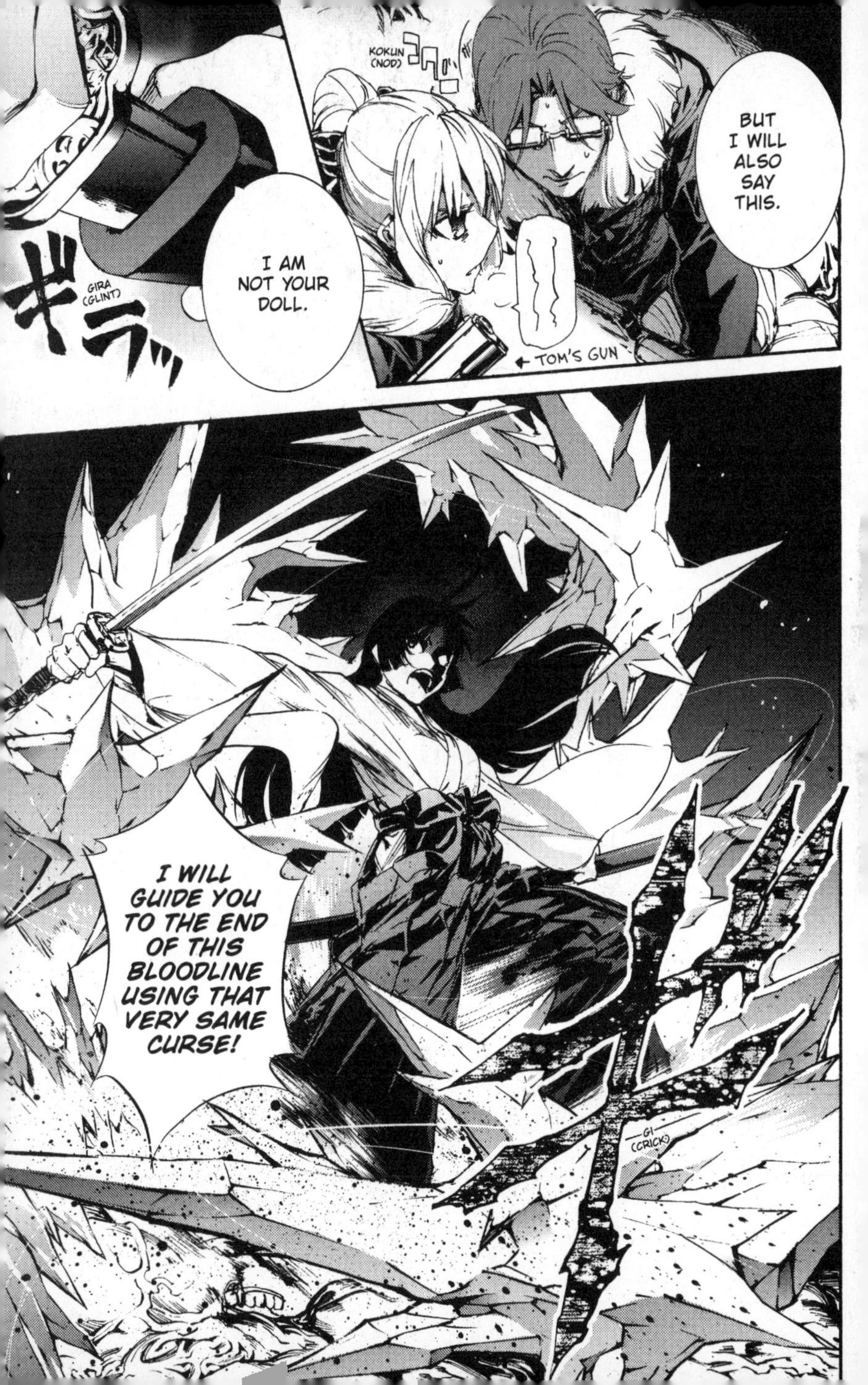
BUT I WILL ALSO SAY THIS.
KOKUN (NOD)
I AM NOT YOUR DOLL.
← TOM'S GUN
GIRA (GLINT)
I WILL GUIDE YOU TO THE END OF THIS BLOODLINE USING THAT VERY SAME CURSE!
GI (CRICK)

SHAAAAAAAAAAAAAAH!!

SHIIGIGH
(CLAAAANG)

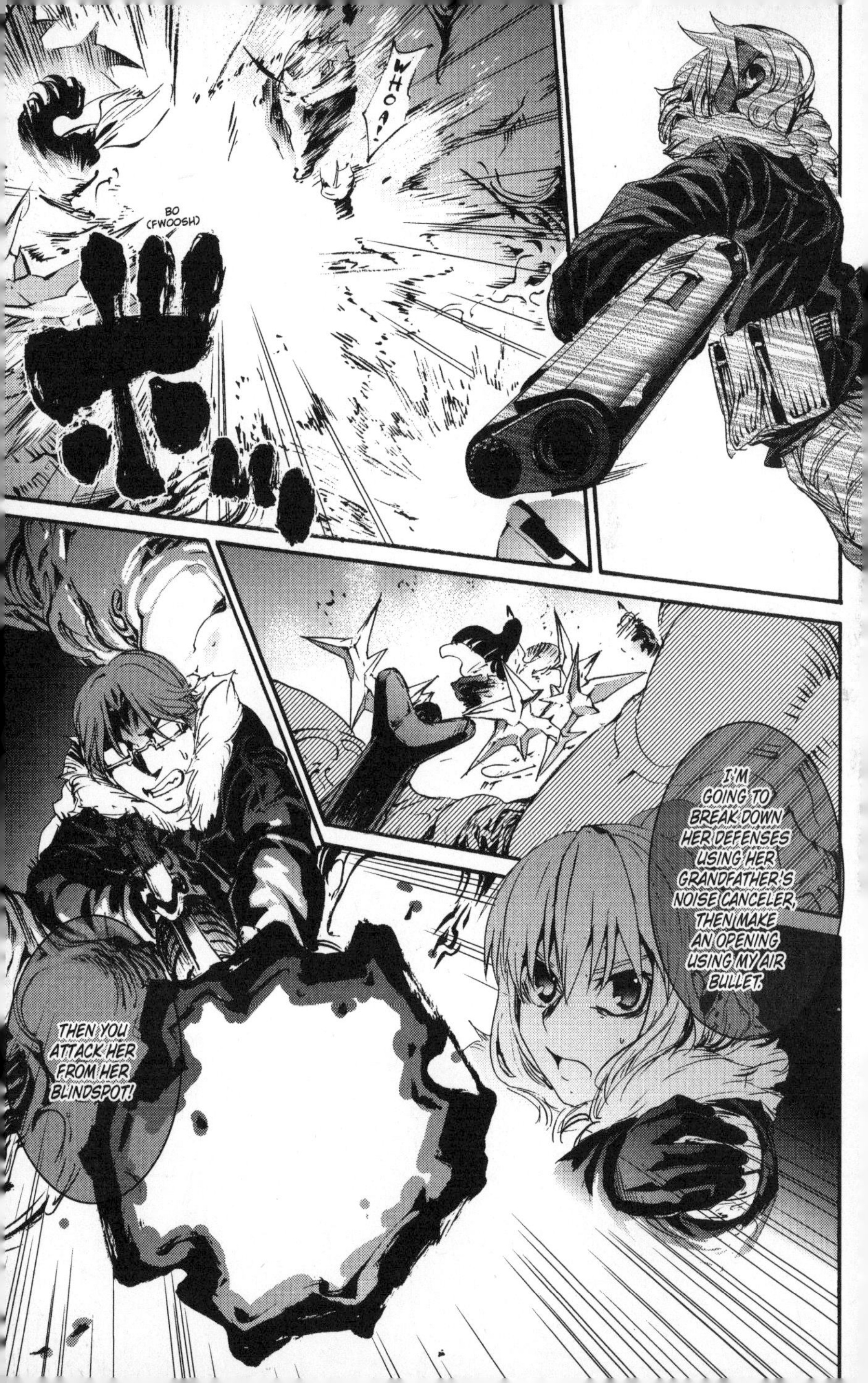
WHOA!
BO (FWOOSH)
I'M GOING TO BREAK DOWN HER DEFENSES USING HER GRANDFATHER'S NOISE CANCELER, THEN MAKE AN OPENING USING MY AIR BULLET.
THEN YOU ATTACK HER FROM HER BLINDSPOT!

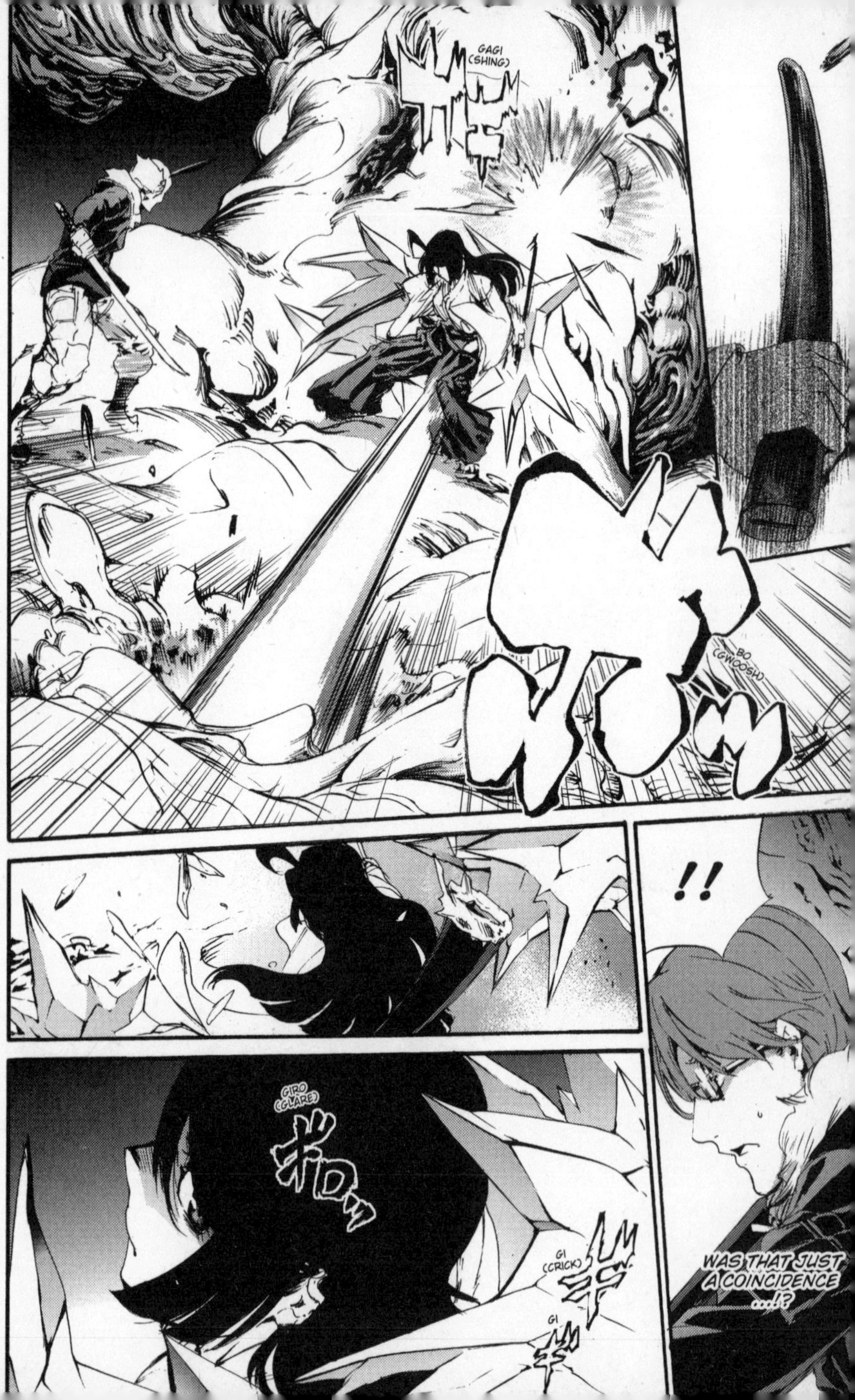
GAGI
(SHING)
BO
(GWOOSH)
!!
WAS THAT JUST A COINCIDENCE ...!?
GIRO
(GLARE)
GI
(CRICK)
GI

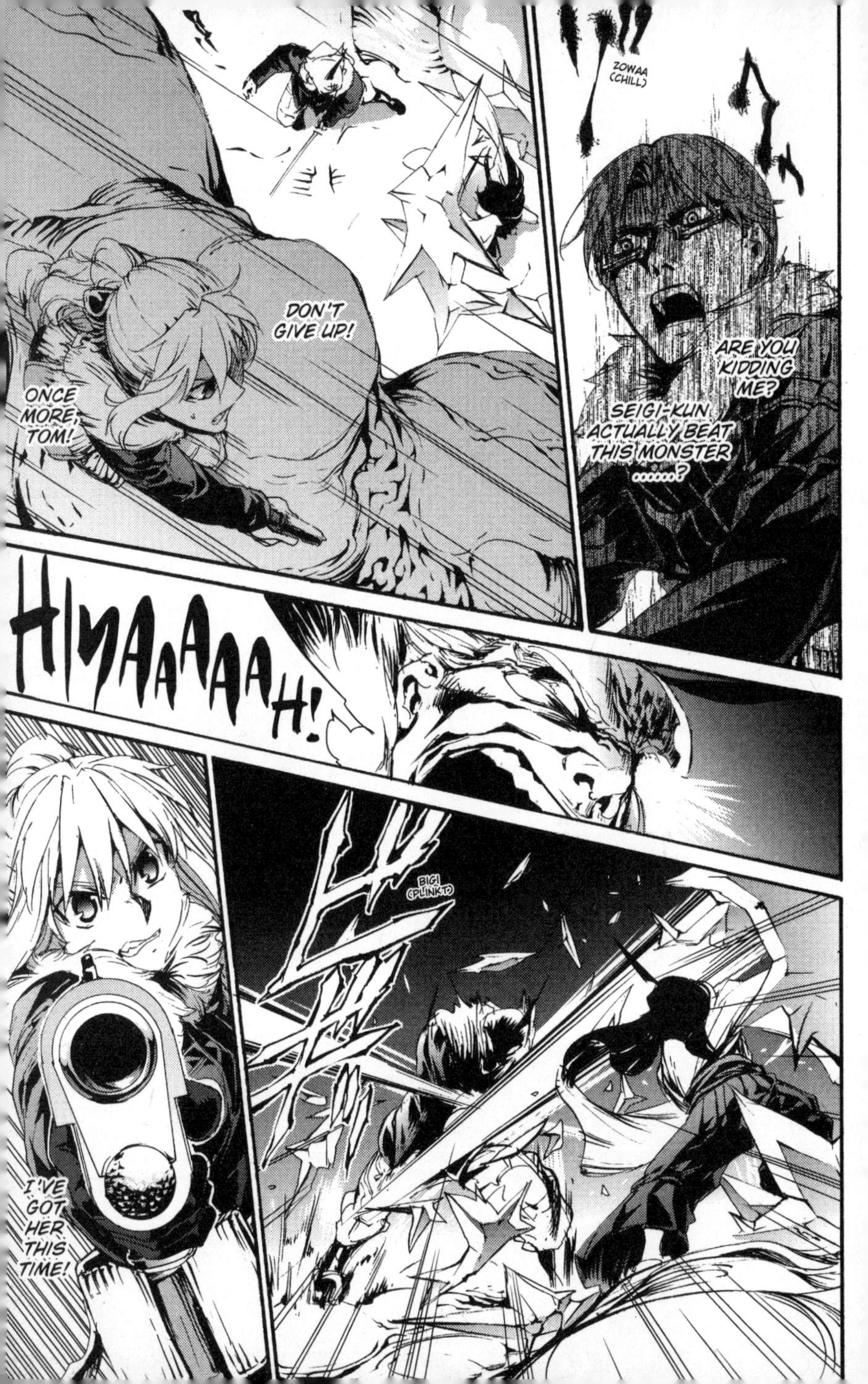
ZOWAA (CHILL)
ARE YOU KIDDING ME?
SEIGI-KUN ACTUALLY BEAT THIS MONSTER ......?
DON'T GIVE UP!
ONCE MORE, TOM!
HIYAAAAAAH!
BIGI (PLINKT)
I'VE GOT HER THIS TIME!

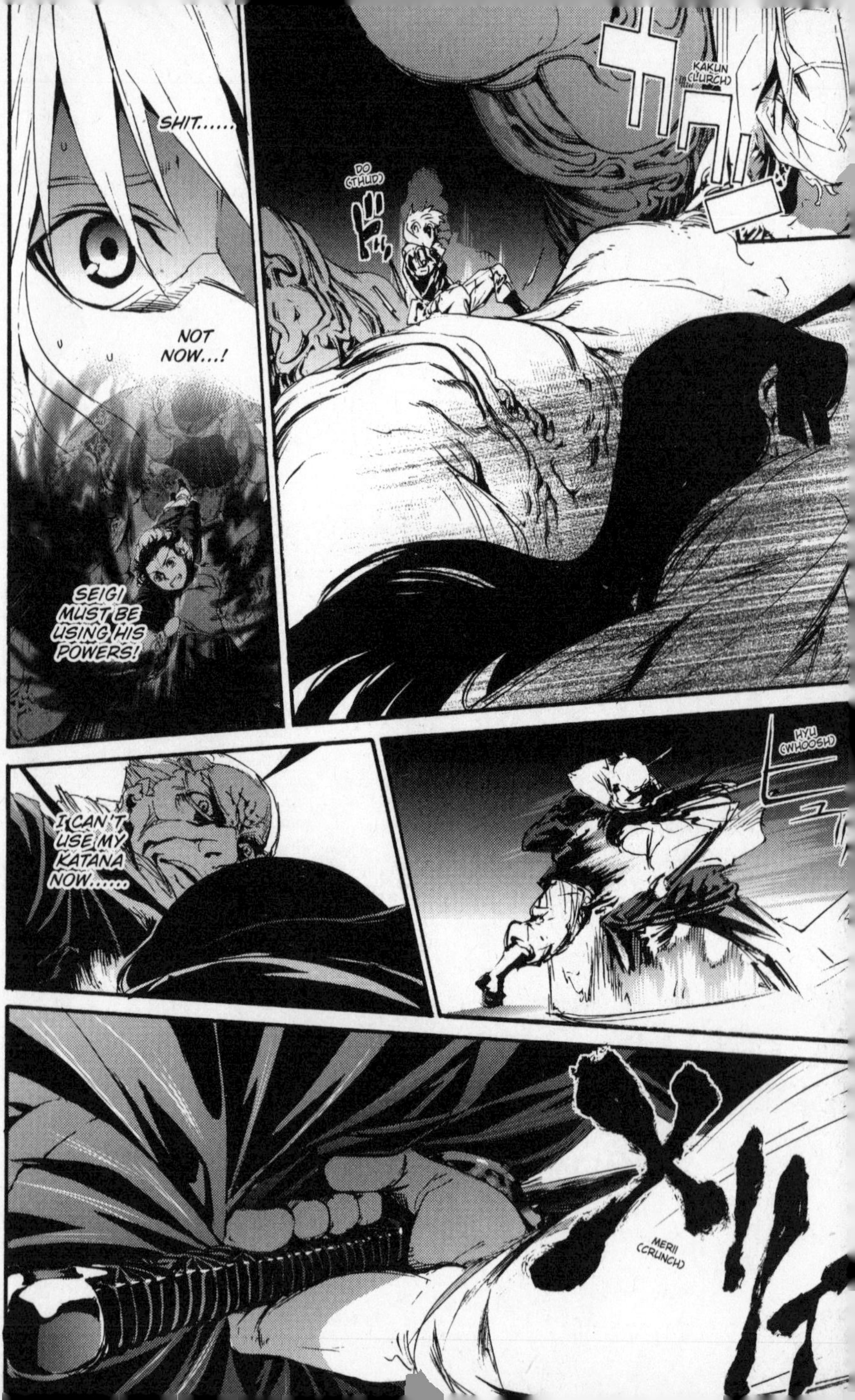
KAKUN (LURCH)
DO (THUD)
SHIT......
NOT NOW...!
SEIGI MUST BE USING HIS POWERS!
HYU (WHOOSH)
I CAN'T USE MY KATANA NOW.......
MERII (CRUNCH)

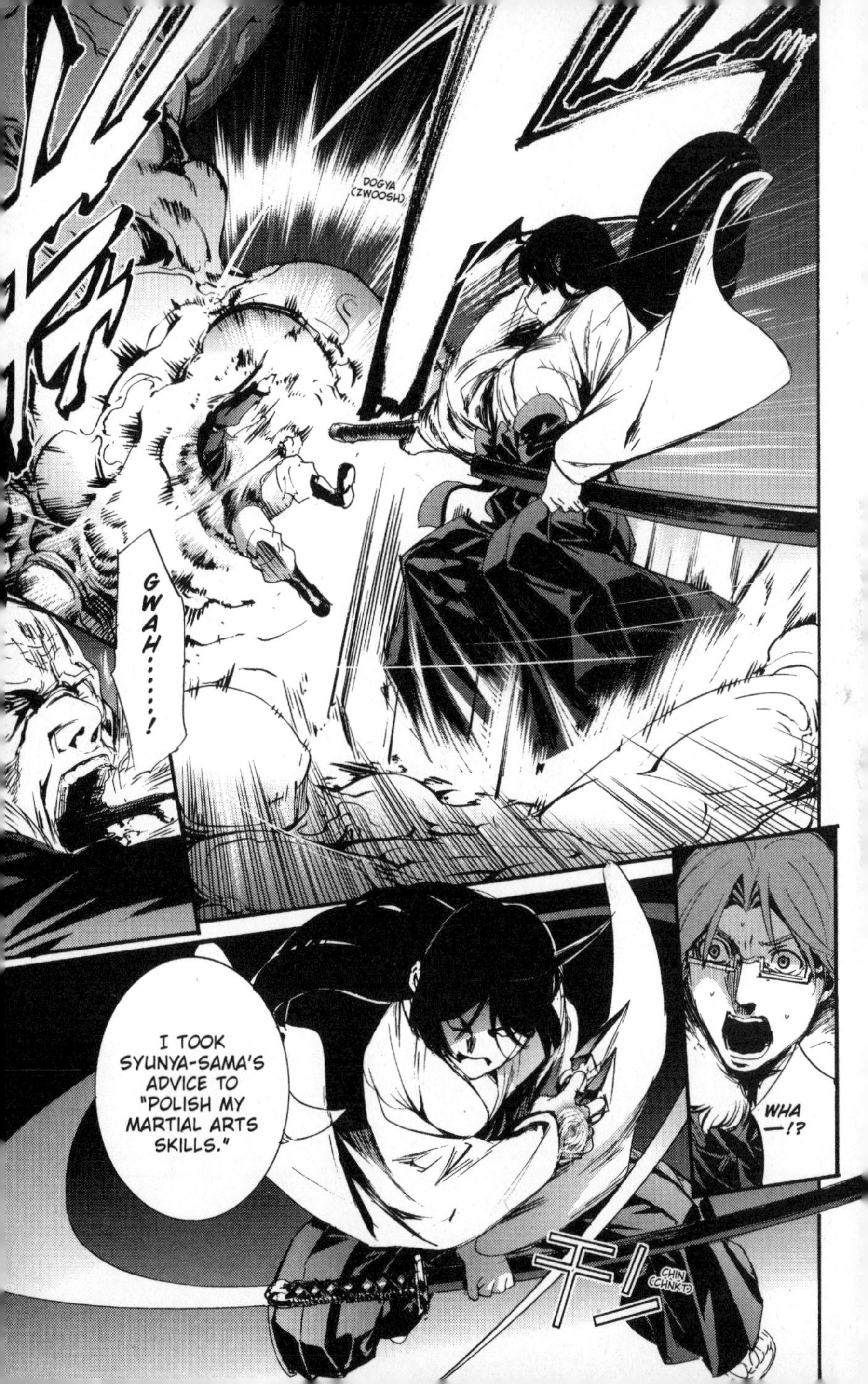
DOGYA (ZWOOSH)
GWAH......!
WHA—!?
I TOOK SYUNYA-SAMA'S ADVICE TO "POLISH MY MARTIAL ARTS SKILLS."
CHIN (CHNKT)

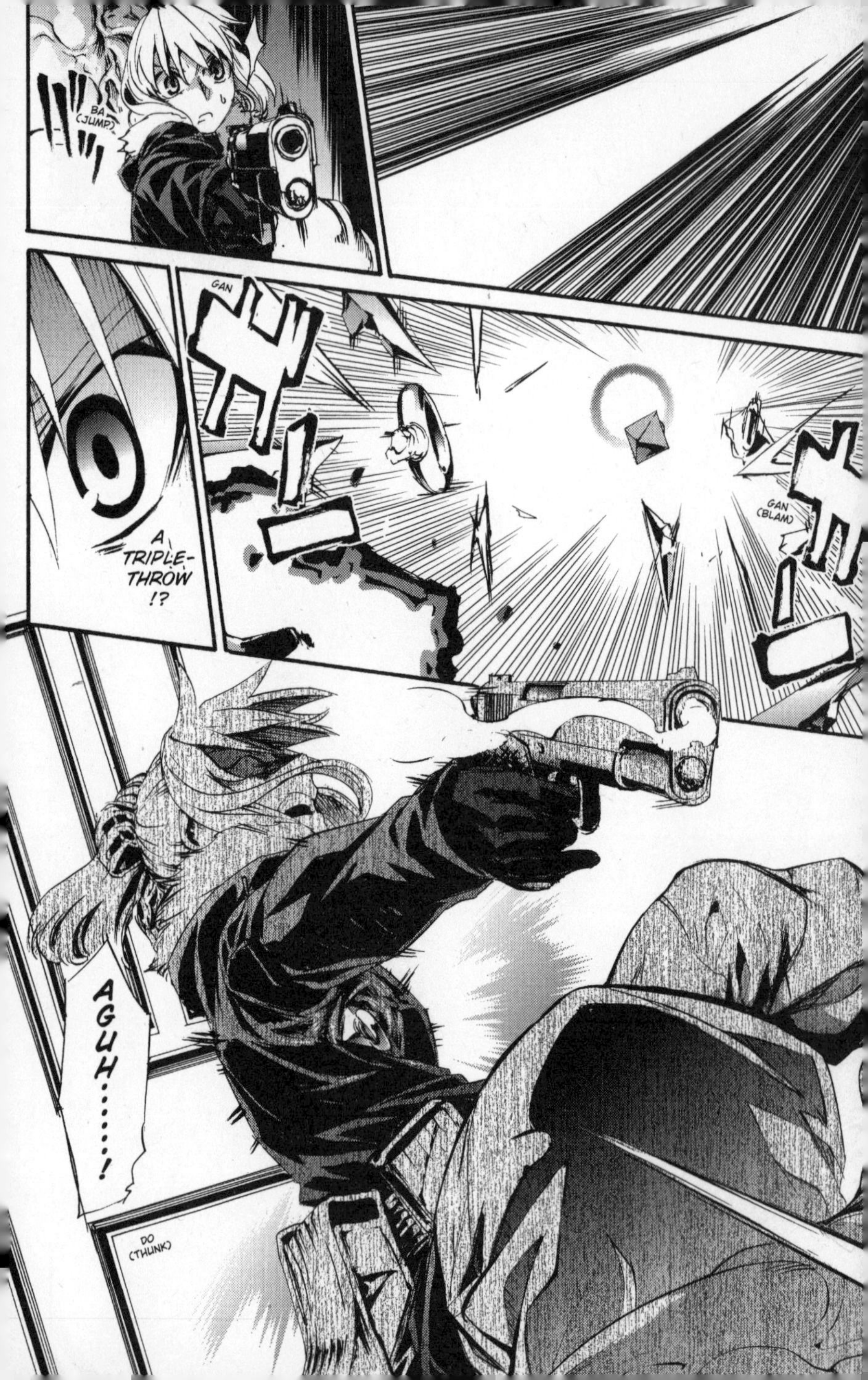
BA (JUMP)
GAN (BLAM)
GAN
A TRIPLE-THROW !?
AGUH......!
DO (THUNK)

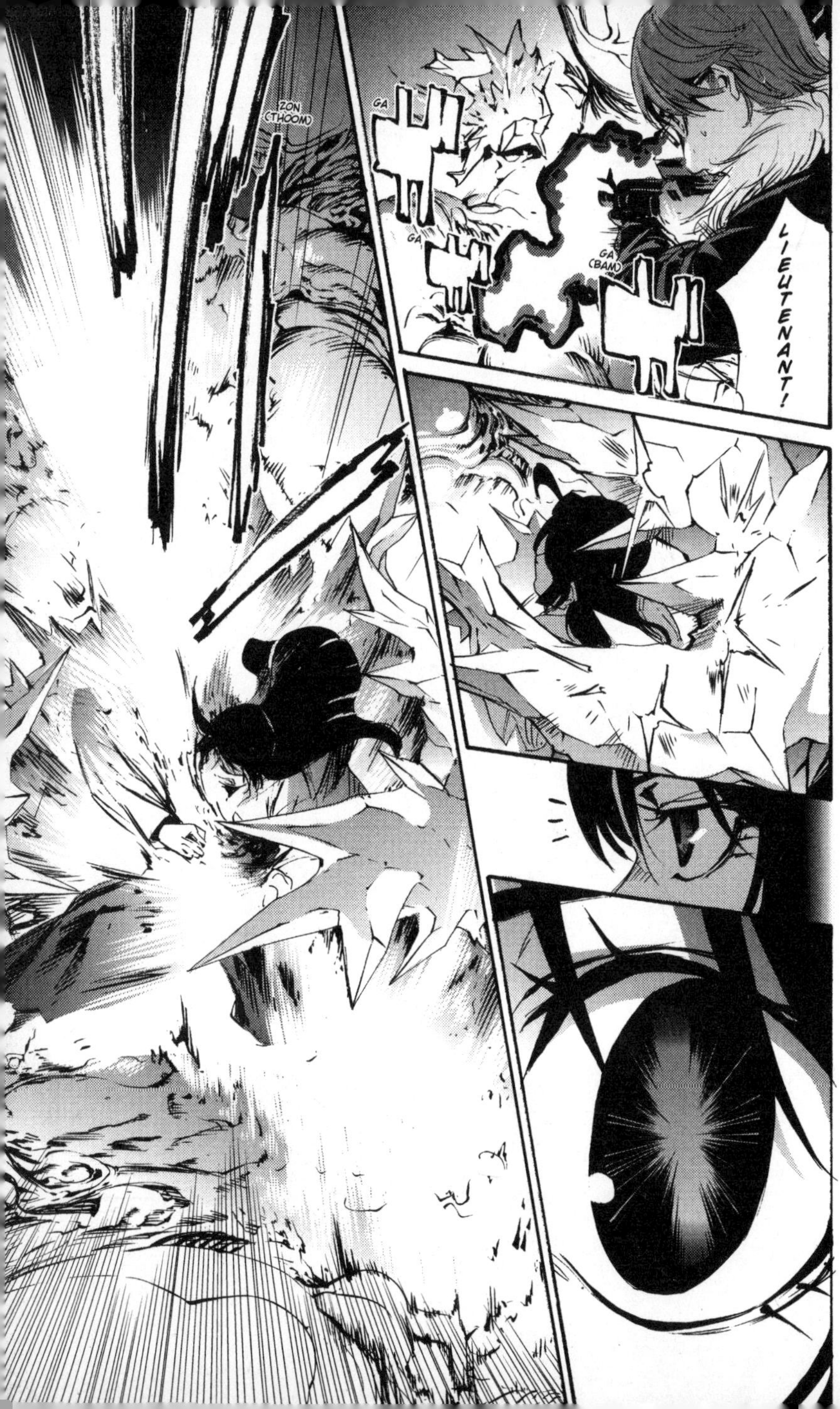
LIEUTENANT!
GA (BAM)
GA
GA
ZON (THOOM)

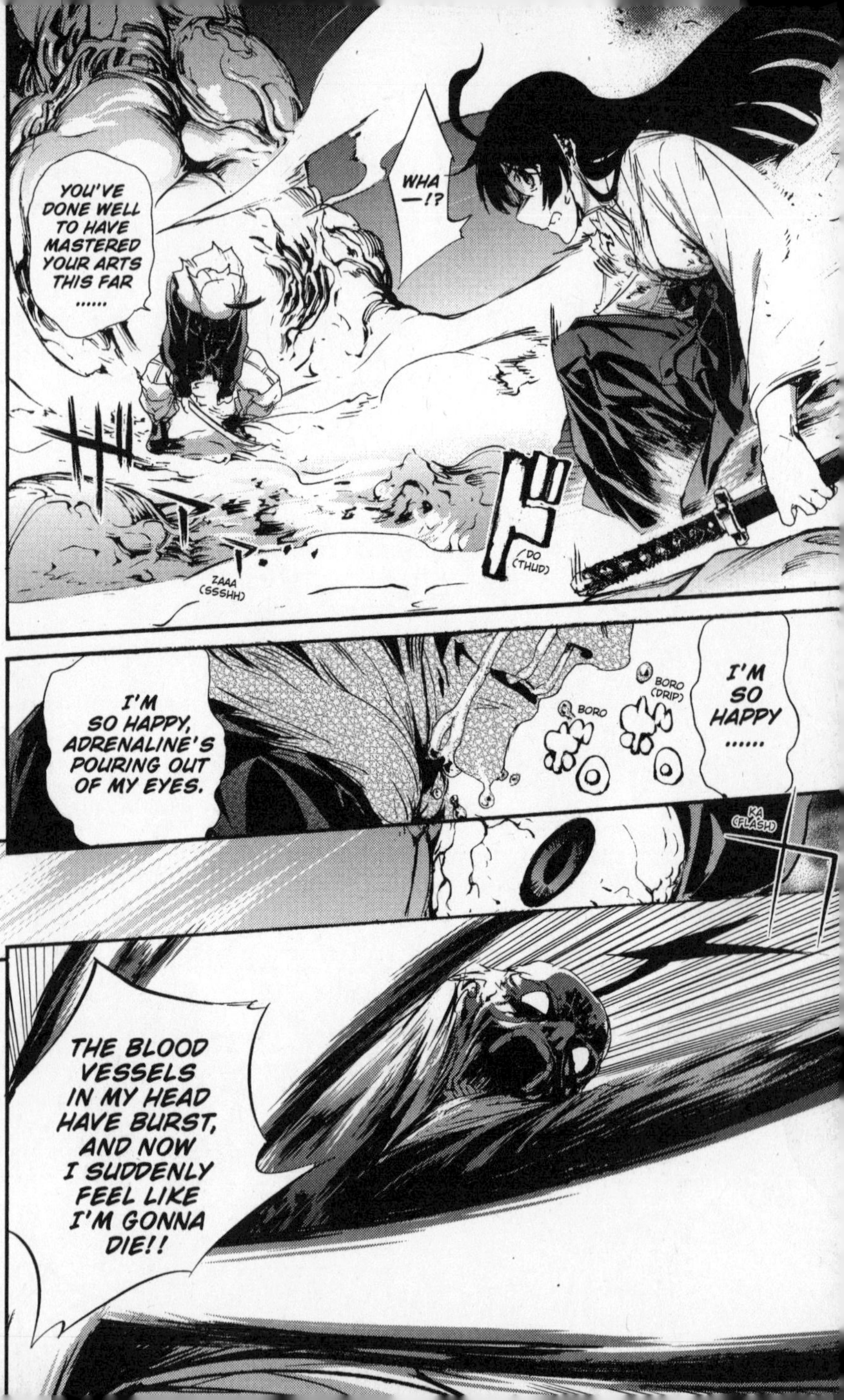
WHA—!?
YOU'VE DONE WELL TO HAVE MASTERED YOUR ARTS THIS FAR ......
DO (THUD)
ZAAA (SSSHH)
I'M SO HAPPY ......
BORO (DRIP)
BORO
I'M SO HAPPY, ADRENALINE'S POURING OUT OF MY EYES.
KA (FLASH)
THE BLOOD VESSELS IN MY HEAD HAVE BURST, AND NOW I SUDDENLY FEEL LIKE I'M GONNA DIE!!

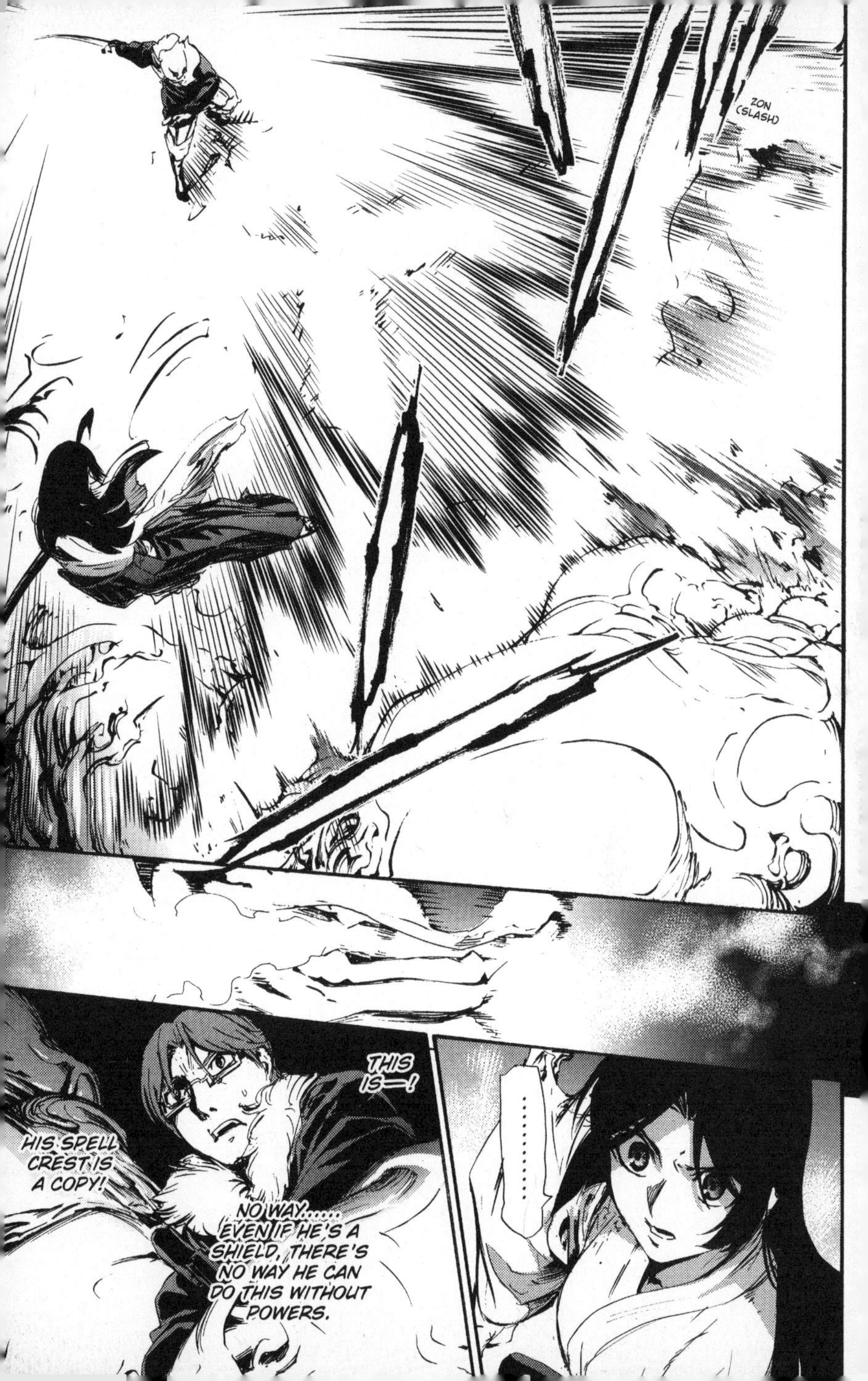
ZON
(SLASH)
......
THIS IS—!
HIS SPELL CREST IS A COPY!
NO WAY...... EVEN IF HE'S A SHIELD, THERE'S NO WAY HE CAN DO THIS WITHOUT POWERS.

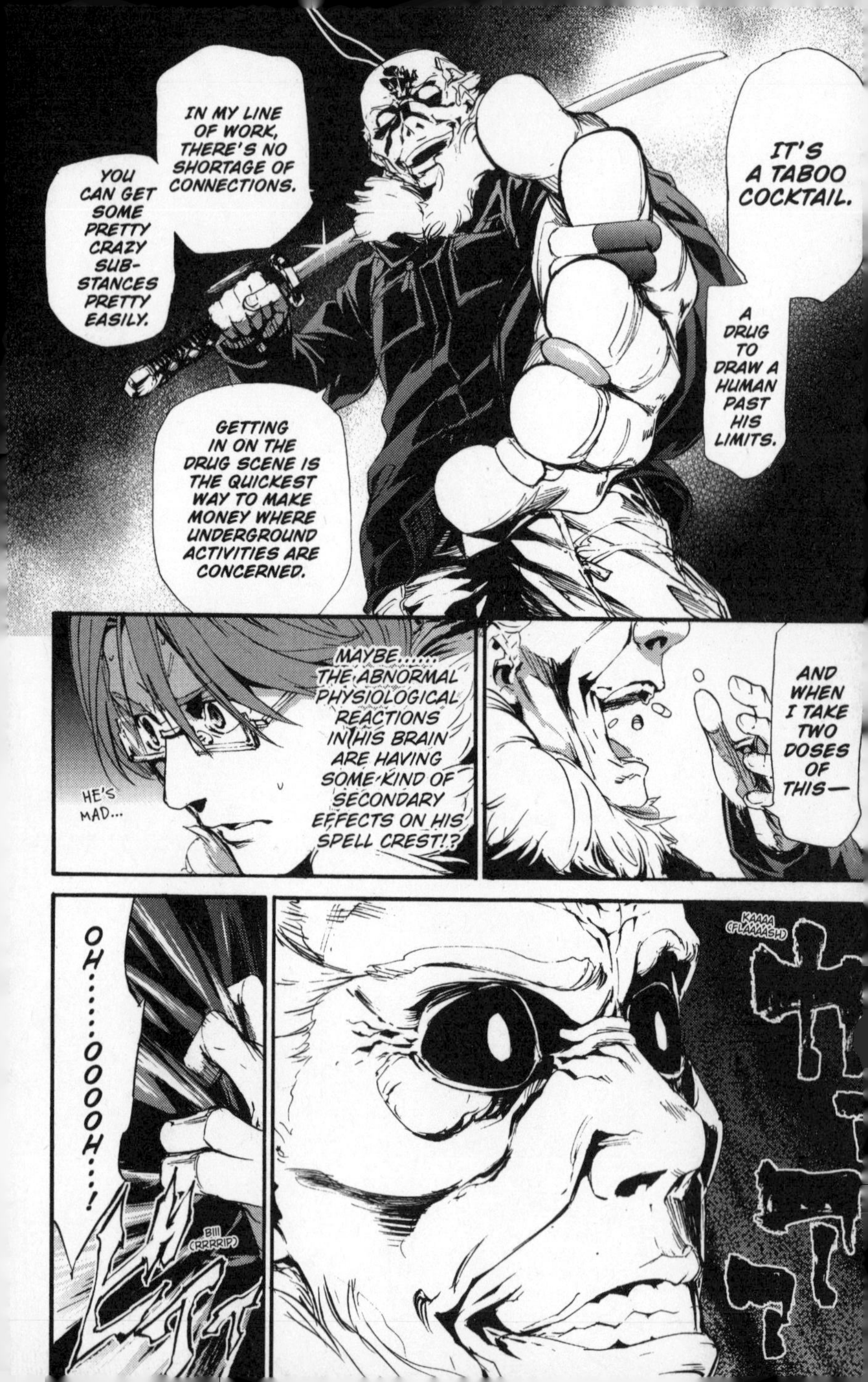
IT'S A TABOO COCKTAIL.
A DRUG TO DRAW A HUMAN PAST HIS LIMITS.
IN MY LINE OF WORK, THERE'S NO SHORTAGE OF CONNECTIONS.
YOU CAN GET SOME PRETTY CRAZY SUB-STANCES PRETTY EASILY.
GETTING IN ON THE DRUG SCENE IS THE QUICKEST WAY TO MAKE MONEY WHERE UNDERGROUND ACTIVITIES ARE CONCERNED.
AND WHEN I TAKE TWO DOSES OF THIS—
MAYBE...... THE ABNORMAL PHYSIOLOGICAL REACTIONS IN HIS BRAIN ARE HAVING SOME KIND OF SECONDARY EFFECTS ON HIS SPELL CREST!?
HE'S MAD...
KAAAA (FLAAAASH)
OH.....OOOOOH...!
BIII (RRRRIP)

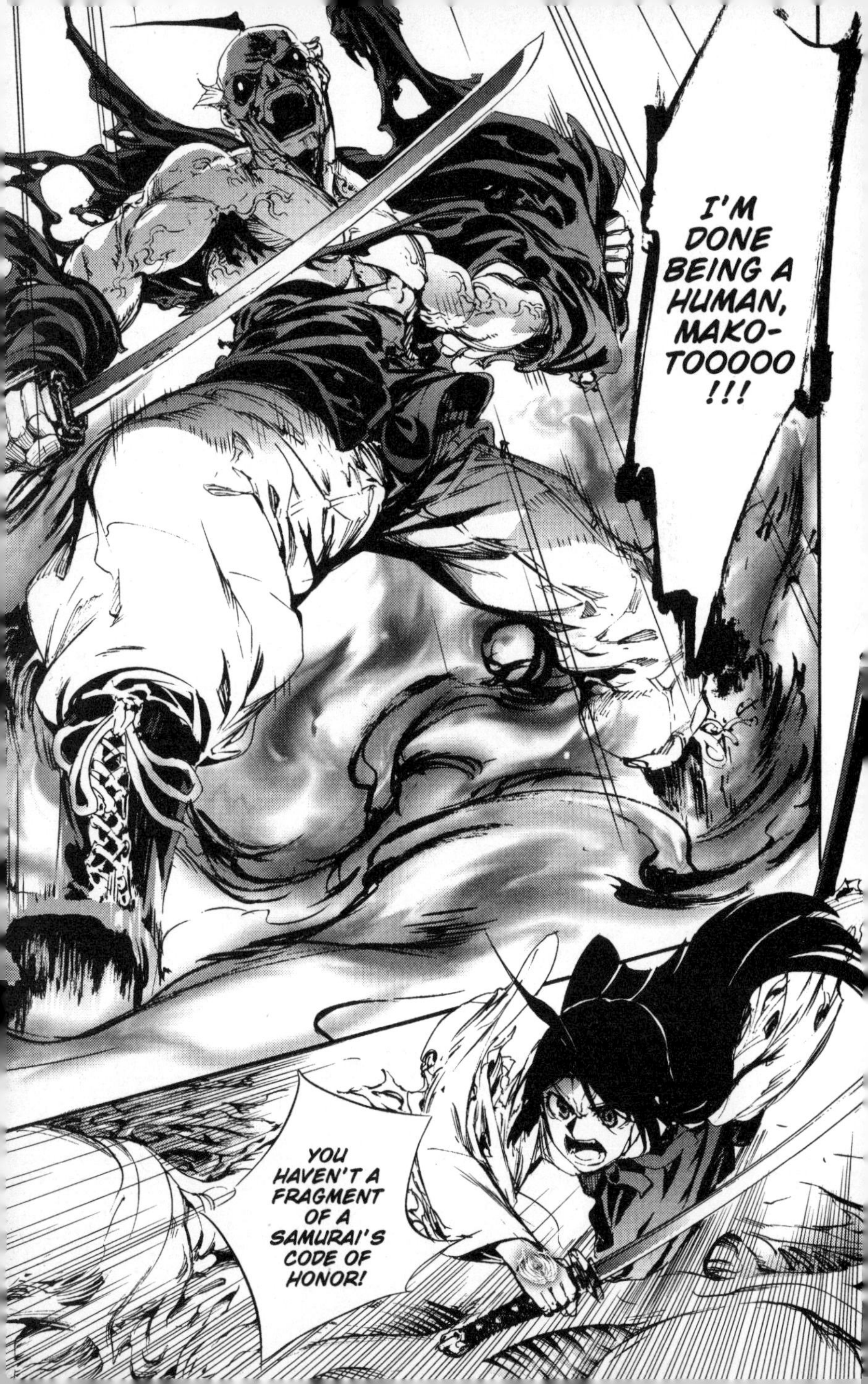
I'M DONE BEING A HUMAN, MAKO-TOOOOO !!!
YOU HAVEN'T A FRAGMENT OF A SAMURAI'S CODE OF HONOR!

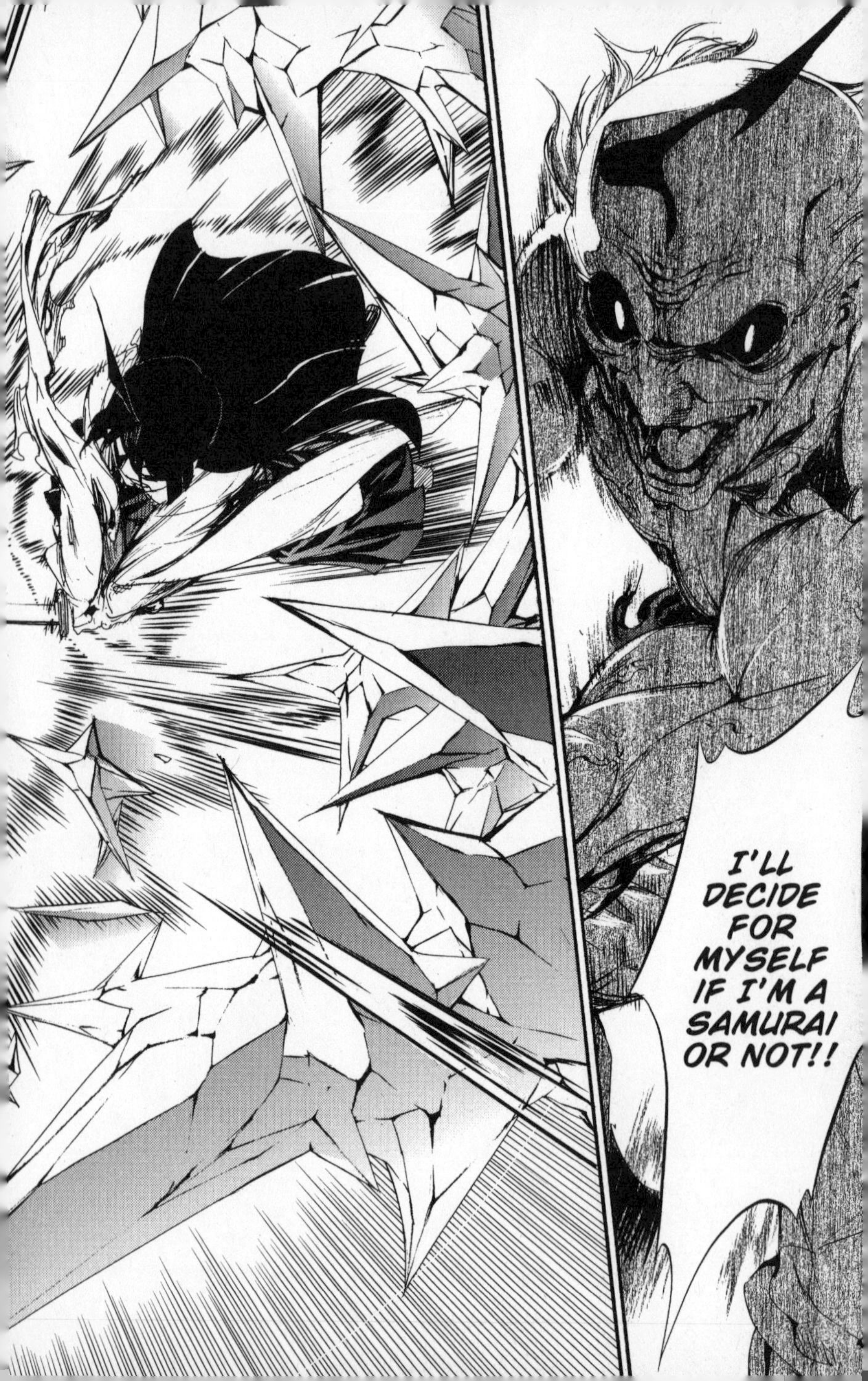
I'LL DECIDE FOR MYSELF IF I'M A SAMURAI OR NOT!!

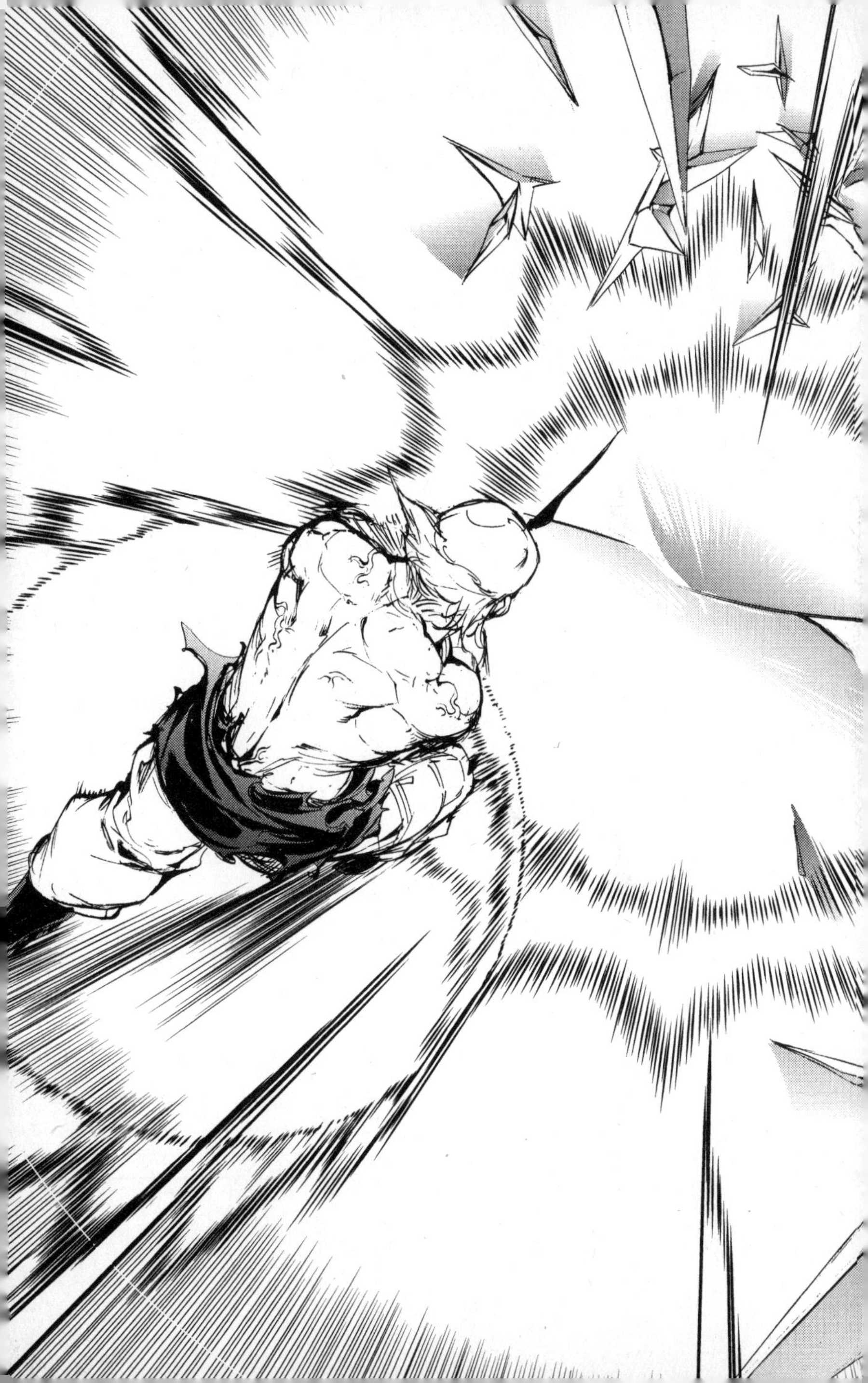

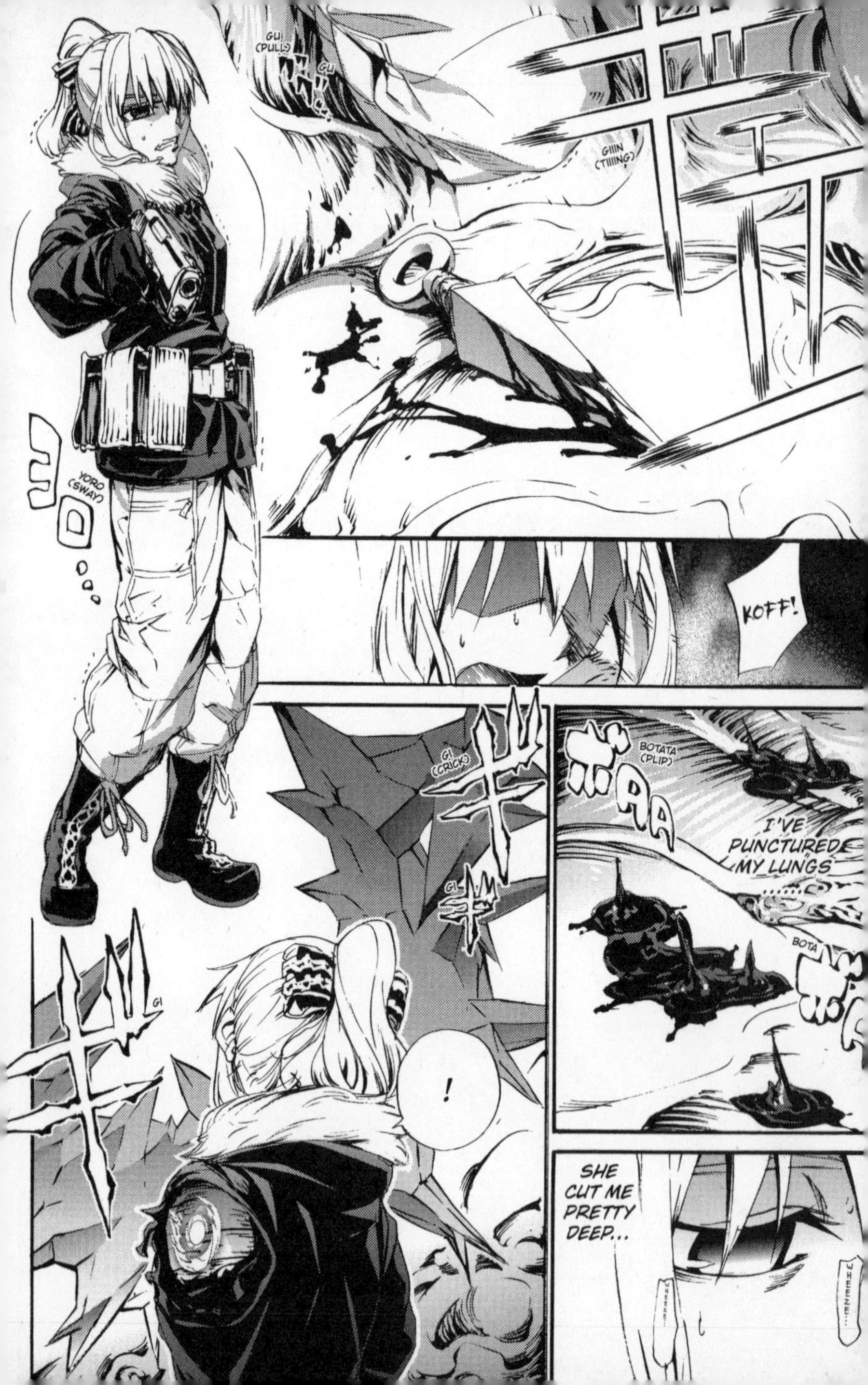

GUI (PULL)
GUI
GIIN (TIIING)
KOFF!
YORO (SWAY)
BOTATA (PLIP)
I'VE PUNCTURED MY LUNGS......
BOTA
GI (CRICK)
GI
SHE CUT ME PRETTY DEEP...
WHEEZE...
WHEEZE...
GI
!

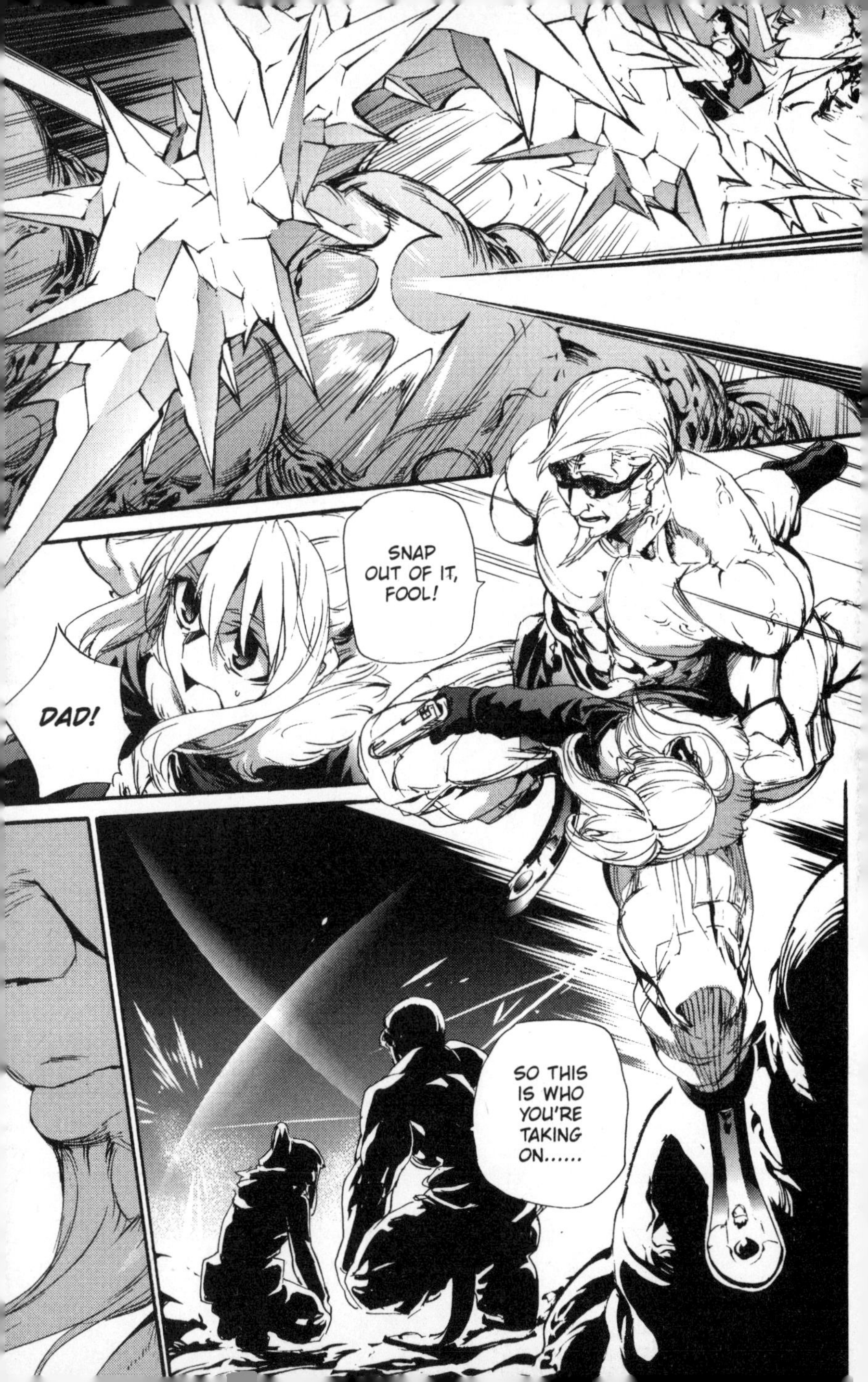
SNAP OUT OF IT, FOOL!
DAD!
SO THIS IS WHO YOU'RE TAKING ON......

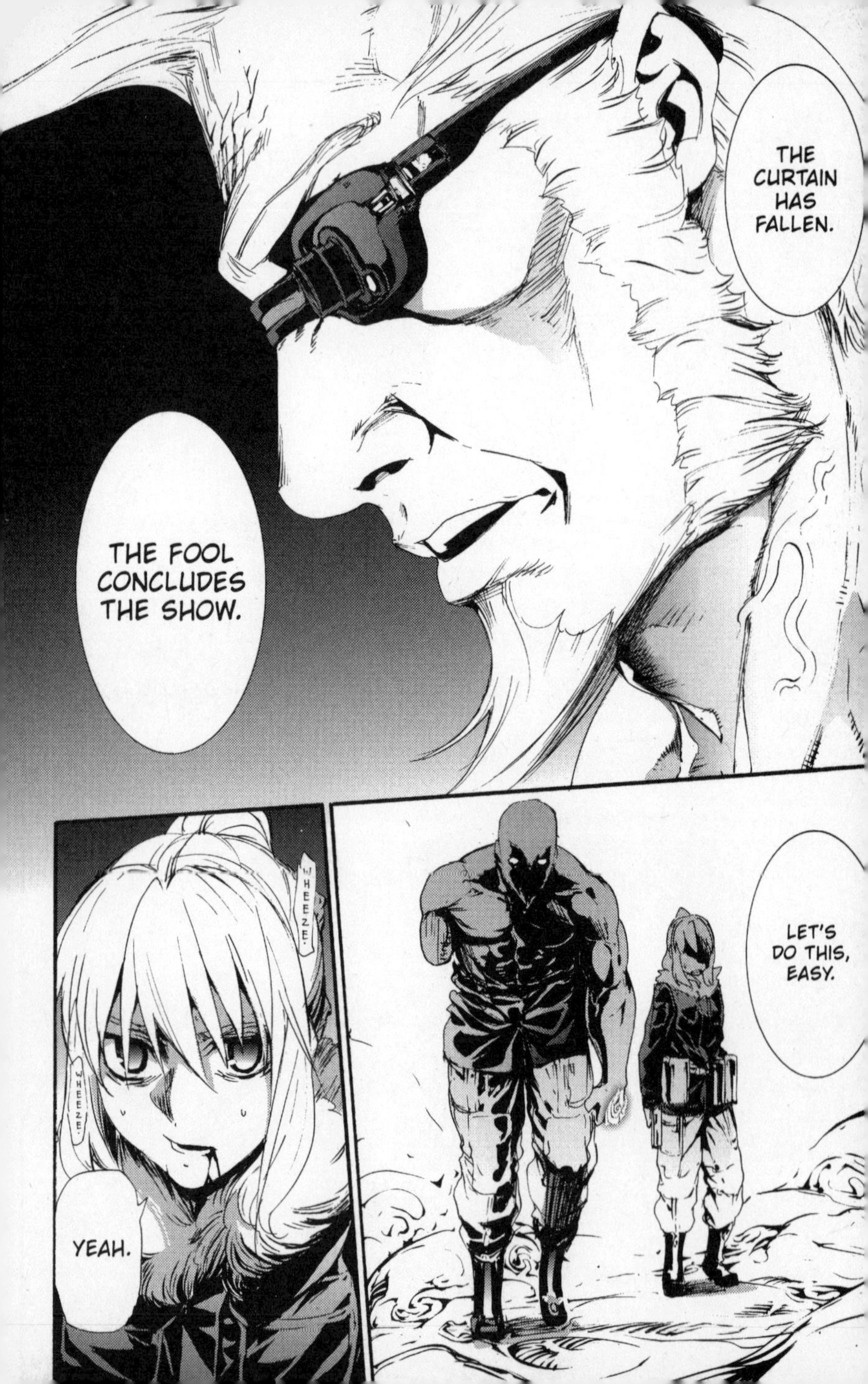
THE CURTAIN HAS FALLEN.
THE FOOL CONCLUDES THE SHOW.
LET'S DO THIS, EASY.
WHEEZE.
WHEEZE.
YEAH.

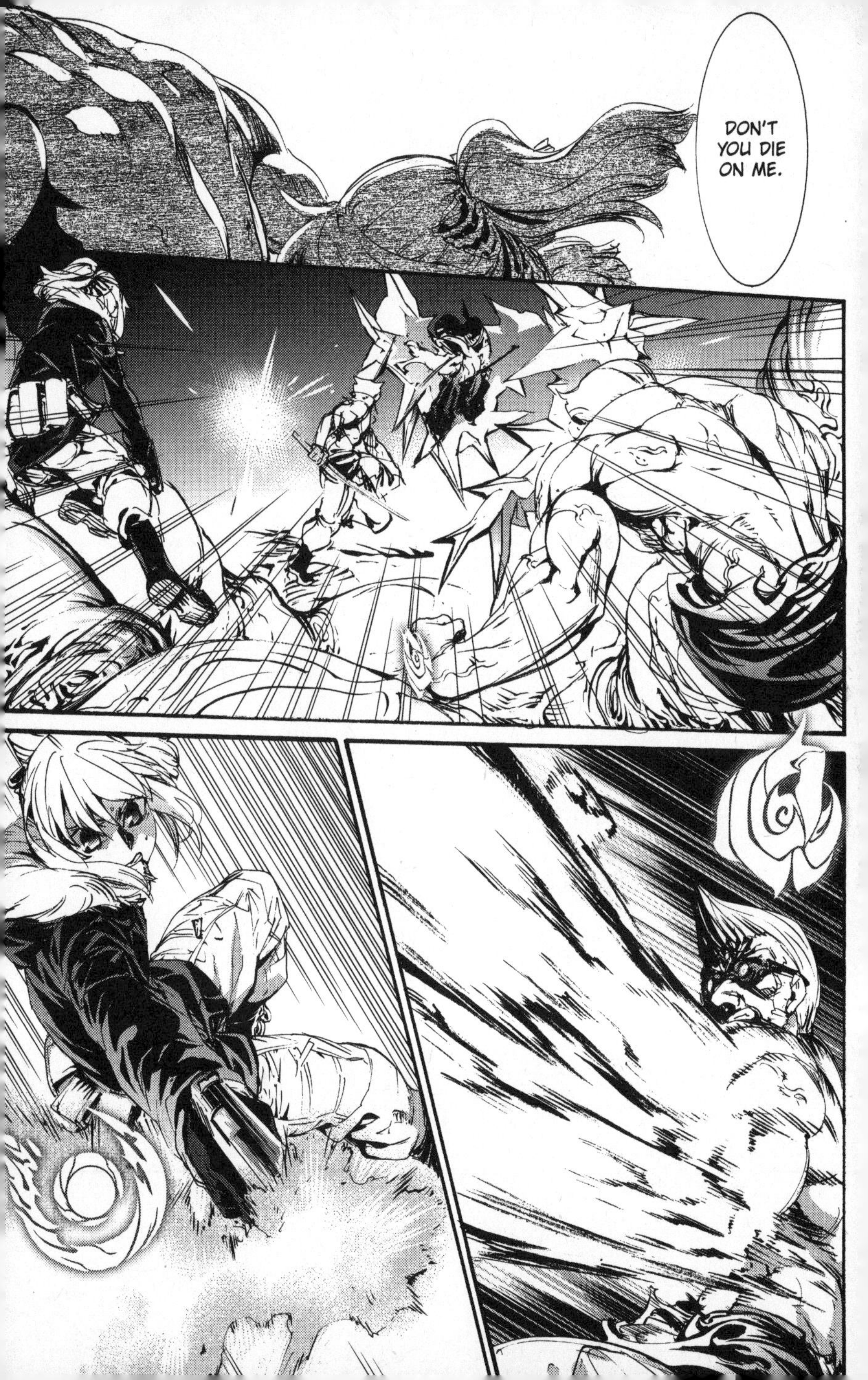
DON'T YOU DIE ON ME.

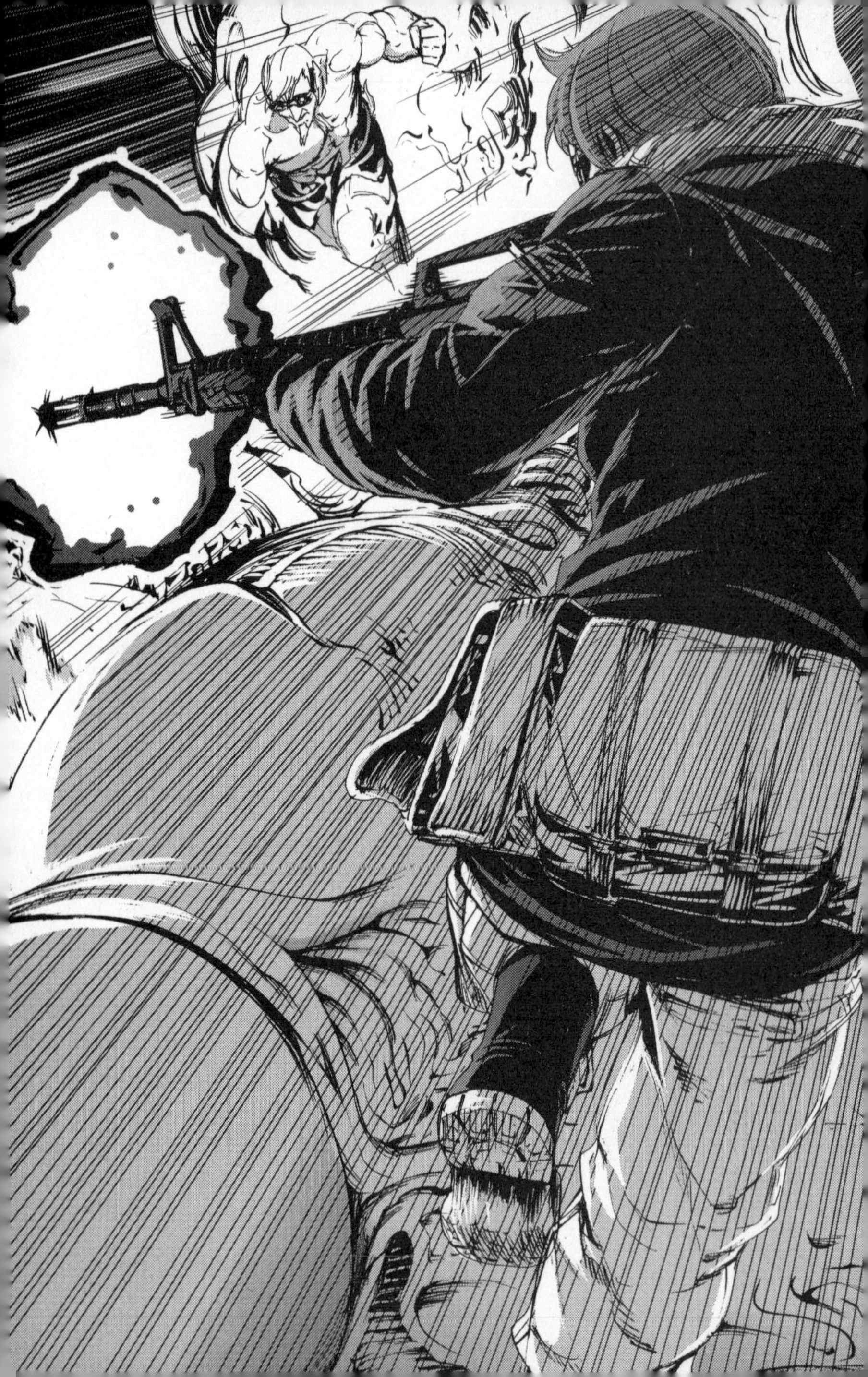

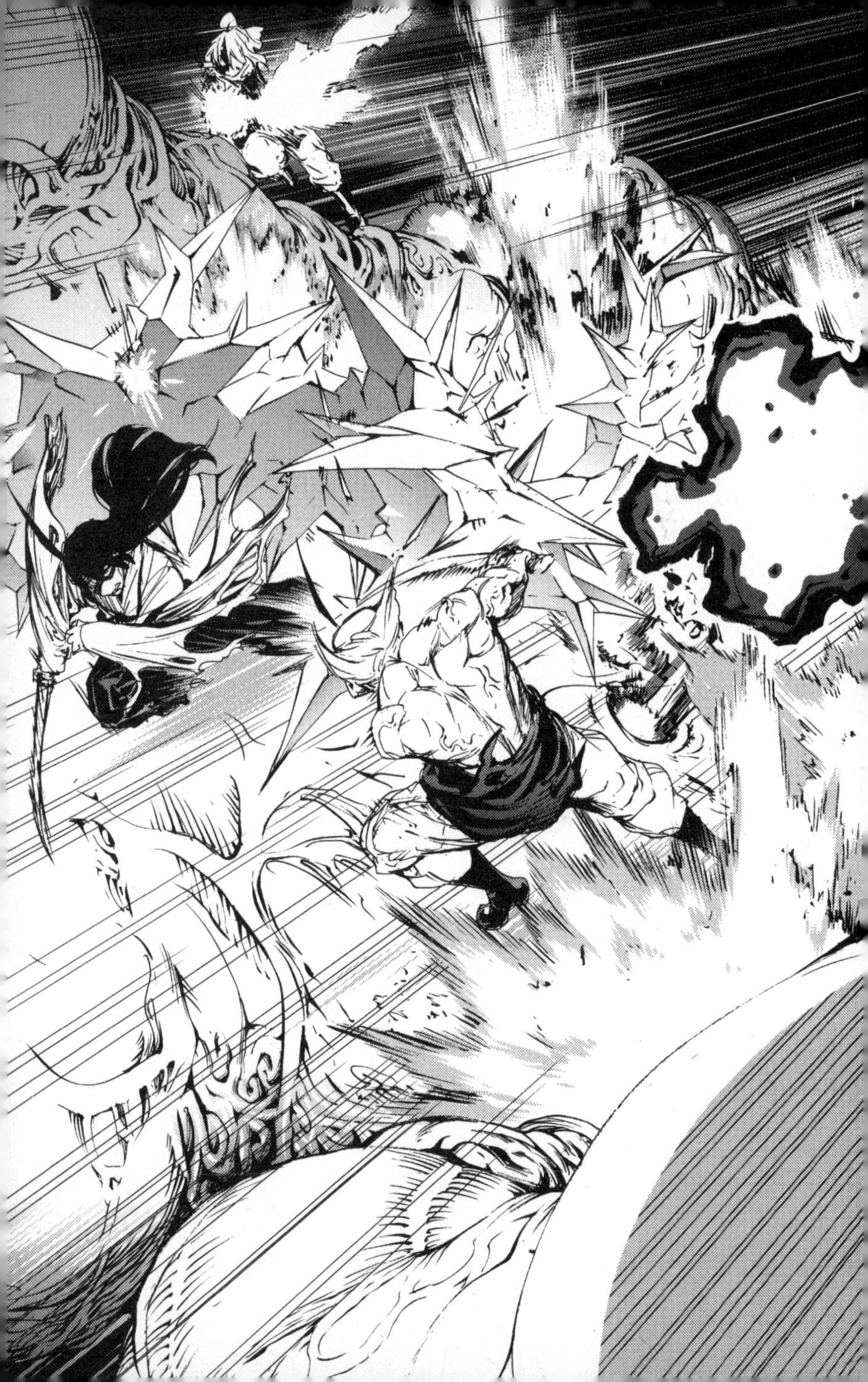

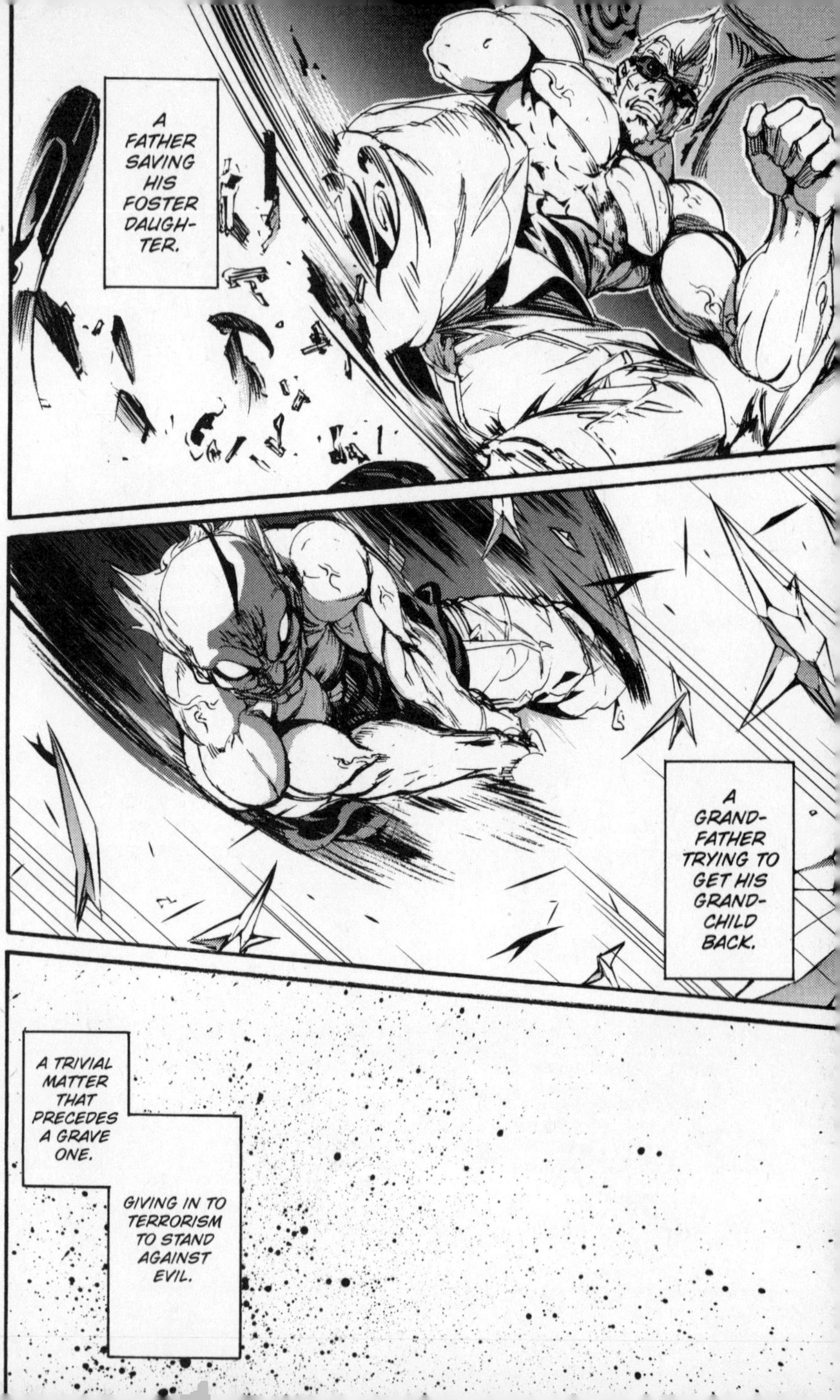
A FATHER SAVING HIS FOSTER DAUGH-TER.
A GRAND-FATHER TRYING TO GET HIS GRAND-CHILD BACK.
A TRIVIAL MATTER THAT PRECEDES A GRAVE ONE.
GIVING IN TO TERRORISM TO STAND AGAINST EVIL.

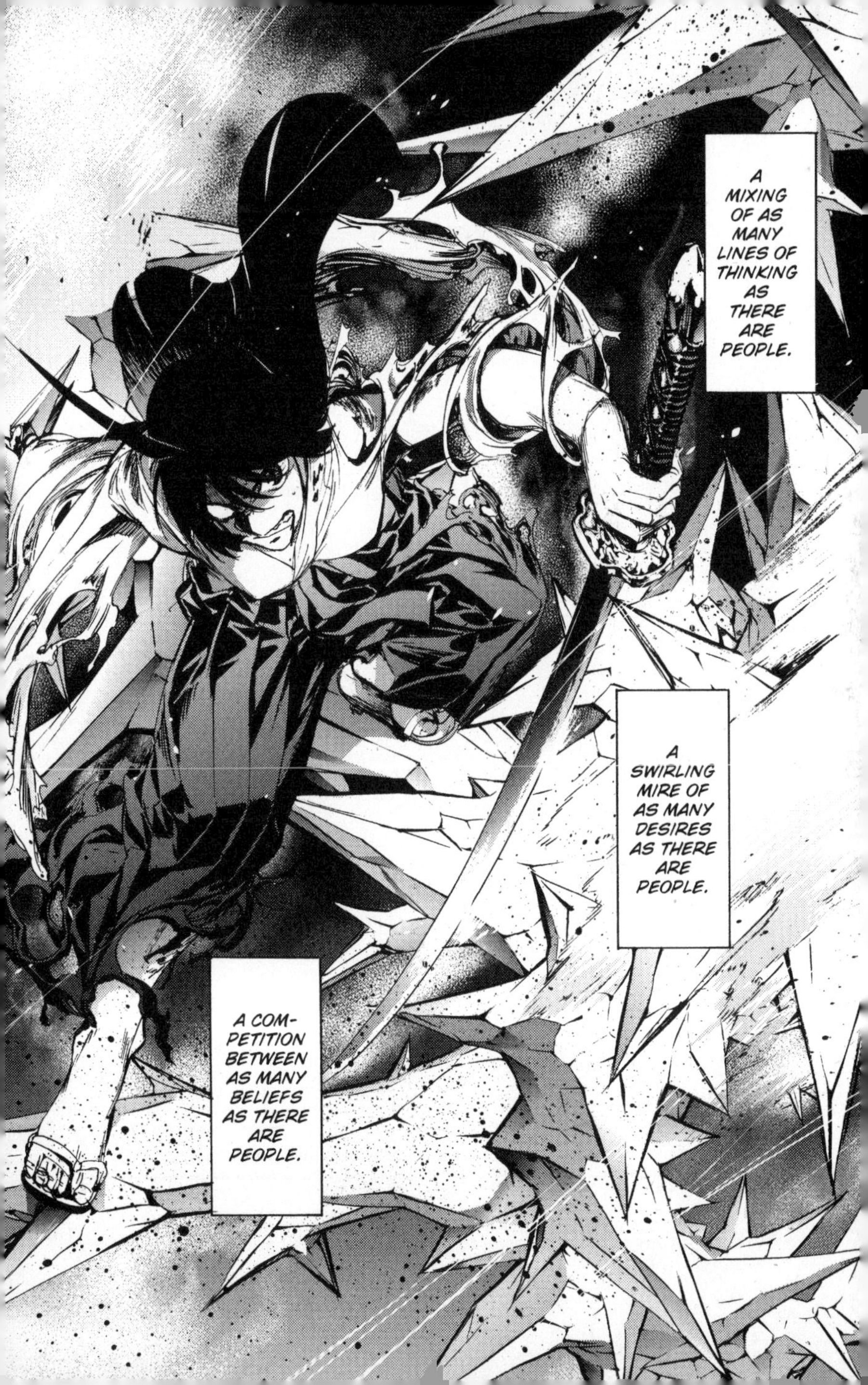
A MIXING OF AS MANY LINES OF THINKING AS THERE ARE PEOPLE.
A SWIRLING MIRE OF AS MANY DESIRES AS THERE ARE PEOPLE.
A COMPETITION BETWEEN AS MANY BELIEFS AS THERE ARE PEOPLE.

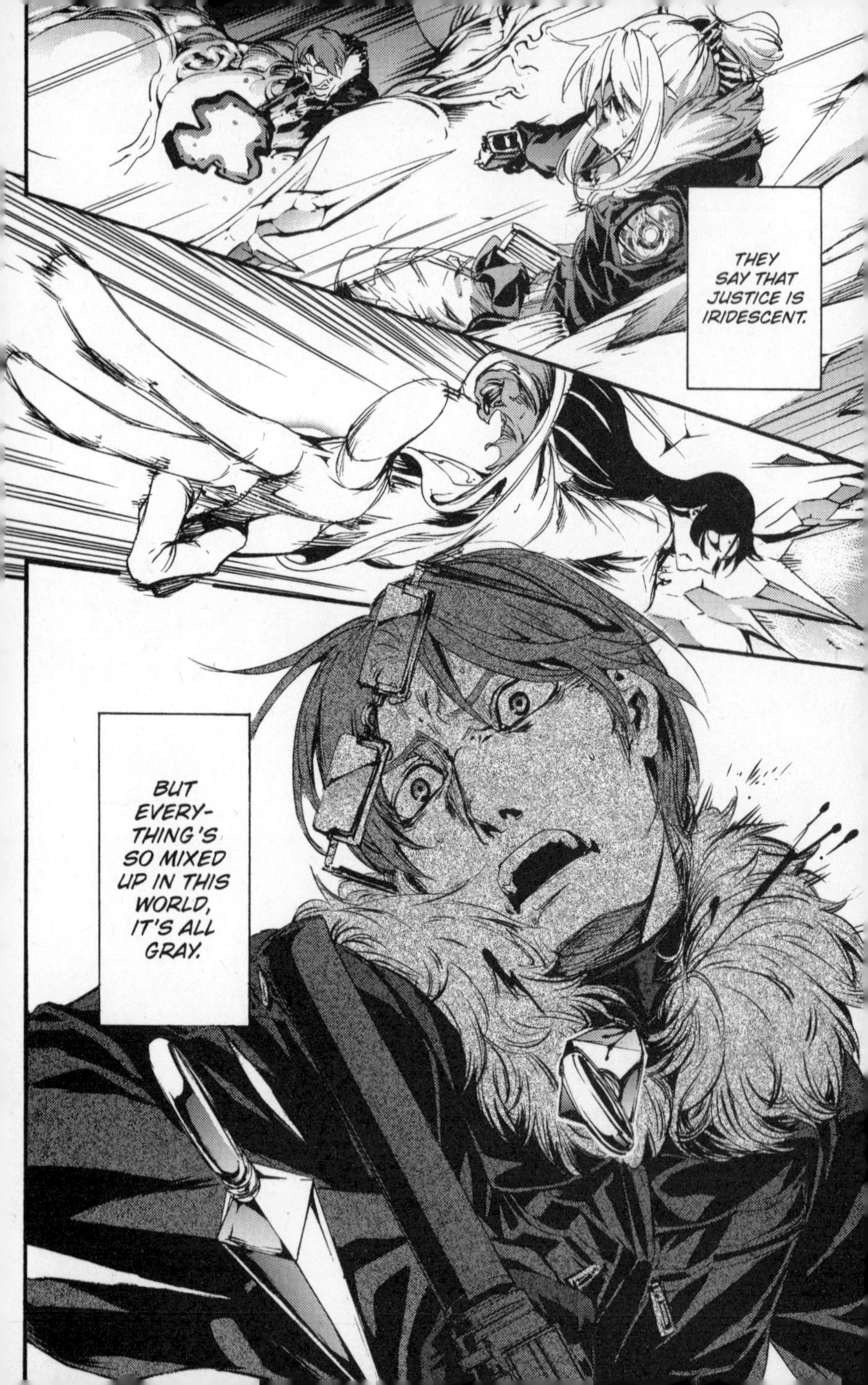
THEY SAY THAT JUSTICE IS IRIDESCENT.
BUT EVERY-THING'S SO MIXED UP IN THIS WORLD, IT'S ALL GRAY.

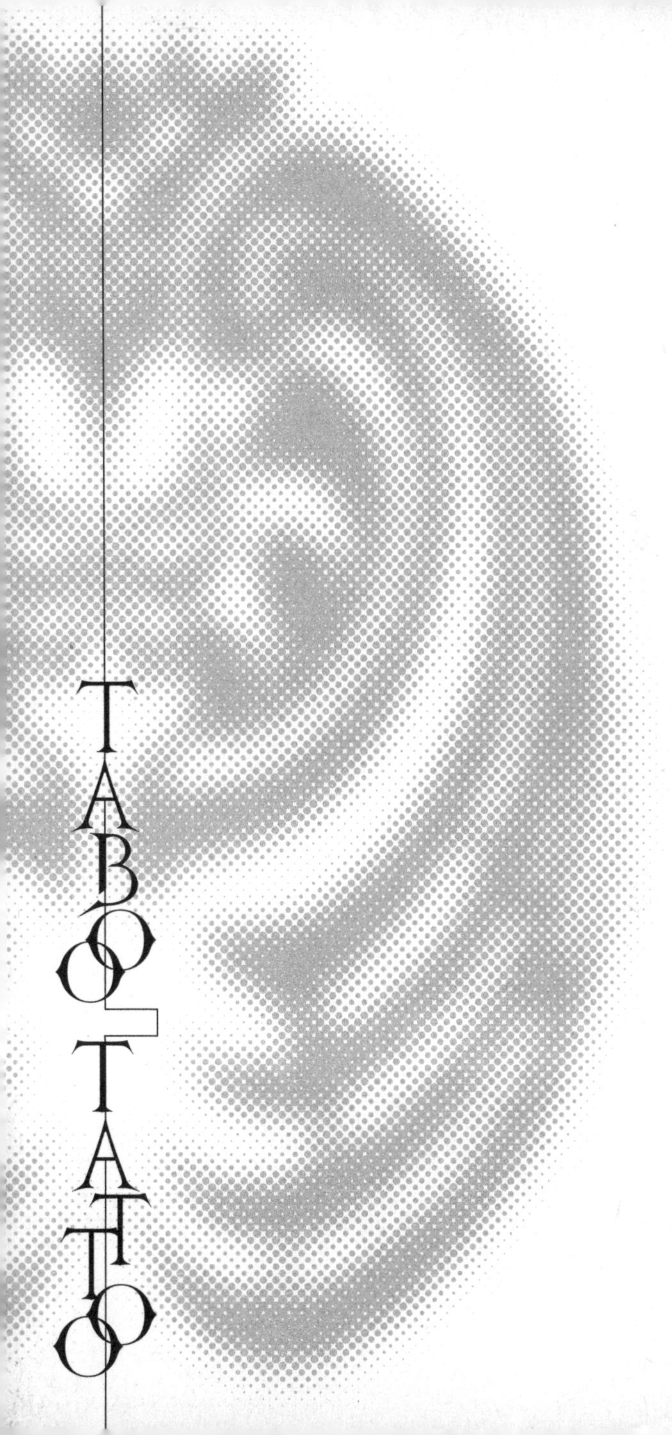

TABOO TATTOO

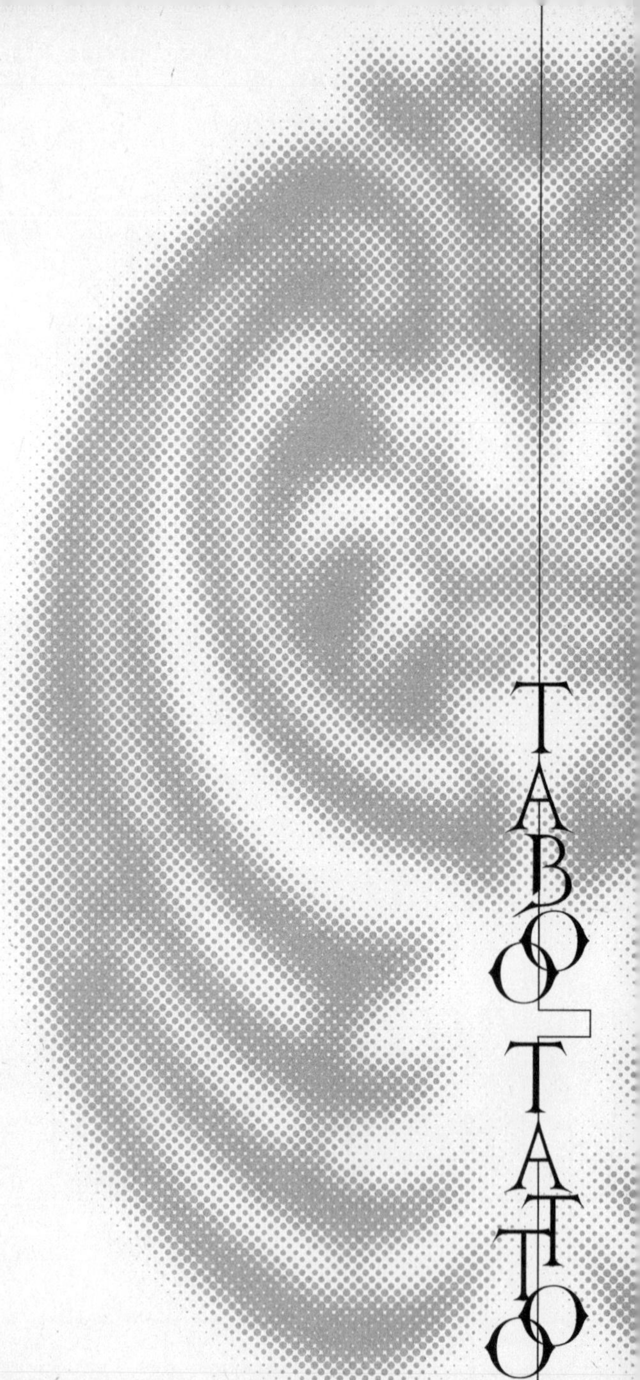

TABOO TATTOO

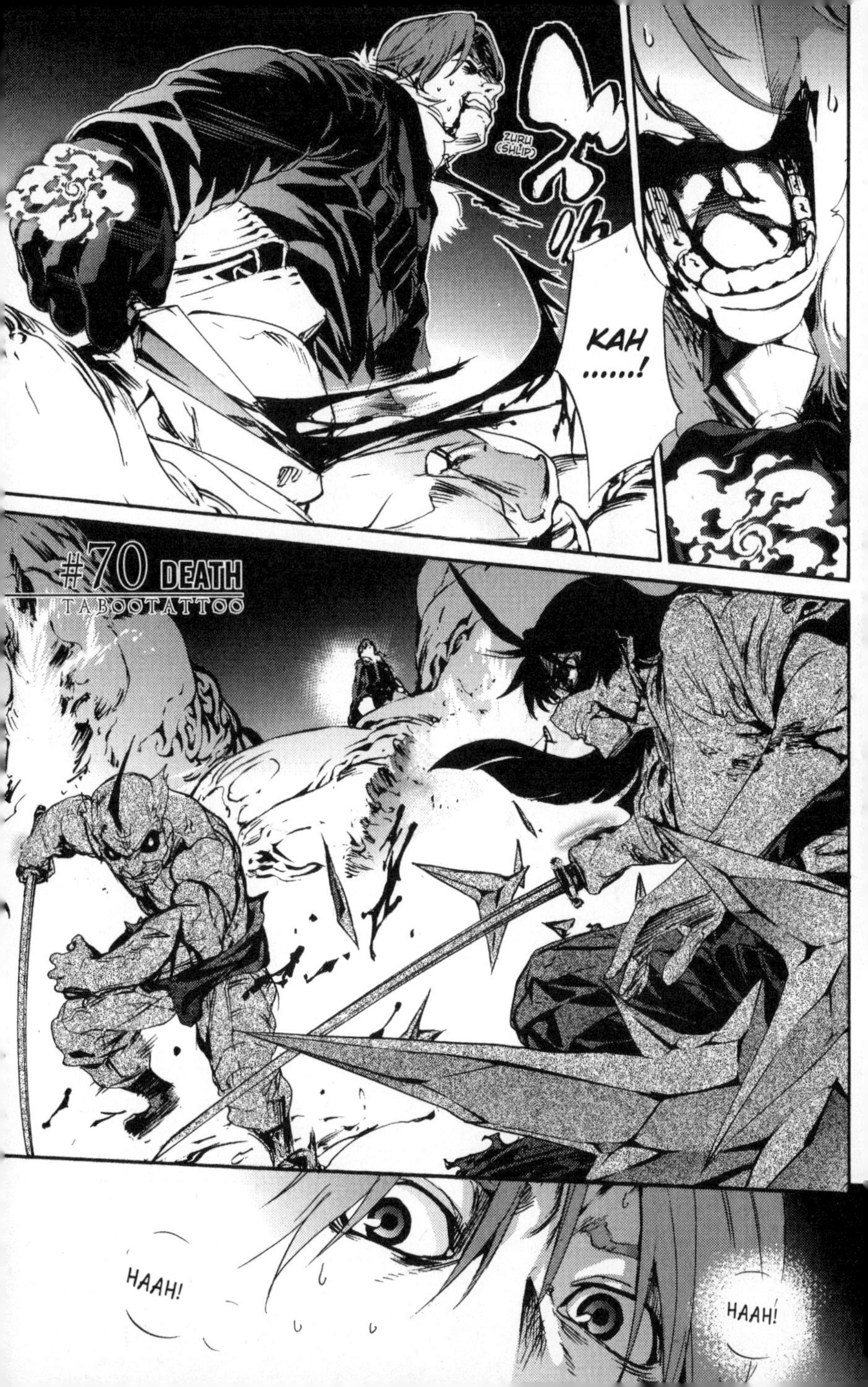
KAH ......!
ZURU (SHLIP)
#70 DEATH
TABOOTATTOO
HAAH!
HAAH!

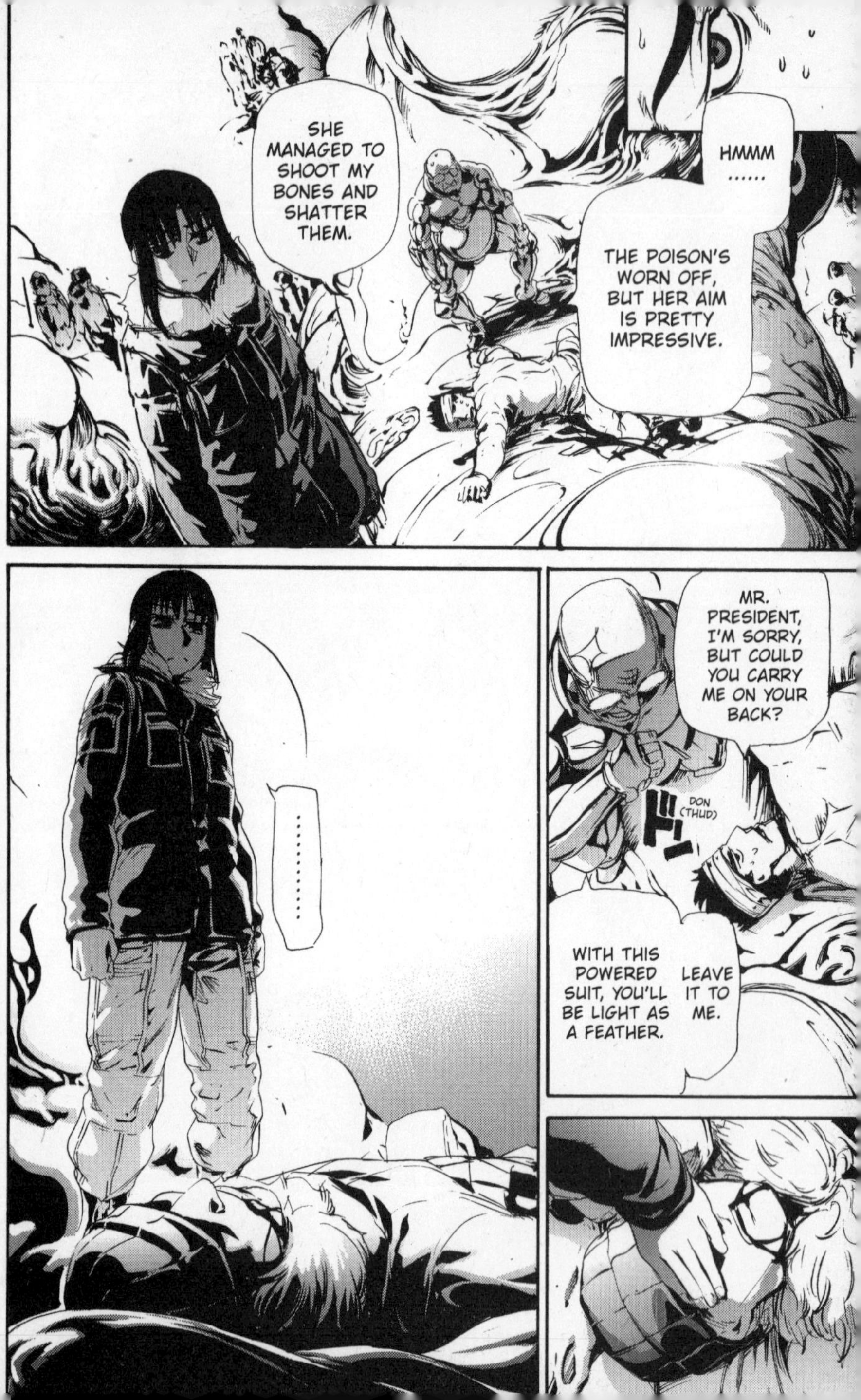
SHE MANAGED TO SHOOT MY BONES AND SHATTER THEM.
HMMM ......
THE POISON'S WORN OFF, BUT HER AIM IS PRETTY IMPRESSIVE.
MR. PRESIDENT, I'M SORRY, BUT COULD YOU CARRY ME ON YOUR BACK?
DON (THUD)
LEAVE IT TO ME.
WITH THIS POWERED SUIT, YOU'LL BE LIGHT AS A FEATHER.
......

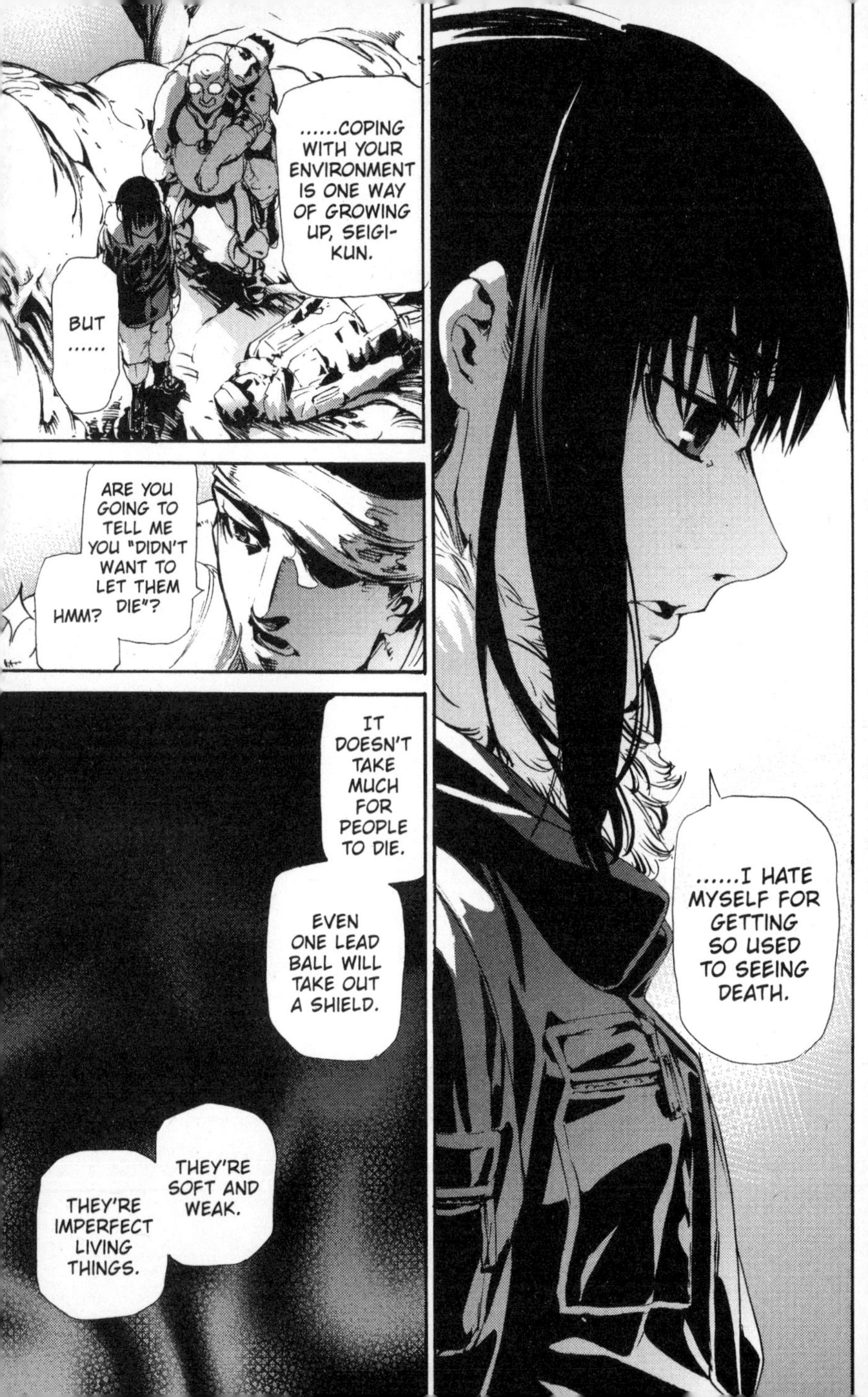
......I HATE MYSELF FOR GETTING SO USED TO SEEING DEATH.
......COPING WITH YOUR ENVIRONMENT IS ONE WAY OF GROWING UP, SEIGI-KUN.
BUT ......
ARE YOU GOING TO TELL ME YOU "DIDN'T WANT TO LET THEM DIE"?
HMM?
IT DOESN'T TAKE MUCH FOR PEOPLE TO DIE.
EVEN ONE LEAD BALL WILL TAKE OUT A SHIELD.
THEY'RE SOFT AND WEAK.
THEY'RE IMPERFECT LIVING THINGS.

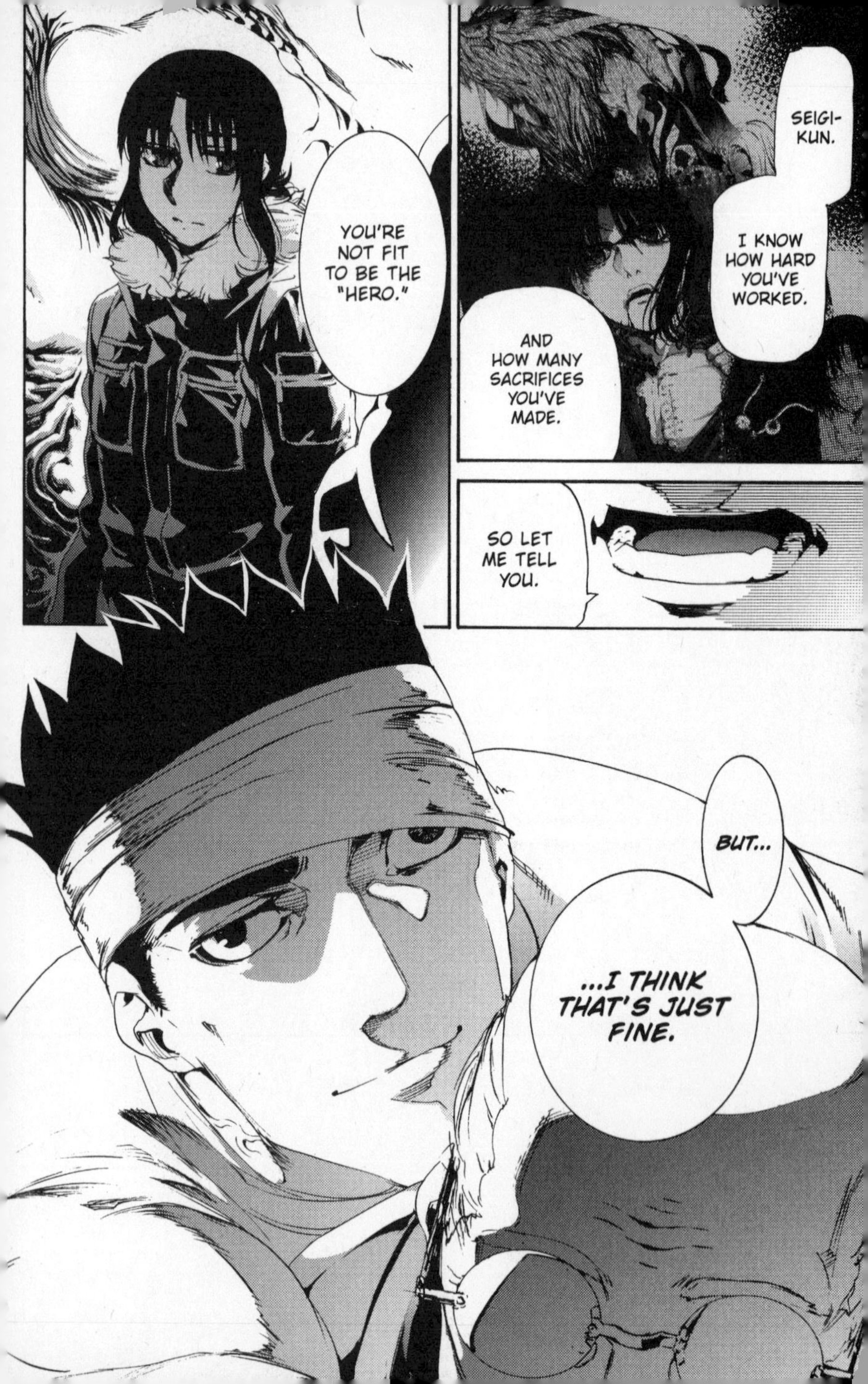
SEIGI-KUN.
I KNOW HOW HARD YOU'VE WORKED.
AND HOW MANY SACRIFICES YOU'VE MADE.
SO LET ME TELL YOU.
YOU'RE NOT FIT TO BE THE "HERO."
BUT...
...I THINK THAT'S JUST FINE.

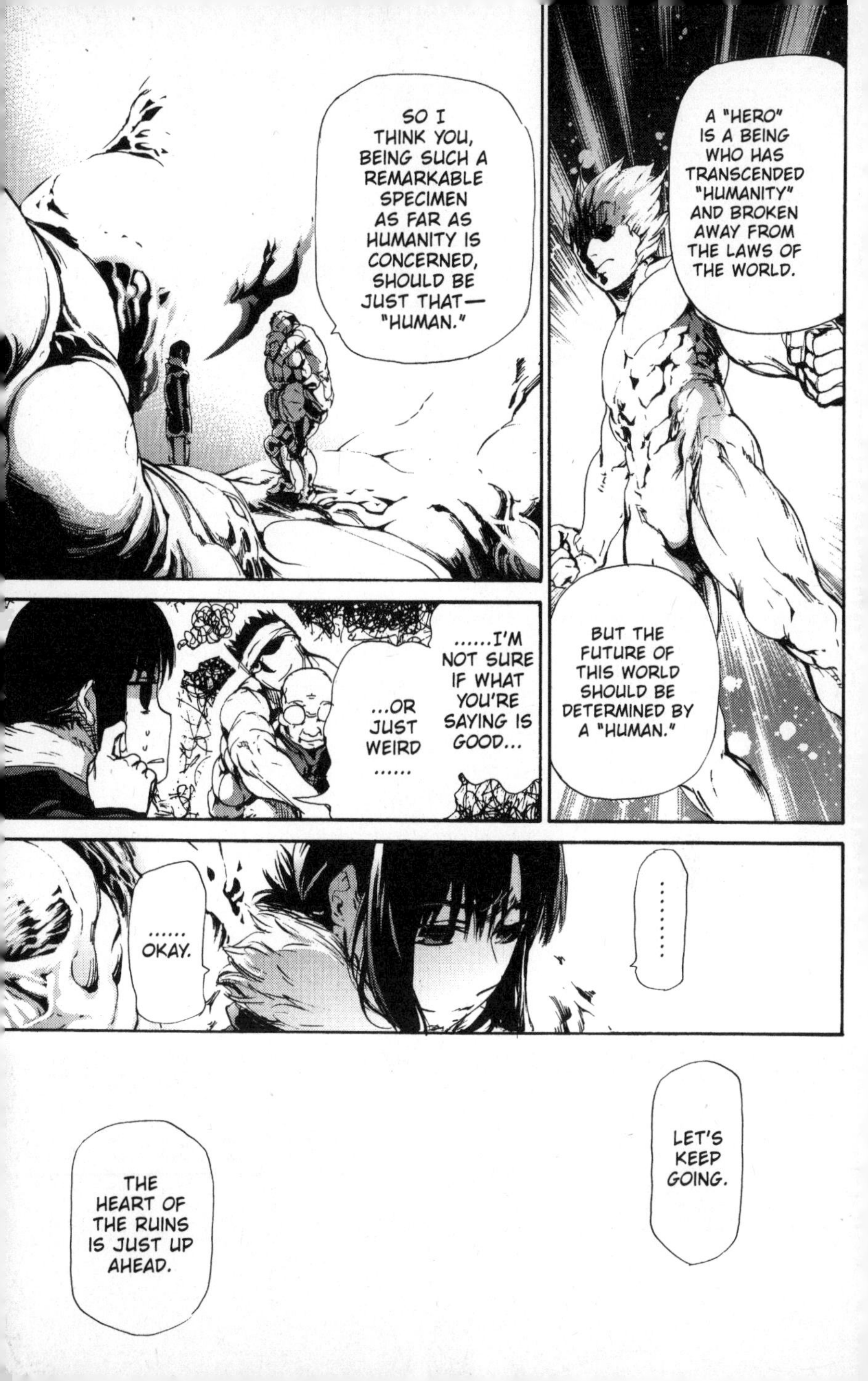
A "HERO" IS A BEING WHO HAS TRANSCENDED "HUMANITY" AND BROKEN AWAY FROM THE LAWS OF THE WORLD.
BUT THE FUTURE OF THIS WORLD SHOULD BE DETERMINED BY A "HUMAN."
SO I THINK YOU, BEING SUCH A REMARKABLE SPECIMEN AS FAR AS HUMANITY IS CONCERNED, SHOULD BE JUST THAT— "HUMAN."
......I'M NOT SURE IF WHAT YOU'RE SAYING IS GOOD...
...OR JUST WEIRD ......
....
...... OKAY.
LET'S KEEP GOING.
THE HEART OF THE RUINS IS JUST UP AHEAD.

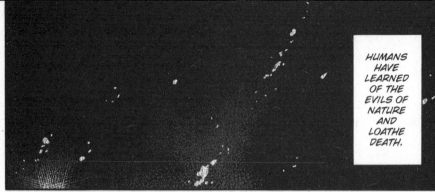

HUMANS HAVE LEARNED OF THE EVILS OF NATURE AND LOATHE DEATH.

THEY'VE LEARNED THE EVILS OF SOCIETY AND LOATHE LIFE.

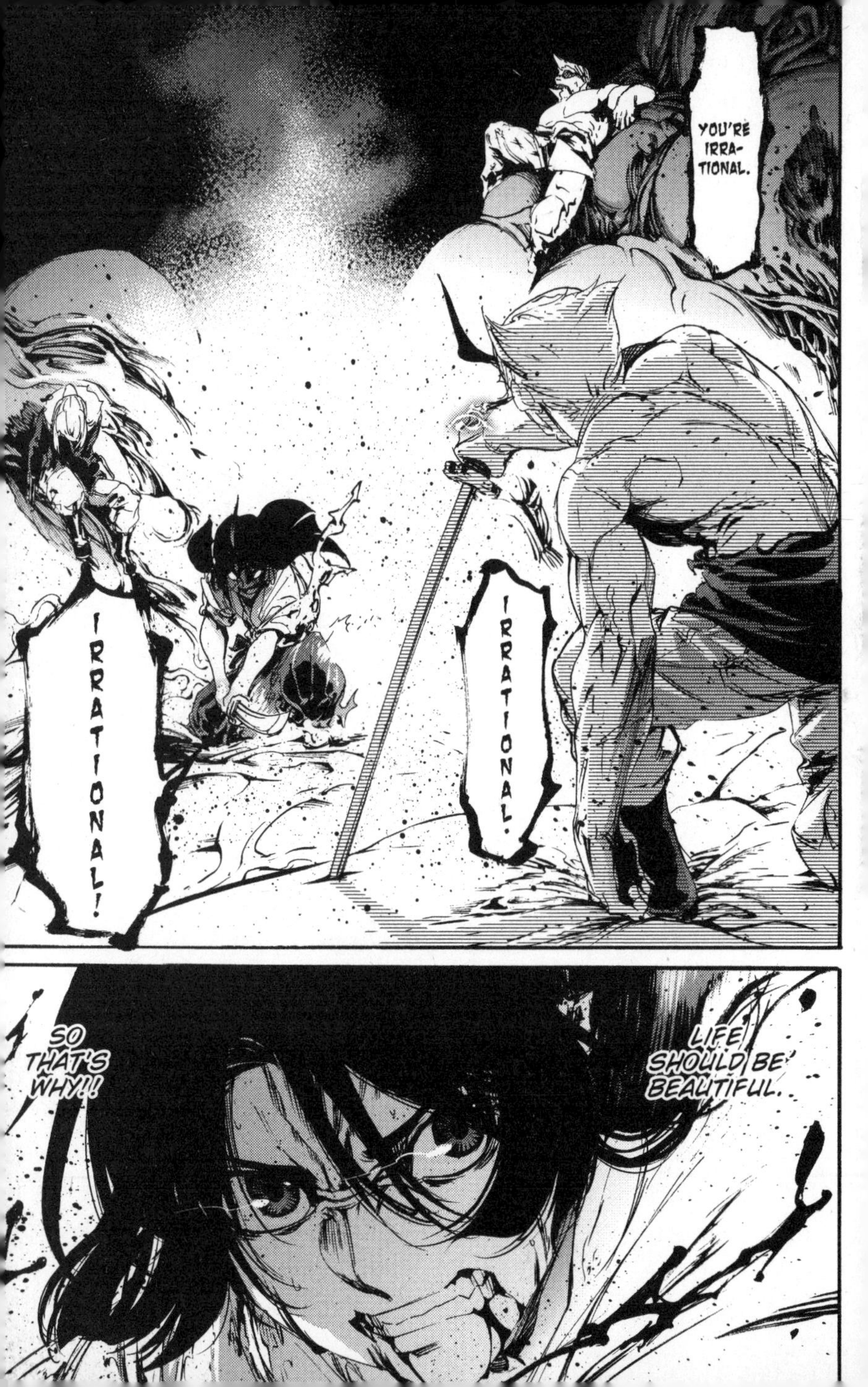
YOU'RE IRRA-TIONAL.
IRRATIONAL.
IRRATIONAL!
LIFE SHOULD BE BEAUTIFUL.
SO THAT'S WHY!!

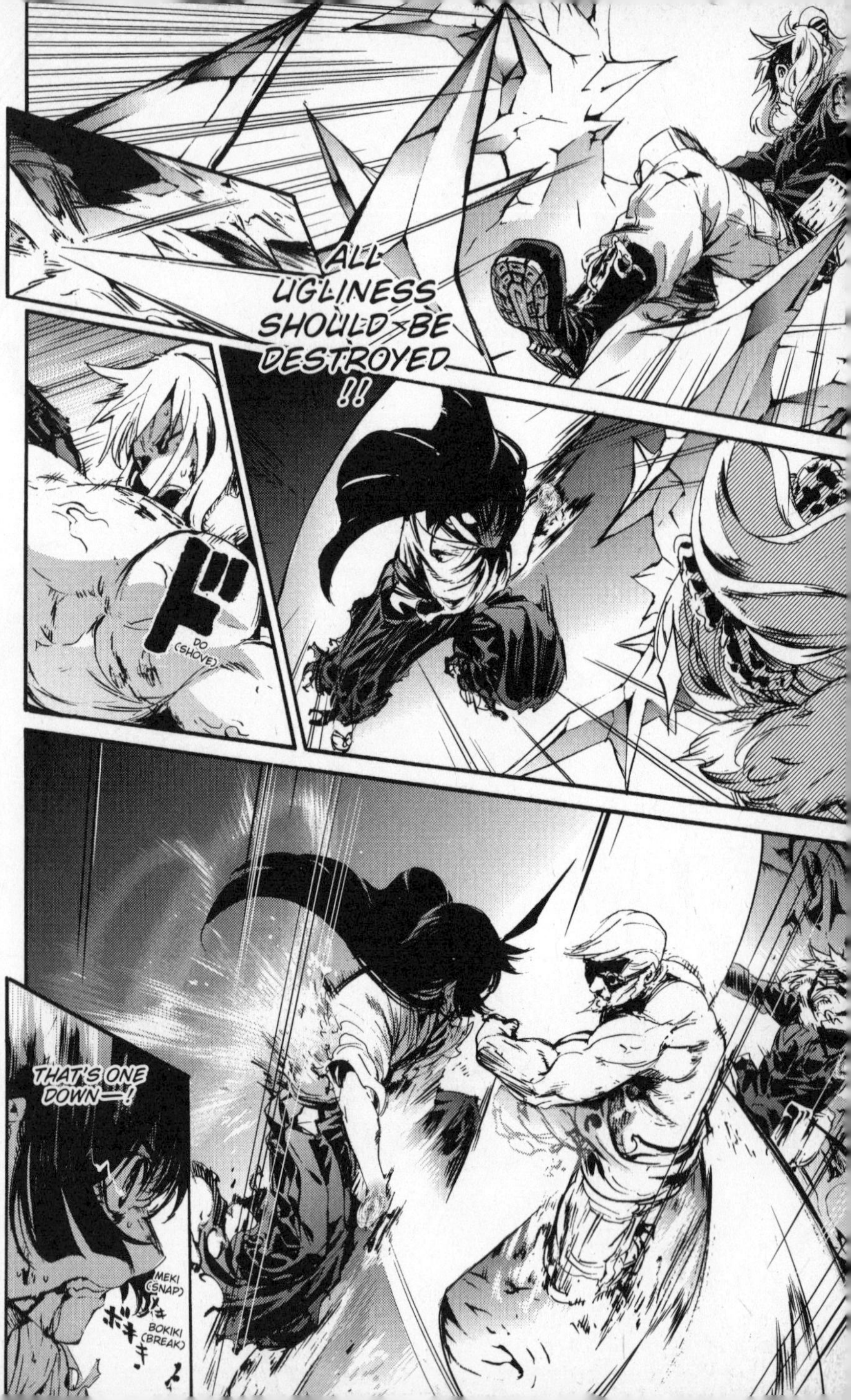
ALL UGLINESS SHOULD BE DESTROYED!!
ド
DO (SHOVE)
THAT'S ONE DOWN—!
メキ
MEKI (SNAP)
ボキキ
BOKIKI (BREAK)

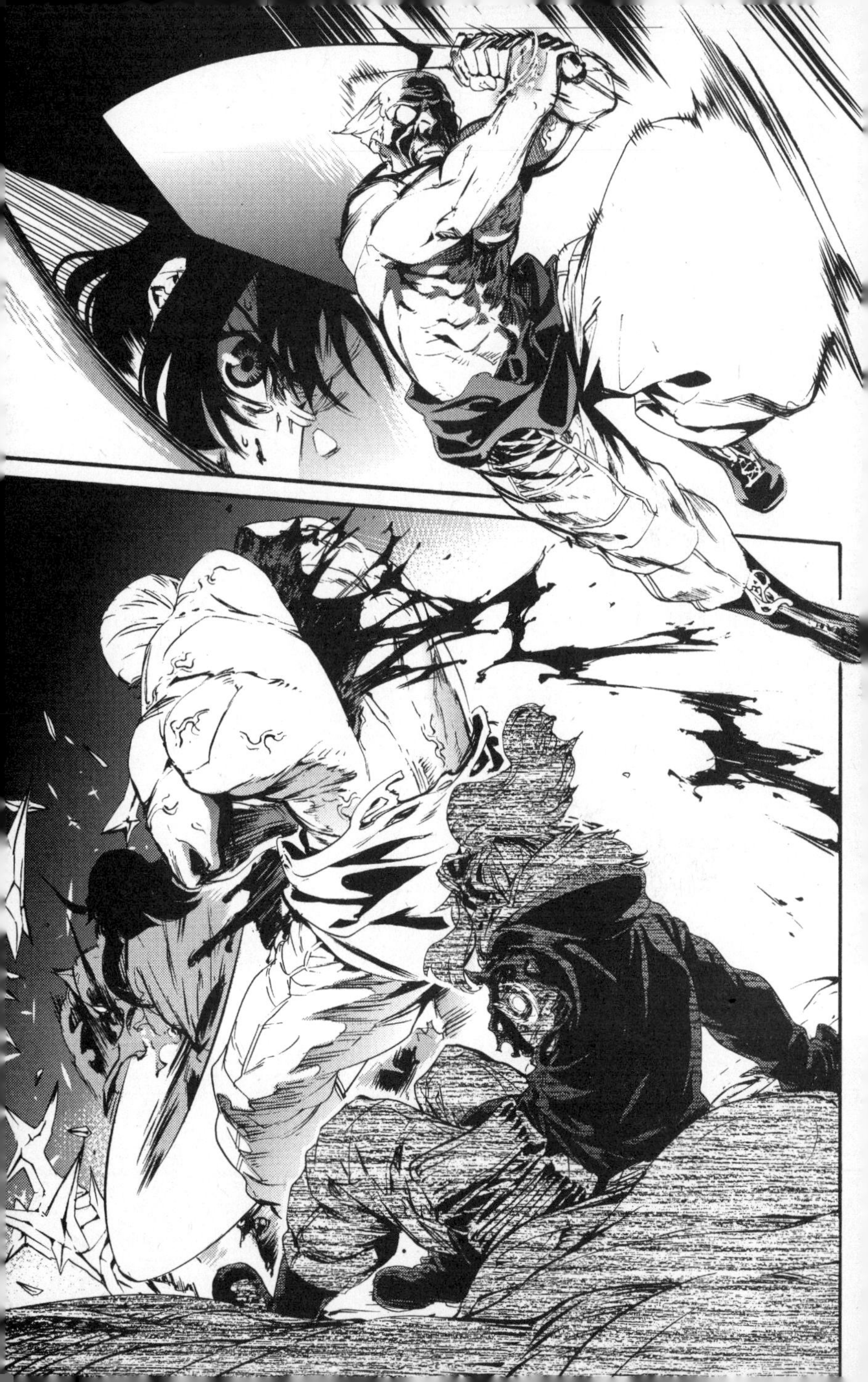

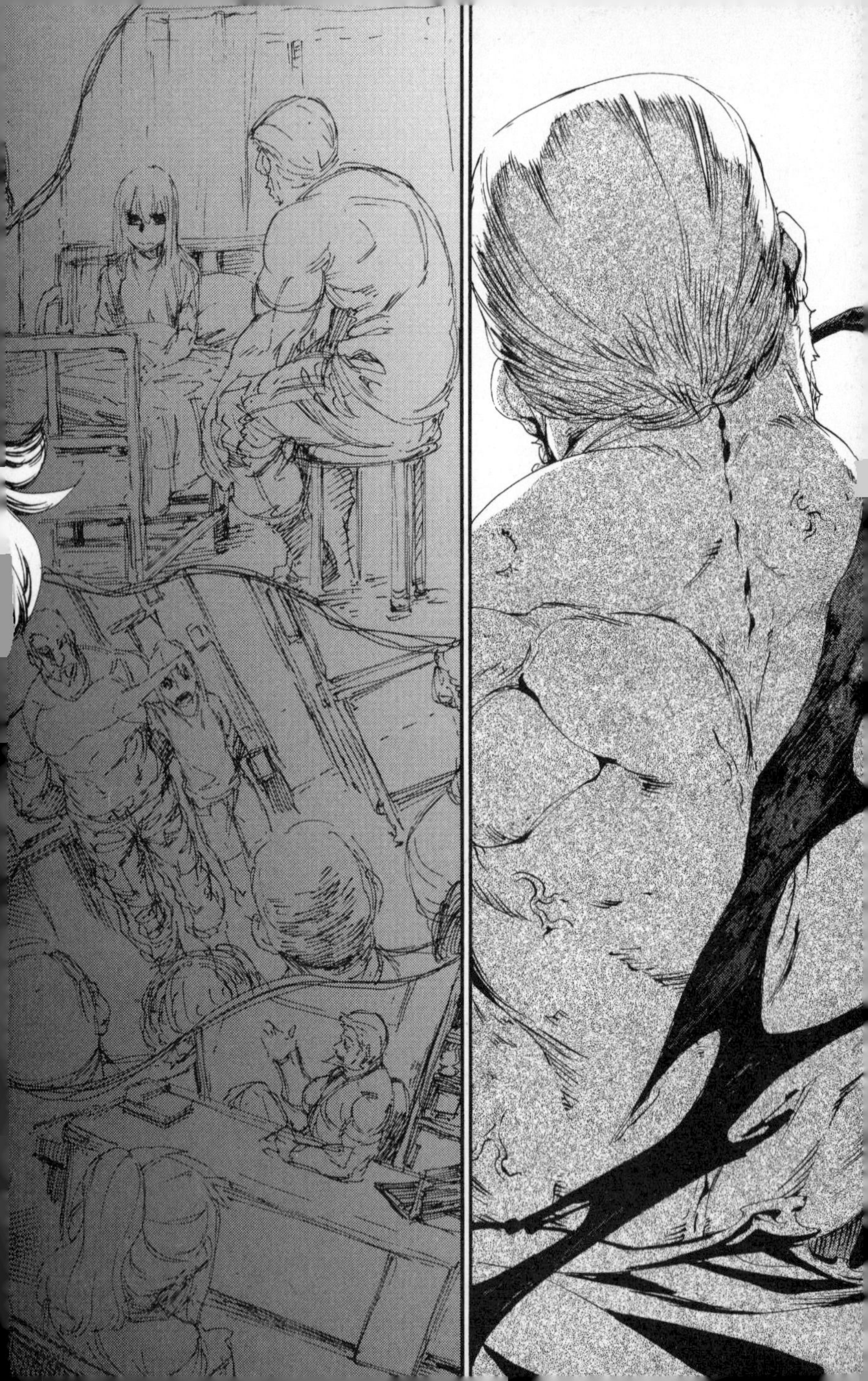

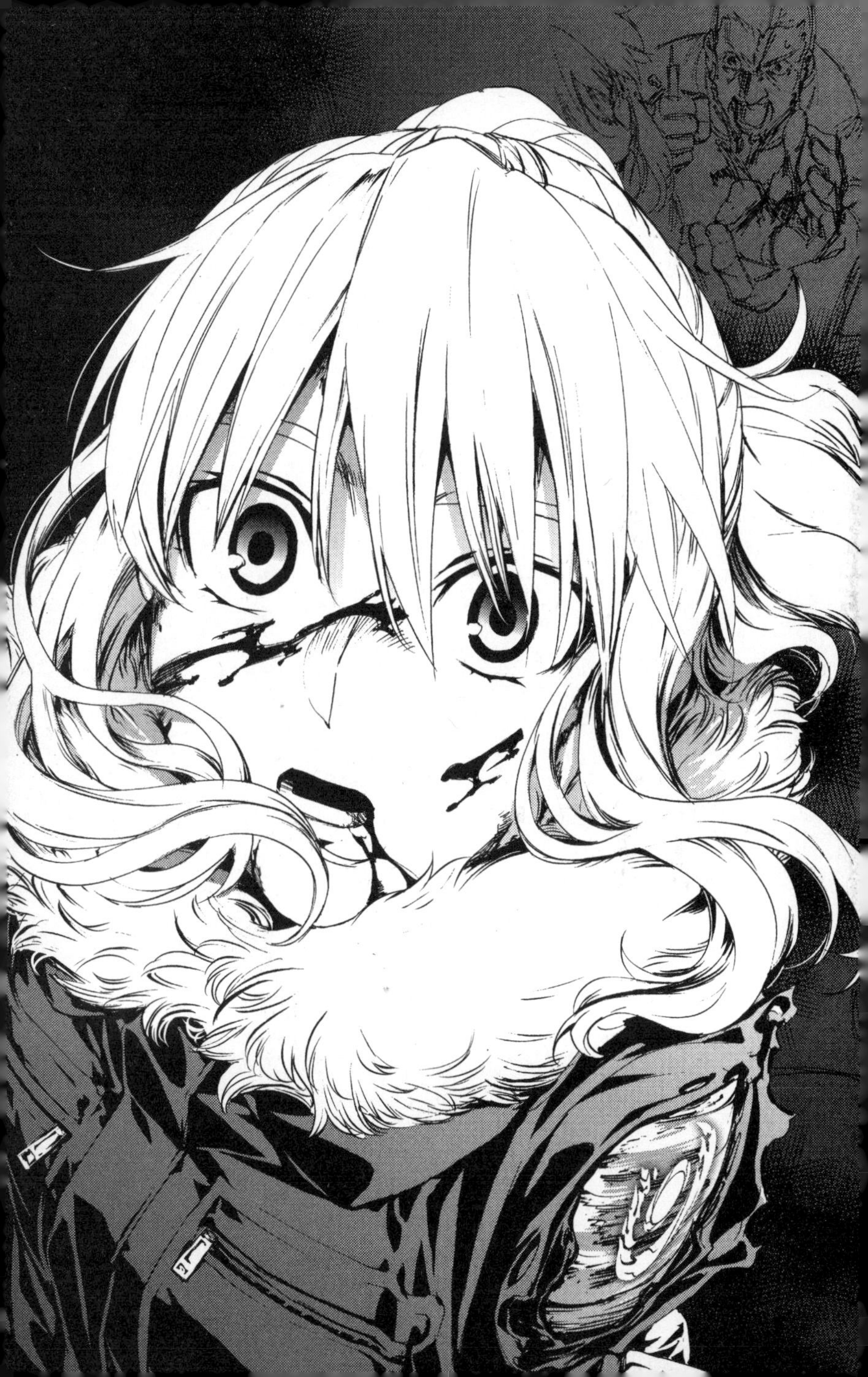

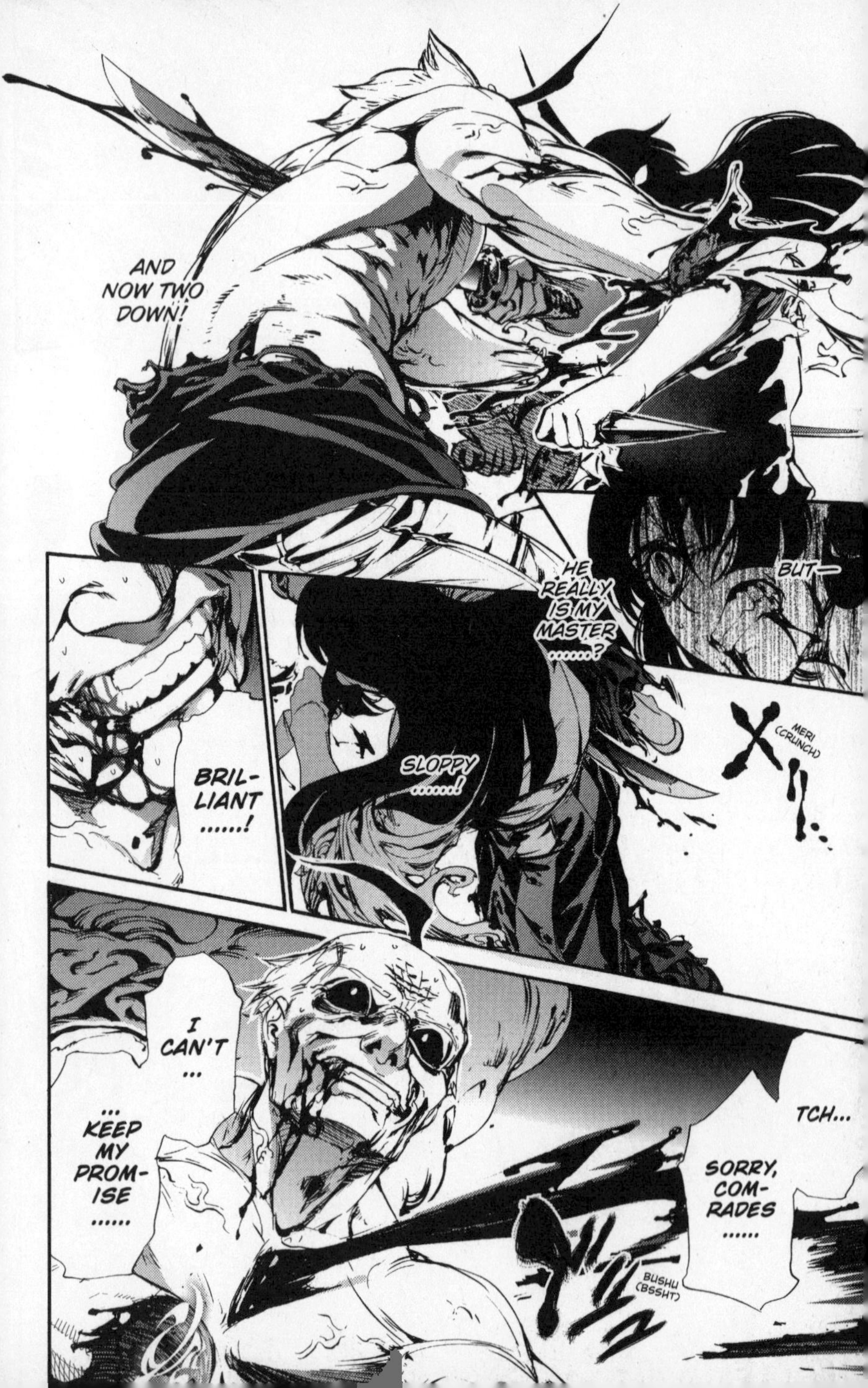
AND NOW TWO DOWN!
BUT—
HE REALLY IS MY MASTER ......?
MERI (CRUNCH)
SLOPPY ......!
BRILLIANT ......!
TCH...
SORRY, COMRADES ......
BUSHU (BSSHT)
I CAN'T ...
... KEEP MY PROMISE ......

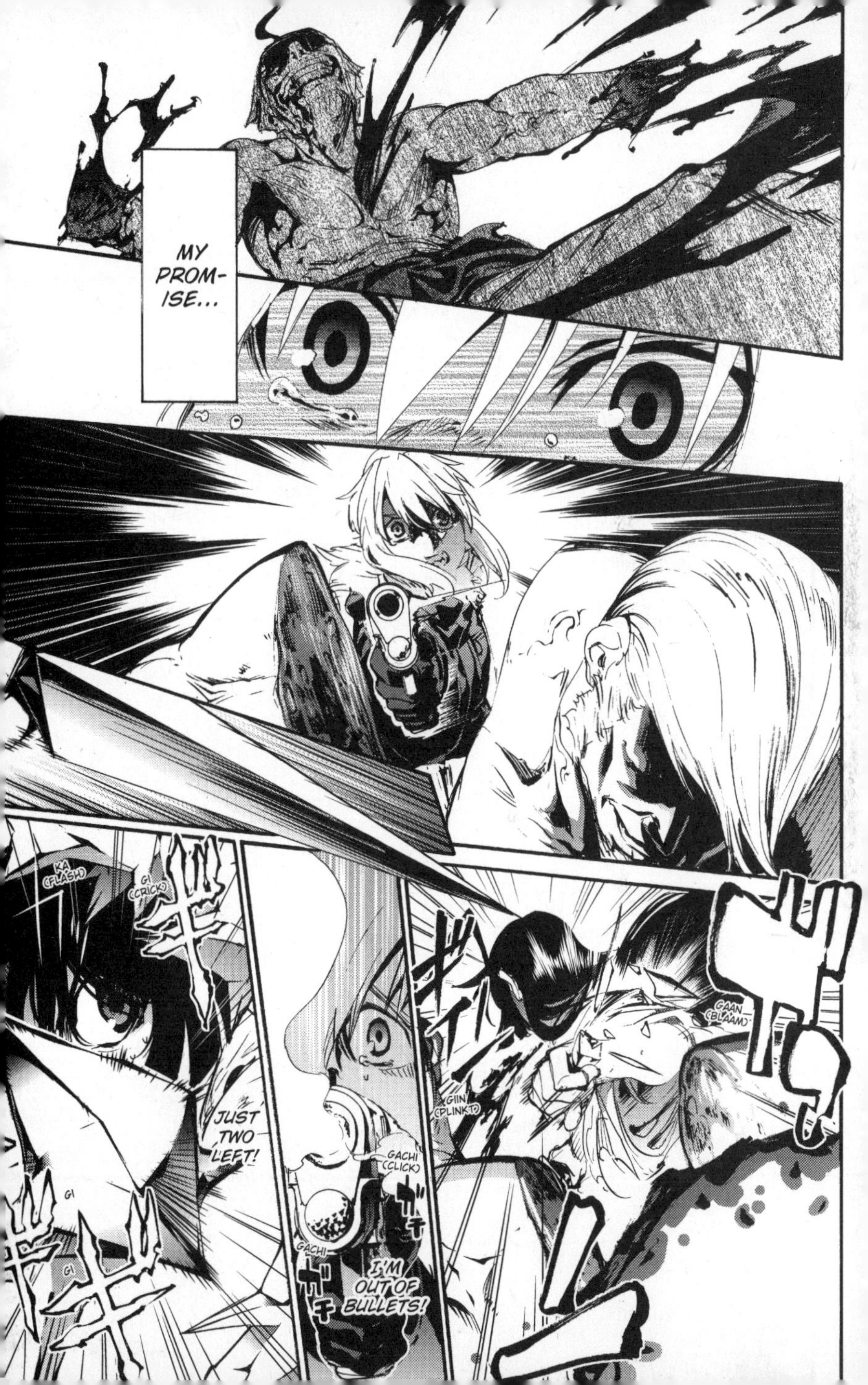
MY PROMISE...
GAAN (BLAAM)
GIIN (PLINK!)
GACHI (CLICK)
GACHI
I'M OUT OF BULLETS!
KA (FLASH)
GI (CRICK)
JUST TWO LEFT!
GI
GI

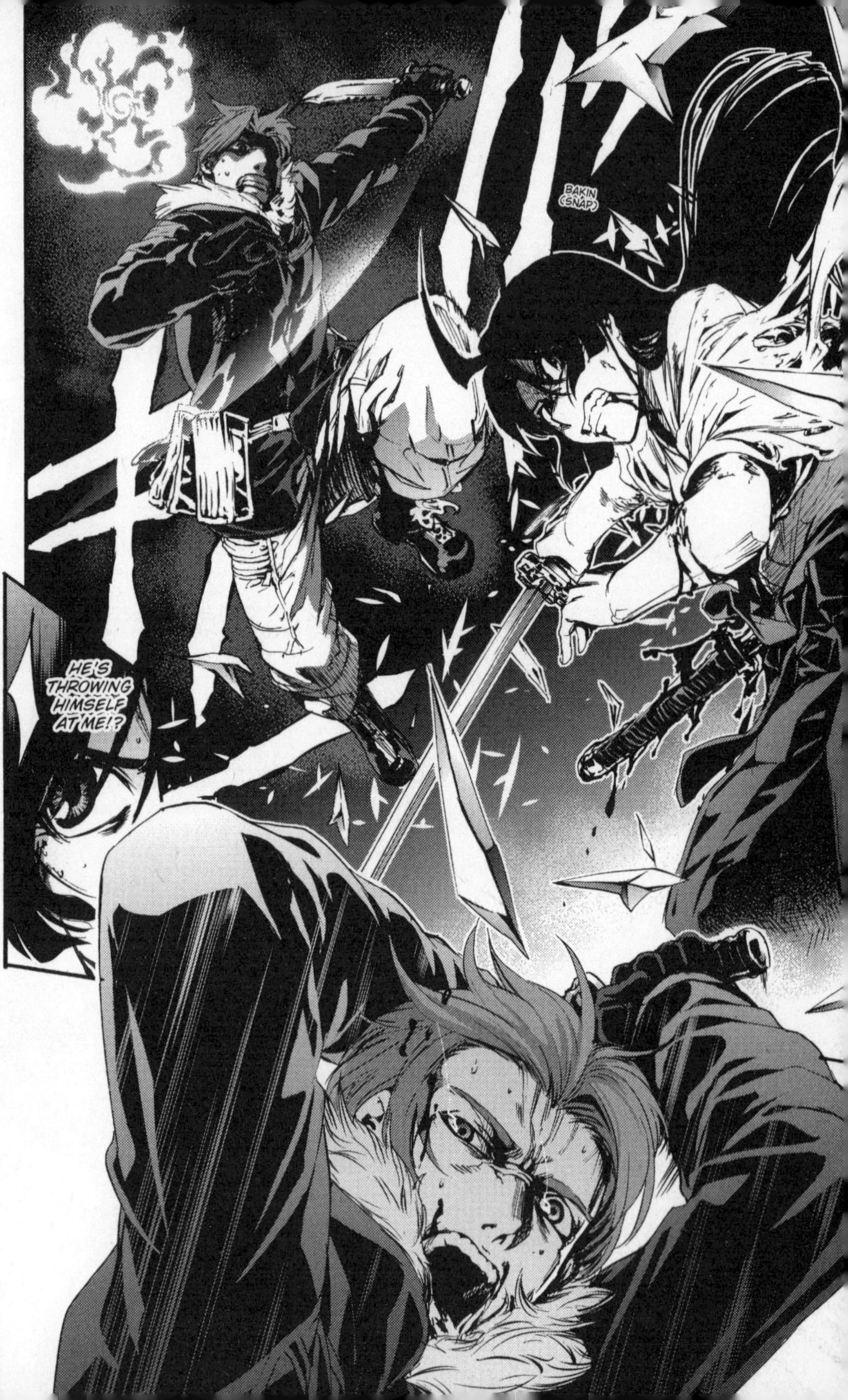
BAKIN (SNAP)
HE'S THROWING HIMSELF AT ME!?

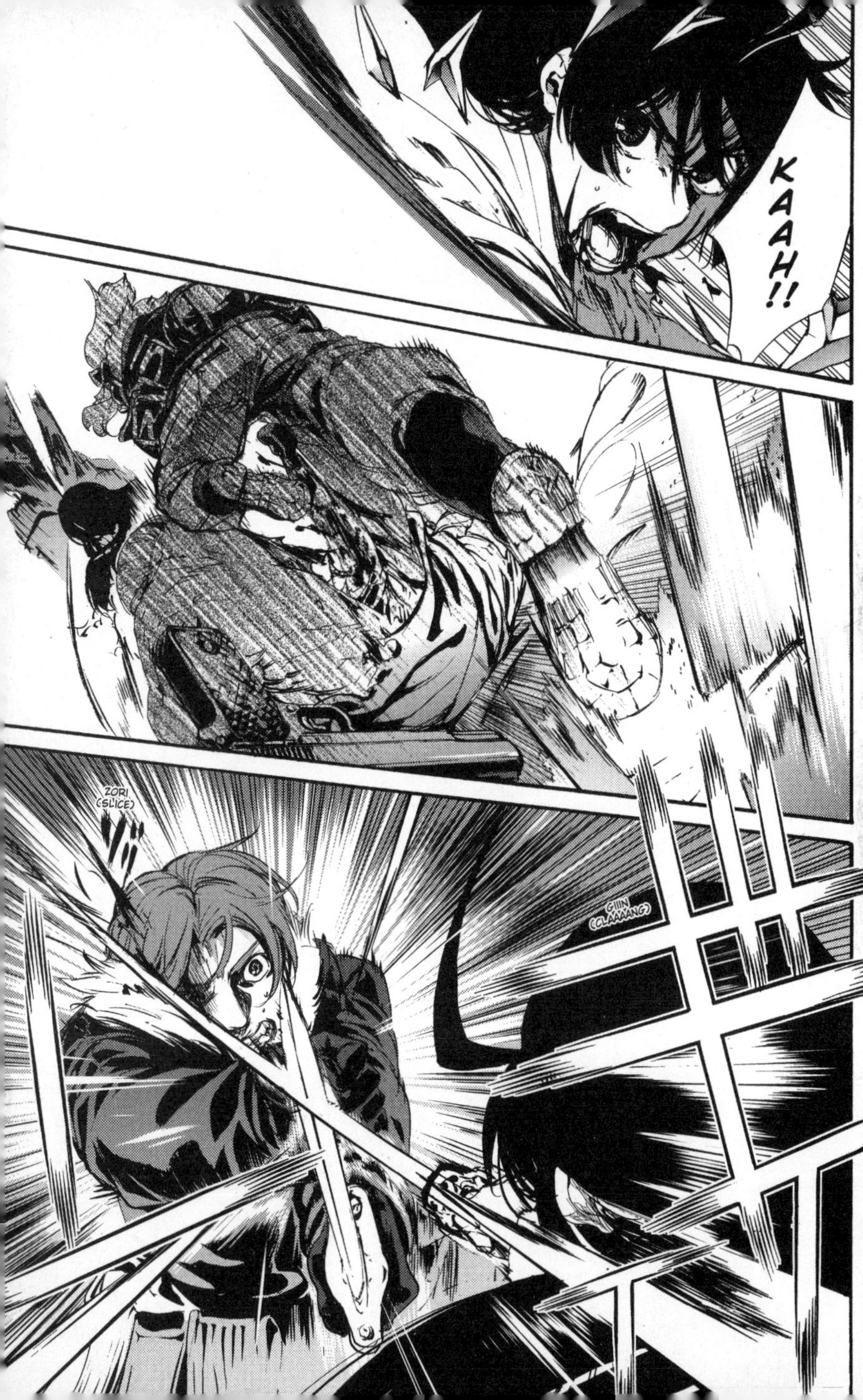
KAAAH!!
GIIIN (CLAAAANG)
ZORI (SLICE)

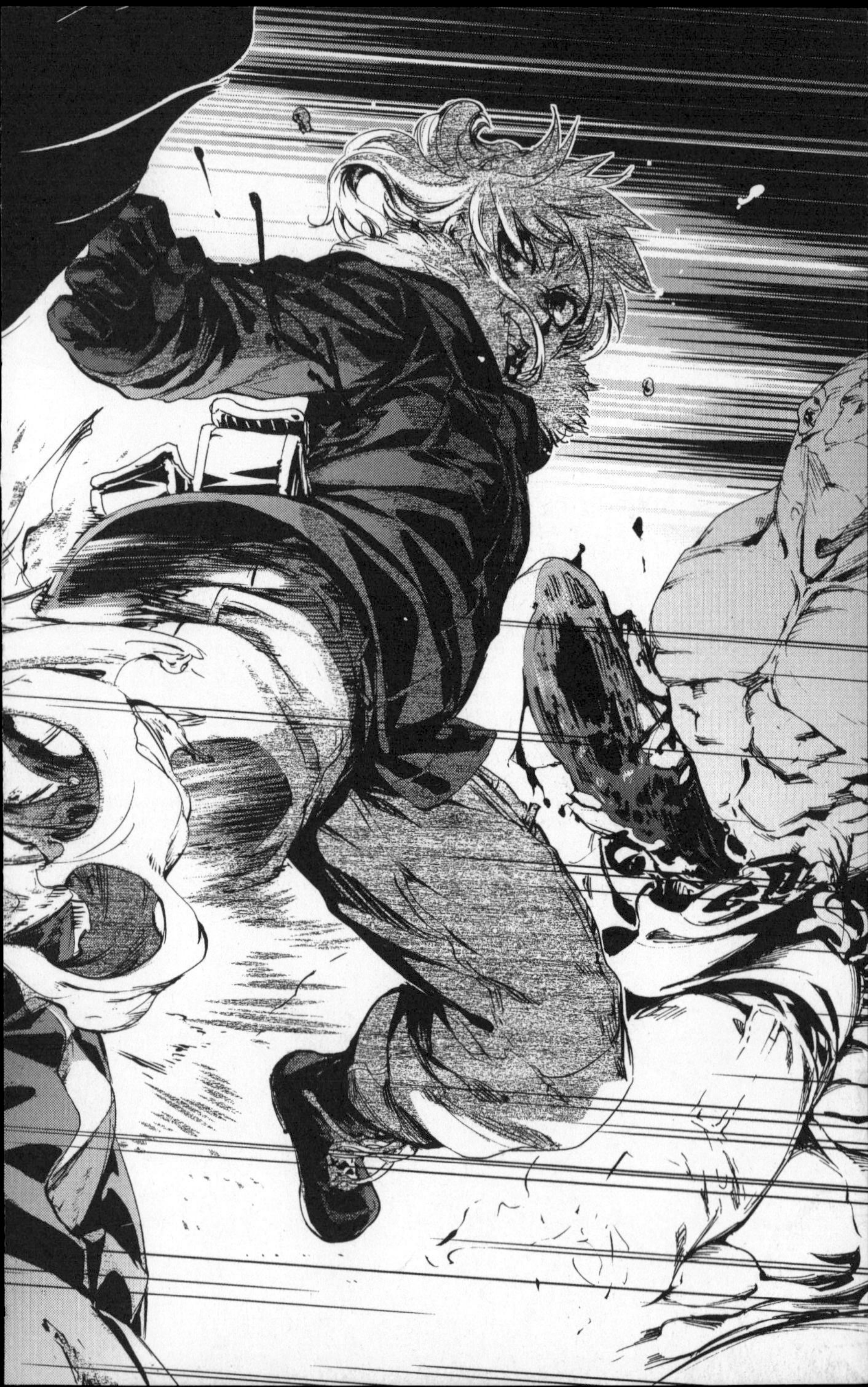

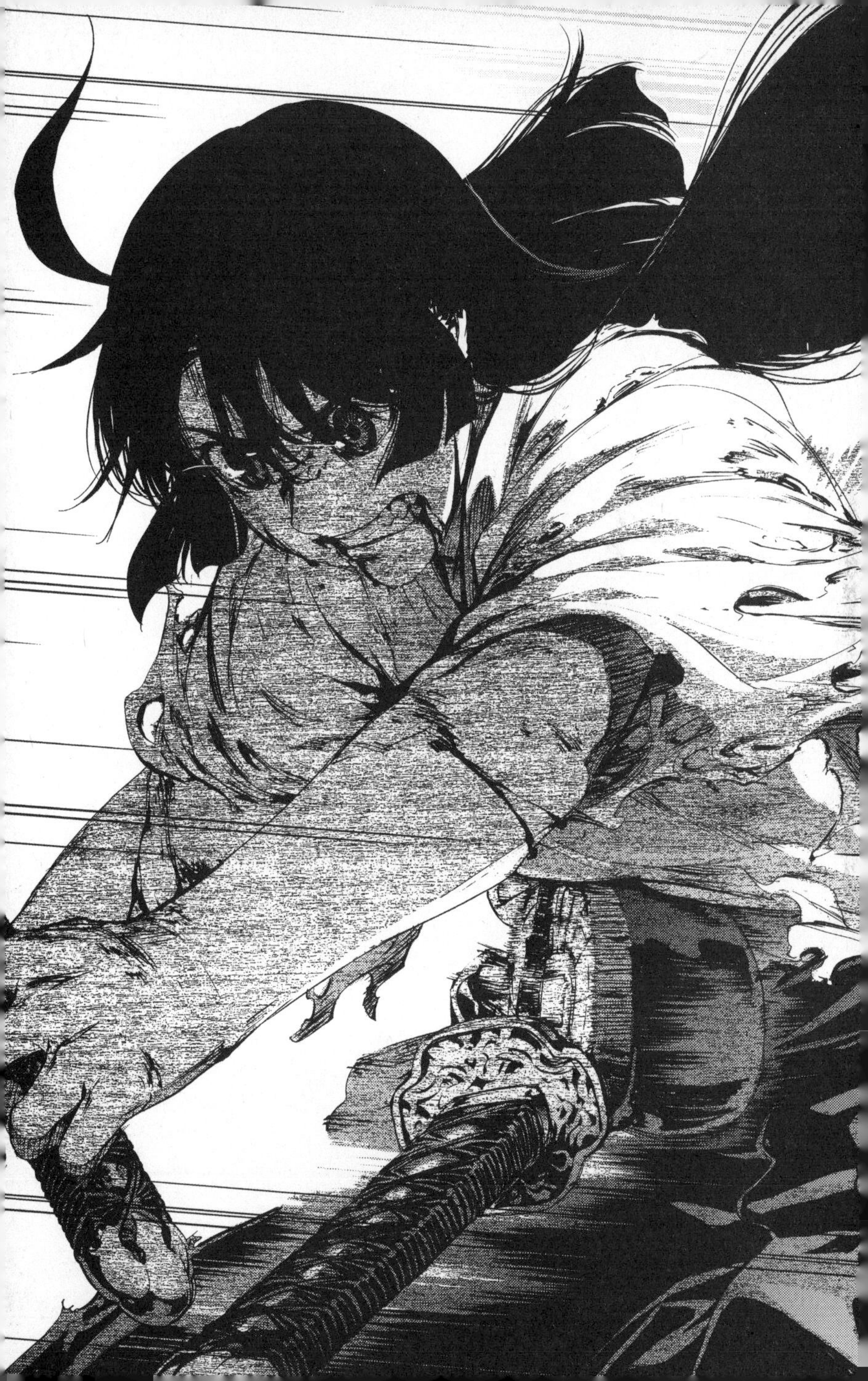

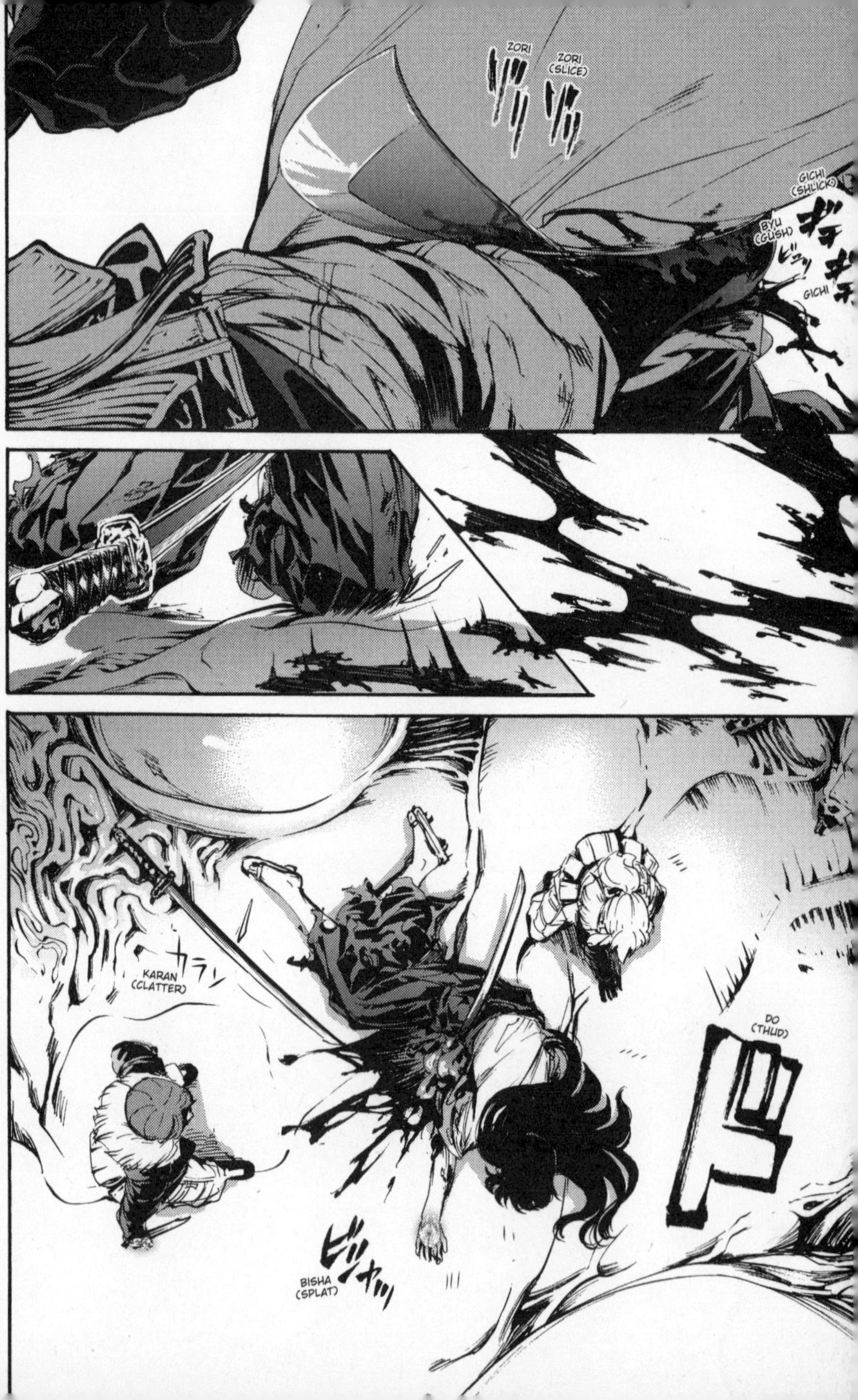
GICHI (SHLICK)
BYU (GUSH)
GICHI
ZORI (SLICE)
ZORI
DO (THUD)
KARAN (CLATTER)
BISHA (SPLAT)

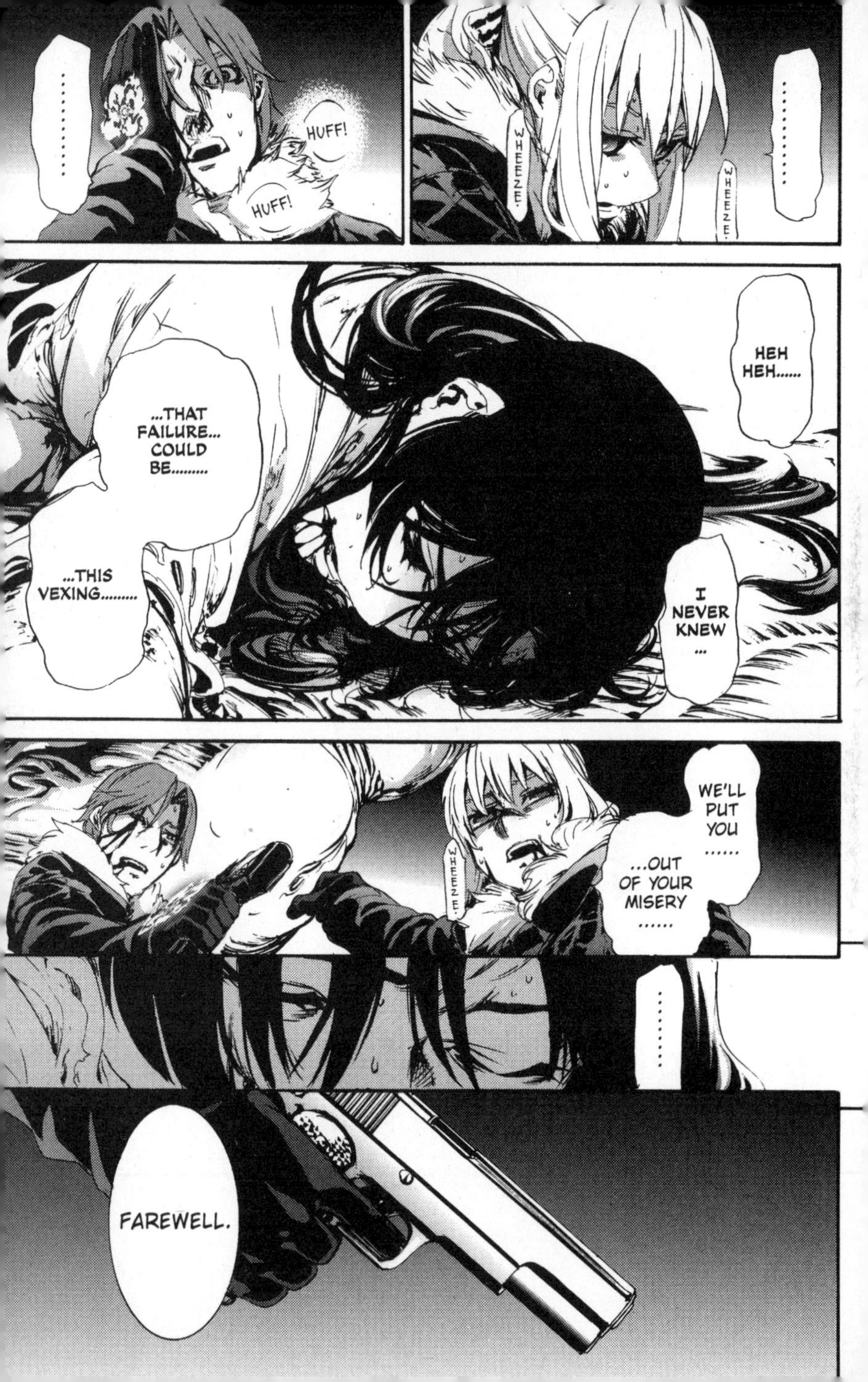
......
WHEEZE.
WHEEZE.
HUFF!
HUFF!
......
HEH HEH......
I NEVER KNEW ...
...THAT FAILURE... COULD BE.........
...THIS VEXING.........
WE'LL PUT YOU ......
...OUT OF YOUR MISERY ......
WHEEZE.
......
FAREWELL.

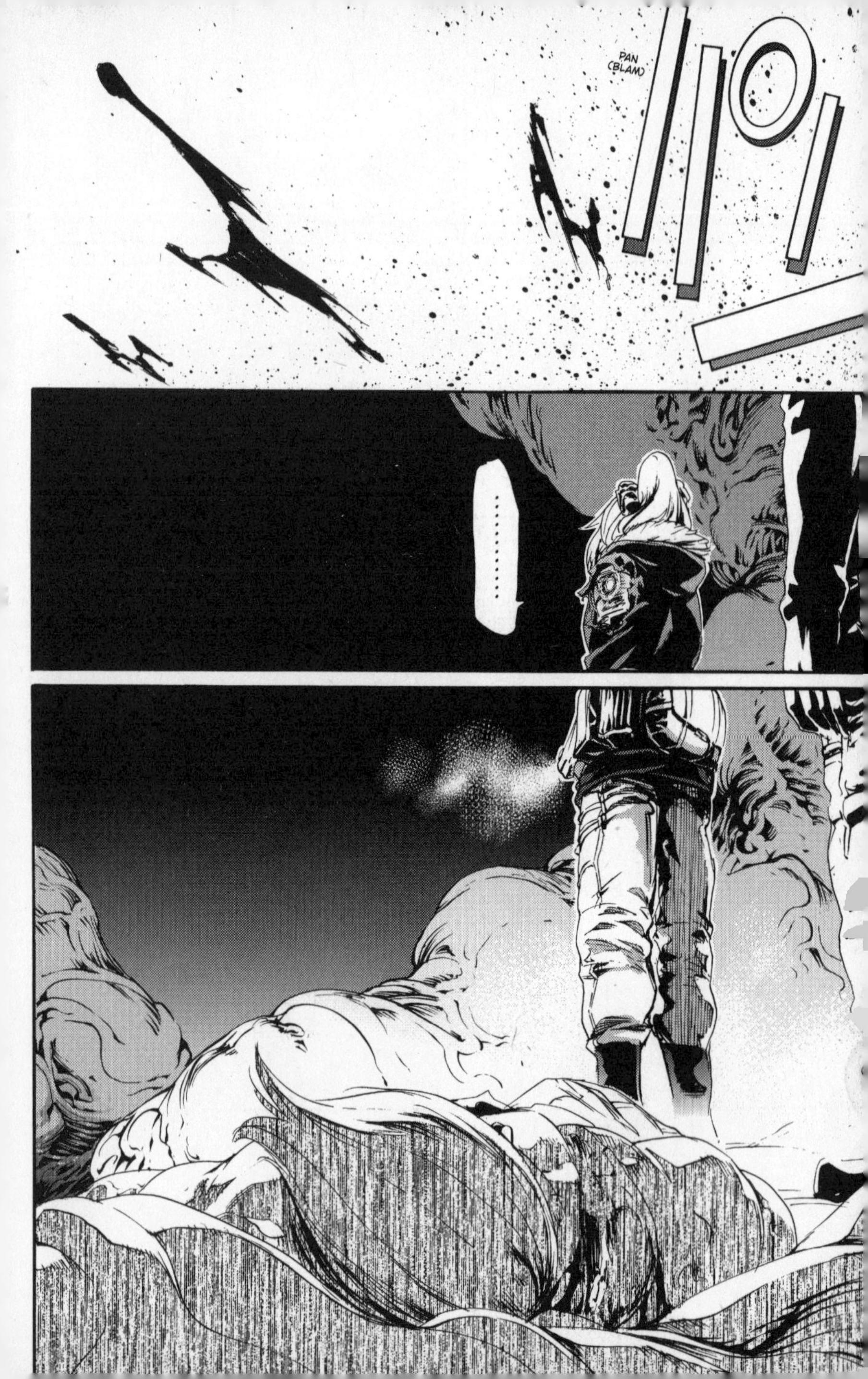
PAN
(BLAM)
……

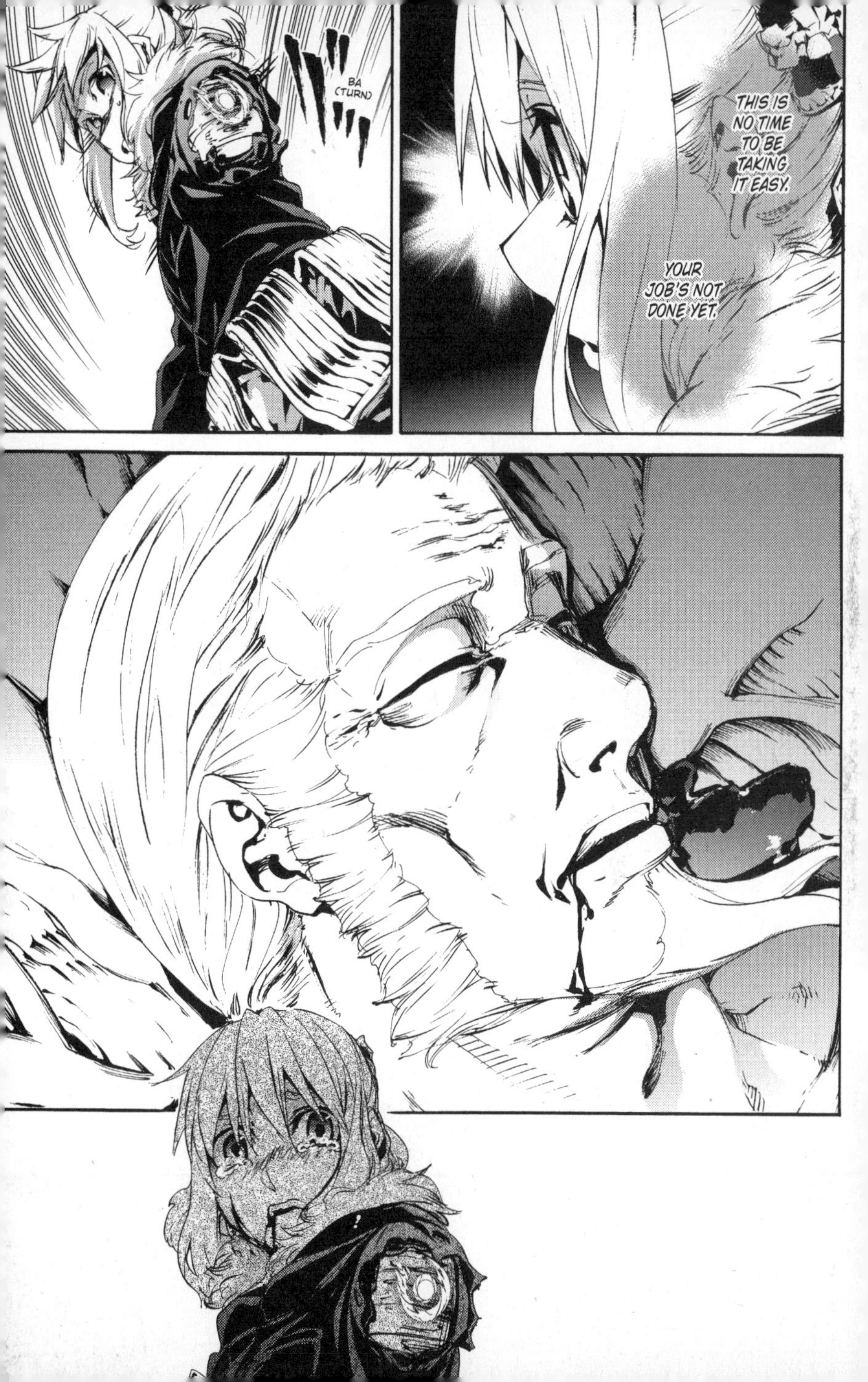
THIS IS NO TIME TO BE TAKING IT EASY.
YOUR JOB'S NOT DONE YET.
BA (TURN)

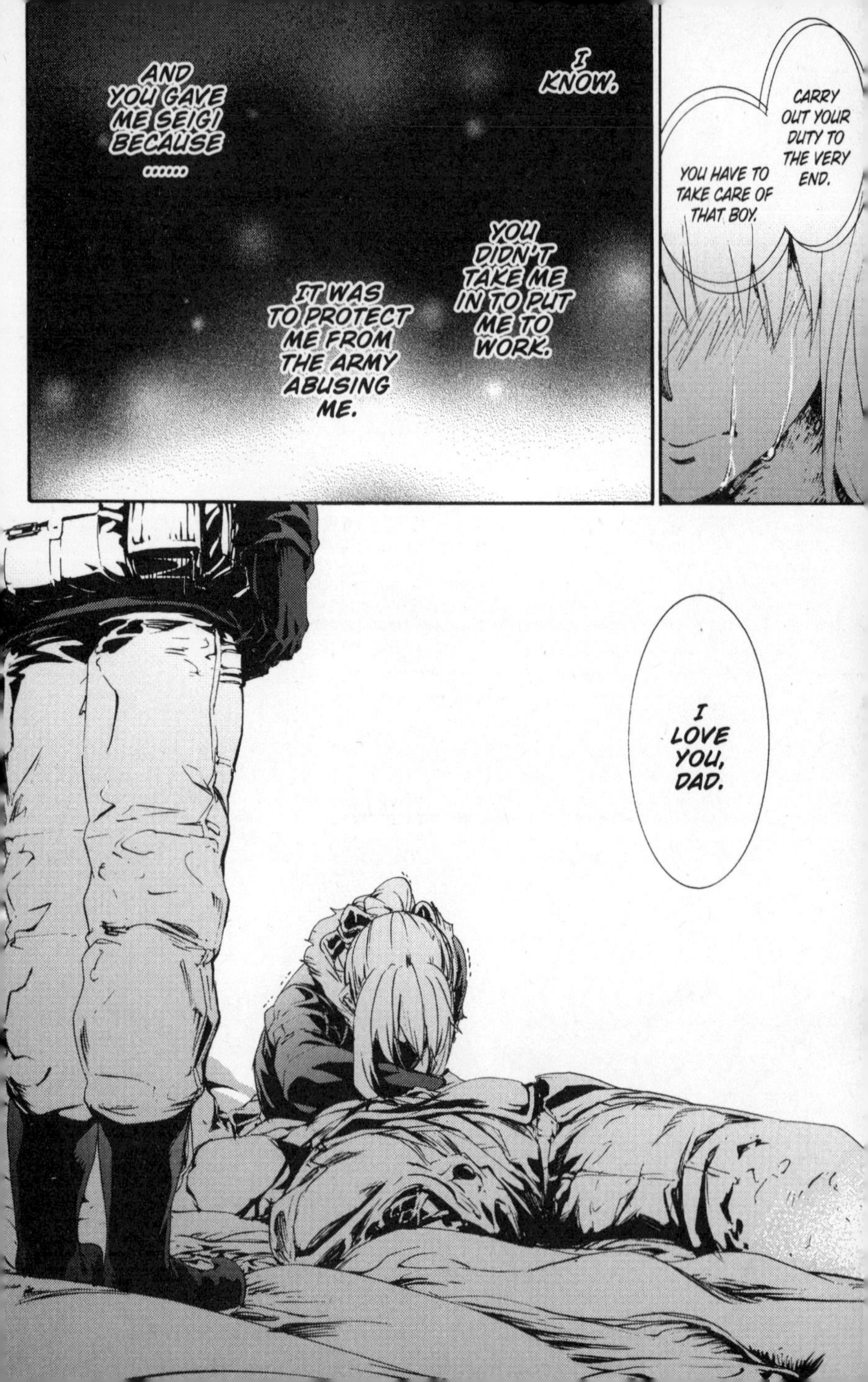
CARRY OUT YOUR DUTY TO THE VERY END.
YOU HAVE TO TAKE CARE OF THAT BOY.
I KNOW.
YOU DIDN'T TAKE ME IN TO PUT ME TO WORK.
IT WAS TO PROTECT ME FROM THE ARMY ABUSING ME.
AND YOU GAVE ME SEIGI BECAUSE ......
I LOVE YOU, DAD.

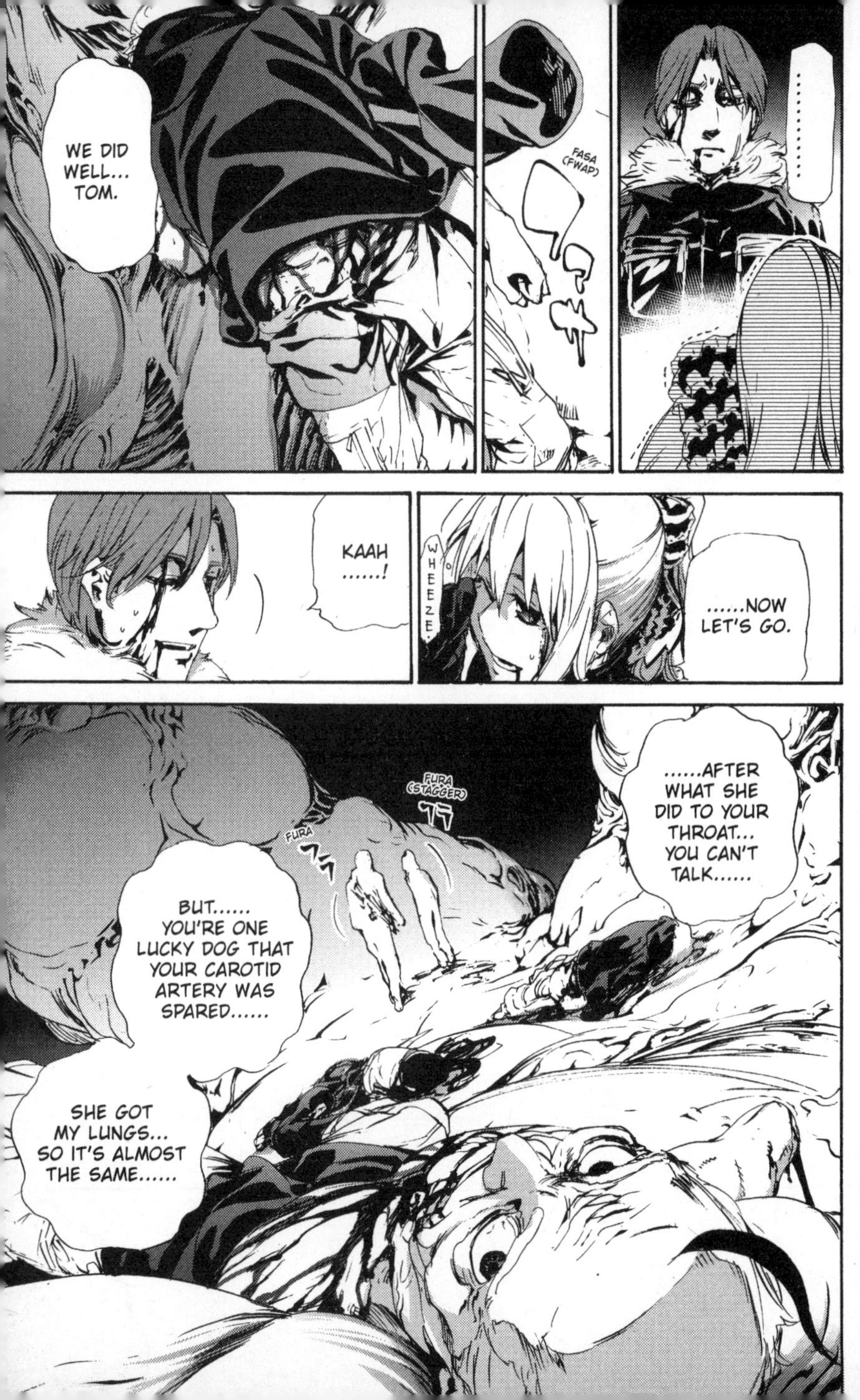
......
FASA (FWAP)
WE DID WELL... TOM.
WHEEZE
......NOW LET'S GO.
KAAH ......!
......AFTER WHAT SHE DID TO YOUR THROAT... YOU CAN'T TALK......
FURA (STAGGER)
FURA
BUT...... YOU'RE ONE LUCKY DOG THAT YOUR CAROTID ARTERY WAS SPARED......
SHE GOT MY LUNGS... SO IT'S ALMOST THE SAME......

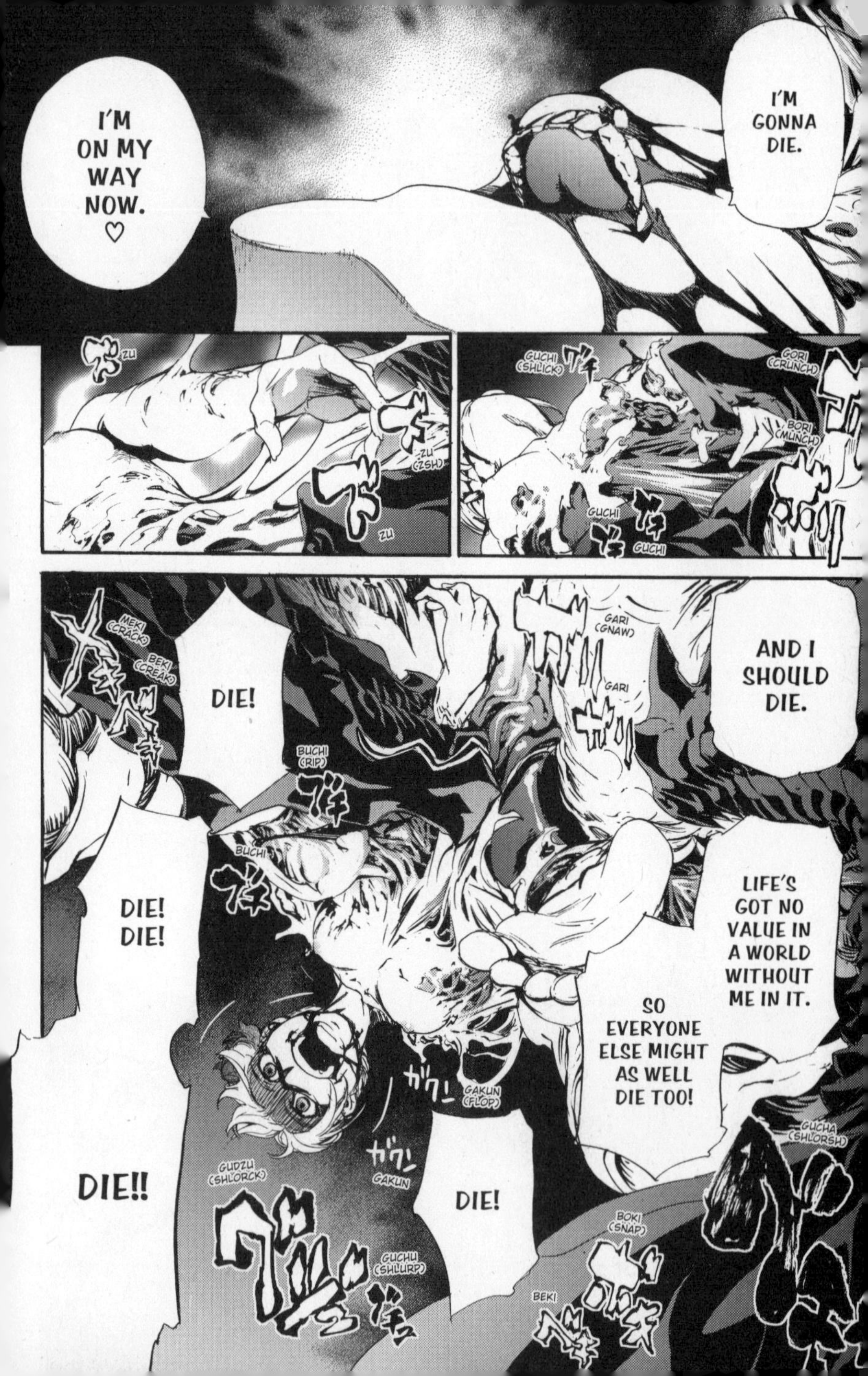
I'M GONNA DIE.
I'M ON MY WAY NOW. ♡
GUCHI (SHLICK)
GORI (CRUNCH)
BORI (MUNCH)
GUCHI
GUCHI
ZU
-ZU (ZSH)
ZU
AND I SHOULD DIE.
GARI (GNAW)
GARI
LIFE'S GOT NO VALUE IN A WORLD WITHOUT ME IN IT.
SO EVERYONE ELSE MIGHT AS WELL DIE TOO!
GUCHA (SHLORSH)
DIE!
BUCHI (RIP)
BUCHI
MEKI (CRACK)
BEKI (CREAK)
DIE! DIE!
GAKUN (FLOP)
GAKUN
BOKI (SNAP)
BEKI
DIE!
GUCHU (SHLURP)
GUDZU (SHLORCK)
DIE!!

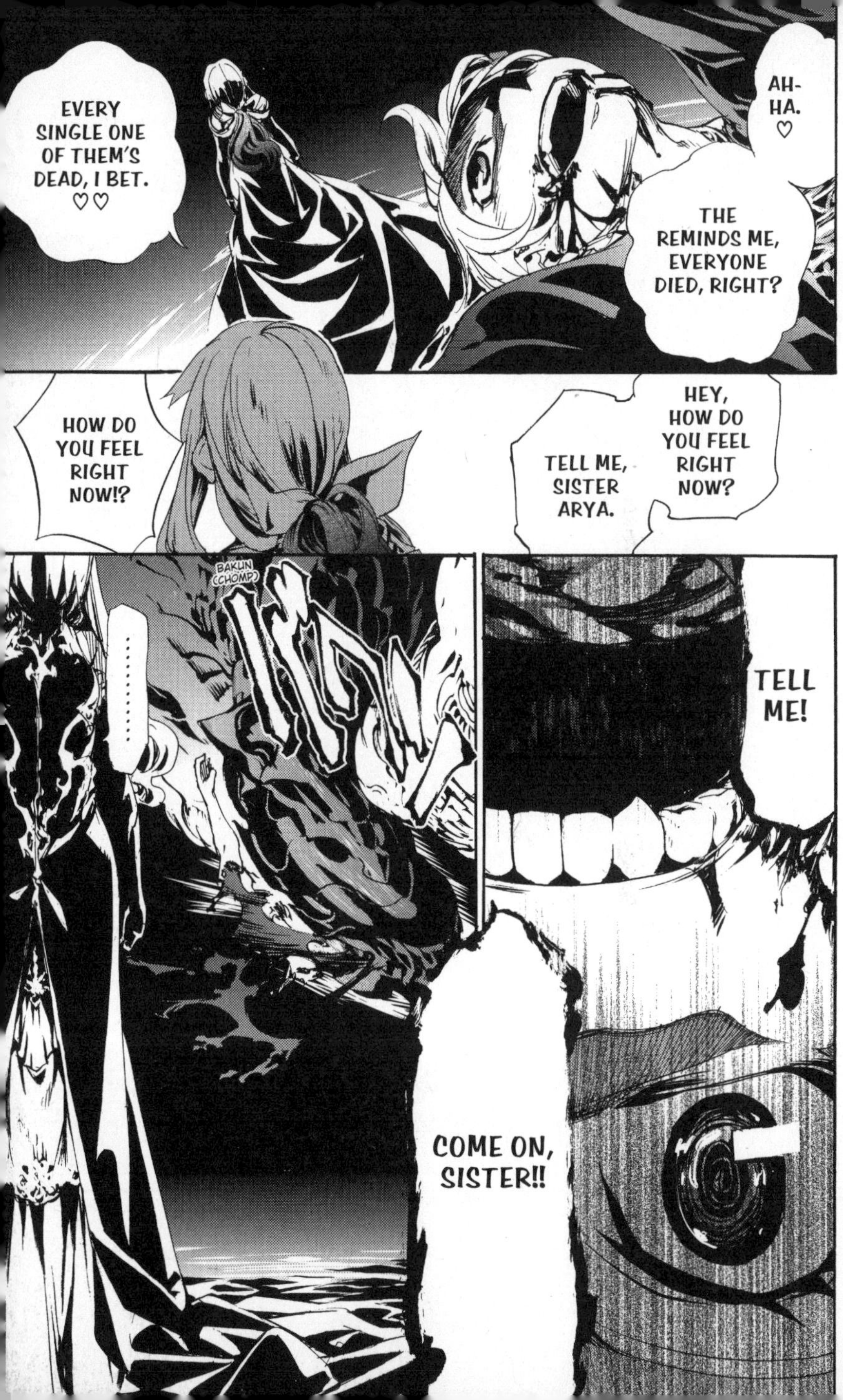
AH-HA. ♡
THE REMINDS ME, EVERYONE DIED, RIGHT?
EVERY SINGLE ONE OF THEM'S DEAD, I BET. ♡♡
HEY, HOW DO YOU FEEL RIGHT NOW?
TELL ME, SISTER ARYA.
HOW DO YOU FEEL RIGHT NOW!?
TELL ME!
COME ON, SISTER!!
BAKUN (CHOMP)
......

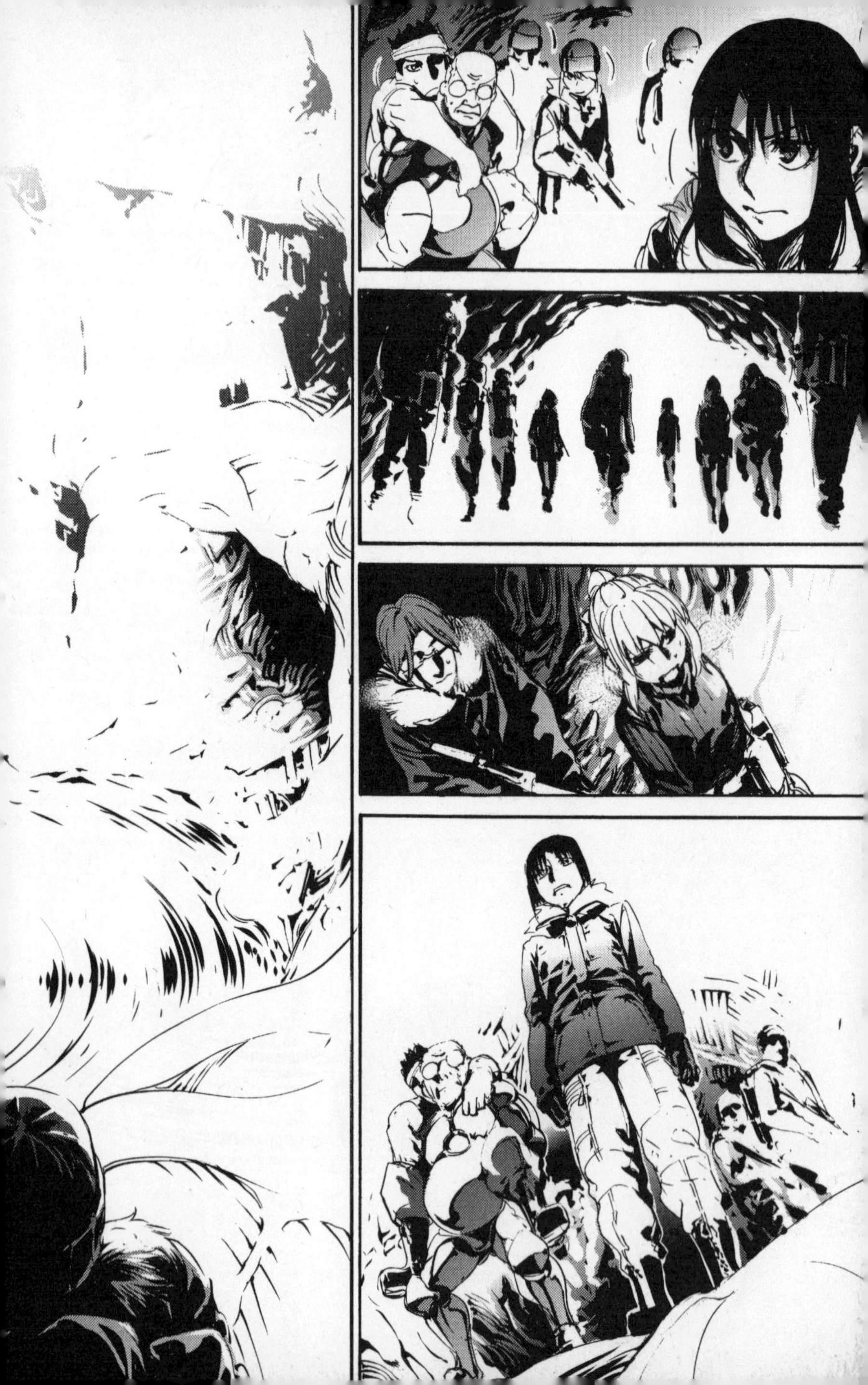

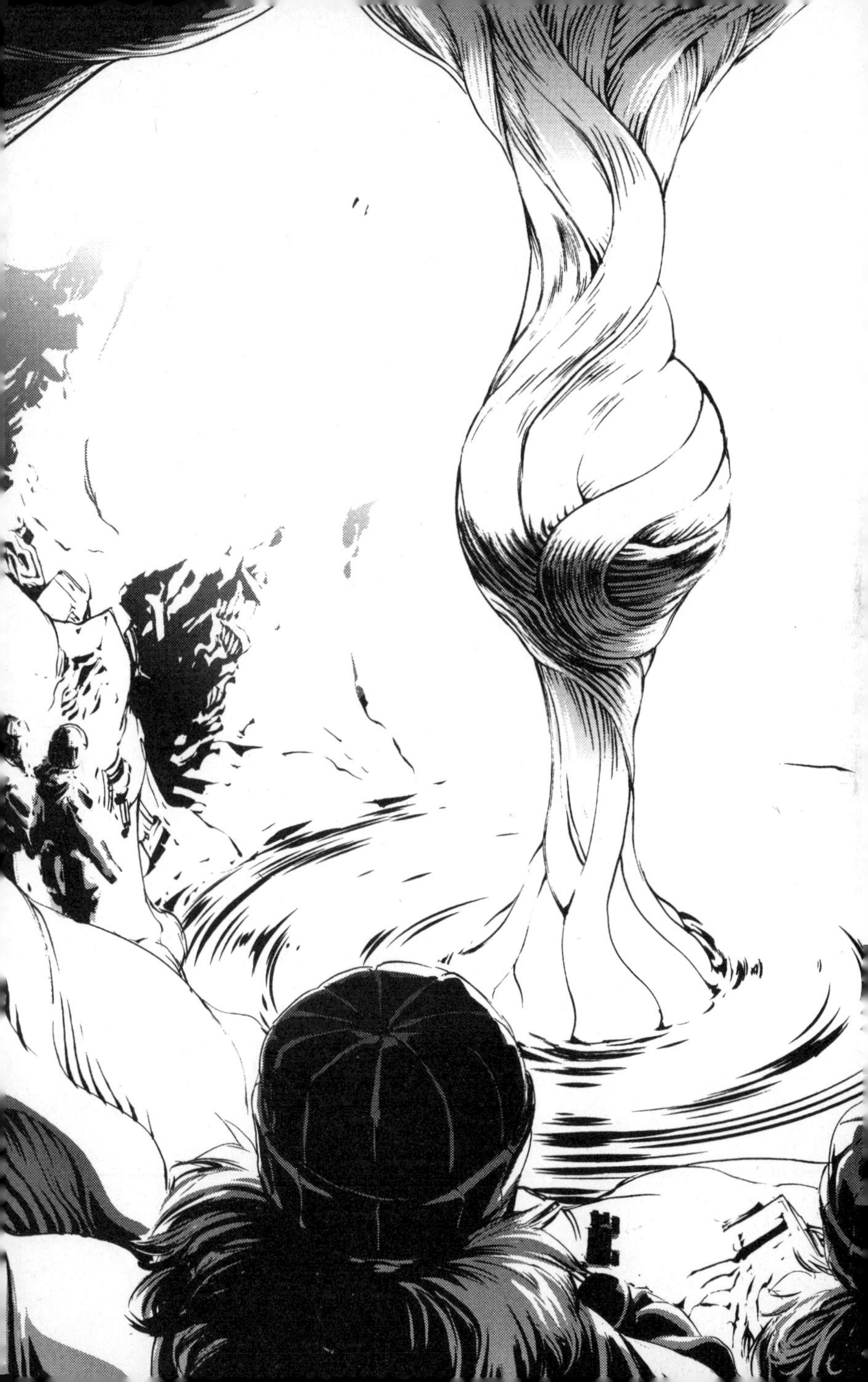

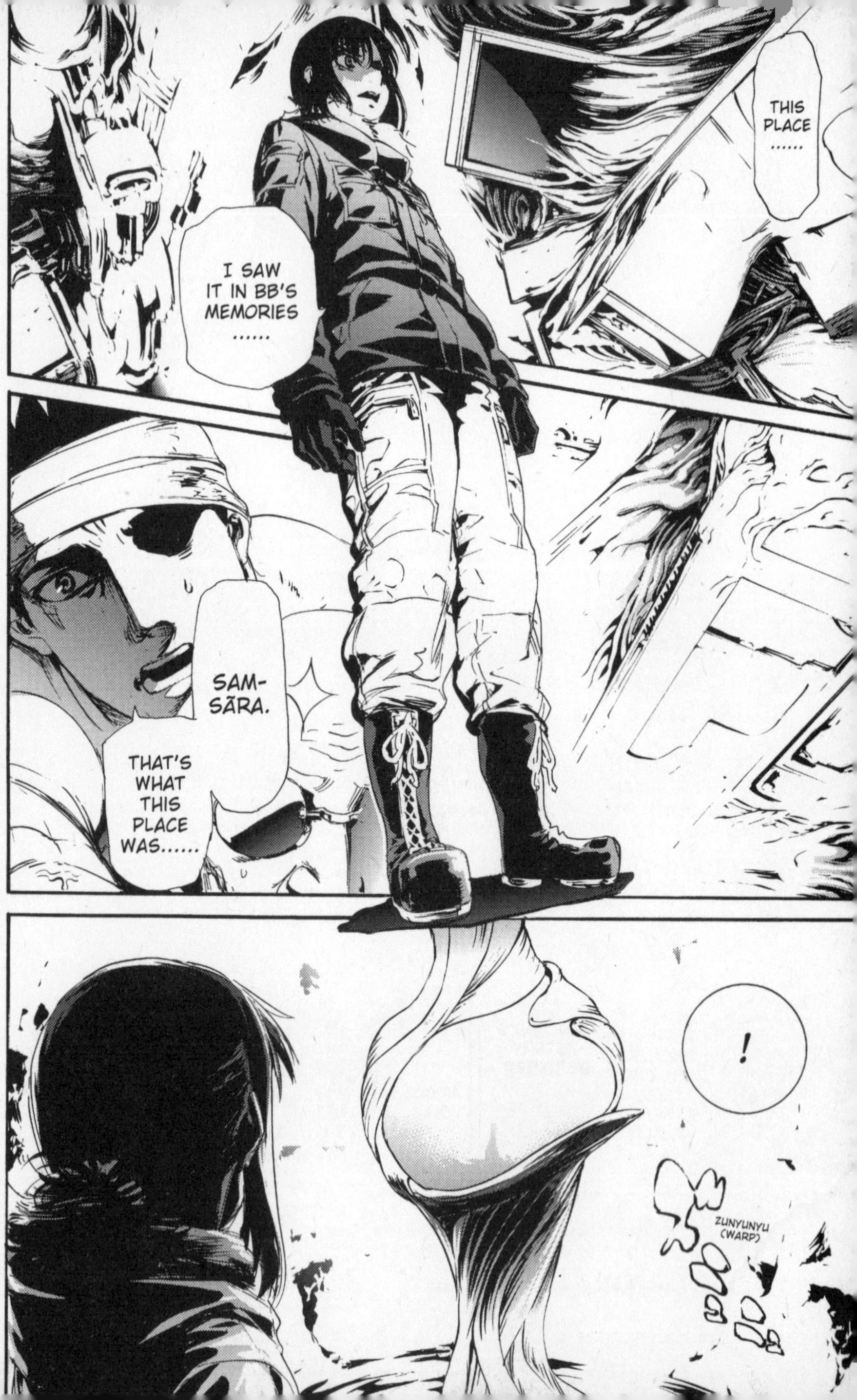
THIS PLACE ......
I SAW IT IN BB'S MEMORIES ......
SAM-SĀRA.
THAT'S WHAT THIS PLACE WAS......
!
ZUNYUNYU (WARP)

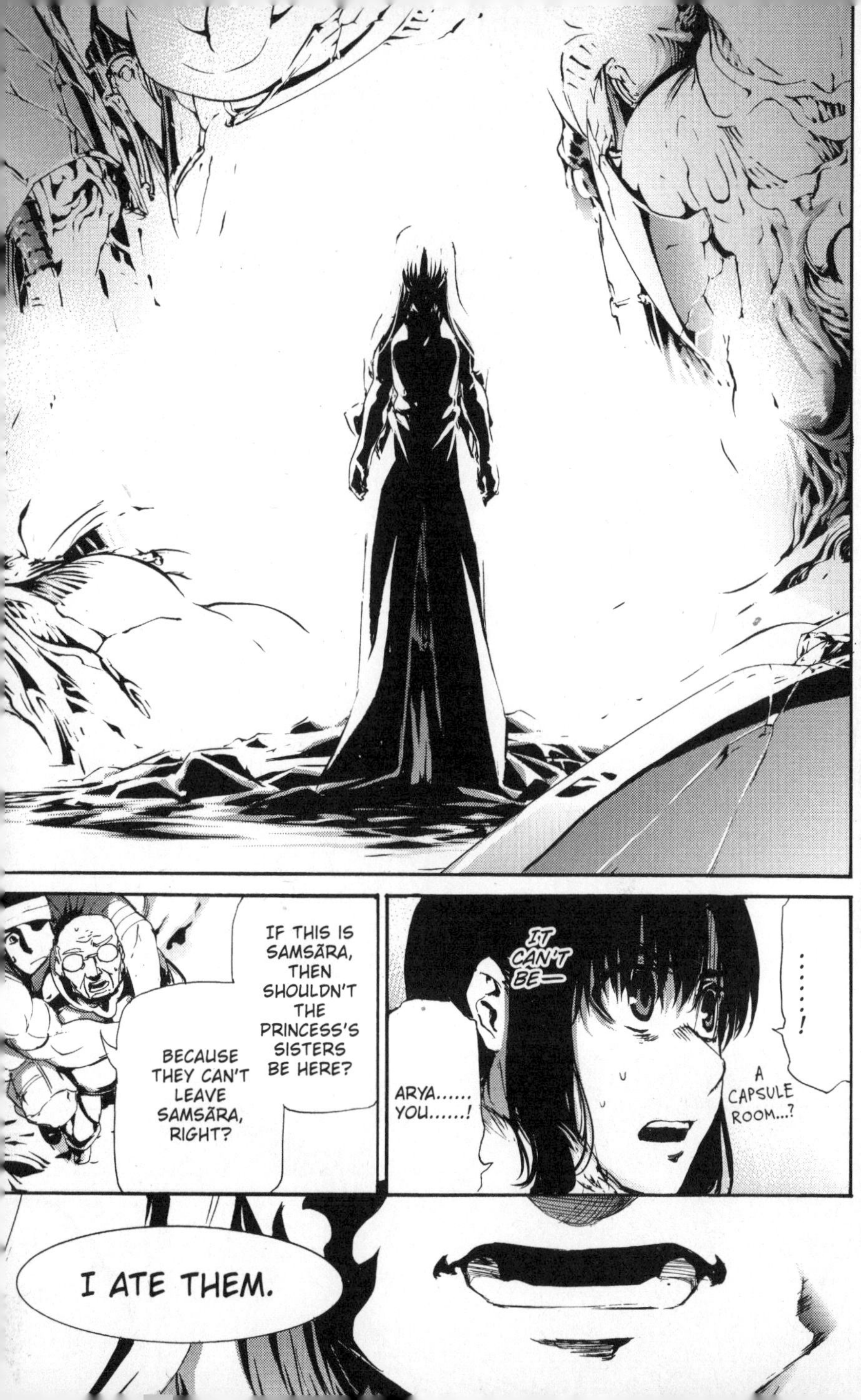
......!
IT CAN'T BE—
A CAPSULE ROOM...?
ARYA...... YOU......!
IF THIS IS SAMSĀRA, THEN SHOULDN'T THE PRINCESS'S SISTERS BE HERE?
BECAUSE THEY CAN'T LEAVE SAMSĀRA, RIGHT?
I ATE THEM.

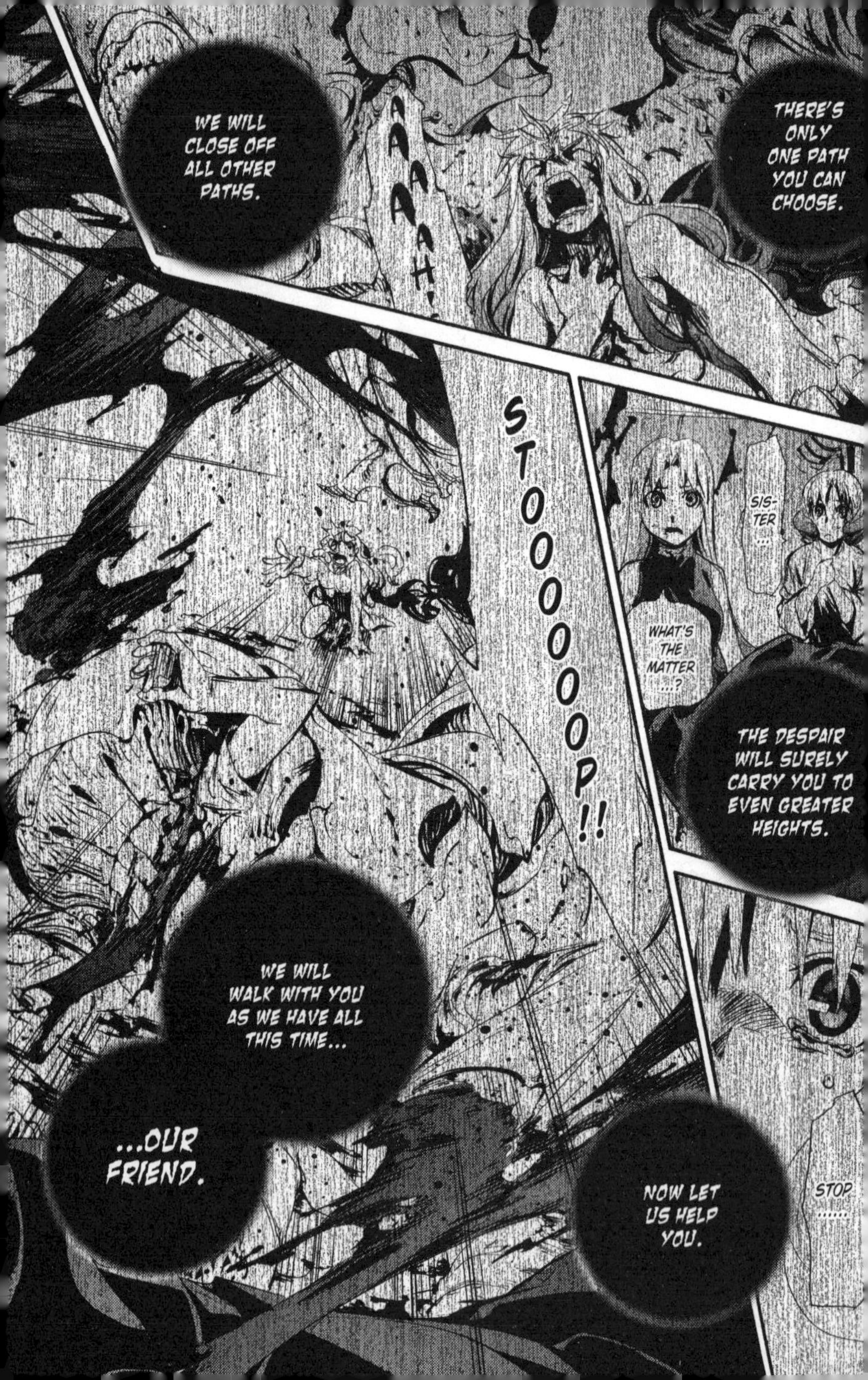
THERE'S ONLY ONE PATH YOU CAN CHOOSE.
AAAAAH!!
WE WILL CLOSE OFF ALL OTHER PATHS.
SIS-TER...
WHAT'S THE MATTER...?
THE DESPAIR WILL SURELY CARRY YOU TO EVEN GREATER HEIGHTS.
STOOOOOOP!!
STOP......
NOW LET US HELP YOU.
WE WILL WALK WITH YOU AS WE HAVE ALL THIS TIME...
...OUR FRIEND.

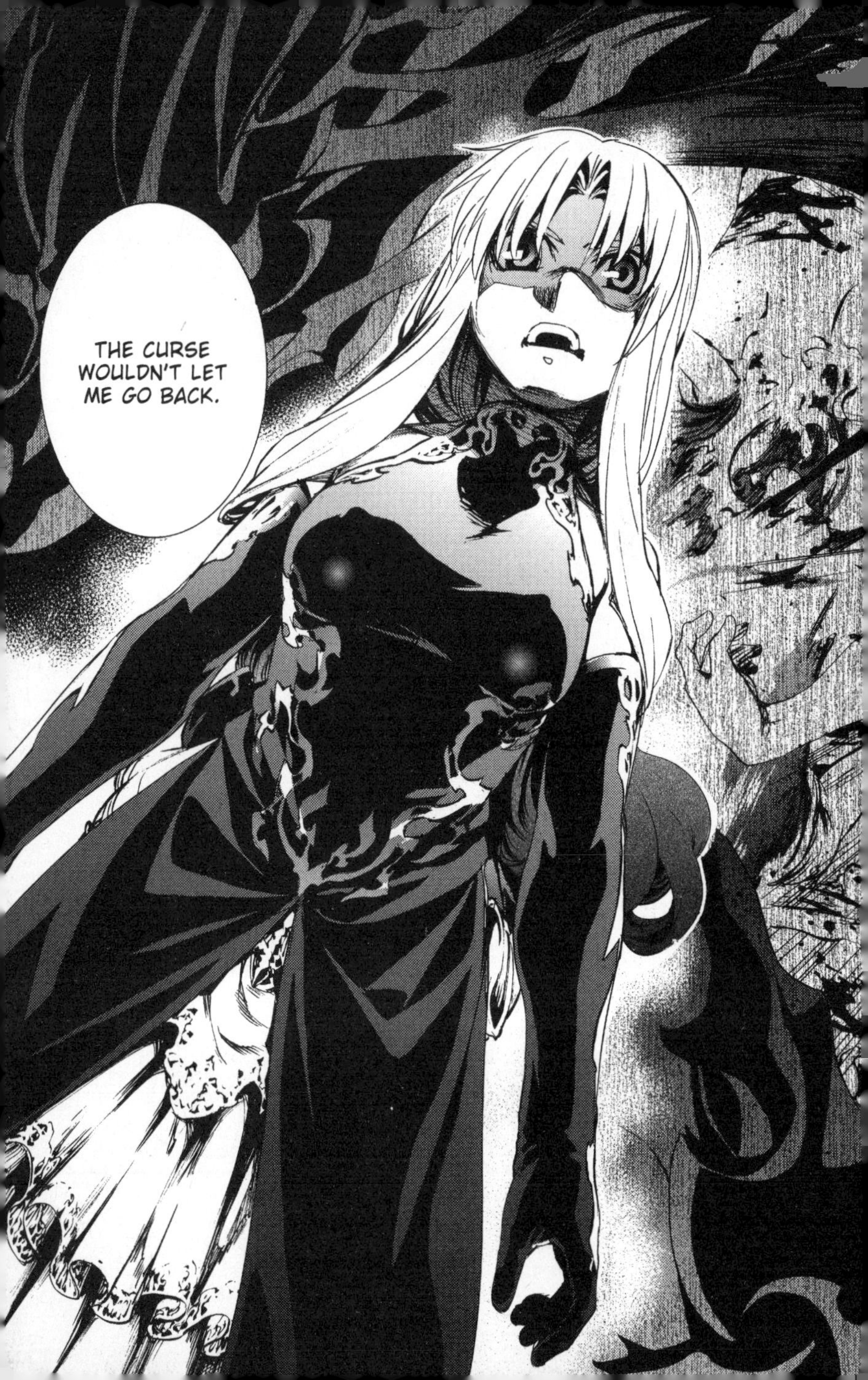
THE CURSE WOULDN'T LET ME GO BACK.

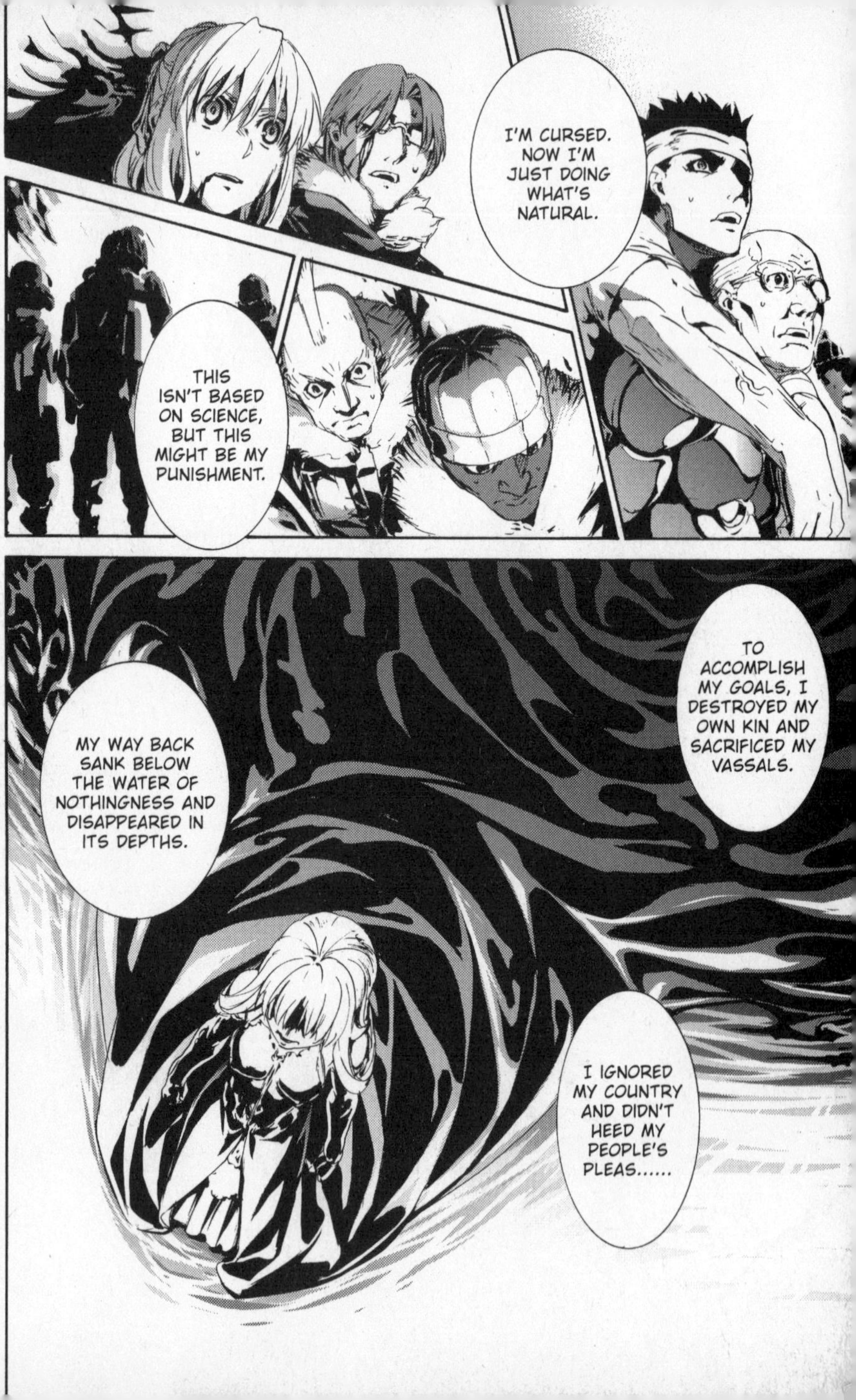

I'M CURSED. NOW I'M JUST DOING WHAT'S NATURAL.
THIS ISN'T BASED ON SCIENCE, BUT THIS MIGHT BE MY PUNISHMENT.
TO ACCOMPLISH MY GOALS, I DESTROYED MY OWN KIN AND SACRIFICED MY VASSALS.
I IGNORED MY COUNTRY AND DIDN'T HEED MY PEOPLE'S PLEAS......
MY WAY BACK SANK BELOW THE WATER OF NOTHINGNESS AND DISAPPEARED IN ITS DEPTHS.

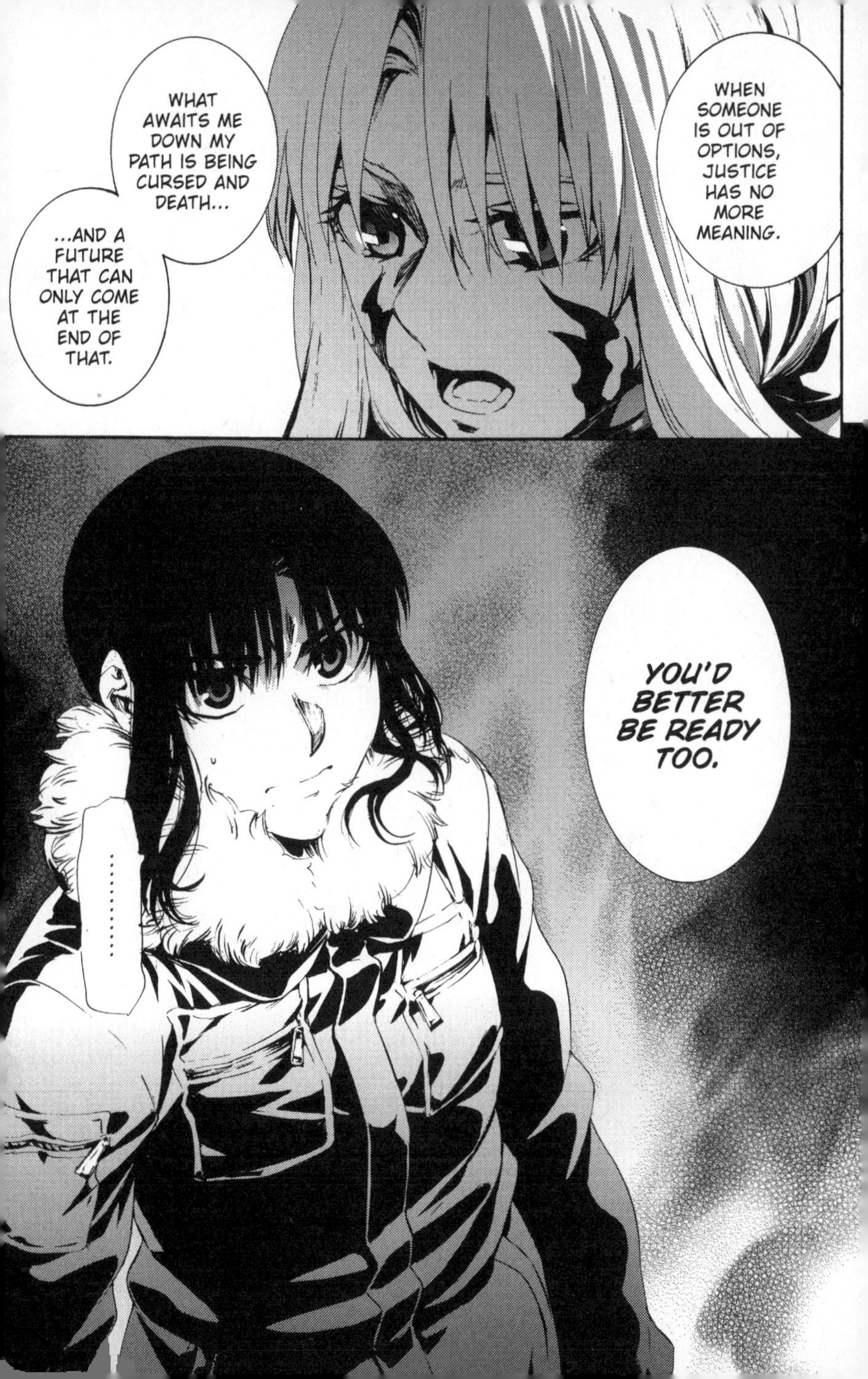
WHEN SOMEONE IS OUT OF OPTIONS, JUSTICE HAS NO MORE MEANING.
WHAT AWAITS ME DOWN MY PATH IS BEING CURSED AND DEATH...
...AND A FUTURE THAT CAN ONLY COME AT THE END OF THAT.
YOU'D BETTER BE READY TOO.
......

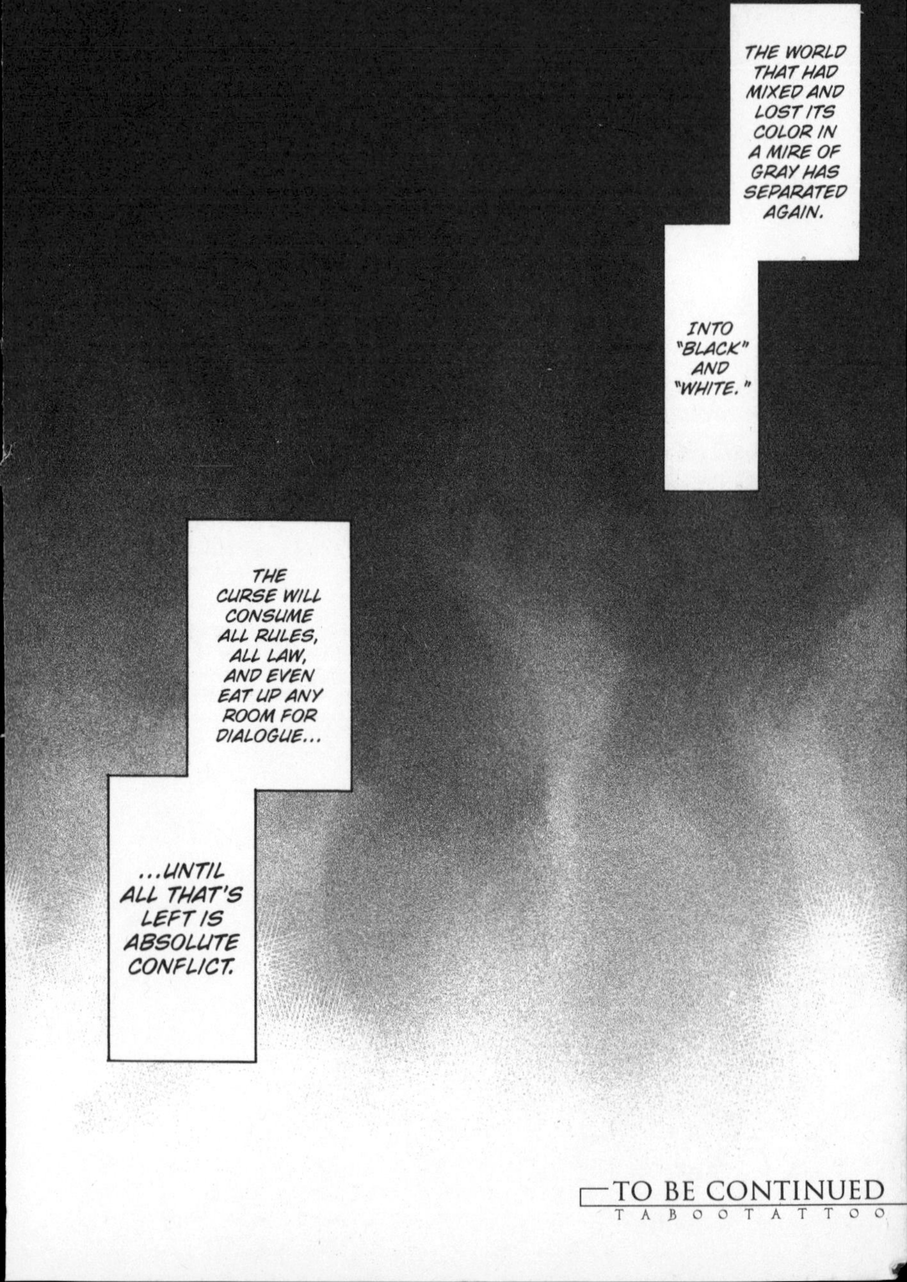
THE WORLD THAT HAD MIXED AND LOST ITS COLOR IN A MIRE OF GRAY HAS SEPARATED AGAIN.
INTO "BLACK" AND "WHITE."
THE CURSE WILL CONSUME ALL RULES, ALL LAW, AND EVEN EAT UP ANY ROOM FOR DIALOGUE...
...UNTIL ALL THAT'S LEFT IS ABSOLUTE CONFLICT.
TO BE CONTINUED
TABOOTATTOO

TABOO TATTOO

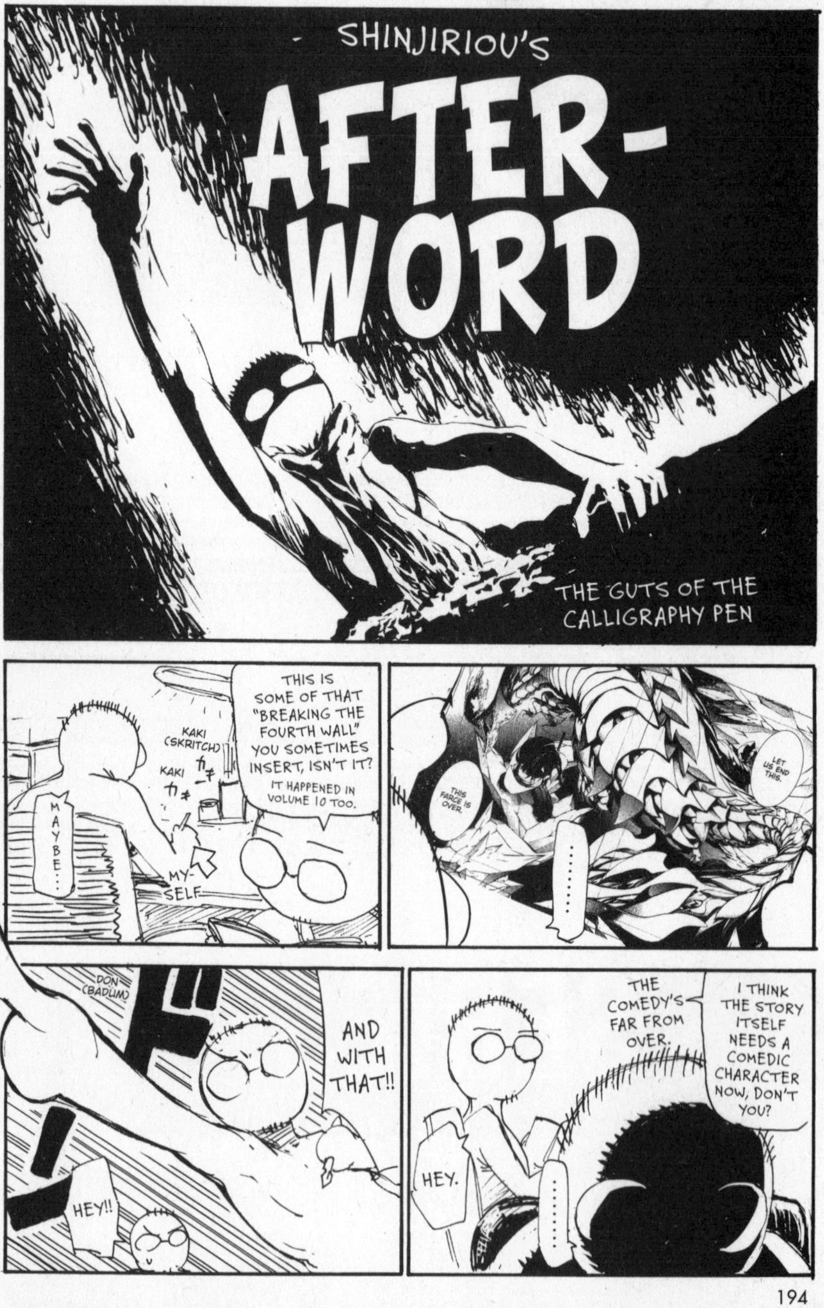
SHINJIRIOU'S
AFTER-WORD
THE GUTS OF THE CALLIGRAPHY PEN
LET US END THIS.
THIS FARCE IS OVER.
......
THIS IS SOME OF THAT "BREAKING THE FOURTH WALL" YOU SOMETIMES INSERT, ISN'T IT?
IT HAPPENED IN VOLUME 10 TOO.
KAKI (SKRITCH)
KAKI
MAYBE...
MY-SELF
I THINK THE STORY ITSELF NEEDS A COMEDIC CHARACTER NOW, DON'T YOU?
THE COMEDY'S FAR FROM OVER.
HEY.
......
AND WITH THAT!!
DON (BADUM)
HEY!!

THE
NEXT
VOLUME
IS THE
END OF
THE
SERIES.

TABOO TATTOO

by SHINJIRO

sbya

Translation: Christine Dashiell • Lettering: Phil Christie

TABOO TATTOO
© Shinjiro 2016
First published in Japan in 2016 by KADOKAWA CORPORATION. English translation rights reserved by Yen Press, LLC under the license from KADOKAWA COPORATION, Tokyo through TUTTLE-MORI AGENCY, Inc., Tokyo.

English translation © 2018 by Yen Press, LLC

Yen Press
1290 Avenue of the Americas
New York, NY 10104

Visit us at yenpress.com
facebook.com/yenpress
twitter.com/yenpress
yenpress.tumblr.com
instagram.com/yenpress

First Yen Press Edition: October 2018

Yen Press is an imprint of Yen Press, LLC.
The Yen Press name and logo are trademarks of Yen Press, LLC.

The publisher is not responsible for websites (or their content) that are not owned by the publisher.

Library of Congress Control Number: 2015952591

ISBNs: 978-1-9753-0054-8 (paperback)
       978-1-9753-0055-5 (ebook)

10 9 8 7 6 5 4 3 2 1

WOR

Printed in the United States of America